Sociology, Work and Industry

Fourth edition

In the fourth edition of this successful and popular text Tony Watson explains how the discipline of sociology contributes to our wider understanding of the variety of contemporary work practices and institutions. The new edition outlines both what has been achieved historically and what is currently being achieved by the sociological study of work. It also sets out a range of concepts, models and other theoretical ideas that students and researchers can apply in their own studies of work and work organisation. Subjects covered include:

- theoretical perspectives on the sociology of work and industry;
- how working patterns have changed since the Industrial Revolution and continue to change in a globalising and technologically innovating twenty-first century;
- work organisations;
- innovations in the structuring of work activities at the enterprise level;
- occupational aspects of the organisation of work in changing societies;
- how people experience and cope with the pressures, insecurities and inequalities of a restructured world of work;
- how challenge and resistance influence the shaping of work in an ever-changing world.

Sociology, Work and Industry has been restructured and updated throughout. It includes a newly written opening chapter which, in addition to explaining the distinctiveness of the sociological perspective, provides guidance on researching and analysing work practices and institutions. It will be essential reading for anybody studying the sociology of work, work organisations and industry.

Tony J. Watson is Professor of Organisational and Managerial Behaviour at Nottingham Business School, The Nottingham Trent University.

Sociology, Work and Industry

Fourth edition

Tony J. Watson

Routledge
Taylor & Francis Group

LONDON AND NEW YORK

First edition published 1980

Second edition published 1987
by Routledge & Kegan Paul Ltd

Reprinted 1988, 1991, 1993 and 1995
Third edition 1995
Fourth edition 2003
by Routledge
2 Park Square, Milton Park, Abingdon, Oxon, OX14 4RN

Reprinted 2004 and 2005

Simultaneously published in the USA and Canada
by Routledge
270 Madison Avenue , New York, NY 10016

Routledge is an imprint of the Taylor & Francis Group

© 1980, 1987, 1995, 2003 Tony J. Watson

Designed and typeset in Univers and Rotis by
Keystroke, Jacaranda Lodge, Wolverhampton
Printed and bound in Great Britain by Bell & Bain Ltd, Glasgow

British Library Cataloguing in Publication Data
A catalogue record for this book is available from the British Library

Library of Congress Cataloging in Publication Data
Watson, Tony J.
    Sociology, work and industry / by Tony J. Watson.–4th ed.
        p. cm.
    Includes bibliographical references and indexes.
    Industrial sociology. I. Title.
    HD6955.W38 2003
    306.3–dc21   2003007044

ISBN 0–415–32165–4 (hbk)
ISBN 0–415–32166–2 (pbk)

Contents

Figures and tables

Figures

Tables

Introduction

Sociology, Work and Industry aims to provide as full as possible an overview of the ways in which sociology can help us understand the role of work in people's lives and in modern societies. The overview offered is set within a characterisation of the nature and key characteristics of sociological thinking and research. This makes it possible for people without a previous sociological education fully to appreciate what is distinctive about the sociological imagination. But, in identifying just how the study of work and work-related institutions fits into the broader sociological discipline, this aspect of the book should be equally helpful to readers with an existing knowledge of sociology. That knowledge should be deepened and enriched by its application to issues of work experience and organisation.

The account of the sociology of work and industry provided by this volume is not just theoretically and methodologically grounded. It is also historically grounded, showing how the original emergence of sociology and the later development of the sociology of work and industry have been inextricably linked to the changing social and industrialising world of which it is a part. This equally entails looking at changing thinking over recent decades, as the pace of change in the world of work has accelerated, as it entails attending to the emergence of industrial capitalist ways of organising social life in the first place. Just because sociologists tend to write currently about, say, issues of worker 'subjectivity' in call centres does not mean that we turn our backs on earlier concerns with labour processes, technological implications thinking or human relations research. And neither does it mean, for example, that in attending to the decline in the contemporary influence of trade unions we forget that there once existed such institutions as the 'closed shop' or that we bury the still relevant and valuable sociological insight that closed shop arrangements and patterns of shop steward representation of the mid-twentieth century were partly the outcome of the exercise of managerial interests and not simply arrangements forced on employers by trade unions. An understanding of matters like these is seen as vital to understanding the rather different, but not radically new, patterns that are currently emerging.

Sociology, Work and Industry also aims to encourage and support readers who are interested in actively applying sociological thinking to the work practices they experience and observe. It is hoped that most readers will find their understanding of their own work practices, and those they see occurring around them, generally *informed* by the knowledge and insights they gain from the book. The various concepts, models and other analytical devices that the book offers as part of its own contribution to the sociology of work and industry, alongside its reporting of the work of others, are there to be *used* by readers as means of making sense of what they see and experience. And it is hoped that they will be especially useful to readers with a more formal research interest in the sociology of work and industry. Alongside the preparation of this fourth edition of *Sociology, Work and Industry*, the author has continued to engage in research on a variety of work and work organisation issues, and much of the conceptualising and theorising presented in the text is thus a live and emergent manifestation of 'sociological work in process'. Sociological research, theorising and sense-making are exciting activities and it is hoped that every reader of this book can, to a greater or lesser extent, make them part of their lives, as they come to terms with and contribute to the shaping of the work activities that they encounter.

1   Studying work and society

People, work and society

Everyone in the world is involved in work in one way or another. People may work in their own small field, growing food to keep themselves alive. They may work in an office or a factory and, after a day working in an employer's premises for a wage or a salary, they may return to do their housework or to work in their garden. Even those who do not themselves perform any of these labours are nevertheless involved with work; as owners of land on which other people work, as investors in industrial enterprises or as employers of servants. To understand the way of life of people living in any kind of society we therefore have to pay close attention to work activities and to the institutions associated with those activities.

> **WORK**
>
> The carrying out of tasks which enable people to make a living within the social and economic context in which they are located.

One of the first things we have to do is to decide what we mean by 'work'. This is not a matter of finding a final and absolute definition of work. The social sciences proceed, like all systematic human inquiry, by deciding what is likely to be the most useful way of characterising the topics being studied. Certain types of economic inquiry in a modern industrialised society might best be conducted by defining work in terms of task-based activities for which people are paid by an employer, client or customer. However, this would exclude all those tasks that we refer to as 'housework' for example. This would be a serious omission given that, in Brown's (1997) words, 'without the enormous volume and unremitting cycle of domestic labour the formal economy of jobs and pay packets would cease to function'. But if, in an attempt to be as inclusive as possible, we included all task-oriented activity in which effort is expended, then we would find our study extending to such activities as walking across a room to switch on a television set or packing a bag to take for a day on the beach. We need a compromise that gives sufficient focus to our studies without limiting them to activities with a formal economic outcome.

For the purposes of sociological study, work can usefully be defined to emphasise, first, its task-related aspect and, second, its association with people making a living.

This way of thinking about work associates it with the expenditure of effort to carry out tasks but it limits it to something that has an economic element – in the very broad sense of dealing with problems of survival in a world of scarce resources. But the notion of 'making a living' implies much more than just producing enough material goods to ensure physical survival. People do not simply extract a living from the environment. In many ways, work effectively transforms environments and, in the process, creates for many people a level of living far in excess of basic subsistence. But it does more than this. It also relates intimately to how people shape their very lives and identities and, indeed, to how they also find their lives being shaped by the circumstances in which they have to work. The work people do becomes closely bound up with their conception of self. In looking at how people 'make a living' we are looking at how they deal with both the economic and the social or cultural aspects of their lives. Work occurs in societies.

SOCIETY

The broad pattern of social, economic, cultural and political relationships within which people lead their lives, typically in the modern world as members of the same nation state.

Each society has its own set of economic and legal arrangements and dominant values, and its members are often pressed to share a degree of communality of identity. Each society also has its own pattern of power and inequality. Precisely where each individual and family fits into that pattern will be fundamental to how they experience work and how well they share in whatever human benefits derive from the work carried out in that society. Nevertheless, in spite of the fact that we typically identify societies with nation states, it is vital to note that it is sometimes more realistic to talk of, say, a 'society' of small farmers to be found in a remote part of a large nation state such as India, and sometimes it is more helpful to think about, say, managerial workers in 'modern industrial capitalist society' as opposed to looking separately at the lives of British, Swedish or American managers. There are significant patterns to be observed within and across nation states. Thus, when we think about 'society' as the subject matter of the discipline of sociology, it is wise to think of it broadly in terms of 'the social' in people's lives – 'social', that is, at the level of the larger patterns of culture, community and political economy within which the smaller scale social interactions and, indeed, individual efforts to 'make a life' and 'make a living' occur. Sociological study looks at all these levels of human existence but, as we shall now see, its characteristic feature is its relating of the small scale, the local, the intimate in people's lives to the bigger social scheme of things – both within and across particular societies.

Thinking about work sociologically

Sociology provides us with a range of insights, concepts, ideas, theories and research findings which help us understand the wide range of work and work-related activities that occur in the context of the broader social and cultural arrangements.

SOCIOLOGY

The study of the relationships which develop between human beings as they organise themselves and are organised by others in societies and how these patterns influence and are influenced by the actions and interactions of people and how they make sense of their lives and identities.

The defining characteristic of the sociological perspective is that it ultimately relates whatever it studies back to the way society as a whole is organised. The essential insight which sociology provides is that no social action, at however mundane a level, takes place in a social vacuum. It is always linked, in some way, back to the wider culture, social structure and processes of the society in which it takes place. These structures, processes, norms and values, with all their related inequalities, ideologies and power distributions, are the source of both constraints and opportunities which people meet in conducting their lives. The better and more widely these cultures, structures and processes are understood and the better the connections between specific actions or arrangements and these basic patterns are appreciated, then the greater is the opportunity for the human control over work, industry and every other kind of social institution.

Let us envisage trying to make sense, sociologically, of a simple piece of 'everyday' work-related human behaviour. A man and a woman get out of a car and walk into an office block. One of them goes into a large private office and closes the door. The other sits at a desk outside that office alongside several other people. The person in the private space telephones the one in the outer office and a few minutes later the latter individual takes a cup of coffee and a biscuit into the person in the inner office. If we were viewing that scene as strangers to the work organisation, whether or not we were formally trained as sociologists, we would be thinking about both the personal and the work relationship between these people: were they a married couple, lovers or simply people sharing a lift to work? We would wonder how this aspect of their relationship related to the authority relationship between them: presumably one of them was 'the boss', was the more highly paid, the more highly trained, and had the right to give instructions to the other. We would here be drawing on our knowledge of 'sociological' matters such as social class, educational and career opportunity structures, bureaucratic authority structures, culturally normal patterns of workplace layout and the patterns of behaviour, rules, assumptions and expectations associated with work activities in this particular society and culture at this particular time in history. If it were the man that entered the private office we might note that standard 'norms' were being followed with regard to gender relationships. But if it were the woman who 'played the role' of the senior person – the presumably higher paid, more qualified individual with greater authority – we might begin to reflect on how this individual has come to challenge established patterns. How had she come to break established norms? What opportunity structures had she used, what barriers had she overcome? To what extent were her actions and her relatively unusual position in the workplace part of a broader pattern of social change? In doing this analysis, we would be thinking sociologically. In asking these questions, we would be asking sociological questions. Further to this, we would be engaging with issues of power and life chances in a way that would not just enhance our 'academic' understanding of relationships at work but would, potentially, offer understandings of possibilities and practices that could inform human choices that might further – or, for that matter, resist – social change.

Choices, constraints and opportunities in work and society

We will return shortly to the potential of sociology for informing human choice. First, however, we need to reinforce the point about working arrangements and social patterns being both the outcomes of human actions and factors helping shape those actions. Sociology has been defined here as something that looks at how human beings organise both themselves and each other. In looking at how people think and behave it looks for cultural patterns and 'structures' in social life. These patterns are seen as both the outcome of the activities of individuals and as something which, in turn, influences, encourages and constrains the individual. If, for example, it was the man in our office scenario who was the more senior of our two social actors he might tell us in an interview that his current role as the organisation's head of information technology was the outcome of a series of *choices* that he personally made in his life. The woman, to whom he gives a daily lift in his company car, might talk to us about how she chose to train and work as an office secretary. As sociological observers we would not want to discount these claims to choice or 'agency' in these individuals' career patterns. Nor would we say that there were no individual choices behind the pattern whereby the great majority of the important 'decision-makers' in this organisation are currently men and most of the secretarial and 'personal assistant' workers are women. Choices have clearly been made. Nobody forced these people into these jobs. Each human individual is an agent, with wants, aspirations and a sense of identity which they bring to any decision to speak or act. But, at the same time, we are likely to be aware that the pattern we have observed is, in some sense, as an outcome of the way the 'society' in which these people grew up channelled male and female children into different spheres of activity. There were clearly pressures on each child from the world around them: from role examples observed as they grew up to the opportunities made available to boys and girls in both education and initial employment.

It is easily possible to see two mutually exclusive alternative types of explanation emerging here: agency and choice on the one hand and structural 'channelling' on the other. Sometimes sociologists talk of making a choice between *voluntarist* and *structural* frames of reference and modern sociological thought is characterised, says Swingewood (2000), 'by a continual tension between . . . a voluntarist model which emphasises the creative and active role of agents, and a structural model which focuses on institutions and processes which constrain and determine the course of action'.

To use terms which have been around as long as there has been social thought, we can speak of explanations which emphasise free will and explanations which stress determinism. This is something that sociologists try to go beyond. What is needed, to develop an explanation of the patterns observed, is an analysis which considers the way these individuals came to shape their career interests and 'choose' their aspirations in the light of their previous experiences in life and what they have learned from the cultural and parental influences upon them to be the appropriate and possible types of work for them to enter. There is an interweaving of individual and social factors, of free choice and of constraint. We might simplify this, as Figure 1.1 does, by saying that individuals make society and society makes individuals.

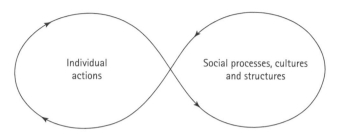

Figure 1.1 Individuals make society and society makes individuals

The dualism between a focus on the individual and a focus on the 'social' does not fully parallel the free will and determinism one, however, because it is possible to talk of an individual's actions being severely constrained, if not determined, by factors such as their individual genetic make-up. Equally, it is possible to see social structures as providing opportunities for individuals to realise their individual interests ('climbing the ladder' of the class structure, say) as well as seeing people constrained by such structures (being excluded from an activity because of one's gender or race, for example). Giddens (1984) usefully suggests we replace the *dualism* of 'agency' and 'structure' with a recognition that the two work together as a *duality* and in continuous processes of *structuration*.

> **STRUCTURATION**
>
> Ongoing processes in which individual initiatives are interwoven into the patterns of human interaction which sometimes constrain and sometimes enable those initiatives.

Human beings are makers of social patterns and are also made by them. These patterns both constrain us and enable us to achieve our purposes. But these patterns or 'structures' are not objectively existing entities outside of human patterns of interaction, even though it may at times feel as if they have this kind of forceful presence. Structuration is an ever-unfolding process.

Sociology is not simply the study of the social, of societies, of social structures. Neither, of course, is it a study of individuals' activities, aggregated in some way to give us a view of societies as little more than the sum of their parts. It is, rather, a study of the inter-relationships between the individual and the social whose greatest potential lies in examining the processes whereby human initiatives and choices shape and are shaped by patterns of human interaction and power.

Work and the sociological imagination

In one of the most influential considerations of what sociology can contribute to human life, Mills (1970b) identified the *sociological imagination* as a way of switching from an initial focus on the private problems of, say, a manufacturing worker faced with redundancy to various contextual *public issues*. These issues range from the state of the international market for manufactured goods and managerial, governmental and trade union policies, to patterns of technological change and the different nature of involvement in that industry of technical and managerial staff on the one hand and manual workers on the other. Sociology, then, shifts the level of focus from that of the close-up on the individual and their working life to that of the 'big picture' of the society and economy in which they live. Sociology is not simply to do with 'painting a picture', however broad that might be. It necessarily goes beyond this to look for regularities, patterns, structures and processes. Sociologists in this case of worker redundancies will want to know about the occupational structure of the industry and the industrial relations processes which go on; they will look at the managerial structures and the ongoing processes of technological change. All this will be set in its historical context and the overall structure of society – in its industrial base, its political-economic system and how it fits into patterns of global change. In analysing these structures and processes the sociologist would try to show how they potentially both constrain people as well as enable people to further their personal wishes, noting how they result from the initiatives of individuals and can also be seen to restrain individual initiatives.

All of this means stepping outside our normal 'everyday' commonsense way of thinking about our working lives and adopting what is perhaps the most basic sociological insight of all; that there is more than one way and one way only for men and women to organise their lives. In other words, the way society *is* is not necessarily the way society *has to be*. In the realm of work this means that the way we currently organise production and distribution does not possess some immutable inevitability. It is only one of a range of possibilities. Baumann and May (2001) refer to sociology's ability to help us appreciate its 'anti-fixating' power. We are reminded, they say, that what we might think of as the 'natural, inevitable, eternal aspects of our lives' have come into being as a result of the exercise of 'human power and human resources'. This, in turn, suggests that social patterns are not 'immune and impenetrable to human action – our own action included'. A world that might have seemed 'oppressive in its apparent fixity' is shown to be a world that could be 'different from what it is now'. We are thus encouraged not to surrender to what might, at first, seem to be irresistible pressures and circumstances.

As we shall shortly observe, the early sociologists were thinkers striving to make sense of the dislocations of their age. Their attempts to make sense of their situation are invaluable to us because, in an historical location more marginal than our own, they were better able to look at the industrial capitalist world in the light of conceptions of alternatives. This is their humanistic significance and their continuing relevance to us today. They were perhaps more aware of alternatives on a societal level than we are because they were better placed historically to contrast the modern and the industrial with the traditional, the urban with the rural, and so on.

Sociology, critique and democratic debate about work

The sociological imagination does not just mean suspending our everyday commonsense assumptions about the world. It also means being wary of styles of intellectual analysis that are more concerned with solving the problems of particular sections of society than with developing an analysis that would be of relevance to members of society more generally. Jacques (1996) points out, for example, that many of the attempts currently being made to theorise work relations are producing their own kind of 'commonsense'. At the heart of this is a standard body of relatively unchanging US-created 'management knowledge' that takes for granted that the key 'work' issue is one of finding better ways to manage employees to enable organisations to achieve high productivity, international competitiveness and 'world class efficiency'. Questions are not asked about the nature and legitimacy of work organisations or, for example, the role of non-managers in 'managing' work, in shaping 'motivations' or acting as social citizens within work arrangements in which relationships are built and balanced. To ask these questions, we might add, does not preclude an interesting issue of efficiency and productivity but it does mean asking 'efficiency and productivity in whose interests?'.

In a powerful attack on tendencies in the sociology of work which play down the plurality of interests at work, Castillo (1999a) points to the Massachusetts Institute of Technology as a key purveyor ('MIT Productions Inc.') of analyses which, in effect, betray the critical legacy of sociology. He sees too many sociologists of work 'penning pastoral odes to just-in-time production, to composing night serenades to work commitment, almost Wagnerian symphonies to flexibility, or Mozartian *divertimenti* to lean production and "high technology work districts"'. There may be a degree of exaggeration here in this attack. There is also perhaps a degree of over-excitement in the polemic (leading to the mistaken idea that Wagner composed symphonies) but, in Wright Mills' terms, the charge here is that the 'private' problems of members of society generally are not being related to broader 'public issues' in much of the contemporary social scientific study of work institutions and practices. In effect, the issues are less 'public' or democratic ones than issues for corporate, and especially American, capitalist interests (cf. Hutton 2002).

If we fully recognise that social arrangements are made by human beings and are not the outcomes of immutable historical forces, we have to be careful about taking the sociology of work into another popular area of reflection on work patterns: making *predictions* about the 'future of work'. Prediction is often seen as a key aim of scientific research and theorising. Castillo (1999b) calls for sociologists of work to *explore* 'work of the future' instead of trying to predict the 'future of work'. The greatest promise of sociology is in making imaginative contributions to exploration and debate rather than producing predictions. This does not mean abandoning attempts to theorise in a scientific manner but perhaps, as Miles (2001) argues, we should evaluate a theory not according to the accuracy of its predictions about change but rather 'according to how far it stimulates debate about that change'. 'Good theories', he suggests, are those that 'bring the sociological imagination to life'. Such a criterion is a very appropriate one to apply to the theories that sociology has produced over its history.

Sociology and the emergence of industrial societies

The sociological imagination is very much a creature of the modern industrialised societies within which it developed as a form of critical reflection on the considerable social changes associated with industrialisation and the growth of capitalism. Sociology emerged in the nineteenth century as both a reaction to and a reflection of certain major social and cultural shifts which had been occurring for some hundreds of years in Europe. For some centuries prior to the emergence of sociology, the glue which held together the fabric of European society, giving it stability and a widespread taken-for-grantedness, had been weakening:

- The Reformation in the sixteenth century saw a questioning of the authority of a centralised Catholic Church and, with the emergence of Protestantism and dissent, came a growing stress on the individual rather than the corporate and the rational rather than the traditional.
- The Enlightenment in the late seventeenth and the eighteenth century brought under rational and critical scrutiny institutions of religion, inequality, kinship, property and monarchy.
- The Industrial and French Revolutions in the late eighteenth and the nineteenth century ensured that all of these institutions were further shaken and indeed often overturned.

A bourgeois revolution occurred in England in 1688 limiting the power of the monarchy and, in France, the monarchy was toppled. Notions of democracy were becoming increasingly popular in the early decades of the nineteenth century but the problem of finding appropriate institutions for democratic politics was increased by the complications introduced by the Industrial Revolution. Capitalism had been growing in strength for centuries but by the early nineteenth century it had become combined with an industrial spirit and associated techniques which carried revolutionary structural implications. Arising partly within and partly from outside the established bourgeois class was the new industrial middle class and, even more threatening to stability, was the appearance of a new social phenomenon – an industrial working class.

Some sense had to be made of these massive processes of change. How could people come to terms with processes of urbanisation, industrialisation, a growing division of labour, secularisation, bureaucratisation, democratisation, national state centralisation and the rest? Sociology can be seen as an intellectual coming-to-terms with these processes and as an attempt to understand their impact.

The potential for a sociological way of coming to terms with these changes had developed during the eighteenth-century Enlightenment period, prior to the full emergence of sociology in the nineteenth century. The scientific aspects of such a venture were implicit in the Enlightenment and its characteristic belief that 'people could comprehend and control the universe by means of reason and empirical research' (Ritzer 2000). But also emerging in this period was the idea that human beings can only be understood in the context of the whole society in which they live. This was an insight that later sociologists were to take up from the eighteenth-century writing of Giambattista Vico. It was also a key idea of the Scottish Enlightenment, and two key figures in this – John Millar and Adam Ferguson – examined changing patterns of work specialisation and division of labour sociologically, stressing the social as well as the economic aspects of these changes and identifying their implications, both positive and negative, for human welfare and work experience (Swingewood 2000, Herman 2001).

A near total breakdown in old assumptions about authority and social order followed the Enlightenment and the Industrial and French Revolutions, a breakdown which called for a reconstruction of the social order. Piecemeal reconstruction was seen as inappropriate, according to Fletcher (1971), when the 'entire fabric of institutions was falling apart' and a need for a 'body of knowledge about society as a totality of institutions' became apparent. It was this need that the founders of sociology were to try to meet. The key concepts or 'unit ideas' of sociology, Nisbet (1970) argues, were all developed as part of an attempt to achieve a 'theoretical reconsolidation' of the various elements on which social order had once rested – kinship, land, social class, religion, local community and monarchy – but which had now been 'dislocated by revolution' and 'scrambled by industrialisation and the forces of democracy'.

Sociologists, in this view, developed concepts like society and community to provide a consolidating or over-arching perspective which would counter the divisive, contradictory and individualistic tendencies of life in this period of emerging modernism. The founders of sociology were preoccupied with the analysis of industrialism and were engaged in creating a 'powerful vision or "image" of a society in the making' (Kumar 1978) and, says Giddens (1971), the overwhelming interest of Marx, Durkheim and Weber was in the 'delineation of the characteristic structure of modern capitalism as contrasted with prior forms of society'. Contemporary sociology has inherited this role and has 'as its main focus the institutions of "advanced" or "industrialised" societies, and of the conditions of transformation of those institutions' (Giddens 1982).

The continuing challenge

It could be argued that the twenty-first century presents us with challenges of coming to terms with social and economic changes that are no less significant than those faced by the creators of sociology almost two centuries ago. Industrialisation continues apace, if unevenly, across the globe and links between different areas and cultures are becoming closer and more immediate with fast-developing information and communication technologies. It sometimes seems that there are few choices left to us about how we live, at the level of the nation state let alone at the level of the local community or family. Technology, international corporations and pressures for capital accumulation sometimes seem to be pushing everyone towards a globalised future within which some will be allocated rich, secure and fulfilling lives at the expense of a mass of materially and experientially impoverished insecure workers and an even more impoverished stratum of economically inactive groups. At other times, we are encouraged to believe that the best of all possible worlds is available to us all, if we take advantage of the great opportunities both for challenging work and exciting recreation made possible by the same technological, commercial and globalising forces. Sociology has to bring us down to earth with regard to all of this. It needs to analyse what is going on and help us make a balanced appraisal of trends. Such analysis and insight can be a valuable resource, informing us and encouraging us to think imaginatively about the alternatives and choices facing us in all aspects of our lives, in our families, our communities and the wider societies of which we are members. How we think about the part that work is to play in our lives is necessarily central to this.

Sociology and the informing of democratic choices about work

What role, then, is suggested for the sociology of work and industry by the above analysis? First, we must recognise that it implies a rejection of a 'servant of power' role. Here, those trained as industrial sociologists would primarily be employed as specialist human manipulators by large organisations in the way Baritz (1960) saw beginning to happen in pre-war America where such people were 'doing what they were told to do and doing it well – and therefore endangering those other personal, group, class and institutional interests which were opposed to the further domination by the modern corporation of the mood and direction of American life'. Sociological knowledge and insight inevitably have a relevance to practical problem-solving in large organisations and can be shown to help solve problems in certain relatively bounded situations (Klein and Eason 1991). One would be naive and wrong to deny the right of any group to make use of knowledge in this way. What can be objected to, however, is the exclusive development of industrial sociology as a manipulative instrument for the pursuit of sectional interests.

An alternative role for the sociology of work and industry would be as a resource which helps those living in the industrial capitalist type of society to understand better the possibilities and choices which exist with regard to how work is organised and experienced in those societies. Its role is thus to inform choice. Here, the subject is not the sole preserve of the expert – be they 'servants of power' or marginalised academic teachers too hung up on their naive political utopianism or too caught up in dense conceptual mystification to be seen as worthy of attention by other than their own acolytes. Instead, it is something to be disseminated through both formal and informal educational institutions and communication media. It becomes something in whose development the individual is first involved as a student, and something which is subsequently drawn upon and further engaged with in their later life and career as employees, managers, voting citizens, trade unionists, self-employers or consumers. It is a resource vital to a democratic society. As Burns (1962) noted about industrial sociology, at a time when it scarcely had a foothold in Britain, it is the sociologist's business 'to conduct a critical debate . . . with the public about its equipment of social institutions'. As Eldridge *et al.* said about the role that industrial sociology might play in coming to terms with economic and social issues emerging later in the twentieth century, 'To show what possibilities may exist for political choices in an active democracy is to exercise the sociological imagination' (1991). Such an imagination is as relevant as ever in the twenty-first century.

In the past, social thinkers were a tiny minority addressing a slightly larger minority of the population. The modern age is one of vastly increased literacy and access to schooling and communication media. This means that critical reflection on the values and institutions of society need no longer be the preserve of the privileged social philosopher or the dilettante intellectual of a leisured class. An ability to be analytical about social, economic and political issues can be developed in every citizen – this furthering the ideal of democratic control of society and its institutions. Institutions of work and industrial organisation are central to the very nature of society and they nowadays require perhaps closer and more rational scrutiny and rethinking than ever before. Sociology, as a science that looks critically, rationally and systematically at aspects of our social lives, has a great deal to offer.

Researching and theorising work patterns and experiences

Sociology as science

Sociology's history unfolded alongside the rise of democratic institutions in Western societies. It is also a result of the rise of scientific ways of looking at the world. Sociology is a science. But what makes it a science is not a sterile value-neutrality or a concern with amassing facts uncontaminated by subjectivity. Neither is it a pursuit of final laws. Sociology uses insight, imagination and even inspiration; it is motivated by moral concern and even by political commitment, and it is characterised by internal debate and rivalries of both method and interpretation, but, in the end, it falls into the category of the sciences rather than the arts.

SCIENCE

A formal, systematic and precise approach to building up a body of knowledge and theory which is rigorous in testing propositions against available evidence.

Sociology is a scientific pursuit because it goes about detecting regularities and because it makes its generalisations on as systematic a basis as possible given its subject matter. This involves the testing of propositions and the basing of statements on evidence – this being collected, explained and interpreted in such a way that others can scrutinise that evidence and make their own judgements on the generalisations which are offered.

Sociology as a science is not essentially different from shrewd practical reasoning about our social lives or radically distinguishable from critical reflections and informed journalistic reflections on social institutions and trends in social change. It is different in degree rather than in essence, in three ways. It is

- more formal, systematic and precise in its observing, classifying, conceptualising and interpreting;
- more rigorous in the extent to which it submits its procedures to critical examination (seeking to falsify rather than prove its tentative explanations for example);
- more committed to building up a body of knowledge and a series of generalisations which go beyond immediate and practical needs. This body of knowledge is, therefore, available to be drawn upon when there is a practical issue to which it may be relevant.

Theory, work and society

Science is concerned to make informed generalisations about the world. These are scientific *theories*. In part these are informed by rational and critical reflection about the world but, most characteristically, they are informed by careful and considered attention to systematically gathered evidence.

THEORIES

Systematic generalisations about the world resulting from the application of scientific procedures.

It is unfortunate that many people use the term 'theory' in a derogatory manner to refer to ideas that do not effectively connect with human practices in the world. Facts about work, some people say, are interesting and useful but once we start to 'get theoretical' we start to become self-indulgent and irrelevant. However, once we recognise that sociological theories are essentially attempts to make sense of how society 'works', the nonsense of this becomes apparent. Indeed, 'facts' about society and work activities cannot really exist separately from the theoretical frames of reference within which they are expressed. How could we in subsequent chapters, for example, talk about the 'facts' of work security and insecurity without a theory of what constitutes 'security' and 'insecurity' in this context. How can we consider the extent to which the world is in fact 'globalising' without some reference to theories of globalisation? How can we even talk about 'work' and 'society' in a theory-free way? The way we conceptualised work and society earlier in this chapter was the start of the broader process of theorising the role of work activities and experiences in modern societies (and, yes, we will have to theorise 'modern' at the appropriate stage). The point of all of this is to deepen our understanding of *what is going on* in the world of work. Surely such an appreciation is valuable to all of us in shaping our social practices.

In the chapters that follow we will come across theories that have largely been developed at the desks of their creators – albeit, we would hope, within a well-informed general awareness of events going on in the social world outside of their libraries. This will tend to be the case in Chapter 2, where the various analytical strands that make up the sociology of work and industry are examined. These 'strands' are, in effect, broad conceptual schemes that we can take out into particular work contexts to make sense of what is going on there. In Chapter 3 we will come across large-scale generalisations about modern societies that are typically derived from critical reflection on broad trends in work aspects of the social world, often using evidence not especially gathered within specially designed 'research projects'. But in Chapters 4 to 8 we will see, in addition to this kind of material, generalisations emerging from specifically designed research projects or 'empirical' investigations. The sociology of work and industry brings together these various styles of investigative and theoretical endeavour.

A range of research methods

Sociologists of work and industry use a variety of techniques of investigation when they undertake empirical research ('empirical' meaning dependent on observation and experience of phenomena rather than reflection on them 'at a distance' so to speak). At one end of a continuum are studies involving the manipulation of existing bodies of statistical information and research projects involving the analysis of quantitative information gathered through questionnaire-based surveys specially designed by the investigators. At the other end of the continuum are studies in which a large amount of time is spent interviewing in depth a small selection of people or projects in which the researchers immerse themselves in the lives of the people they are studying by becoming participant observers. In between these contrasting styles of investigation are studies in which relatively large numbers of people are interviewed by research teams to gather both quantitative information and more qualitative material, 'qualitative' information typically taking the form of statements made by the people interviewed or observations made by the researchers themselves during the process of investigation.

Sometimes the research goes for *breadth* of coverage by looking at large numbers of instances of whatever is being studied or by checking samples large enough to be statistically representative of larger patterns. And at other times the concern is to achieve *depth* of understanding by giving attention to close details of particular *cases*. Case studies might examine particular work organisations, particular events or even particular individuals. The logic of such work is to get a detailed understanding of the processes that occur when, say, two work organisations merge, a new occupation establishes itself or an individual rises from being an ordinary worker to taking over the leadership of a large trade union.

We will come across studies in subsequent chapters which use some of these different approaches to develop our understanding of what is generally 'going on' in the work and industrial aspects of societies and the work dimension of people's lives. It is possible, however, for a variety of techniques to be used within one study. Say we wanted to understand better what is generally happening in telephone 'call centres', a growing area of work in modern societies. A research team might be established in which one member looks at employment statistics across a range of developed and less developed economies, whilst another interviews workers and managers in call centre companies, another implements a postal survey of members of the public who use or are contacted by such organisations, and a fourth member of the team obtains a job in a call centre to learn at first hand about working in such a setting. Within this research design, it might be decided to take time to look in depth at a selected case study call centre which has a generally good reputation as an employer and to compare this with one which has a bad reputation, this part of the study being concerned to learn something of the variety of work designs and work experiences occurring in this growing employment sector.

Our imagined multi-technique research project would be influenced by current theories of, say, work design, organisational change and job 'choice'. The information it produces would be analysed to develop further our theoretical understanding of these matters as well, of course, to present to the public and to policy-makers broad insights about what is occurring in an important aspect of contemporary employment. However, things are not as straightforward as our imagined case of a research project might imply. Sociologists who study work, industry, occupations, organisations and employment relations often differ from each other in quite significant ways in the assumptions which they bring to their studies.

Methodological assumptions

We have just noted the range of different methods that sociologists of work use. But they also vary in the *methodological* assumptions they bring to their research and theorising. Unfortunately, the term 'methodology' is often used simply to mean 'method'. It is unfortunate because it tends to divert people from some very important issues that need to be considered before a 'method', in the sense of an investigative technique, is chosen. Methodological assumptions are ones about the very nature of the 'realities' that we study, about how we can 'know' those realities and how we can make valid or 'truthful' generalisations about the social world on the basis of the very limited materials that we gather (whether these be number from surveys or statements and observations collected in 'field work'). There are many complexities involved here but it is vital to any student of the sociology of work to have a basic understanding of the main methodological choices that every researcher and theorist has to make.

The choice is often taken to be one between 'positivism' and 'interpretivism' (sometimes the latter being labelled 'phenomenology', which is really only one version of interpretivist thinking). The term 'positivism' is often used to refer to any research which uses quantitative methods and is sometimes condemned for a naive belief in the validity of the social facts that it collects, regardless of the theoretical assumptions to which those alleged 'facts' relate. But this is, as Turner (2001) stresses, a 'gross distortion' of what was intended by Auguste Comte, the original advocate, in the 1830s, of a positivist sociology (and, indeed, the inventor of the word 'sociology'). Comte conceived of sociology as a theory-driven activity. Data collection would be a means of formulating laws – laws that would enable positive social progress to be made and would replace superstition and guesswork as the basis for making decisions about the control of society. Positivists continue to seek 'covering law' types of generalisation about the social world, working on the assumption that the social world is not fundamentally different from the natural or physical world and that the social sciences can therefore adopt procedures similar to those of the natural sciences.

If positivism, as a term, has been misrepresented and misunderstood at times, interpretivism has fared little better. All too often it is thought of as research that uses 'qualitative' rather than quantitative materials, with the researcher recognising that they have actively to interpret the material they collect rather than let the 'facts speak for themselves'. This is not necessarily incorrect but it is utterly to miss the point about interpretivist sociology. Of course the interpretivist researcher acknowledges the need to interpret their research materials. But so do most non-interpretivists. But the essential difference between positivists and interpretivists is that, whereas positivists see the social world as amenable to research procedures not dissimilar to those of the natural sciences, interpretivists do not. They see the social world as different in nature from the physical world. It therefore needs to be studied in a different way. Most significantly, this is because human beings, whose actions form the subject matter of social science investigations, are thinking, sense-making, decision-making beings who could potentially choose to defy the predictions of social scientists. In the social sciences human beings study human beings, we might say. This is quite a different matter from human beings studying rocks, plants or planets. Humans, unlike physical entities, make interpretations for themselves of what is happening in the world. It is the *interpretive* or meaning-making interactions of people that interpretivist sociologists focus upon.

'Reality' for the interpretivist is something created by human beings through their interactions and cultures. But positivists take the position that there is a social reality existing independently of the ways in which people in society interpret their circumstances. They are thus said to be methodological realists. But positivism is not the only methodological realist option. An alternative realist position that is attractive to some sociologists of work and industry is that of *critical realism*. If we take the key methodological choice to be between realism and interpretivism, as set out in Table 1.1, we can see that there are not two but three possible methodological positions for the researcher and theorist to choose from: interpretivism and two variants of methodological realism – positivism and critical realism.

Table 1.1 Realist and interpretivist social science methodologies

Realist methodologies	Interpretivist methodologies
Assume that social reality exists independently of how people make sense of it – or investigate it. • *Positivism* devises covering laws about social reality through testing hypotheses – propositions that can be tested against systematically gathered data which are typically analysed using quantitative methods • *Critical realism* attempts to identify the structures, processes and *causal mechanisms* that operate beneath the surface of social reality and which are a constitutive part of that reality	Assume that social reality is the outcome of people's interactive and interpretive activities – how they socially and pragmatically 'construct' and negotiate meanings and patterns of relationship. Theoretical approaches that work within these broad assumptions include: • Weberian sociology (originating in Germany in the early twentieth century) • Symbolic interactionism (originating in America in the early to mid-twentieth century) • Poststructuralism (originating in France in the late twentieth century)

In Chapter 2 we will examine six strands of thinking that contribute to the sociology of work and industry. They vary in various respects but an important differentiating factor is the basic methodological stance that their proponents have tended to adopt. The managerial-psychologistic and the Durkheim-systems strands have more or less followed positivist assumptions whilst the Weber-social action, the interactionist and the discursive strands follow interpretivist principles. The critical realist approach that has emerged in recent years, very much influenced by the philosophical writings of Bhaskar (1986, 1989), incorporates some of the key ideas of Marxian thinking. One of its attractions to sociologists of work is that it stresses the reality of the underlying mechanisms of the capitalist mode of production whilst recognising that, at a level above this, interpretive processes and social construction processes do play a significant role in shaping social patterns and processes (Ackroyd and Fleetwood 2000). It might therefore seem, at first sight, to be a compromise between realist and interpretivist positions. It is, however, very firmly rooted in realist thinking, granting to patterns and causal processes outside of human actions a real and solid existence.

To illustrate how acceptance of each of these three sets of methodological assumption might influence the design of a research project, let's imagine three different researchers planning a research project on the relationship of people's age and experience of work.

- The positivist researcher might design a large survey in which a questionnaire is posted to a sample of people, the sample being 'stratified' to ensure that there is a representative coverage of different age groups and occupations. Questions would be asked about respondents' age and about the extent of their agreement with a variety of printed statements about work satisfaction and dissatisfaction. Once collected, these responses would be treated as *data* – unproblematic 'givens' or 'findings' – which could then be statistically analysed to test the hypothesis that, say, job satisfaction increases with age in high status occupations and decreases in age in low status occupations. If the 'data' or 'findings' supported the original contention, then the researchers might say that they had developed a new 'theory' about age and job satisfaction. Strictly speaking, what they would have created would not be a theory but a covering law. This would take the form of a statement about the relationship between work and age possessing a degree of predictive power: reading it would suggest to each of us, in our particular occupational context, how our happiness at work is likely to change as we get older.
- The critical realist would tend to be more strongly influenced from the start by existing theories (in the sense of generalisations about how the social world 'works'). They might use either, or both, quantitative and qualitative techniques to reveal, say, how ideologies influenced by the interests of employers in capitalist societies influence younger, and hence fitter and more flexible, people to regard their work positively whilst older, and potentially less productive, workers are discouraged from wanting to stay at work. Drawing on both existing theoretical assumptions about the social world and on the information gathered in the research, attempts would be made to identify the causal or 'generative' mechanisms within capitalist class and employment relationships using concepts like capital accumulation, labour process and false consciousness. These mechanisms would be taken to have a 'real' existence of their own, a reality operating at a deeper level than the actions and interpretations of the employers and workers involved.
- The interpretivist might arrange a series of face-to-face interviews with people of different ages and in different occupations. They might, additionally, attempt to spend time with some of these people in the workplace, or in a leisure context, in order to note how in group interactions they talk to each other about their work and their lives. It would not be assumed that words that people spoke in the research context constituted 'data' – unproblematic 'given' statements of what people actually feel or think. They would be treated as statements made in a particular context and at a particular time. The researcher sets out to interpret what was said to them in the light of how they believe the subject was interpreting the context in which they spoke and how they were, at the time of their speaking, choosing to present a particular image of themselves

to the researcher and perhaps to other people present. In the analysis of this research material, great attention would be given to the language used by the subjects, as well as other symbols like 'body language' and the clothing worn by subjects. This would be used to construct an understanding of how the people make sense, for themselves and for others, of the relationship between age and the experience of work. The 'reality' of the relationship between one's age and one's work experience is thus treated as something that emerges from human interactions, socially negotiated understandings and available discourses. It does not exist 'out there' separately from the people who bring that reality into existence. Taking this position does not mean, however, that the interpretivist cannot use concepts such as ones of structure, society or, for that matter, capitalist labour process. They might do this, but, unlike the critical realist, the interpretivist would regard these terms as sense-making concepts for analysing the world sociologically rather than as 'actually existing real things'.

Coping with the variety of orientation in the sociology of work and industry

From our examples of three possible research approaches it is apparent that there are significant variations of *methodological orientation* within the sociology of work and industry. There is also a variety of *theoretical orientations* – as we see in the six 'strands' of thought to be examined in Chapter 2. How is one to come to terms with a subject where there is such a variety of orientation? First, these tensions can be regarded as creative ones, and the multi-faceted nature of sociological study seen as healthily reflecting and forcing us to confront the multi-faceted nature of human society itself. Second, the notion of a sociological imagination (see p. 6) can bring a significant sense of unity to this variety. Whatever emphasis we adopt, we need to remember that sociology is essentially about relating the lives of particular individuals and the occurrence of specific and local events to wider patterns of society and the converting of 'private problems' into 'public issues'.

To undertake our own research does not necessarily mean having to join one or other of the various 'camps' that sociologists tend to set up with others of similar methodological or theoretical orientation. It has nevertheless been suggested that the various theoretical, methodological and political orientations of people studying the organisation of work are fundamentally incompatible with each other and that each researcher needs to locate themselves within one particular box or *paradigm* (a cluster of assumptions about sociological knowledge), choosing between a functionalist paradigm, an interpretive paradigm, a radical humanist paradigm or a radical structuralist paradigm (Burrell and Morgan 1979, Jackson and Carter 2000). Some researchers are happy to move back and forth between these various paradigms to find insights to apply to their area of study (Hassard 1993) whilst others wish to seek integration across them all to find a shared set of assumptions that provide a single frame of reference for studying work and the way it is organised (Pfeffer 1993, Donaldson 1996b).

A further approach is to reject the very notion of paradigms as irrelevant to the social sciences and to follow instead a strategy of *pragmatic pluralism* (Watson 1997). This encourages the researcher to utilise concepts and ideas from a whole range of different social science perspectives and traditions as long as, first, the chosen concepts are helpful in understanding the particular aspect of social life being studied and, second, as long as they are brought together in a clearly expressed frame of reference which has internal conceptual consistency and methodological integrity. The researcher needs to be particularly clear that they are not, for example, claiming at one point that interview materials they have collected are 'data' (i.e. unproblematic 'given' facts) and, at another, claim to be doing interpretivist analysis (which insists that such material can only be analysed with reference to the particular context in which it was uttered and in the light of the 'presentation of self' processes that were engaged in by both the interviewer and the interviewee in that context). To put it another way, one cannot try to be a methodological realist and a methodological interpretivist at the same time.

The structure of *Sociology, Work and Industry* has been devised to do justice to both unities and varieties of emphasis in the sociology of work and industry. The concern of this first chapter with achieving such a purpose is continued across the next seven chapters. Table 1.2 is intended to show how this is to be done. It recognises that, in addition to the six strands of thought that make up the sociology of work and industry, there are six areas of study to which these broad ways of thinking are applied. The six strands of thought (which form the subject matter of Chapter 2) are mapped in Table 1.2 against the six areas of study that form the subsequent six chapters which focus, each in turn, on:

- the industrial-capitalist and 'modern' nature of contemporary societies;
- the organisational dimension of work structuring;
- changes in the organising and managing of work;
- the occupational dimension of work structuring;
- the patterns of meaning, opportunity and experience of work in modern society;
- the tendencies to conflict and resistance in work relations.

To try to find some overall patterns across all of this, Table 1.2 offers a matrix identifying how the six strands of thought each bring a distinctive emphasis to the six substantive areas studied by the sociology of work and industry.

Table 1.2 How the six strands of thought in the sociology of work and industry bring different emphases to the six areas studied by the subject

	Work, society and change: Ch 3	Work organisations: Ch 4	The changing organisation and management of work: Ch 5	Occupations and society: Ch 6	Work experiences, opportunities and meanings: Ch 7	Conflict, challenge and resistance in work: Ch 8
Managerial psychologistic emphasis on		Increasing managerial effectiveness through satisfying the economic wants or psychological needs of workers			Causes and correlates of job satisfaction	Overcoming worker 'resistance to change'
Durkheim–systems emphasis on	The 'organic' division of labour in modern societies	Organisations as 'systems' of roles	Social/cultural integration of individuals into enterprises	The role of occupational groupings in maintaining social cohesion	Work meanings and experiences related to one's life in society as well as in the workplace	The management of conflict within industrial relations systems
Interactionist emphasis on	Division of labour as part of the moral order of society	Organisations as 'negotiated orders'		The significance of 'dirty' or deviant work	Identities and subjective careers	Defence of self and resistance to power of others
Weber–social action emphasis on	Rationalisation of life in modern industrial capitalist societies	The bureaucratic nature of organisations and the tendency towards unintended consequences of managerial initiatives		The tendency of groups to pursue social closure to further shared interests	The role of work 'orientations' in work-related behaviour	The inevitable plurality and clash of interests and values in social life
Marxian emphasis on	The exploitative nature of capitalist societies	Managerial shaping of labour processes in organisations to serve interests of the property owning dominant class		Decline of the social division of labour	Work a source of human fulfilment only when a non exploitative social order has been established	
Discursive emphasis on	The power of 'modernist' discourses in social life	The social construction of the 'realities' of organisational activity	Managerial use of discourses to define worker 'subjectivities' or identities	Occupational ideologies and discursive resources	The interplay and competition between different discourses in the shaping of identities, interests and social actions	

2 The sociological analysis of work and industry

Six strands of thought in the sociology of work

Sociology, it was established in Chapter 1, is a discipline which has developed to provide a critical understanding of industrial capitalist societies. An interest in work and how it is both organised and experienced has always been central to this project. A single and fully integrated industrial sociology or sociology of work has not emerged, however. Sociologists of work have varied in their methodological and theoretical orientations along the lines considered in the previous chapter. They have also differed in their primary interests; with some focusing on large societal patterns of work organisation and others focusing on more 'micro' aspects of work behaviour and experience; with some prioritising issues of conflict, exploitation and inequality and others prioritising issues of workplace and team co-operation; with some concentrating on structural factors influencing work activities and others concentrating on the role of human agency and 'subjectivity'. It is nevertheless possible to see some pattern in all of this. To avoid the artificiality of allocating different researchers and writers to 'schools' whilst still recognising the need somehow to bring together contributions which appear to have something in common, we can use the notion of *strands* of thought.

Table 2.1 identifies six strands of thought that we need to be aware of if we are to appreciate both the variations and the continuities in the sociological study of work. The arrows crossing some of the 'boxes' in the table indicate developments which have been influenced by more than one of the theoretical strands. In the case of three of the strands we see approaches which have been especially influenced by a particular founding figure of sociology, Durkheim, Weber or Marx. The first strand, however, contains what are usually seen as quite separate and indeed contrasting styles of thought. These strange bedfellows are brought together here to represent a style of thinking about people and work to which the five other strands can be seen as reacting and going substantially beyond.

CHAPTER TWO

Table 2.1 Six strands of thought in the sociology of work and industry

Strand of thought	Application and development
Managerial-psychologistic	Scientific management (Taylorism)
	Psychological humanism
Durkheim-systems	Human relations
	Systems thinking in organisational analysis
Interactionist	Occupations and professions in society
	Organisations as negotiated orders
	Ethnomethodology
Weber-social action	Social action perspective on organisations
	Bureaucratic principles of work organisation
	Orientations to work
Marxian	Individual experiences and capitalist labour processes
	Structural contradictions in society and economy
Discursive	Discourse and human subjectivity
	Postmodern organisations

The managerial-psychologistic strand

Strictly speaking, neither of the two approaches brought together here are part of a sociology of work and industry. Yet they are vitally important to an understanding of the development of industrial sociology as it became a significant area of study in the twentieth century because they have provided an ever-present general style of thinking with which sociologists have to come to terms and to which they seek to provide a critical alternative. Scientific management and psychological humanism are the ghosts at the banquet, in effect. It is much easier to appreciate the sociological guests at the feast if we have a good view of these strictly non-sociological approaches which tend to haunt such events. Scientific management and psychological humanism are at first sight diametrically opposed in underlying sentiment and assumptions about human nature. But they are both relatively individualistic styles of thinking about work and are both concerned to prescribe to managers how they should relate to their employees and should organise workers' jobs. They both concentrate on questions of 'human nature' and fail to recognise the range of possibilities for work organisation and orientation that people may choose to adopt, depending on their priorities in life. To this extent they can be regarded as *psychologistic*.

> **PSYCHOLOGISM**
>
> A tendency to explain social behaviour solely in terms of the psychological characteristics of individuals.

The concern of each of the approaches is to harness scientific method to discover and make legitimate what are, in effect, techniques of manipulation rather than disinterested concerns with understanding.

Scientific management

The leading advocate and systematiser of what he named scientific management (and others frequently call 'Taylorism') was F.W. Taylor (1856–1917), an American engineer and consultant. Taylor's importance to the modern organisation of work has to be set in its historical context. The increasingly rationalised division of tasks and the mechanisation of work reached a point at the beginning of the twentieth century where the need to co-ordinate human work efforts not surprisingly invited the attentions of individuals interested in applying scientific and engineering criteria to the human sphere as they had to the mechanical. Taylorism encouraged a view of the industrial worker as an economic animal who could be encouraged to act as a self-seeking hired hand and who would allow managers to do their job-related thinking for them. If this could be achieved, especially through the use of output-based and potentially high-level rewards, the management would work out the most efficient way of organising work, tying the monetary rewards of the work to the level of output achieved by the individual. This would produce results which would benefit employer and employee alike, removing the likelihood of conflict and the need for trade unions.

Scientific management involves:

- the scientific analysis by management of all the tasks which need to be done in order to make the workshop as efficient as possible;
- the design of the jobs by managers to achieve the maximum technical division of labour through advanced job fragmentation;
- the separation of the planning of work from its execution;
- the reduction of skill requirements and job-learning times to a minimum;
- the minimising of materials-handling by operators and the separation of indirect or preparatory tasks from direct or productive ones;
- the use of such devices as time-study and monitoring systems to co-ordinate these fragmented elements and the work of the deskilled workers;
- the use of incentive payment systems both to stabilise and intensify worker effort;
- the conduct of manager–worker relationships at 'arms-length' – following a 'minimum interaction model' (Littler 1982).

Taylor's successors within scientific management modified his refusal to accept a place for organised labour in the workplace, but the approach has always retained its individualistic emphasis. Books on management thought and much management teaching imply that scientific management, on being shown to fall short psychologically, was consigned to the history of management as a thing of its 'classical' past. This is far from the case, however, when it comes to the practicalities of job design in the modern world. Systematic research carried out in the 1950s and followed up in the 1970s (Davis and Taylor 1979) on a representative sample of American companies showed that job design practices in manufacturing continued to be dominated by a concern to minimise the unit production time in order to minimise the cost of production. Job design criteria included skill special-isation, minimal skill requirements, minimum training times, maximum repetition and the general limiting of both the number of tasks in a job and the variation within those tasks and jobs. Braverman (1974) claimed that scientific management and its associated deskilling, because of its association with the logic of capital accumulation, will continue to dominate the capitalist working world. Research carried out in a wide variety of contexts to test Braverman's analysis has shown that alongside attempts to give workers greater choice and relative autonomy in certain work contexts, the deskilling logic of scientific management is still applied to many easily routinised work activities.

The psychologistic assumptions of scientific management (which are also looked at in Chapter 4) are illustrated by reference to Taylor's concept of 'soldiering' as described in *The Principles of Scientific Management* (1911a). Soldiering in Taylor's sense is 'the natural instinct and tendency of men to take it easy'. When this is combined with people's economic interests and the failure of managers to design, allocate and reward work on a scientific basis, it leads employees to get together and rationally conspire to hold production down. They do this to maximise their reward without tempting the incompetent management to come back and tighten the rate (which only needs tightening because it was originally guessed at and not fixed scientifically). This is 'systematic soldiering' and is an inefficient evil. It is not, however, seen as an inevitable phenomenon. If the manage-ment relate directly to each individual and satisfy their personal self-interest then they will get full co-operation. A proper understanding of human nature, it is implied, would demonstrate that this is the case. And the application of technical solutions to human problems in this way makes it unnecessary to tackle them politically. Taylor, and other engineers of his time, aspired to taking politics and contest out of work relationships, effectively 'redefining industrial conflict as a mechanical problem' (Shenav 1999). These aspirations were cultural as well as political. Scientific management fostered a social movement which, as Taksa (1992) puts it, 'would facilitate the creation of a unified industrial culture unmarked by class divisions or conflict, a culture characterised by imposed notions of consensus'. Contemporary interests in 'culture management' (Chapter 5, pp. 129–31) keep much of this spirit alive.

Psychological humanism

The prescriptions offered to managers by this group of writers and researchers are based on rather different assumptions about human psychology than those seen in scientific management. Psychological humanists argue for achieving organisational efficiency not through the exclusion of workers from task-related decision-making but by encouraging their *participation* in it with, for example:

- non-managerial workers becoming involved in setting their own objectives;
- jobs being 'enriched' by reducing the extent to which they are supervised and monitored;
- more open and authentic colleague relationships being developed, particularly in 'teams'.

These ideas have become popular with more 'enlightened' managers since the writings, manuals and training films of a group of American psychologists and management consultants encouraging such an approach began to have an influence in the 1960s. It can be seen as the opposite of scientific management but, in some ways, it is a mirror image of it. It bases its approach to human work behaviour on a theory of human nature, and one of the popular early writers of this school made quite clear the equivalence of the two opposing propositions by labelling them, alternatively, Theory X and Theory Y.

McGregor (1960) characterised the scientific management type of approach, which is adopted by unenlightened managers, as based on Theory X. This sees human beings as naturally disliking work and therefore as avoiding it if they can. People prefer to avoid responsibility and like to be given direction. They have limited ambitions and see security as a priority. The manager therefore controls and coerces people towards the meeting of organisational objectives. The effect of this is to encourage the very kind of behaviour which managers wish to avoid: the employees' passive acceptance of the situation may be encouraged, leading to a lack of initiative and creativity on their part, or their resentment may be fuelled and hence their aggression and lack of co-operation. But Theory Y, which McGregor advocated and which social science research was said to support, states that people are not at all like this but would generally prefer to exercise self-control and self-discipline at work. He believed this would occur if employees were allowed to contribute creatively to organisational problems in a way which enabled them to meet their need for self-actualisation.

The notion of a *self-actualisation need* within all human beings is central to the writing of Maslow (1954) whose starting point was the belief that scientific investigation of human behaviour should be oriented towards releasing in people the various potentials they possess. The basic scheme, which has been taken from Maslow and used by numerous 'enlightened' management writers and teachers, is the 'hierarchy of needs' model (Watson 1996). This suggests that there are five sets of genetic or instinctive needs which people possess and that as one satisfies most of the needs at one level one moves up to seek satisfaction of the needs at the next level:

- at the first level there are *physiological needs*, such as for food, drink, sex and sensory satisfaction;
- at the second level, there are *safety needs* which motivate people to avoid danger;
- at the third level, there are what Maslow calls *love needs*; these include needs to belong and to affiliate with others in both a giving and a receiving sense;
- at the fourth level, there are *esteem needs* which cover prestige, status and appreciation coming from external sources as well as internal feelings of confidence, achievement, strength, adequacy and independence;
- at the fifth level, there is the need for *self-actualisation*, which is the desire to realise one's ultimate potential.

SELF-ACTUALISATION

'To become more and more what one is, to become everything that one is capable of becoming' (Maslow 1943).

The needs-hierarchy model was influenced by Maslow's earlier studies of monkeys and of the way certain individuals, human or primate, come to dominate others. He believed that some individuals have a greater inherited propensity to self-actualise than others. Natural biological elites would thus come to rise to the top in society and, Cullen (1997) argues, Maslow's theory effectively 'justifies managerial power, and enables managers to adopt motivation practices that appear to be responsive to employee needs while at the same time absolving them of accountability for the ineffectiveness of their practices'. In spite of these ideological undertones, or perhaps because of them, Maslow's model is frequently used as a stick with which to beat traditional managerial approaches, these being seen as failing to obtain employee co-operation because they do not provide the intrinsically and naturally sought rewards which employees 'need' once they have satisfied their basic low-level requirements. An influential example of such thinking is Herzberg's 'Motivation-Hygiene' or *two-factor theory of work motivation* (1966) which was originally based on a study of engineers and accountants who were asked to describe events in their working lives which made them feel good or made them feel bad. Herzberg suggested that the factors which made them feel good when they were present were different from those which made them feel bad when they were absent.

Herzberg went on to differentiate between:

- contextual or 'hygiene' factors like salary, status, security, working conditions, supervision and company policy which can lead to dissatisfaction if 'wrong', but which do not lead to satisfaction if 'right';
- content or 'motivation' factors such as achievement, advancement, recognition, growth, responsibility and 'the work itself'. These have to be present, in addition to the con-textual or 'hygiene' factors, before satisfactions can be produced and people motivated to perform well.

These 'motivators' clearly relate to Maslow's 'higher level needs' whilst the hygiene factors only satisfy the 'lower level' ones. Managers are therefore encouraged to see that getting 'right' such matters as wages, supervision and working conditions would produce little by way of positive motivation. Instead, the 'motivators' have to be built into the very way jobs are designed. Jobs should be enlarged and managerial controls over how they are performed reduced. Workers themselves would set targets, plan the work and, as far as possible, choose the working methods to be used. This represents a complete reversal of the job design principles advocated by scientific management, as we shall see when we look at job design issues in Chapter 5.

Discussion

At first sight it might appear that those interested in scientifically investigating work behaviour have a fairly simple task here: that of testing these two propositions about work and human needs to find the validity of either scientific management's 'Theory X' or the psychological humanists' 'Theory Y'. Alas, says the sociologist, this cannot be done. Such an attempt would involve reductionism and psychologism in its belief that understanding work behaviour is a matter of reaching a correct understanding of human nature – a set of principles about people which would apply to all human beings in all circumstances. In so far as there is such a thing as human nature it is much more complex than this and leads people to act very differently in different circumstances. To a much greater extent than other animals, humans are what they make of themselves. They are not without instinctive drives or innate physiological needs. But these are overridden by cultural norms, social rules and identity related preferences. Within these, individuals may sometimes seek the assurance of safety and sometimes seek the stimulation of danger, sometimes pursue self-aggrandisement and sometimes indulge in self-abasement. Our socially or culturally defined nature is far more important than any universal 'human' or species nature. We have socially mediated wants rather than built-in needs.

In evaluating scientific management and psychological humanism we confront a paradox. In effect, both are right and both are wrong. To make sense of this statement, we must add the words *depending on the circumstances*. By circumstances we mean the structural and cultural factors that are central concerns of a sociological approach to analysis. Thus, (a) if we have on the one hand, a culture which lays major value on money and an industry structured on the basis of mechanisation and minute task-specialisation, it is possible that people will deliberately choose to do such work and will happily accept close supervision and a degree of boredom in return for cash; (b) if, on the other hand, we have a wider culture which places central value on personal autonomy and sees work as a key to identity, then we might expect the scientific managers to lose out to the self-actualisers as guides to appropriate managerial policy.

In practice, we find a mixture of these circumstances in modern societies. Consequently we need a more sophisticated sociological approach to studying work behaviour and attitudes. The work orientations perspective that we will meet shortly in this chapter (pp. 40–1) was in part intended to meet this need but, for the moment, we must stress that the choice which is made to adopt either cash-reward-oriented or self-actualising work organisations is not a scientific one. It is to a large extent a value or a political choice. The role of sociological analysis is to inform that choice with a consideration of what is possible in what circumstances.

The Durkheim-systems strand

In contrast to the psychologism of the first strand of thinking, there is a rejection in the second strand of attempts to understand social patterns through a focus on human individuals and the 'needs' which they are all said to share. Instead we see an emphasis on the social system of which individuals are a part. The social system may be that of the society as a whole or, alternatively, it may be that of the work organisation or even a sub-unit of the organisation. The key idea is the essentially sociological one of concentrating on the patterns of relationships which exist between people rather than on the people as such. This insight is apparent in the early proto-sociologists of the Scottish Enlightenment with Adam Ferguson, for example, noting the system-like character of the emerging industrial workshops whose logic was one in which the workers' minds were less significant than their acting as components of a social 'engine' (Swingewood 2000). But the broad emphasis on patterns of human relationship reaches its peak in the history of sociology with Emile Durkheim and it provides the theoretical underpinning of what is often identified as the first recognisable 'school' of industrial sociology, that of human relations. More recently it has inspired systems approaches to both industrial relations thinking and to the sociology of organisations.

Emile Durkheim

Emile Durkheim (1858–1917) is often described as the sociologist *par excellence*. In this we see his importance and perhaps the major problem with his work. His position as the first sociologist to hold a university professorship meant that there was considerable pressure on him to establish the distinctiveness of the new discipline. This fact probably explains in part his over-heavy stress on science (which, he believed, can give moral guidance) and his over-emphasis on the 'reality' of an autonomous and externally existing 'society'. Ideas which stress the primacy of community over the individual have a strong ideological and conservative potential, but to picture Durkheim as an intentionally con-servative thinker in this way is quite wrong. He was concerned neither to return to the past nor to justify the status quo. Yet he was strongly reacting to certain aspects of the prevailing individualism of his age. On a methodological level he was opposed to psychological reductionism, showing that even a highly individual act like suicide has to be understood in terms of the extent of the individual's integration into a community or group rather than by simple reference to the individual's mental state. To study social life one had to isolate and examine 'social currents' and 'social facts'. These are to be seen as *things* and as existing external to individuals, exerting constraint over them. Values, customs, norms, obligations and suchlike are to be considered in this way.

Perhaps most influential in taking Durkheim towards an over-emphasis on the structural side of the agency–structure relationship was his morally inspired reaction to the disintegrating effects of the egoism and self-interest which he saw developing in the European societies of his time. He saw the organic solidarity so necessary for a healthy society being threatened by *laissez-faire* economics and a utilitarian philosophy which encouraged an egoism strongly contrasting with the healthy kind of individualism which could exist in an industrialised society. A 'healthy' individualism could exist as long as that society provided regulation, directing principles or norms. Without this we have the pathology of *anomie*.

ANOMIE

A form of social breakdown in which the norms that would otherwise prevail in a given situation cease to operate.

The particular form of anomie which worried Durkheim was one in which the 'organic integration' of society would be threatened by unrestricted individual aspirations and hence a lack of any kind of social discipline, principle or guiding norms.

Human relations

Durkheim's analysis of anomie and his concern about social solidarity and integration was a major influence on the work of Elton Mayo (1880–1949) who has come to be seen as the leading spokesman of the so-called human relations 'school' of industrial sociology. Whereas Durkheim's sympathies were not with the ruling or managerial interests of capitalist society, Mayo's were. In place of Durkheim's seeking of social integration through moral communities based on occupations, Mayo put the industrial work-group and the employing enterprise, with the industrial managers having responsibility for seeing that group affiliations and social sentiments were fostered in a creative way. Like Taylor, Mayo was anxious to develop an effective and scientifically informed managerial elite. If managements could ensure that employees' social needs were met at work by giving them the satisfaction of working together, by making them feel important in the organisation and by showing an interest in their personal problems, then both social breakdown and industrial conflict could be headed off. Managerial skills and good communications were the antidotes to the potential pathologies of an urban industrial civilisation.

The context of the contribution of the human relations group was the problem of controlling the increasingly large-scale enterprises of the post-war period and the problem of legitimating this control in a time of growing trade union challenge. The faith of the scientific management experts in a solution which involved the achieving of optimum working conditions, the 'right' method and an appropriate incentive scheme proved to be too blind. Practical experience and psychological research alike were indicating the need to pay attention to other variables in work behaviour. Here we see the importance of the Hawthorne experiments.

The Hawthorne investigations had been started in Chicago by engineers of the Western Electric Company's Hawthorne plant. They had investigated the effects of workshop illumination on output and had found that, as their investigations proceeded, output improved in the groups investigated, regardless of what was done to the lighting. In 1927 the Department of Industrial Research of Harvard University, a group to which Mayo had been recruited, were called in. Their enquiry started in the Relay Assembly Test Room where over a five-year period a wide range of changes were made in the working conditions of a specially segregated group of six women whose job was to assemble telephone relays. Changes involving incentive schemes, rest pauses, hours of work and refreshments were made, but it was found that whatever changes were made – including a return to original conditions – output rose. The explanation which was later to emerge has been labelled 'the Hawthorne effect'. It was inferred that the close interest shown in the workers by the investigators, the effective pattern of communication which developed and the emerging high social cohesion within the group brought together the needs of the group for rewarding interaction and co-operation with the output needs of the management. This type of explanation was also encouraged by the other stages of the investigation. The employee interviewing programme was seen as showing that many of the problems of management–worker relationships could be put down to the failure to recognise the emotions and the 'sentiments' of the employees, and the study in the Bank Wiring Observation Room was taken to show the part played by informal social group needs in worker restriction of output. The Hawthorne studies were most fully reported by Roethlisberger and Dickson (1939) and their reports and interpretations can be compared with those of Mayo (1933) and Whitehead (1938). We have already noted the relationship between Durkheim's ideas and those of Mayo but perhaps a more important influence on all of these interpreters was the classical sociologist Pareto (1848–1923). A key figure in the Harvard sociological circles of this time was the biologist and translator of Pareto, L.J. Henderson. He introduced the thinking of this former Italian engineer to those Harvard thinkers who, at the time, were highly receptive to ideas that might counter those of the liberals or Marxists (Gouldner 1971). The effects of Pareto (via Henderson) on this early form of industrial sociology were two-fold:

1   The suggestion that workers' behaviour can be attributed to their 'sentiments' rather than to their reason. Apparently rational behaviour, like Taylor's 'systematic soldiering', referred to earlier, could be better understood as deriving from irrational fears, status anxieties and the instinctive need of the individual to be loyal to his or her immediate social group. The problems did not arise from economic and rationally perceived conflicts of interest and were therefore not open to solution through 'scientific' management.
2   An emphasis on the notion of *system*, this conveniently according with the holistic tendencies of Durkheim. Here we have the organic analogy with its stress on integration and the necessary interdependence of the parts and the whole. Only by the integration of the individual into the (management-led) plant community could systemic integration be maintained and the potential pathologies of the industrial society avoided.

Human relations industrial sociology has been widely criticised for such things as its managerial bias, its failure to recognise the rationality of employee behaviour and its denial of underlying economic conflicts of interest (see Landsberger 1958). The investigations which were carried out have also been examined and found wanting (Carey 1967). Some of the writers in the tradition are more vulnerable to criticism than others, but what cannot be denied is the enormous influence these researchers, and especially Mayo, had on subsequent social scientific investigation of industrial behaviour (Smith 1987). The 'Mayo legacy' remains in management thinking, especially in human resource management (HRM) (see Chapter 5, pp. 108–11), and the concern of that approach with getting workers to 'adjust' so that they are 'integrated' into organisations whose 'goals' they identify with (O'Connor 1999). Although the Hawthorne works in Chicago have now been replaced by shopping malls, researchers on work organisations are turning back to the classic studies carried out there as they debate a range of theoretical and methodological issues which were initially raised by this work (Schwartzman 1993). Gillespie (1991) argues that we can most usefully regard the accounts and discussions of the Hawthorne experiments as 'manufactured knowledge' in which Mayo and his fellow human relations writers drew on their social scientific investigations to construct a 'message' – one which played down the possibility of an active role for workers, especially a collective role, and which stressed the role of managers as experts in control.

Systems thinking in industrial sociology

Durkheim's message to sociologists was that they should look beyond the individuals who compose society to the level of the underlying patterns of social activity. The institutions, which are part of this pattern, are to be studied not only to locate their 'genesis' but to understand their 'functioning' – that is, the contribution of the parts of the society to the continuation and survival of the whole.

SYSTEMS THINKING

A way of viewing social entities as societies or organisations as if they were self-regulating bodies exchanging energy and matter with their environment in order to survive.

The idea of looking at society itself or at industrial organisations as social systems (and, later, as socio-technical systems) is rooted in the old organic analogy which views society as a living organism constantly seeking stability within its environment and has come down into contemporary sociology through the work of Durkheim, Pareto and various anthropologists working in the Durkheimian tradition. One of the most influential sociologists of the twentieth century, Talcott Parsons (1902–1979), who was much taken up with biological analogies, was a member of Henderson's Harvard 'Pareto Circle' along with Elton Mayo. His influence was considerable, establishing an intellectual ambience in which a significant proportion of contributions to industrial and organisational sociology were fashioned. Added to this has been the increasing popularity of cybernetics in the industrial world and a growing interest within management thought in the so-called 'general systems theory' of von Bertalanffy.

The greatest impact of systems thinking in the sociology of work and industry was undoubtedly on the study of work organisations. Between the mid-1950s and 1970 or so the view of the formal organisation as an open system functioning within its 'environment' virtually became an orthodoxy shared by various different schools of organisation theory. These include the socio-technical systems approach and the very influential contingency approaches that we will look at in detail later in Chapters 4 and 5. The systems approach, essentially, amounts to the replacement of the classical managerial metaphor which sees the organisation as a rationally conceived machine constructed to meet efficiently the goals of its designers with the metaphor of the organisation as a living organism constantly adapting in order to survive in a potentially threatening environment. Systems views are still widely followed in the study of organisations even if their use is sometimes more implicit than explicit (Brown 1992). They have two major strengths:

- They properly recognise that organisations are much more than the official structures set up by their initiators. They are, rather, patterns of relationships which constantly have to adapt to enable the organisation to continue.
- They stress the importance of close interrelationships between the different parts, or 'subsystems', of the organisation. The tendency for changes in one part of a system to have implications for its other parts is strongly emphasised.

The influence of systems thinking in industrial relations has been less long-lasting, at least among those taking a more sociological view of industrial conflict. The British Oxford school of industrial relations writers, whose most significant impact came with their influence on the Donovan Commission (see p. 213), used a systems approach (Schienstock 1981).

However, such an approach was made more explicit in the American tradition based on the model offered by Dunlop (1958). This locates all industrial disputes and their management within an 'industrial relations system' which is made up of four elements: groups of actors (managerial, worker and outside, especially governmental, agencies); a context; an ideology which binds the system together; a body of rules which govern the behaviour of the various actors.

Central to this industrial relations system, and central to the kinds of objection which have been made by sociologists to the approach, is the notion of the ideology which holds the system together. This, according to Dunlop, is the set of ideas and beliefs 'commonly held by the actors' involved. To the sociologists of the generations active after the mid-1960s who were turning away from orthodox systems-oriented sociologies of the Durkheimian and 'structural-functionalist' type towards the power and conflict-oriented insights of Weber and Marx, this was to over-stress heavily the degree of consensus which exists in modern societies about work and its rewards. It was felt that the sociologist should set issues of industrial conflict much more in the context of the basic power and material inequalities of society as a whole and give attention to the role of domination, exploitation and class conflict in work relationships.

Corporate cultures

An important development in management thinking which emerged in the 1980s and continues to influence organisational management (Chapter 5, pp. 129–31) urged managers to develop 'strong' cultures in their organisations (Peters and Waterman 1982; Deal and Kennedy 1982). This, in part, took up the recognition by Barnard (1938), a management writer associated with the Human Relations group at Harvard in the 1930s, of the importance of developing a sense of belonging and common purpose within organisations. Barnard contrasted the type of social integration he felt necessary for the successful performance of industrial organisations with Durkheim's notion of *anomie*. This was manifesting itself within industrial enterprises where there was a lack of clear corporate norms of conduct pulling people into managerially desirable co-operative social action. The later advocates of strong corporate 'cultures' similarly wanted to create conditions in which people's individualism would flourish through their finding meaning as members of a corporate community. In this there would be a reconciling of the social and the individualistic aspects of human beings along the lines that Durkheim envisaged as a component of social solidarity at a societal level (Ray 1986). The association by critics of the management culture writers of their tendency to 'subjugate the individual to the collective' (Ray 1986; Dahler-Larsen 1994) with Durkheim's understanding of social solidarity is not warranted, according to Starkey (1998), if we recognise how Durkheim's later work gave fuller attention than his earlier work to how an interplay between different interests, as opposed to an overcoming of differences, contributes to the achievement of social integration.

Discussion

Although they can be accused of using over-simplified versions of Durkheim's ideas for critical purposes rather than fully appreciating the sophistication of his thinking, later sociologists have seen the key weakness of the Durkheim-systems strand of thinking as a tendency to over-emphasise integration and consensus both within societies and within work organisations at the expense of attention to underlying conflicts and fundamental differences of interest. Differences of interest are recognised but interest groups tend to be conceived within a 'pluralist' political model which sees the parties in conflict as being more or less evenly matched in power terms. As we shall see in later chapters, contemporary approaches to understanding industrial capitalist societies, work organisations and industrial conflict, attempt to give a more balanced view through attending to basic power structures and patterns of inequality as well as to matters of co-operation and shared norms.

Systems models are not only increasingly seen as one-sided in their over-emphasis on integration and consensus. They are often seen as too readily viewing the organisation, or the society of which it is a part, from the point of view of managerial or other dominant interest groups. Often implicit in analyses of social relationships as 'systems' is a concern to identify ways of maintaining that system. Conflicts and differences over anything more than minor matters of adjustment thus become seen as pathologies – or sicknesses of the organism – which have to be cured if the organism is not to die. This tendency is not inevitable, however, since highly oppositional, and especially revolutionary, analyses are fond of talking about 'the system', usually implying a wish for the system to 'die'. Such radical types of systems thinking are, of course, no less one-sided than their managerial counterparts.

Systems thinking is valuable in its stress on structures and patterns in social life. It is therefore a useful corrective to over-individualistic and 'psychologistic' approaches to explanation. However, it faces the danger of over-reacting to individualistic perspectives. It is always in danger of leaving out of the analysis the people involved. Structures come to replace human beings as the focus of attention so that the approaches which make up this present strand of thinking do not really meet the criteria established for a successful sociology in Chapter 1. In making human individuals secondary or derivative of the social system in which they are located, systems approaches tend to pay insufficient attention to the degree of interplay which goes on between individual initiative and social constraint in human societies. Systems views tend to fall especially short when it comes to taking into account the extent to which the social world is the creation of interacting individuals and groups assigning *meanings* and making interpretations of their situations. To consider an approach which gives prime emphasis to meanings and to interaction rather than to systems and structures existing outside the individual, we now turn to a quite different strand of the sociology of work and industry.

The interactionist strand

The interactionist strand has its roots firmly in the sociology department of Chicago University in America. Theoretically, the interactionist perspective, with its focus on the individual, the small group and on meanings, is almost a polar opposite of the Durkheim-systems strand described above. Yet in the contributions of interactionist sociologists to the study of work, we find important continuities with the work of Durkheim. This continuity can be seen in a common interest taken in occupations as central social institutions and also in a recognition of the importance of the division of labour in society. But to appreciate fully the interactionist approaches to work, it is necessary to give an account of the theoretical approach of the wider school of sociology of which these sociologists of work are a part – the school of symbolic interactionism.

The Chicago school and symbolic interactionism

The particular brand of sociological theory known as symbolic interactionism has developed alongside the more empirical study of work which has taken place within the same Chicago circles. The origins of the approach lie in the work of Cooley (1864–1929) and Mead (1863–1931) and its basic position is that the individual and society are inseparable units; their relationship is a mutually interdependent one, not a one-sided deterministic one. Human beings construct their realities in a process of interaction with other human beings. Individuals derive their very identity from their interaction with others.

SYMBOLIC INTERACTIONISM

The study of social interaction which focuses on how people develop their concept of self through processes of communication in which symbols such as words, gestures and dress allow people to understand the expectations of others.

According to the symbolic interactionists, all interaction and communication is dependent on the use of symbols such as words, gestures, clothes, skin colour and so on. The infant acquires an identity – a consciousness of *self* – through the socialisation or social learning process. This process involves the internalisation of symbols, which are organised round the concept of self to make social life meaningful. Awareness of self is acquired through 'taking on the role of the other'. It is through taking on the role of the other, particularly what are called 'significant others', that we learn about the expectations which others have of us. This helps us in deciding what role we will play in any given situation. Similarly, by taking the role of the other, we learn what to expect of that other. To orient us as we make our way through life we look to a variety of what are termed reference groups and as we move through a series of situations which bestow identity on us we are said to follow a career. Not surprisingly this concept of career is, as we shall see in Chapter 7 (pp. 195–6), a key contribution of this theoretical perspective to the sociology of work.

The man who established the investigative tradition of the interactionist strand was Park (1864–1944), a former journalist who encouraged researchers to make detailed ethnographic observations of both normal and deviant Chicago life in the participant observation tradition previously confined to anthropological studies of tribal life. In this and in his Durkheimian interest in what he called the 'moral order' (an ordering of expectations and moral imperatives which tend to routinise interaction) he influenced Everett Hughes (1863–1931) (Hughes 1958, 1994). Where Durkheim tended to look to occupations as offering possible solutions to the problem of social order, Hughes tends to take the study of occupations as his starting point; his way into learning about society. He is seen as an inspiration by contemporary researchers whose 'workplace studies' in settings such as news rooms, hospitals, air traffic and rapid urban transport control centres are closely examining how 'the social and interactional organisation of workplace activities, ranging from paper documents to complex multimedia systems, feature in day-to-day work and collaboration' (Heath *et al.* 2000).

Hughes' approach is to focus on the social drama of work – the interaction which takes place at work – taking note of the problems or tensions which are created by the work itself and by its social situation. The concern then turns to how the individual copes with or adapts to those problems, and especially, relates them to the problem of maintaining their identity. Here, perhaps, is the great fascination of this approach, a fascination which will become apparent in Chapter 6 when we look at how members of different occupations cope with the particular problems of their work. Hughes encouraged his students to focus on the offbeat, the 'dirty' or the deviant types of occupation (in the notorious Chicago 'nuts and sluts' tradition). This was not only because these occupations are interesting in their own right but because their study can highlight factors of general relevance to work experience which we might not notice in more conventional kinds of work where we too easily take them for granted. Thus, for example, when later on we consider the way prostitutes heavily stress the extent to which they control their clients in order to maintain self-respect, we are prompted to consider just how this may also be done in the more normal service occupations which we come across – the retail worker, the garage mechanic or the nurse. Light is thus thrown on the significance of the common tendency of car mechanics to insist that any theory put forward by the motorist about what is wrong with their car cannot be correct. Expertise must be protected to defend the mechanic's sense of self-respect *vis-à-vis* the client just as the female prostitute must protect her sense of emotional non-involvement to defend her notion of 'self' and personal autonomy *vis-à-vis* the male punter.

Organisations as negotiated orders

Interactionism has perhaps made its most significant contribution to the understanding of work organisations with its notion of the organisation as a negotiated order (Watson 2001c). The concept was developed by Strauss *et al.* (1963) as part of a study of a psychiatric hospital showing how 'order' in the hospital was an outcome of a continual process of negotiation and adjustments between doctors, nurses, patients, social workers, patients' families and administrators. Organisational rules and hierarchies play a part in the patterning of life in organisations but the overall organisational order is one that emerges out of the processes whereby different groups make use of rules, procedures and information in the day-to-day negotiations that occur between them about what is to happen in any given situation at any particular time.

> ### NEGOTIATED ORDER
>
> The pattern of activities which emerge over time as an outcome of the interplay of the various interests, understandings, reactions and initiatives of the individuals and groups involved in an organisation.

The hospital study was criticised for a failure to ground organisational analysis in its wider political, social structural and historical context (Day and Day 1977). Strauss (1978), however, took up the criticism of the earlier study and developed a style of organisational analysis which would cover not just mundane and local differences between parties involved in an organisation but would identify more basic or 'endemic' conflicts affecting them. The original hospital study was influenced by an earlier interactionist study of asylums in which Goffman (1961) showed that within 'total institutions' like prisons, monasteries and mental hospitals, in which inmates' lives and identities are almost totally dominated by organisational rules, even those in the least powerful positions in organisations nevertheless 'make out' and defend their identities in spite of the determination of the 'system' to reduce them to a cipher. Strauss's later work made use of Dalton's (1959) classic participative observation study of managers and how they make covert deals and secret bargains and generally engage in 'sub-processes of negotiation'.

Ethnomethodology

Ethnomethodology might be seen as taking interactionist insights to their logical conclusion. It combines the thinking of the Chicago school with ideas from the European tradition of phenomenological philosophy and with insights from Weber's methodological thinking.

> ### ETHNOMETHODOLOGY
>
> The study of how ordinary members of society in their everyday lives make the world meaningful by achieving a sense of 'taken–for–grantedness'.

Ethnomethodology denies any objective reality to social phenomena. It suggests that there are no such things as societies, social structures or organisations. Instead, there are conceptions of this type within the heads of ordinary members of society which are *made use of* by these 'members' in carrying out their every day purposes. Thus, as Bittner (1965) suggested, for example, we should see the idea of 'the organisation' as a commonsense construct of ordinary people rather than as a scientific concept, and we should concentrate on how people exploit the concept to make sense of what it is they are about. We do not follow organisational rules and procedures but carry out a whole range of personal projects which we then 'make sensible' by claiming to be acting in accordance with the organisation's requirements.

Ethnomethodological thinking has been applied by a number of researchers to organisational settings. It was applied by Silverman and Jones (1976) to show how interviewers in a job selection process 'made sensible' the decisions they reached by utilising 'typifications' like 'acceptable behaviour' or 'abrasive behaviour'. It plays a key part in the new workplace studies which examine the minutiae of workplace activities and the ways in which technologies are developed and used (Luff *et al.* 2000). It has also had an impact in the occupational sphere in the study of the work of scientists and the ways in which scientific knowledge emerges from the processes whereby scientists work together to produce 'accounts' of the physical world (Woolgar 1988). Neither the science produced by scientists nor the decisions arrived at by the job selectors are to be seen as outcomes of a rational analysis of an objective 'reality' but reflect the mundane sense-making work which all humans beings do all the time.

Perhaps ethnomethodology's importance is far greater than is implied by the very limited number of people in the sociology of work and industry who wholeheartedly adopted it. The impact of the ethnomethodologists' powerful critique of conventional sociology which was mounted in the early to mid-1970s was to make sociologists much more sensitive than they had been to the dangers of turning conceptual abstractions like 'society', 'class' or 'organisation' into concretely existing 'things' which have a life of their own outside people's minds.

Discussion

The interactionist strand of the sociology of work and industry clearly pays great attention to individuals and their role in social life and it pays very necessary heed to the human interpretative process which the more structural or systems-oriented approaches considered earlier tend to neglect. The approach is clearly not psychologistic, but we do have to ask whether, in turning attention away from social wholes, it is doing sufficient justice to the influence on human interaction of those ongoing historical processes and 'structures' of power and material interest which provide the context for the individual and their social role. To see how an interest in social meanings and individual motives can be combined with a more power-conscious and historically aware perspective we must return to the European tradition and the contribution of Max Weber.

The Weber-social action strand

This strand of sociological thinking takes into account both the meaningful activity of the individual and the larger-scale questions of historical change and economic and political conflicts. Despite the early interest shown by interactionists in the societal 'moral order' and the overall division of labour, their interests have subsequently proved to be largely confined to the group or occupational levels. They tend not to relate meanings at the micro level to historical and cultural patterns at the macro level. A concern with such a relationship is basic to the work of Weber, however.

Max Weber

The work and ideas of Max Weber (1864–1920) have been much misunderstood and misrepresented. This is partly because of the incompleteness of his written works, his awkward style of writing, his ambiguity on various issues, his tendency to separate his political writing from his sociological work and, especially, because of the fact that his work was brought back into contemporary sociology largely via American sociologists who wished to use the name of this impressive European figure to legitimate their own positions or interests. Thus we find Weber misinterpreted at times as one who totally opposed Marx's position on the nature and rise of capitalism; one who denied the importance of class divisions in society by arguing that a plurality of interest groups counter-balanced each other; as one who 'advocated' bureaucracy as 'efficient'; as one who was an armchair thinker without interest in carrying out empirical investigations; and as one who encouraged the sociologist to be a neutral and uncommitted individual. There is some element of truth in each of these interpretations but each of them tends to suggest quite the opposite of what was his essential position.

Weber's advocacy of value-freedom and his attempts to fill out (rather than totally contradict) the one-sidedness of Marxian thinking have to be understood in the light of his social and historical context. In trying to separate scientific analysis from political interpretation and advocacy he was reacting to contemporary academics whom he saw as abusing their academic status, and he was interested in relegating sociological study to a role which was secondary to moral thinking and political activity. His reaction to the Marxist thinking of his time was not to try to demolish it but to take from it what was most useful in understanding modern capitalism whilst balancing its emphasis on material factors with fuller consideration of the role in history of ideas, individual agents and culture. It is true that, in his more political writings, he showed a clear preference for capitalism over its socialist alternative, but his enthusiasm for capitalist social organisation was not much greater than that for socialism. Both of them involved the threat to individual freedom which he saw in bureaucracy. Such was the fatalism and pessimism which runs through Weber's world view (Turner 1996).

Weber defined sociology as the study of *social action*. The discipline should examine the ways in which people, through the attribution and inference of subjective meanings, would be influenced by each other and thereby oriented in their actions. Weber avoided talking of 'structures' or 'systems' and he related these social meanings to the wider society through the concept of a 'legitimate order'. This is a patterning in social life which individual actors *believe* to exist and to which they may conform. To understand how the order becomes valid to actors it has to be seen within the human meaning-creating processes which, in turn, have to be related to the conflicts and power struggles which take place in a world where there are a variety of material interests. The interplay between ideas and interests is basic to Weber's sociology. The sociologist,

- as a first stage of investigation, attempts to gain an interpretative understanding (*verstehen*) of actors' behaviour;
- as a second stage of investigation, moves to a causal explanation. Since the actors who are being studied think in causal terms about what they are doing and because they

base their actions on certain rationally based assumptions of regularities in the world, some causal explanation of their behaviour is possible.

Weber's sociology is informed by a set of philosophical assumptions about the world which include a view of reality as infinitely diverse and as involving the existence of fundamental conflicts of value, interest and perspective. Social life is thus characterised by perpetual conflict, struggle and the exercise of power. Humans are seen as rational beings pursuing ends, but there is no direct relationship between their efforts and the resulting social order. There is a *paradox of consequences* in social life.

PARADOX OF CONSEQUENCES

The tendency for the means chosen to achieve ends in social life to undermine or defeat those ends.

This tendency for the social means chosen by humans to achieve their ends often to fail to meet such purposes, or even to undermine them, is profoundly important for our understanding of the role of bureaucracy in modern societies, as we shall see in Chapter 4 (pp. 86–7, 89–92). It is also essential to his most famous substantive work.

In Weber's famous study, *The Protestant Ethic and the Spirit of Capitalism* (1965), to which we will return (Chapter 3, pp. 57–9), we see how the ideas developed by individuals such as Luther and Calvin, who were primarily concerned with religious and spiritual ends, had the unintended consequence of helping to foster a 'spirit of capitalism' and an increasingly rationalistic world view, one of the consequences of which was the eventual undermining of religious belief. The ideas which encouraged asceticism contributed to a later materialism in Western culture which would have horrified those who first set out these ideas. But Weber, in this kind of analysis, is not suggesting that ideas autonomously wing their way through history, changing their form as they go. It is their coming together with the material interests of historical actors which gives ideas force. Weber talks of an 'elective affinity' between ideas and interests: people tend to choose, develop or adopt ideas which fit with their material interests – these interests in turn being influenced by available ideas. Weber is by no means replacing Marx's stress on material interests as a force in history with an equally one-sided stress on ideas. Instead, he is showing that the cultural or subjective aspects of social life have to be seen as equal partners in any analytical scheme.

Weber sees a process of *rationalisation* underlying Western history.

RATIONALISATION

A trend in social change whereby traditional or magical criteria of action are replaced by technical, calculative or scientific criteria.

With rationalisation, social life is 'demystified' or disenchanted, rational pursuit of profit motivates work behaviour and efforts are increasingly co-ordinated through bureaucratic means. All this means that people more and more use calculative devices and techniques as means towards the achieving of ends (these are *formally rational* means) – the division of labour, sets of rules, accounting methods, money, technology, and so on. However, because of the ever-present tendency for unintended consequences to occur, these often turn out not to lead to the goals for which they were intended (thus making them *materially irrational*). In fact, the means may subvert the very ends for which they were designed. This may be difficult to understand and it is perhaps not surprising therefore that many writers on organisations have taken Weber to mean that bureaucracy is 'efficient', thus implying that he was unaware of its tendencies to develop 'dysfunctions' – tendencies towards inefficiency (Albrow 1970). Weber was in fact pointing merely to the *potential superiority* of bureaucracy as an administrative instrument (its formal rationality) whilst being fully aware that it could manifest features which rendered it materially irrational, even going so far as to threaten individual freedom in a society with an attachment to such a goal or value. But this misunderstanding of Weber (perhaps partly deriving from a failure to realise that his ideal-type construct of bureaucracy was an intentionally one-sided representation) has been such that it has led to the development of one whole area of industrial or organisational sociology, and therefore part of the present strand. This is the work in the tradition of Merton's analysis of the so-called dysfunctions of bureaucracy (see Chapter 4, pp. 90–1).

Weber's perspective allows us to take into account the individual social actor whilst seeing ideas and actions in the context of the vast political and dynamic patterns of history. The great sweep of Weber's interests (note that he applied his historical and comparative approach to both Western and non-Western societies) does not mean, however, that he was uninterested in detailed empirical investigation. He was, in fact, closely involved in what might have become one of the classical studies of industrial sociology – factory studies which predated the Hawthorne studies by twenty years or more. Weber was interested in investigating a range of issues which are very close to those which have become central to industrial sociology in practice only some fifty or sixty years later (Eldridge 1971b). Weber's 'Methodological Introduction' to the proposed study shows an intention to study the effects of large-scale industry on the 'individual personality, the career and the extra-occupational style of living of the workers', thus taking into account the 'ethical, social and cultural background, the tradition and the circumstances of the worker'. All this is set in the context of economic, technical and capital-investment patterns in a way which is still very relevant to industrial sociology today.

Orientations to work

The Weberian strand of specialised industrial sociology could well have started early in the century had Weber's research investigations not been abandoned. But more recent sociologists have applied a generally Weberian perspective to industrial questions and carried out studies very much in the spirit of Weber's own projected work. Especially important here were the *Affluent Worker* studies of Goldthorpe *et al.* (1968) which gave sociology the important concept of 'orientation to work', a notion which links actions in the workplace and the external community and cultural life of employees.

> ### ORIENTATION TO WORK
>
> The meaning attached by individuals to their work which predisposes them to think and act in particular ways with regard to that work.

The orientations perspective takes the employee's own definition of the situation as an 'initial basis for the explanation of their social behaviour and relationships' (Goldthorpe *et al.* 1968). Much earlier thinking about industrial behaviour tended to focus on the assumed 'needs' of workers, whether these be the economic needs focused on by scientific management (see pp. 23–4), the social needs focused on by human relations writers (pp. 29–30) or the self-actualisation needs focused on by the psychological humanists (pp. 24–5). And there was a trend in the 1960s for the technological context in which people worked to be treated as a determinant of attitudes to work (Chapter 7, pp. 180–3). Goldthorpe and colleagues reacted against all of this, stressing the importance of the meanings that workers take into the work situation in the first place. Thus an individual in a life situation where earning money might be a priority over personal work satisfaction might *choose* to undertake unpleasant but highly paid work but, at another stage of their lives, where economic imperatives are less significant to them, they might opt for work that allowed them more scope to express their own identities, develop their capacities or simply enjoy the company of other people at work. The research on which this was based, and subsequent research which has built upon and developed the overall approach, will be considered in Chapter 7. But the concept of work orientation will also be used to re-conceptualise so-called managerial efforts to 'motivate' workers in Chapter 5 (p. 191).

Discussion

Weber's relevance to the sociology of work and industry lies in his concern with the interplay that occurs between the agency or voluntaristic aspects of social activity and the wider cultural or structural patterns within society (Chapter 1, pp. 4–5). It has taken the sociology of work decisively away from the managerial orientations of its early strands and relates the study of work and industry to concerns with some of the basic 'dilemmas of modernity' (Ray and Reed 1994). It furthers an essentially sociological concern with how work behaviour and patterns fit into the wider political, social and cultural context. A similar concern leads others to retain a commitment to the analytical potential of Marx's thinking. For some sociologists who want a critical and historical perspective on work Weber does not fit the bill. His anxious desire to separate sociological analysis and political evaluation is partly responsible here. His arguments were seen as being used too often to justify what more critical thinkers saw as the indifference of much mainstream sociology to the persisting inequalities of the modern world and the constant tendency for the ever present underlying conflicts to manifest themselves. In addition to this we have the range of misrepresentations of Weber which prevailed and these, together with Weber's self-identification as a bourgeois and his own political nationalism and antipathy towards socialist reorganisation, have led to an understandable reluctance to look behind the complexities and ambiguities of his writing to find a perspective which, in analytical terms, extends rather than rejects the strengths of Marxian thinking. The extreme subtlety, ambiguity and complexity of Weber's analysis, we have to recognise, does reduce the analytical value of his perspective in some ways. The full potential thrust of a Weberian perspective in sociology is perhaps only possible when combined with some of the more immediately coherent insights which are offered by Marxian thinking.

The Marxian strand

Since its first appearance on the intellectual and political scene, Marxist and Marxian thought has influenced the development of sociology (Marxist to mean after Marxism and Marxian to mean after Marx). Marx and Engels created one of the most influential theories of social life ever made available to those trying to make some kind of systematic sense of the modern industrialising world. Its influence in contemporary sociology can be understood as part of a reaction to an earlier tendency of much academic sociology to be consensus-oriented, to be non-critical at best and justifying the status quo at worst, and also to its tendency to restrict its attention to the 'social' at the expense of the economic and political. Much of the older sociology was also seen to be too static and tending to ignore history.

Marx and Engels

Underlying the ideas of Karl Marx (1818–1883) and Friedrich Engels (1820–1895) is an assumption about the nature of human beings. This is the assumption that human beings achieve the fullness of their humanity through their labour. It is through labour – an essentially social process – that the human world is created. This is the basis of Marx's 'materialism'. However, the conditions under which labour is performed make a crucial difference to the extent to which the human being is fulfilled. Under capitalism workers are forced into an unequal relationship with the owner of capital, to whom they sell their labour power. The relationship is unequal, since the owner of capital always has sufficient means of subsistence whether production goes ahead or not, whilst wage workers are dependent on work being available to them. Furthermore, the employer requires workers to do more work than the workers themselves would need to do to meet their own needs; that is, the capitalist *extracts the surplus value* and in this way exploits the workers. Work within a capitalist context does not allow the workers the creative fulfilment which labour could potentially give them. Since the workers do not use tools and materials which are their own and since they neither own nor control the products of their labour any more than they have control over the methods which they apply in their work, they cannot achieve their potential self-realisation. They are thus *alienated* (Chapter 7, pp. 176–7). Although this condition clearly has subjective implications, fundamentally it is an objective condition. A contented worker is no less alienated in this sense than a frustrated one.

Marx sets the above ideas in a historical model of the way in which one form of society develops to a point where it is superseded by another (for example, feudalism is transcended by capitalism which, in turn, is transcended by socialism). These ideas are also set in a structural model of capitalist society – or, more accurately, a capitalist mode of production. This is represented in Figure 2.1.

According to Marx, it is the nature of the economic base which characterises a society. The way in which production is organised and the social relations accompanying that organisation are the more decisive factors – ideas, culture, law and politics being secondary. This again illustrates the materialist basis of Marx's work and perhaps indicates how the rather crude accusations of 'economic determinism' have come to be made against him. His approach is often described as 'dialectical materialism' and the dialectical element of the analysis can be illustrated here by pointing to the tendency of the base to contain within it conflicts and contradictions which represent the seeds of its own destruction (or, rather, supersession). The dialectic operates in history by the growth of one thing out of another in such a way that the new comes into conflict with the old, leading to its overthrow. Thus the bourgeoisie, we might say, created the proletariat but, in so doing, created the condition for its own overthrow.

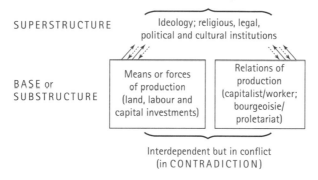

Figure 2.1 The capitalist mode of production

Marx sees the capitalist mode of production as inherently unstable and ultimately doomed. A close reading of Marx's later economic writing makes it clear that this demise of capitalism could well be a very long way off and that the dominance of capitalism in the early twenty-first century is quite consistent with Marx's long-term thinking (Desai 2002). Capitalism may be a long way from coming into full bloom. The roots of the eventual superseding of capitalism have been in the ground from the start, however. They lie in the fact that the social relations of bourgeoisie and proletariat are relations of fundamental conflict since their relationship is a one-sided and exploitative one. All of those who sell their labour power are, objectively, members of the proletariat. They are all 'exploited'. The proletariat is thus a 'class in itself', but they will not act as a class – so releasing themselves from exploitation – until they overcome their 'false consciousness' and become aware of their common interest. Class action is therefore dependent on the growth of class-consciousness. The proletariat will become a 'class for itself' and act out its historical destiny through creating socialism. To recognise the full force of the notion of *contradiction* in Marx we have to note that the efforts of the bourgeoisie themselves, to a considerable extent, hasten their own demise. For example, the bringing together of larger and larger numbers of employees into ever larger work units will create the very conditions in which workers, through being thrown together, can become aware of shared economic and political interests. Thus class-consciousness increases and the challenge to the prevailing order is invited.

Marxian industrial sociology and labour process analysis

Marx's key concepts of class, exploitation, labour process and alienation played a growing part in the sociology of work and industry after the mid-1960s, sometimes being used as analytical instruments and sometimes in a more directly Marxist way when their discussion is tied to an interest in actually affecting consciousness. There has been an especially strong Marxist attention to various aspects of conflict at work (Beynon 1984; Nichols and Beynon 1977) and Hyman has exerted considerable influence through his persuasive attempts to establish a Marxist political economy of industrial relations (1989). The greatest impact of the ideas of Marx on modern industrial sociology has undoubtedly been through the use of his concept of 'the labour process' to develop a perspective which combines interests in employee behaviour, employment relations and questions of work design and organisation.

THE CAPITALIST LABOUR PROCESS

The design, control and monitoring of work tasks and activities by managers acting as agents of the capital owning class to extract surplus value from the labour activity of employees.

It is assumed that capitalist employment is essentially exploitative in attempting to take from working people the 'value' which they create through their labour and which is properly their own. In managing the labour process to fulfil this function, managers follow the logic of the capitalist mode of production whereby the need for capital accumulation demands employers' constant attention to subjugating labour in order to extract enough profit from it to enable the employer to survive within the capitalist market economy.

A central role in stimulating the application of this kind of analysis of modern work activity was played by Braverman's (1974) application of it to various trends in work design. Braverman's thesis was that the pursuit of capitalist interests has led to a general trend towards deskilling, routinising and mechanising of jobs across the employment spectrum, from manufacturing to retailing and from design to clerical work. Industrial engineers are seen as going from strength to strength as they apply the deskilling logic of Taylorism to work tasks. They are helped along in this by the personnel and human relations experts who act as fellow manipulators and as a 'maintenance crew for the human machinery' rather than as any kind of check upon or reaction to work degradation. Braverman links these work design processes to class analysis by reference to Marx's argument that the working class will become increasingly homogeneous. He suggests that, through the process of deskilling and work degradation, all employees will find themselves in increasingly similar positions and distinctions between blue-collar and white-collar, technical and manual, production and service workers will become increasingly blurred. Taylorism continues to be rampant and is aided and abetted by modern electronic techniques which are continually reducing the need for capitalist employers to depend on human skills and hence reducing their need to reward employees in any but a minimal and straightforwardly economic way.

Research following up Braverman's resurrecting of an interest in the capitalist labour process has shown trends of deskilling and up-skilling occurring simultaneously, the existence of these opposing trends not necessarily being seen as undermining the basic assumptions of labour process analysis but, instead, as refining it by showing that in some circumstances capitalist interests are better served by upgrading work and in others by downgrading it (Friedman 1977; Edwards 1979). At the theoretical, as opposed to the empirical level, effort has been made to overcome the weaknesses of the basic Braverman version of labour process thinking. Not only did that perspective fail to recognise that owning interests may, in certain circumstances, see it as advantageous to upgrade rather than downgrade jobs, it also portrayed managers as much more omniscient and united than they really are, tended to romanticise the skilled craft worker of the past and under-played the ability of workers to defend themselves against managerial strategies. The trend within labour process thinking has therefore to recognise that a range of contingencies or circumstances intervene between the deeper tendency of labour to be managed in the interests of capital and the actual practices that are followed. Burawoy, for example, recognises that the extraction of surplus value with its implications for employer–worker conflicts at a deeper level necessarily requires a degree of aligning of employer–worker interests at the level of the workplace (1985). Thompson (1989) acknowledges that whilst there are basic structural pressures to accumulate capital this does not directly determine patterns of control and resistance in the workplace. And Edwards (1990) stresses that the way events unfold at the level of day-to-day behaviour is pressured by 'structured antagonism' rather than fully shaped by it.

Some of the most contested changes that have occurred within labour process thinking have been those made by researchers turning to the poststructuralist work of Foucault to cope with the alleged failure of labour process analysis otherwise to give a full account of human agency or, as it is called in this context, *subjectivity*. The dispute that has arisen here again takes us back to the basic tension in sociology between voluntaristic and structural emphases when trying to explain social behaviour, and we will return to it once we have introduced and explained poststructuralist thinking.

Discussion

The ideas of Marx and Engels constitute more than a sociological theory. Marxism can be seen as providing a particular method of analysis – one which does not divide polity, economy and society and one which attempts to unite theory and practice. Despite the fact that Marx wanted to bring together theory and practice, sociologists can nevertheless derive a great deal of analytical value from Marx and Marxian thought, without necessarily accepting Marxist evaluations or programmes for action. In doing this, however, the sociologist is clearly differentiating their enterprise from that of the Marxist and, given the central concern of Marx and Engels with human labour and their interest in relating individual experience to large-scale matters of history, economy and societal power structure, it would be surprising if there were not major insights to be gained with regard to the sociology of work.

A difficulty with this strand of the sociology of work for those who do not share Marxist political values can result from its primary concern with problems of class, exploitation and large-scale historical change and the implicit (sometimes explicit) interest in seeing existing political-economic patterns overthrown. It can be felt that the concepts which are deployed to analyse specific situations therefore tend to be selected to highlight issues relevant to these problems and, consequently, play down issues which are not felt to be of strategic political relevance. However, many of the issues which are under-emphasised within the Marxist frame of reference or 'problematic' are areas of considerable importance when it comes to examining actual work or employment problems at a particular point in history – even if in the 'final instance' they may not be regarded as crucial to those hoping for the overthrow of capitalism. There are people who will look to the sociology of work and industry for insights relevant to their concerns with such matters as organisational redesign, the improvement of workplace relations and the attempt to reduce ethnic or gender discrimination within the existing basic social and economic system. Marxist and Marxian thought has useful insights to offer on questions such as these. Such insights are perhaps more likely to be taken up if they are offered alongside insights and concepts from other theoretical and value traditions within the sociology of work and industry.

The discursive strand

The discursive strand of thinking about work and organisations contains a range of approaches which have in common an emphasis on the role of language in social life. The particular notion of 'discourse' that is used varies from theorist to theorist (Alvesson and Karreman 2000). One general way of conceiving of discourses, however, is to see them as elements of human culture which arise over time and *frame* the way various aspects of the world are understood so influencing the way people act with regard to that aspect of their reality.

> **DISCOURSE**
>
> A set of concepts, statements, terms and expressions which constitute a way of talking or writing about a particular aspect of life, thus framing the way people understand and act with respect to that area of existence.

We might say, for example, that there is a discourse current in modern society that encourages people to believe that they have a 'human right' to find 'personal fulfilment' in the work they do 'for society'. Certain people might be encouraged by these ideas to act in certain ways with regard to work. But it might be observed that there is another discourse in existence alongside this first one; a discourse that speaks of work as an unpleasant necessity that produces incomes enabling people to support their families and to find personal satisfaction in the non-work part of their lives. Some people may be more influenced by this way of 'framing' their work involvement and hence act differently from the first group. Members of society do not simply and passively 'read' this discursive framing, of course; they also contribute to the shaping of these ideas and ways of talking about the world and the ways in which they change – with their language use affecting their actions and their actions affecting their language use.

The basic insight captured in this broad notion of discourse can be incorporated into some of the other strands of thinking we have considered, especially the Weberian one. We will return to this point shortly, but, first, need to recognise that the concept has come to the fore largely as a result of postmodern and poststructuralist thinking being brought into the sociology of work and industry.

The postmodernist perspective and poststructuralism

The postmodern perspective has its roots in the French intellectual tradition of *post-structuralism*, an approach which puts the consideration of human language and how it is used at the centre of the study of all aspects of human existence. It builds upon the key insight in the linguistics of Saussure (1974) about the 'arbitrariness of the sign' – the recognition that there is no necessary connection between a word (or other sign) and what it stands for. The word 'book', for example, does not connect with the item which you at this moment have in front of you apart from the social convention that such a sound, to an English speaker, is conventionally taken to stand for such objects. In poststructural or postmodern thinking, reality itself comes to be treated as if it were a text; as a set of arbitrary signs which are not tied into a pre-existing reality. This implies that there is no basic truth outside language and that there is no reality separate from the way we write and talk about the world. There are no universal human values and we cannot rely on overarching systems of thought, like science or religion, to give us a basic understanding of the world and to provide guidance on how to act within it.

POSTMODERNISM

An approach to the world which rejects attempts to build systematic explanations of history and human activity and which, instead, concentrates on the ways in which human beings go about 'inventing' their worlds, especially through language and cultural innovation.

Postmodernism rejects the main ideas of the Enlightenment, the change in Western thinking that led among other things to the emergence of sociology itself. There is a turning away from the Enlightenment principles that constitute *modernism*.

In modernism *expertise* becomes important in achieving human progress with key roles going to scientists, technocrats and administrators. And *grand narratives* like those of Marxism or Freudianism emerge to offer blueprints for making the world a better and more easily controlled place. Postmodernism reacts against all of this. It encourages what Lyotard

(1984) calls a stance of 'incredulity towards metanarratives' and, in effect, encourages us to look at the world in terms of the way we 'make it up' through talk, speech and other communicative behaviour.

> ## MODERNISM
>
> An approach to dealing with the world based on the application of rational and scientific analysis to social, political, economic and industrial institutions in the belief that this can lead to greater human control over the world and thus bring about general progress in the condition of humankind.

Foucault and human subjectivity

Postmodern and poststructuralist perspectives are said to 'decentre the subject'. They question the notion of an autonomous thinking and feeling human subject who acts upon the world from a position of a confident belief in an essential and unique personality or 'self'. Poststructuralists stress the way the human being's notion of who and what they are is shaped by the discourses which surround them. Foucault (1980) observes historically how various discourses have exerted power over people by creating the categories into which they are fitted: 'the homosexual', 'the criminal', the 'mentally ill'. Such notions help people define what they are and create notions of how such people should be treated by others. This is clearly relevant to people as workers and employees. To designate a worker as 'a loyal employee', for example, is clearly to frame for that person a reality that supports particular workplace power relations and encourages certain behaviours as well as beliefs that are consonant with that order.

From a Foucauldian perspective, say McKinlay and Starkey (1998), 'truth and knowledge are weapons by which a society manages itself' and they argue that perhaps the greatest impact of this perspective on the study of work organisation and management has been on the critical study of accounting where accounting is seen as 'a set of practices and a discourse which aims to disaggregate the organisation and lay the actions of all its members open to critical scrutiny, comparison and modification' (Miller and O'Leary 1987; Hoskin 1998). We will return to the role of discourse in shaping human subjectivities in work contexts in Chapters 7 (pp. 196–7) and 8 (pp. 230–1). But it is important to note here that some of the key contributors to the labour process element of the Marxian strand of thinking about work have turned to Foucault to develop labour process thinking.

The turn to Foucault by some of those interested in labour processes has caused some of the most heated debates seen in the history of the sociology of work and industry. In this development, *subjectivity* has been a key notion.

> ## SUBJECTIVITY
>
> The notion that individuals are continually developing, in the light of the discourses surrounding them, of who they are and how they fit into the social world.

The employee's subjectivity or 'their ability to make decisions in the context of social constraints' (Grugulis and Knights 2001) is, say Knights and Willmott (1989b), 'directed narrowly, and in a self-disciplined fashion' towards actions that give people a 'sense of security and belonging'. The employee's subjectivity is 'a product of disciplinary mechanisms, techniques of surveillance and power-knowledge strategies' and the tendency is for individuals to become isolated from each other or 'individualised'. This insight has been refined by its main authors (Knights 2001; O'Doherty and Wilmott 2001a and 2001b), challenged by researchers both unsympathetic (Smith and Thompson 1998) and broadly sympathetic to the approach (Sosteric 1996; Ezzy 1997; Newton 1998; Wray-Bliss 2002) and debated (Parker 1999; Jaros 2001). But the most powerful attack on this general direction of analysis has come from authors who share the labour process background of these writers but who see the change of focus 'beyond the political economy of capitalism to some existential self' as a serious *diversion* from the important issue of understanding the potential for role human agency within the constraints of capitalist employment relationships (Thompson and Smith 2001). A particularly significant result of this diversion, the critics argue, is that the potential for workers to challenge, resist or generally 'misbehave' is seriously underestimated (Thompson and Ackroyd 1995; Ackroyd and Thompson 1999). This line, in turn, is contested by Knights and McCabe (2000), as we see in Chapter 8 (p. 230).

Discussion

Postmodernism as a way of looking at the world and associated claims that the world is moving into a new epoch of postmodernity (Chapter 3, pp. 69–70) have been received with varying degrees of acquiescence and disdain by industrial and organisational sociologists. Thompson (1993), for example, described both trends as a 'fatal distraction' and a retreat by sections of the intelligentsia from engagement with important issues in the world. He describes postmodernism as a reactionary trend. Although there are progressive dimensions to postmodernist thinking – the decentring of the sovereign subject, the exploration of multiple identities and the challenge to traditional hierarchies of knowledge – the interest in 'multiple realities' and the making of multiple interpretations of the world leaves a situation where, in effect, the world becomes 'all things to all people'. If we let this become the case, Thompson argues, it would allow us no opportunity to take action to change that world.

An alternative approach is to play up the virtue of those aspects of postmodern analysis which Thompson was willing to label progressive. The most significant idea in the postmodernist style of analysis is the notion that, as Hassard and Parker (1993) put it, 'the world is constituted by our shared language and . . . we can only "know the world" through the particular forms of discourse our language creates'. This has great appeal to many social scientists who have, as Gergen (1992) suggests, a yearning for an alternative to modernist and romanticist beliefs that there are 'essentials of the universe' which can be discovered through observation and reason and which are then *reflected in* or represented by language. Within modernism, language is in some way secondary to that which it 'describes'. Gergen points to a whole range of ways in philosophy and the social sciences, from the type of ethnomethodological thinking we met earlier to ideas such as those of Foucault which reject this position. All of these can be seen as part of a 'postmodern transformation' reversing 'the modernist view of language as picturing the essentials of reality'. Language now loses its 'servant' or 'picturing' role. It is part of a process whereby people, through joint action, make sense of the world. In effect, we cease to speak of language as something which *describes action* and see language as *action in itself*.

It might be helpful to label this broad approach one of *soft postmodernism*. Hancock and Tyler (2001) identify as a 'core proposition' of full-blooded postmodernism (alongside the rejection of Enlightenment aspirations, the primacy of language and commitment to a 'pluralist politics of difference') an 'epistemological perspectivism that considers all knowledge claims as relative to their linguistic and cultural context' which means that 'all claims to knowledge . . . become contingent and temporary'. But this tendency to make all truths relative inevitably threatens the very idea of a social science. And what Parker (1993) has called the 'extreme ethical-political relativism' of 'hard' postmodernism, together with its tendency to refuse to see a social world beyond the 'texts' that people write and speak, makes it unacceptable to many sociologists (sociology itself being an enterprise to which we might expect hard postmodernists to deny legitimacy). A soft postmodernism, on the other hand, does not reject the existence of a social world beyond language, 'however precarious and fluid that latter may be' (Tsoukas 1992). It retains a concern with reason and analysis but recognises, along with Weber (above pp. 39–40), the limits of formal rationality. It recognises the centrality and power of language, without suggesting that there is nothing in the world beyond the words we use to talk about it. It comes to terms with the plurality of interests and perspectives in the world but does not descend into a moral relativism where any one idea or activity is said to be as good or right as any other. Postmodernism considered in this 'softer' way can indeed be seen as a perspective developed *within* modernism rather than as something which supersedes it. Baumann (1992) points out that we might see it as *modernism coming to terms with itself* by recognising what it had tried to deny; its own discovery that 'human order is vulnerable, contingent and devoid of reliable foundations'.

Although it is useful to consider the notion of 'soft postmodernism' as a way of incorporating poststructuralist insights about language and discourse into sociology, it might, on reflection, be wise to drop the terminology. As Hancock and Tyler (2001) point out, it represents 'little in the way of a radical departure from other well-established interpretive . . . research strategies within the social sciences'. It is close to the notion of the 'social construction of reality' (Berger and Luckmann 1971; Gergen 1999) with its recognition that people 'make the social world' at the same time as their own notions of who they are and what they are doing are 'made by' the social world. And the concept of discourse is fully compatible with social constructionist thinking.

SOCIAL CONSTRUCTION OF REALITY

The process in which people, through cultural interaction, give meaning to the world – a world that may well exist beyond language but which can only be known and communicated by people through language-based processes of cultural interpretation and sense-making.

The concept of social construction becomes especially helpful when we come to consider the nature of work organisations. We all treat the organisations we work in, shop in, are born and die within as being 'real'. Yet they are not entities that we can touch, feel, hear, smell or throw up in the air. And the same can be said of all the other aspects of society that sociology considers. Whatever we may feel about poststructuralist and postmodern thinking, it can be argued that the concept of discourse which emerged from it is an invaluable addition to the broad conceptual vocabulary of sociology, helping us cope with the level of social reality that mediates between that of *culture* at the relatively 'macro' level and the social interactions and interpretive actions of individual and groups at the more 'micro' level. In our lives we are more influenced by the discourses that surround us, rather than by a single overarching 'culture'. And few human individuals can be identified as shaping the cultures of our societies. But it is much less unreasonable to expect to look to sociological analysis to help us identify the role of specific human actors and interest groups in shaping the discourses and discursive resources available to us all to make sense of our lives and activities.

Sociology emerged as a characteristically modernist activity with the project of applying reasoned analysis to the changes which were coming about with industrialisation and helping people make a better world within the new possibilities which were emerging. This aspect of the 'enlightenment project', so powerfully defended by Habermas (1987), need not be totally abandoned, as a hard postmodernist position would suggest. But social science is inevitably going to play a much more modest role in helping social change and achieving human control over circumstances than was once hoped. The sociology of work and industry can helpfully be characterised as a bundle of *discursive resources* that people can use in various ways to create their own interpretations and understandings of the world with which they have to deal. It is a world full of ambiguities, paradoxes and contradictions which will never finally be 'sorted out', classified or pinned down in terms of sociological laws. The various perspectives or strands of thought in the sociology of work and industry covered in this chapter all have something to offer and will form the arguments and analyses contained in subsequent chapters.

3 Work, society and change

CHAPTER THREE

The nature of modern societies

The sociological study of work has always played a central part in sociology. It has necessarily done this, given that sociology emerged and developed as a way of coming to terms with fundamental changes associated with industrialisation and the rise of capitalism, as we saw in Chapter 1. Changes in the way work is organised and experienced have been at the heart of the social and historical shifts with which sociology has always engaged. The most significant historical shift has been the rise of *industrial capitalist* societies. It is a more useful way to characterise the modern form of social organisation in terms of 'industrial capitalism' than by prioritising either 'industrialism' or 'capitalism'. It is especially important to recognise that it was a conjunction of capitalist forms of activity and industrial methods of production that led to many of the most significant social changes which have occurred in the modern period of world history. And attempts to develop a socialist alternative to capitalist ways of running industrial economies – a very significant part of twentieth-century history – can only be understood as both reactions to industrial capitalism and as challenges to the dominance of industrial capitalist principles in the world.

It can be argued that it is simpler to characterise modern societies as 'industrial societies'. But to do this is to play down the extent to which industrialised societies are the way they are as a result of the growth of capitalism. Industrialism, in anything like the sense in which we have seen it in both market and command economies, would never have come about but for capitalism. Also, there are major objections to the concept of 'industrial society' which derive from the way this term has tended to be used ever since its first appearance. The term is far from being a neutral term. It supports the image of an industrial Leviathan, a Prometheus unbound, marching through history (Badham 1984). The idea of an industrial society is very much associated with an evolutionary perspective which ignores the part of human initiatives and interests in shaping history.

Evolutionary views of industrialisation imply that it is a 'natural' process. Such a suggestion gives industrialism a certain legitimacy deriving from an implied inevitability and a potential, if not always realised, benevolence. Two of the earliest sociologists, Saint-Simon (1760–1825), who coined the term 'industrial society', and his one-time disciple Comte

(1798–1857) suggested theories of change in which societies are seen as passing through stages. In both cases the final – and favoured – form is the industrial and scientifically based social order. The ideas of the Saint-Simonians influenced later thinkers as different as Durkheim and Marx. Durkheim attempted his understanding of the industrial world by examining its evolution from less complex societies whilst, in England, Herbert Spencer (1820–1903) combined the biological metaphors of organicism, growth and evolutionism to show how 'militant society' develops into the more moral industrial society in which individual freedom can flourish. 'Growth' and 'progress' views of industrialisation imply that it is natural, inevitable and universally beneficent.

A further problem with the concept of 'industrial society' derives from its association with an assumption that the industrial nature of production in any society is the prime determining feature of social structure and culture. It may well be that technology does have certain imperatives with regard to social organisation but it would be a mistake to prejudge the existence of these at this stage as a result of the way in which we choose to conceptualise the social form with which we are concerned. We have to decide on the basis of analysis which features of our society are essentially concomitants of industrial technology and which relate more to the capitalistic aspects of social activity.

When we turn to the concept of 'capitalism' we similarly meet a number of problems. Not least of these is the pejorative loading which the word carries. This is largely a result of the fact that it has been the critics of capitalism who have used the term, whilst its defenders have preferred such expressions as 'market economies'. However, there is no reason why the concept cannot be used analytically. Both the major theorists of capitalism, Marx and Weber, recognised that capitalist activity has occurred in various forms and settings historically, but both of them became centrally concerned, as we are here, with the relatively modern phenomenon in which capitalistic activity becomes a predominant factor underlying the way in which whole societies are organised. Marx's characterisation of the capitalist mode of production was described in the previous chapter and central to it is his emphasis on the way in which the property owning bourgeois class buy the labour-power of a propertyless proletariat to meet their own ends. Weber fills out this picture. Whilst placing less central emphasis on the importance of property interests he nevertheless recognises their importance. However, he stresses the way in which, under modern capitalism, formally free labour is organised on a rational basis: the work of free citizens is administered on a routinised and calculative basis not known in any other kind of economic system.

From the work of these two major thinkers, Marx and Weber – one the arch antagonist and the other a partial defender of capitalism – we can draw out several key features that are basic to modern capitalist societies:

- ownership and control of wealth (and therefore the means of production) is in private hands;
- there is a relatively free market;
- the pursuit of profit is a key motivator of economic activity;
- the capacity to work of those without capital is 'sold' to those who own capital – or to their agents.

And in capitalist societies:

- there is a basic inequality in the distribution of resources with certain social groups controlling the means whereby wealth is produced, whilst
- most other social groups possess a capacity to work under the direction of others, this being their only means of earning a living,
- those earning their living as employees are subject to the systematic and calculatively rational pursuit of return on capital by those who own or control that capital and buy people's capacity to work.

The predominance of these features could not have occurred, however, without their conjunction with industrialisation. Thus we get the following working conceptualisation of the form of society with which we are concerned:

> **INDUSTRIAL CAPITALISM**
>
> A form of society in which large-scale or complex machinery and associated technique is widely applied to the pursuit of economic efficiency on a basis whereby the capacity for work of the members of some groups is sold to others who control and organise it in such a way that the latter groups maintain relative advantage with regard to those resources which are scarce and generally valued.

Baechler (1975), after his detailed examination of the analysis of capitalism by both Marx and Weber, concluded that the specific and defining feature that belongs only to the capitalist system is 'the privileged position accorded the search for economic efficiency'. We must note that 'efficiency' can only be understood in terms of specific goals and that the privileged significance given to the pursuit of economic ends over other values such as religious, military or political ones, is privilege given to the fulfilling of goals which may not be shared equally by all members of society. For example, it is quite common to see employees – at various occupational levels – becoming unemployed as a result of their employers' conscientious pursuit of efficiency. Reducing manning levels or the deskilling of work is clearly in the interests of efficiency, but it is not necessarily 'efficiency' from the point of view of those experiencing job or skill loss. Whether or not such actions are to be judged efficient or otherwise at the level of whatever goals are widely shared within a society is a judgement which, ultimately, can be informed by social scientists, but cannot be made by them.

The emergence of industrial capitalism

From feudalism to capitalism

It has been a conventional and indeed valuable method used by sociologists to accentuate the characteristic features of industrial capitalist societies by comparing these with some notion of a feudal society. The most famous attempt to do this is that of Ferdinand Tönnies (1855–1936) who contrasts the modern form of association or society (*Gesellschaft*) with the older, traditional, small-scale community (*Gemeinschaft*).

Table 3.1 Tönnies' notion of a transition from community to association

Community (Gemeinschaft)	Association (society) (Gesellschaft)
• Small-scale, intimate, stable	• Large-scale, individualised, rapidly changing
• Rural	• Urban
• Religious and traditional	• Scientific and rational

To fill out this simple image of transition we can look back to the pre-industrial and pre-capitalist world, remembering that in doing this we are considering a world that has left us images of life that still underlie many of our contemporary ideas about how human lives could be lived.

People undoubtedly worked very hard to survive in the medieval period. But this work was performed on a basis which fundamentally differs from that which we take as normal today. Work was seen more as an inevitable burden than as a way of 'developing' oneself. It was not a duty to work hard nor was hard work a way of improving oneself. Hard work was done because survival demanded it. Further, there was little separation of home and workplace and a quite alien notion would have been that of 'working for' an employer. This does not mean that the rich did not exploit the poor but that even the poorest and most exploited serfs tended to have their own land to work – even if they were forced to supplement the income derived from this with some wage labour. However exploitative relationships might have been between social groups, the hierarchical relationship existing between people was nevertheless based on a certain recognised mutual dependence and some sense of reciprocity. There was a commitment from both sides of the master–servant relationship of a diffuseness quite lacking in the modern employment relationship (Fox, 1985). The essential feature of work was that it was performed to meet clearly and generally recognised needs and its rhythms were given by natural and immediate human needs, like the need for food, shelter and clothing, or by the rhythms of nature in the shape of the changing seasons, the needs of animals to be milked or crops to be harvested.

The most advantaged groups of this period not only had the greatest share of wealth, which was predominantly in the form of land and the comforts which accrued from that land, but they were also served by a church which provided ideologies helping to stabilise social order. Christianity itself contained much which might have encouraged challenge to the feudal order and such challenges indeed did arise in combination with Christian 'heresies' and millenarian hopes on a number of occasions. However, the Roman Catholic Church and its doctrines, which put its priests as intermediaries between individuals and their destinies, was able to counteract challenges with organic models of society like that developed by Aquinas in which each person plays his natural part in the wider scheme of things. In an organic view of society, each person serves or contributes to this scheme for the sake of the whole community. Those who rule are merely doing so for the benefit of the community. Given a largely illiterate society and the insecurities resulting from dependence on agricultural production and dangers of war and disease, it is easy to see how the Church, with its near monopoly on literacy, could maintain a stabilising affinity between ruling interests and the realm of ideas.

All processes of social change involve conflicts and competition between social groups. Throughout history, groups form around common interests and the formation and activities of groups are closely involved with processes whereby ideas are developed and expressed. Advantages with regard to scarce and valued resources are sought and, once they have achieved these, the advantaged groups attempt to regularise and make legitimate their advantage in the face of challenges from rival groups. Applying this basic theory of social change, we should expect to see groups arising within feudalism to challenge the feudal order and the advantages of the feudal lords. Peasant groups did indeed provide such challenges at different times but this was not the challenge that prevailed. Instead, the challenge came from the one part of feudal society which was not fully incorporated into the feudal order. This was the urban trading element which contained a class whose interests did not fit with a stable, landed and rural order. It was among the growing bourgeoisie of later feudal society that we find an economically motivated group with interests which potentially challenged the status quo. This was a group lacking social legitimacy and which needed to find appropriate ideas to give force to its motives and thus power to its pursuits of economic ends, as well as to give itself legitimacy in its own eyes and those of others.

Protestantism and the spirit of capitalism

The following account of the interplay between interests and ideas in the rise of capitalism attempts to recognise both underlying sociological trends and historically specific factors that came into play. Holton (1985) has noted a tendency towards disguised evolutionism in the accounts of both Marx and Weber and called for a 'conjunctural' approach that does not allow the search for a 'prime mover' to lead to the ignoring of specific historical circumstances. And Baechler et al. (1988) make a similar point, emphasising specific features of north-western European medieval society which made capitalist initiatives a possibility:

- political pluralism – given the lack of a dominant single power,
- stability – resulting from the common ideology of the Church,
- good communications between areas,
- a system of marriage and family based on couples – this encouraging economically active households,
- emphasis on individualism, this going far back into history in the case of England.

Weber's immensely important study, *The Protestant Ethic and the Spirit of Capitalism* (1965) is best understood in the context of his broader investigation of the chain of events which led to the emergence of modern capitalism. If one looks at his *General Economic History* (1927) and at *Economy and Society* (1978), especially his chapter on 'the city', it is clear that he sees the influence of Protestantism as just one factor to be put alongside the type of change in city life alluded to above, the growing separation of home and workplace and many other technical and commercial factors. Greenfield (2002) follows Weber's emphasis on the role of cultural factors in the emergence of modern economic systems but puts her emphasis less on religious beliefs than on doctrines of nationalism, arguing that nationalistic ideas, first in England and later in other countries, spurred on the expansion of trade and the pursuit of economic efficiency.

Weber's original emphasis on cultural factors can be seen as arising from his concern to counter the one-sided materialism and the determinism of Marxian accounts of the rise of capitalism. He therefore chose to emphasise the part played by ideas in social change. His concern was to show how the congruence of certain material interests and particular ideas produces forces leading to change. He brings into historical analysis the variable of human agency, countering any tendency towards determinism with an emphasis on human motivation. Weber recognised that interests, not ideas, govern human conduct (Bendix 1965). Nevertheless he sees world views created by ideas frequently acting 'like switchmen indicating the lines along which action has been propelled by the dynamics of interest'. In his version of Goethe's concept of *elective affinity* Weber suggests that people adopt ideas to fit in with their interests.

The spirit of capitalism, aided by the Protestant ethic, brought a new force and a new legitimacy to the proto-capitalists of the cities. It encouraged hard work not just in order to meet basic needs or to produce short-term capital gain but as a virtue or duty in its own right. A religious doctrine which suggests that one is serving God by following one's mundane tasks in a self-disciplined and efficient way and which combines this with a demand for an ascetic or frugal form of existence has obvious potential for fostering such a spirit and indeed encouraging the accumulation of capital. One makes money by hard work and application but confidence of membership of the elect is risked if one slacks in one's efforts or if one over-indulges in the fruits of one's labours. The fruits of labour are not now hedonistic ones but confidence of salvation. Under Catholicism a 'calling' from God involved transcendence of the mundane but the novel Calvinist notion of seeing one's mundane work itself as a 'vocation' overturned this. The almost revolutionary change in religious thought brought about by the Reformation was its removal of the Church and its priests as intermediaries between the individual and God. In a sense, every one was to be their own priest and the demand was now less that one should be guided in one's actions by the Church hierarchy than that one should look to one's own conscience in deciding how one should act.

There had been earlier tendencies in Christianity which looked to 'motives of the heart' in this way but such ideas were only able to take root once there were social groups well placed to sustain opposition to prevailing values, and 'in a society where custom and tradition counted for so much, this insistence that a well-considered strong conviction overrode everything else had a great liberating force' (Hill 1974). Protestantism does not cause capitalism but gives force and legitimacy to the pursuit of economic interests by already emerging social groups. As Hill puts it, 'the protestant revolt melted down the iron ideological framework which held society in its ancient mould. Where capitalism already existed, it had henceforth freer scope.' Weber's whole point is to show how the ethical posture of inner-worldly asceticism engenders within certain groups 'already involved in the practice of business . . . a certain occupational ethic' (Poggi 1983). This is 'the spirit of capitalism'.

At this stage it is worthwhile to pause and consider just why looking back so many centuries to changes in theological thinking should be relevant to a study concerned with work and industry today. Attention to these matters is justified by the need to locate the roots of norms and values which underlie the culture of industrial capitalist society. Protestantism played a major part in liberating people from the forces of tradition – forces which ensured that by and large one played one's allotted role in a drama scripted elsewhere. This laid a massive stress on the individual, on a striving for individual achievement, on human competitiveness. Campbell (1987) has argued that the particular form of 'sentimental' (as opposed to Calvinist) Protestantism prevalent among the English middle class contained within it the seeds of modern consumerism. A 'cult of sensibility' developing within these beliefs led to a concern with good taste and a following of fashion which, in turn, led to a strong demand for luxury goods. And alongside all these shifts was the unleashing of what Weber sees as a basic process which runs through all subsequent social change in Western Europe: the process of *rationalisation* (Chapter 2, pp. 39–40). This process involves a replacement of the criterion of tradition (we do this because it is the way it has always been done) with a criterion of rationality (we must work out the most efficient means of achieving this end). We will meet this idea again shortly in the more contemporary form of 'McDonaldisation'.

RATIONALITY AND CHANGE

The criterion of rationality involves submitting decisions and actions to constant calculative scrutiny and produces a continuous drive towards change.

The essence of rationality is *calculation*, and, historically, this process led to the undermining of the primacy of religious or magical thought (including, ironically, those forms which gave impetus to this process) and is a force pushing forward the growth of science and technology together with an accompanying expansion of the technical division of labour and the bureaucratic organisation of work.

It is interesting to note that many of the changes made in contemporary work organisations, especially changes which lead to the replacement of human skills or even basic human involvement at all, by technology and advanced techniques of control, are frequently described by those implementing such changes in terms of 'rationalisation'. The disturbance to human lives caused by these programmes can be seen as part of the long-running tendency of Weber's process of rationalisation and its accompanying individualism, materialism and acquisitiveness given such impetus by the Protestant Reformation to threaten social solidarity. The modern 'work ethic' – a secularised form of the old Protestant ethic – has long been seen as posing a threat to social cohesion or solidarity (Rubenstein 1978).

Social groups and the rise of industrialism

We have to be careful in looking at the importance of changing ideas not to underestimate the extent to which their force only becomes manifest when they interact with changing material and political conditions. If we turn our attention towards England, where the Industrial Revolution was later to occur, we see a rising bourgeoisie challenging the old order in such a way that, by 1688, their political action and parliamentary triumph had brought about a bourgeois revolution. The wealth of this rising class was made possible in part by other aspects of the decay of feudalism. Massive rural changes were displacing increasing numbers from the land (as many as half a million by the mid-seventeenth century) and from traditional crafts. People were thus made available as wage labour for employment or as domestic manufacturers to be exploited by merchants. These commercial groups were not unopposed in their ascendancy, of course, and it was the very opposition of established groups to their interests which helped mould them into, effectively, a coalition of interest. England had a relatively permeable class structure by general European standards and this encouraged aspirations towards advancement (Israel 1966). The Crown, however, pursued a policy of suppressing middlemen and the 'proto-industrialists' in ways which increased the revolutionary challenge to the established order. This threat was increased by the driving of various proto-industrial cliques into a united front, their consolidation being 'promoted by this clear perception of a common foe, the Establishment' and they were helped in their new solidarity by Puritanism which was, as Israel puts it, 'the only available ideology that could effectively legitimise opposition to church and state simultaneously'. Here again we see the dialectical interplay of interests and ideas.

Opposition to the rising groups had also helped foster the scientific spirit. The effective forbidding of non-conformists entering Oxford and Cambridge after 1660 encouraged the application of minds away from traditional academic pursuits towards pursuits of a more rationalising spirit. But to see the resulting scientific developments *leading to* the Industrial Revolution would be mistaken. Nevertheless, the conditions were set for yet new social groups to emerge and apply with a vengeance the rationalising spirit to employment and to manufacture. Studies of the early industrial entrepreneurs suggest that a large proportion of them were from relatively low origins and, like their merchant predecessors, they too found the opposition of ruling groups 'an important stimulus to the formation of this social class' (Bendix 1963). Yet whilst Foster (1974) shows the importance of money made in the previous century of capital accumulation in the establishing of new manufacturing concerns in Oldham, Crouzet (1985) produces evidence to suggest that very few pioneer industrialists came from either the upper or the working classes. Most rose from the lowest strata of the middle class and, servicing the larger new firms, were numerous small firms led by members of a 'reserve army of capitalists' who probably had even humbler origins.

What clearly did occur in the latter part of the eighteenth century in Britain was the beginning of a great leap forward of the capitalist spirit, a revolutionary advance facilitated by the new processes of industrialisation. In what is probably best seen as an alliance between the established capitalist groups and some of the new thrusting industrial men who managed to establish themselves with these groups, a massive initiative was taken with fundamental structural and cultural implications.

The specifically novel development of the Industrial Revolution was the bringing together of the now available *wage labour* in special premises to work under the supervision of the employers (or their agents), using the employers' tools and machinery and their raw materials. The impression is frequently given, following the lead of Adam Smith's *Wealth of Nations* (1776), that the splitting down of work tasks among the employees in these factories simply follows some 'logic of efficiency'. In contrast to this, it can be argued that this division of labour was not the result of a search for a 'technologically superior organisation of work but for an organisation which guaranteed to the entrepreneur an essential role in the production process' (Marglin 1980). There is thus no determining force making the appearance of the factory inevitable. There is, rather, a choice on the part of certain people to provide themselves with a niche in society – one which involved the control and co-ordination of the labour of others in the pursuit of capital accumulation and their own material advantage. It was no technological imperative that brought people into factories and set under way new methods of work organisation. Human interests and ideas, including ideas about how technologies could be developed, worked together to change societies and the division of labour within societies.

Industrialisation and the changing division of labour

A key concept used in the analysis of social change since the early stage of industrialisation has been that of a division of labour. It focuses attention on how particular tasks are carried out by particular people – this pattern being seen as undergoing significant change with industrialisation.

THE DIVISION OF LABOUR

The allocation of work tasks to various groups or categories of individual.

Durkheim (1984, originally 1893) saw the division of labour as central to the nature of a society's solidarity – the way in which a society achieves integration. In a simple society there would be little occupational differentiation with, say, most of the women carrying out one basic task, most of the young men occupied in another general task and so on. A similarity of outlook would develop between people, most of whom are engaged in more or less similar activities. Social order and stability would thus be maintained through *mechanical solidarity*. However, in the vastly more complex industrialising world where a large range of specialised occupations have developed, each with distinctive ideas, norms and values, a similarity of outlook cannot be depended upon to hold society together. The source for stability is to be found, instead, in the inevitable interdependence of members of occupations one with the other. Bakers depend on butchers for their meat, butchers on the bakers for their bread, and so on. We thus have integration through *organic solidarity*.

Although Durkheim saw the occupational principle as offering a basis for integration in modern society in this way he nevertheless began to note how the increasing emphasis on material advancement and sectional interests of his own time tended to undermine social solidarity, leading, in particular, to the moral confusion and purposelessness which he conceptualised as *anomie*. But Durkheim treated such tendencies as pathological rather than as essential features of industrial capitalism. The more closely we look at Durkheim's assumed source of social order in modern societies – the organic solidarity achieved by interdependent occupations – the more we come to realise that the structure and dynamics of industrial capitalism can be better understood in terms of interests, power and control. The attachment of people to the prevailing social order is more realistically seen as deriving from their dependence on the material rewards to be gained from their relationship not to occupations but to bureaucratic work organisations, whether this relationship be more one of submitting to control within an organisation, exercising such control or servicing the organisation in some direct or indirect way.

Consideration of the division of labour in the Marxian tradition has seen the increasing specialisation of tasks which accompanies the capitalist labour process as essentially disintegrative. An important distinction is made between the general or *social* division of labour and the detailed or *technical* division of labour.

SOCIAL DIVISION OF LABOUR

The allocation of work tasks at the level of society, typically into trades and occupations.

TECHNICAL DIVISION OF LABOUR

Task specialisation within an occupation or broad work task.

The technical division of labour has generally been seen as involving a splitting down of tasks within a former craft at the initiative of employers or their agents in order to increase the efficiency of the enterprise – efficiency as conceived by those extracting a surplus (Braverman 1974). The dividing of tasks *within* occupations, with its alienating effects, is often seen as fundamentally different from the dividing of tasks *between* occupations – the latter constituting a healthy and necessary part of any human society.

Technology, science and social change

Sociological analysis recognises the importance of human interests in introducing changes in the division of labour and instigating technological change. It also recognises that new technologies are not just new machines. In spite of this, technology is frequently spoken of in terms of the physical devices or 'hardware' that people use when carrying out tasks. Sociologically it is seen as involving much more than this.

Technology in this sense is often brought into the kind of determinist views of history and social change like that of Kerr *et al.* (1973) in their talk of the 'iron hand of technology'. And there is a popular tendency to invest technical inventions and their associated technique

---

TECHNOLOGY

The tools, machines and control devices used to carry out tasks and the principles, techniques and reasoning which accompanies them.

---

with causal power (McLoughlin 1999). Hill (1988) has described this as part of the 'tragedy of technology', something which is experienced as a 'remorseless working of things'. Individual human action appears to be 'so completely enframed within the technical properties of systems that there seems to be no way that the individual can stand outside and kick the system into new life or wrestle it into a trajectory that departs from the apparently intrinsic system expansion that has characterised industrial history'.

The view of technology as having causal power is often encouraged in the educational process. Many of us in our early history lessons at school are encouraged, for instance, to see the scientific inventions which were made in the period of the Industrial Revolution as key causal factors in the occurrence of that revolution. Technical changes in both of these cases might indeed constitute *necessary conditions* for the social changes with which they are associated, but it is mistaken to regard them as *sufficient conditions* for change. When considering the major economic advances which occurred in Europe in the eighteenth and nineteenth centuries, we have to ask why the level of technical sophistication achieved by the Chinese in ancient times did not lead to industrialisation. The answer must be in terms of human initiative. No powerful, or potentially powerful, Chinese group *chose* to apply their knowledge to economic ends.

It was pointed out by Hobsbawm (1969) that the early Industrial Revolution was technically rather primitive. He suggested that what was novel was not technical innovation but 'the readiness of practical men to put their minds to using the science and technology which had long been available and within reach'. The motor of change was not the machinery itself or new scientific knowledge but the motivation of these practical individuals. The novelty was 'not in the flowering of individual inventive genius, but in the practical situation which turned men's thoughts to soluble problems'. Hill (1988) claims that science did not play a role as a leading edge in industrial progress until after the Second World War when existing markets for capitalist expansion were saturated. The early inventors were, in fact, 'more motivated by curiosity than "practical intent"'. Sociologically, it is helpful to speak of the 'social shaping of technology' (McKenzie and Wajcman 1985) and to recognise that in the emergence of any given technology a whole range of social factors, individual and group interests come into play and interact with each other.

Although technology is in itself only a means, a mere device, it is difficult to see its role as a neutral one in human affairs. Although technologies do not have any inherent properties or *essences* of their own (Grint and Woolgar 1997) we often experience them as if they did have an independent kind of 'existence' that can impact upon our lives. *Actor-network theory* recognises this and goes as far as abolishing the distinction between human and inanimate actors; people, machines, techniques and operational principles can be analysed as equivalent actors in a network of activities (Latour 1987). Latour (1993) says that the distinction between the natural and the social world can be regarded as a myth of modernism and when one sees a surveillance camera swivelling to 'watch us' as we cross a car park or hears somebody pleading with their personal computer (or perhaps a particular piece of software within that computer) not to 'mess them about' one appreciates the power of this insight. In actor network terms, the computer and the operator are both 'actants', doing their work within a network of numerous other actants – human and non-human – in their work organisation. There is a constant interplay between 'hard' technological artefacts and their organisational and social contexts. This interplay is equally important when we come to look at technology within work organisations. Technology and organisation can perhaps best be seen as 'fluid and interlocking *processes*' in which 'technology and organisation evolve and overlap together rather than separately or in opposition to each other' (Scarborough and Corbett 1992). And, indeed, work organisations are often designed as if they were 'big machines' in themselves. They are conceived within what Hill (1988) calls the *technology text*; 'the design principles of human organisation' are those of

- efficiency,
- instrumentally powerful, controlling information flows,
- standardisation – to make this 'system' work.

Technology may be a means towards certain ends, then, but the meeting of ends implies the fulfilling of human material interests, and all human material interests do not coincide. One man's airfield takes another man's land and one woman's capital requires another woman's labour. Thus the importance of technology in human life can only be appreciated once it is set in the context of social, economic and political relationships. Machinery itself can do neither good nor harm to human beings – it is what human beings do to themselves and to each other with machinery that is crucial. Any argument about the logic of industrialism, the inevitability of technological change or the automatic unfolding of 'progress' has to be treated with suspicion. And we also have to be careful not to over-estimate the extent to which changing technologies bring about fundamental changes in societies in the forms such as 'post-industrialism', 'computer revolutions' or the arrival of an 'information age'.

Industrial capitalism: change and transition

In the same way that early sociologists observed a transformation occurring in societies as they industrialised, thinkers have suggested further transformations in industrial societies which are significant enough to warrant recognition of the approach or the arrival of a new type of social order, in one sense or another.

Post-industrialism and the information society

One of the most influential statements of this kind, suggesting that advanced industrial societies were entering a new phase in their development in the latter part of the twentieth century, was made by Bell (1974). Out of this has come the still influential notion of a post-industrial society.

POST-INDUSTRIAL SOCIETY

A type of economically advanced social order in which the centrally important resource is knowledge, service work has largely replaced manufacturing employment, and knowledge-based occupations play a privileged role.

The characteristic features of the post-industrial society are to be found in the spheres of technology, the economy and the social structure. The economy undergoes a shift from being a predominantly manufacturing one to a service one. In technology the new science-based industries become central. And in the social structure we see 'the rise of new technical elites and the advent of a new principle of stratification' (Bell 1974). The suggestion is that a new type of occupational structure develops in which white-collar workers outnumber blue-collar ones and in which the professional, scientific and technical occupations become predominant.

In this new type of society, 'theoretical knowledge' becomes the basis for innovation and policy-making. Post-industrial society is thus a 'knowledge society' and those occupations that possess theoretical knowledge are expected – on the principle that knowledge is power – to come to exert a controlling influence on society. With the diminution of the manual working class, a relatively stable order is expected to follow as social and economic policy is rationally formulated and as individuals are tied into the social order through the operation of the meritocratic system of rewards which must accompany an occupational structure dependent on recruiting individuals with high ability. The potential for satisfaction at work is increased, it is claimed, by the increased opportunity created by the expanding service sector for people to relate to other people in their jobs rather than to machines.

Bell's assumptions about the changing nature of the work people *actually* do can be strongly questioned. Qualitative inferences about the nature of occupational life are made on the basis of statistical trends whereby tasks are allocated to official categories which tell us little about what people actually do in their work (Gershuny 1978). The greatest weakness in Bell's thesis, however, lies in his assumption that there is anything novel about the centrality of knowledge to economic and working life. The growth of industrialism and the rise of capitalism were both dependent on the increasing application of rational-calculative thinking to social life. Thus the growth of scientific and technical qualifications among the population is all part of the rationalisation process which Max Weber saw as characterising Western history over several centuries. This is recognised in Castells' (1996, 1997, 1998) major overview of the sociological implications of information and communication technologies (ICTs) and his notions of 'the information age' and 'the network society' (Castells 2000).

Castells distinguishes between the 'information society', which is not new, and the *informational society* which differs from what has come before because the generating, processing and transmitting of knowledge-based information has become 'the fundamental sources of productivity and power' (1996). This developed in the 1980s with the emergence of 'informational capitalism' which has since taken on a global form (albeit with considerable regional differences). It is the 'networking logic' of ICTs that gives them a 'planetary' significance – with the gains made from global flows of capital becoming more significant than those that were made from the production of goods. And whereas, in the older forms of capitalism, the challenge to capitalism came from members of working classes resisting their exploitation, the challenges to informational capitalism come from a variety of social movements concerned to protect or advance their *identities*, rather than their material interests. However, opposition from, say, environmentalist, feminist or gay groups does not come from outside the networked social order; such groups will only be able to pursue their identity projects through the use of information technologies and networks.

Castells' work has been challenged on the grounds that it is not supported by empirical evidence and is poorly theorised (Abell and Reyniers 2000). And in pointing to significant continuities between the role played by ICTs and modern technologies generally and noting the continuing salience of long-standing patterns of social inequality, Golding (2000) argues that the sociology of the future, in these areas, is very much the sociology of the present. This is not to say, however, that new information and communication technologies are not having a significant impact at the level of work experience and work organisation, as we shall see in Chapter 5.

Post-Fordism

Like the concepts of post-industrialism, information or network society, post-Fordism has been used to characterise changes in work and society over the last quarter of a century. Although Fordism is clearly connected to developments made in the earlier part of the twentieth century in Henry Ford's car factories, 'Fordism' has come to be used as a term describing a whole way of organising industrial societies that came to prominence in the second part of that century. At the level of the workplace Fordism follows such scientific management or 'Taylorist' principles as the use of a detailed division of labour, intensive management work-planning and close supervision (Chapter 2, pp. 23–4) and extends these considerably in the close attachment of the individual to their work station and in the mechanising of work handling. But it goes beyond Taylorism, which tends to treat labour strictly as a commodity, by making a connection between labour management policy and attention to markets. Fordism was essentially a mass production process which recognised that the people it employs are part of the market for its products. It therefore recognises the necessity of taking an interest in the lives of workers as consumers as well as producers. And this involves nation states in adopting policies and creating institutions, such as those of the 'welfare state', that develop citizens as both fit and healthy producers and acquisitive consumers.

> **FORDISM**
>
> A pattern of industrial organisation and employment policy in which (a) mass production techniques and an associated deskilling of jobs is combined with (b) treatment of employees which recognises that workers are also consumers whose earning power and consumption attitudes – as well as their workplace efficiency – affect the success of the enterprise.

Fordism involved a recognition of the need to develop working-class 'social consumption norms' which would stabilise the markets for the products of mass production industries (Aglietta 1979). The mass consumption market has to be created and stabilised to fit the mass production organisation of the factory. But such regimes are seen as being replaced by post-Fordism.

POST-FORDISM

A pattern of industrial organisation and employment policy in which skilled and trusted labour is used continuously to develop and customise products for small markets.

In 'regulation theory' (Aglietta 1979; Lipietz 1987; Boyer 1988) post-Fordism is related to the ways in which particular 'regimes of accumulation' in capitalist societies are supported by specific 'modes of regulation'. Different relationships are said to emerge between these two structural elements as Fordism begins to fail and is replaced by post-Fordism:

- The *Fordist regime of accumulation* in which standardised products for price-competitive mass markets are mass produced with largely semi-skilled labour is supported by a *Fordist mode of regulation* in which there is state macro-economic regulation, public welfare provision and the institutionalising of collective bargaining.
- The *post-Fordist regime of accumulation* replaces the Fordist one with an emphasis on quality-competitive production for shifting and differentiated markets using qualified and highly skilled flexible labour, and is supported by a *post-Fordist mode of regulation* in which there is reduction in state intervention in labour markets, a shift of responsibility for welfare provision from the state to employers or private individuals and a more flexible and varied approach to employment relations.

Fordism is widely seen as hitting difficulties in the later part of the twentieth century. The economic recession of the 1970s and 1980s could be seen, for example, as part of a general economic downswing associated with a crisis in the Fordist approach to production and consumption. And the emergence of new information technologies at this time presented a way out of this difficulty. Blackburn *et al.* (1985) pointed out that information technology made an economic upswing possible by enabling 'the mechanisation, at high levels of productivity, of more flexible production of a higher level of variety of products'. This would involve work redesign and an upgrading of jobs. The work of different organisational sub-units would be integrated by electronic methods and there would also be a change in the pattern of consumption, especially in the service industries. In this way ICT offered an opportunity to sever 'the Fordist link between mass-production and economies of scale' by allowing 'the production at lower costs of smaller but still economic batches of both goods and, most significantly, services'. The physical concentration of workers in large units would no longer be necessary to enable cost-effective production to occur.

Sociologically, this theory is useful in that it relates specific manifestations of 'restructuring' to broader structural trends and, in relating the regime of accumulation to the mode of regulation which supports it, a possible relationship is suggested as developing between institutions of work and industry and broader societal ones. Although it still has overtones of economic determinism, it usefully draws attention to possible links between the economic and the political spheres – as long as these are not seen as too mechanistic and as operating in only one direction. The theory is, however, also vulnerable to criticisms of over-simplification because of its dualistic style of analysis; and when we look at more detailed and local studies of restructuring such as that of Bagguley *et al.* (1990), who examined restructuring in two particular towns, there is less evidence of changes being 'driven by capital' than the neo-Marxist theories would suggest. These researchers argue that although economic factors are central to what they saw occurring, they are far from the whole story. Local, ethnic, political, gender and class factors play a significant role. And Beck (2000) sees with the collapse of Fordism and the growth of a destandardised, fragmented, deregulated and plural 'underemployment system' in which neither the state nor trade unions can protect people from risk and insecurity, an opportunity for a 'multi-activity society' to be developed. In this 'brave new world of work' housework, family work and voluntary work would be 'prized alongside paid work' and new communities of interest developed outside the formal world of organised work and industry. Gorz (2002) also argues for movement towards a multi-activity society and culture along such lines, seeing this as an alternative to the pressure which post-Fordist employment puts on the worker to sell their 'whole self' to the corporation. Whereas under Fordism the worker simply sold their labour-power to the employer, the post-Fordist employer would seek a level of commitment and initiative that would threaten workers' identity and personal autonomy.

Flexible specialisation

Flexible specialisation (Piore and Sabel 1984; Piore 1986) is similar to post-Fordism but extends the idea in several ways.

FLEXIBLE SPECIALISATION

An approach to employment and work organisation which offers customised products to diversified markets, building trusting and co–operative relationships both with employees, who use advanced technologies in a craft way, and other organisations within a business district and its associated community.

Those identifying a trend towards flexible specialisation see the breakdown of the mass markets associated with Fordism leading to a use of computer-controlled production equipment for the small batch production of high quality, customised products for discrete or specialised market niches. The speed and economies possible with microelectronic technology allows firms to respond rapidly to changes in demand and to combine low unit costs with non-repetitive manufacturing. For this to succeed, workers have to be competent across a range of tasks and be prepared to switch between these as demand requires. Recomposition of tasks leads to reskilling of labour and the revival of craft traditions. Co-operative relationships are developed not only with the employees, however, but with other organisations and institutions within the firm's business district. Collective services relating to training of labour, low-cost finance, marketing and research and development are shaped in the district in such a way that firms both co-operate and compete with one another.

Patterns of flexible specialisation in this sense have arisen in districts of Germany and Italy and its advocates see a potential for its principles spreading into larger organisations as these perceive a need to react to changes in consumer demand. The picture painted by Piore and Sabel has been criticised as over-optimistic, of giving an over-simplified account of the alleged period of mass production and of under-estimating the costs of computer controlled production (Williams *et al.* 1987). Sabel and Zeitlin (1997) later updated the thesis that affinities are appearing in modern times with what occurred in the early stages of 'mechanisation' and they move away from the evolutionary tone of the earlier work to stress the role of human choices and identities in developing a world of more flexible possibilities. In spite of this, there is still power in earlier arguments that British traditions and general approaches to business are not conducive to a flexible specialisation approach (Hirst and Zeitlin, 1991), and case studies of firms introducing technical innovations and work reorganisation carried out by Tailby and Whitson (1989) suggest that the outcome for workers has been 'job losses, more oppressive supervision and higher levels of stress', this leading them to comment that the 'alleged universally beneficial results of flexible specialisation, to say nothing of the idea of the newly autonomous worker, are questioned by such findings'. On the other hand, it has been suggested there is growing evidence that these broad principles are having an impact and are, as Starkey and McKinlay (1989) put it, 'being widely appropriated by manufacturing managements in their diagnosis of product market segmentation and work organisation'.

Postmodernity

In Chapter 2 we encountered postmodernism as a way of looking at the world – a style of social and cultural analysis. Sometimes, however, it is used to characterise a recent stage in human history, something that might be better labelled *postmodernity*.

POSTMODERNITY

An alleged state into which the world is moving which departs from the key organising principles of modernity.

Postmodernity sees a reshaping of activities across the globe with trends towards both globalisation and more localised activity. A greater plurality of interest groups appears, 'image' and consumption play a key role in people's consciousness with pleasure replacing the old emphasis on work as a virtue in its own right. Work organisations become much more decentralised and people's experience within them changes.

Discussions of postmodernity pay attention to various ways in which *fragmentation* of existing patterns can be seen to be occurring in the world – although there is also attention to some countervailing trends within this. As the association of a concept of postmodernity with *postmodernism* as a way of thinking about the world (explained in Chapter 2) would imply, a concern with changes in human knowledge plays a key role here, as it did with claims about post-industrialism. Lyotard's (1984) claim that the basis of legitimacy of 'modern' knowledge is withering away is crucial here. Postmodernity is associated with 'heterogeneity, plurality, constant innovation, and pragmatic construction of local rules and prescriptives agreed upon by participants, and is thus for micropolitics' (Best and Kellner 1991).

Like Castells' notion of the network society, and the globalisation thesis to which we shall shortly turn, 'postmodernity' tends to be associated with increasing movements of capital across the world and the way this puts considerable limits on what nation states can do. Such trends, say Lash and Urry (1987), lead to a 'disorganisation of capitalism' as economic activities within a nation state become decreasingly amenable either to state management or to working-class-based political initiatives. The claim of these authors that there is a general move from an era of 'organised capitalism' to one of *disorganised capitalism* has a cultural element as well as an economic one. Lash and Urry observe the 'disorganising' effects of a postmodern culture, with its fetishising of cultural images which they see as tending to fragment people's cultural or class identity. In spite of the fact that analyses such as these touch on significant changes occurring in contemporary life, especially in the cultural field, they are vulnerable to the same criticism made earlier of information-related attempts to identify a new epoch in human history. They are also vulnerable to the criticisms that are made of claims that the world is moving into a *globalised* epoch.

Globalisation, convergence and internationalisation

Globalisation is a concept which is increasingly used to label changing ways in which different parts of the human world relate to each other. Implicit in this is the idea of a world whose various parts are becoming increasingly like each other. Although 'globalisation' is a fairly recent notion, the idea of convergence is by no means new. One of the most influential analyses in this vein was that of Kerr *et al.* (1973, originally 1960) and Kerr (1983).

THE CONVERGENCE THESIS

Societies which industrialise become increasingly alike in their social, political and cultural characteristics as well as their work organisations.

A compelling logic underlying industrialism is identified. This means that whatever choices are exercised by human beings they cannot avoid, in the long run, having the technology of industrialism without a whole set of concomitant structural and cultural features. Industrial technology is seen as requiring a highly skilled and professional labour force that is controlled by a range of norms and rules. For this labour force to exist and to be motivated there must be a certain kind of open educational system accompanied by social mobility and relative social equality in society at large. This society will inevitably be a large-scale one with the consequent requirement for close government involvement but with overall consensus being achieved through the development of values of progress, science, mobility, materialism, a work ethic and, especially, pluralism. No one group dominates the world of 'pluralistic industrialism'. Various groups compete but do so within an accepted web of rules with the government holding the ring. Following from this is the suggestion that in many basic respects all societies which are industrialised must, because of the very logic of industrialism, become similar.

A strand of this style of thinking is carried over into some of the attempts to make sense of how the world was changing with the collapse of authoritarian states in central and eastern Europe and in Latin America in the late twentieth century. Fukuyama (1992), for example, analysed these changes in terms of 'the endpoint of mankind's ideological evolution and the universalisation of Western liberal democracy as the final form of human government'. Political forces and, in particular, a broad 'liberal project', were seen as significant, but so were the economic benefits of industrialism and the emergence of 'a single market for German cars, Malaysian semiconductors, Argentine beef, Japanese fax machines, Canadian wheat and American airplanes'.

Discussions of globalisation also combine attention to economic changes in the world with political and cultural changes.

GLOBALISATION

A trend in which the economic, political and cultural activities of people in different countries increasingly influence each other and become interdependent.

Political changes following the end of the Cold War and changing patterns of international tension (Bobbit 2002) bring about new patterns of military alliance which influence contacts between peoples in different parts of the world. And the *cultural* dimension of international changes is stressed by Robertson (1992) who defines globalisation as 'the compression of the world and the intensification of consciousness of the world'. He analyses the ways in which the trend towards global consciousness develops at local levels as people look outwards towards the world. He questions the thesis that globalisation represents a growing domination of the world by Western rationality. The considerable role of religious movements across the globe, examined by Robertson, is strong evidence of the survival of a powerful 'local' level of consciousness. This exists, however, alongside the international popularity of various forms of entertainment and the ubiquity of certain fast food 'outlets' (Waters 1995). And there is empirical evidence for convergence of time-use patterns, at least in the developed world, with Gershuny (2000) showing that across the twenty societies he studied there has been a *national convergence* and shared general increase in leisure (as opposed to work), a *gender convergence* in which women do a greater proportion of domestic work than men, and a *status convergence* in how time-use varies between social groups.

If there were full economic globalisation, national governments would become powerless in the face of the international market and national and local elites would lose their power and influence to international 'capital'. Multinational corporations – ones with a base in a particular country – are undoubtedly increasingly influential in the world, moving people, money and jobs around the world to suit their own interests (Gray 1998). Globalisation would entail these being replaced by transnational corporations whose management is internationally recruited and who moves business activities about the world regardless of interests in any one country. However, it is clear that the major business corporations in the world are still located in particular countries. Although large corporations move investments about the world and build international markets, they are still recognised as being 'Japanese companies' or 'American corporations'.

Hirst and Thompson (1996) argue that an international economy certainly exists but not a 'globalised' one. They demonstrate that national and international markets have not been replaced by a global free market, and Whitley (1994) observed that, given the 'continued importance of national political, financial, labour and cultural systems in structuring economic relations within and across market economies', the 'separation of an international level of economic organisation has not developed'. It is not, he adds, likely to do so 'as long as national and regional institutions remain significant and different'. And in a later study, Whitley (2000) shows the extent to which business systems across the world continue to vary. He identifies five types of business system – fragmented (Hong Kong), co-ordinated industrial districts (parts of Italy), compartmentalised (Anglo-Saxon countries), state-organised (Korea) and highly co-ordinated (Japan) – and produces evidence to suggest that little convergence is occurring between these, in spite of financial and economic internationalisation.

The changing significance of service work

It is important when looking at statistics indicating shifts from manufacturing to service work to note much of the apparent increase in service employment (increases in numbers of managers, technologists and other professionals) is associated with an increase in activities aimed at improving the efficiency of systems of material production. In pointing this out, Gershuny (1978) also noted that service requirements are often being met by increased production by manufacturing industry. For example, people tend to buy a washing machine, putting demand on the manufacturing sector, instead of taking the washing to a laundry and creating laundry service employment. And when it comes to the experience of work in the two sectors there are both continuities and differences.

The fast-food restaurant is a prime example of principles of industrial manufacturing being applied to service work, thus giving us continuity between experiences in the two sectors. Taylorist principles underpin the operation of the fast-food restaurant. Labour in such restaurants is 'highly rationalised, and the goal is the discovery of the best, the most efficient, way of grilling a hamburger, frying chicken, or serving a meal' (Ritzer 1993). As Ritzer (1993, 1998) observes, McDonald's, the best-known fast-food business, did not invent these ideas, but combined them with the principles of bureaucracy and the assembly line 'to contribute to the creation of McDonaldisation'. And industrial manufacturing principles of mechanisation, rationalisation and routinisation are not only applied to fast-food service work but also to banking, retailing and other services work in a way which means that service work is tending to extend 'manual industrial labour' rather than erode it (Beynon 1992). Yet, as Ritzer points out, in response to Smart's (1999) criticisms of his McDonaldisation thesis, these tendencies towards 'McDonaldised standardisation' are occurring in the world at the same time as post-Fordist moves towards greater flexibility may be occurring in other 'sectors of society' (Ritzer 1999).

In contrast to claims about the continuity between manufacturing and service, Allen and du Gay (1994) concentrate on the ways in which service work differs from manufacturing work. It is a 'hybrid' type of activity in that it combines with its *economic* function a *cultural* one (culture being involved with the 'production of distinct meanings'). Thus, a profitable service relation 'is one in which distinct meanings are produced for the customer' and service work can be seen as developing its own technologies – 'soft' ones of 'interpersonal and emotion management'. This means that service work has its own characteristic types of skill, involving predispositions and capacities which are aimed at making it possible for them 'to win over the "hearts and minds" of customers'. This argument is helpful in enabling us to recognise service work as something distinct and existing in its own right, so to speak, rather than as something always to be subordinated conceptually or evaluatively to the 'real work' of manufacturing.

However, it needs to be pointed out that a great deal of work in manufacturing organisations, especially in the managerial and marketing spheres, involves the types of 'people skill' that is traditionally associated with service work. Frenkel *et al.* (1999), in recognising a general rise in the proportion of people engaged in service rather than manufacturing work, observe the increasing importance of *front-line service workers*, both as a proportion of the workforce and as a reflection of the 'strategic' role they play 'at the interface of the organisation and its customers'. Work, these researchers argue, is generally becoming more complex. In part this is because of increasing demand for more customised products and services and is partly the result of the growing use of ICTs combined with the increasing costs of labour. And an important consequence of this shift is that higher level skills will be required of an increasing proportion of workers, with a consequential shift in bargaining power on the part of those workers.

4 Work organisations

CHAPTER FOUR

The organisational principle of work structuring

Work organisations are crucial to the way modern industrialised societies are structured. Central to the history of modern societies is a trend whereby work tasks are increasingly carried out within bureaucratised corporations and formally structured enterprises that employ people to work under the instructions of organisational managers. Organisations are at 'the centre of gravity of contemporary society' (Strati 2000). And the work tasks performed by organisations are not just those of industrial production but ones involved in the administration of government and the birth, education, leisure and welfare of people throughout their lives. A high proportion of modern people earn their living through their employment by a formal work organisation and, after work, they go to shops owned and run by similar organisations, they enjoy entertainment provided by organisations and they seek help from them when they find themselves in difficulty. Thus much of the 'structuring' or patterning of modern lives, both within work and outside it, involves what we might call the organisational principle of work structuring.

THE ORGANISATIONAL PRINCIPLE OF WORK STRUCTURING

Patterns of work activity which are the outcomes – intended and unintended – of institutional arrangements in which some people conceive of and design work and then recruit, pay, co-ordinate and control the efforts of other people to fulfil work tasks.

The increasing dominance of this aspect of the shaping of modern societies is closely associated with the historical shift discussed in Chapter 3 from a *social division of labour* in societies (where tasks are shared out *across* a range of occupations) to a *technical division of labour*. The technical division of labour involves task specialisation *within* what we still tend to call occupations but where, in practice, 'who does what and how' is decided by organisational managers, engineers, supervisors and other technical experts rather than by the guardians of occupational, guild or trade traditions.

The trend over recent centuries, then, has been for the organisational principle of work structuring to push aside the *occupational principle* of work structuring; one which emphasises the way in which people with similar skills, traditions and values co-operatively conceive, execute and regulate work tasks. The occupational principle has not disappeared from the way work is structured in modern societies. It most visibly survives in certain trade-based trade unions, in certain 'professional' groups and in public perceptions of certain distinctive types of job. These matters will be examined in Chapter 6, where we will also demonstrate the value of using the notions of occupation and occupational structure as sociological concepts that can help us analyse and understand work and working lives in modern societies. It will become clear in that chapter that changing occupational patterns in societies are very much the consequences of changes made in organisations and the various organisational and employment initiatives that the managers of corporations have pushed forward (the focus of Chapter 5).

To analyse sociologically any given area of life, such as that of work organisations, we have to meet the very basic requirement identified in Chapter 1 of fully recognising the interplay which occurs between the patterns, regularities or structuring of social life and the varied interests, initiatives and values of the individuals who create and operate within this structuring. To understand work organisations sociologically, therefore, we need to see them as overall patterns of regular behaviour which include the whole range of informal, unofficial and even illegitimate actions and arrangements that occur. This is why the above characterisation of the organisational principles of work structuring recognised that the work structures we see in modern societies are the result of both intended and unintended efforts by organisational managers. It is highly inappropriate and *partial* (in both senses of the word – inadequate and biased) to see organisation structures as just the formal arrangements which are portrayed in the management's organisation chart, rule book and official operating procedures. This all too often happens in standard organisation and management writing and teaching and it is as unhelpful as a way of conceptualising organisations to those who are interested in managing organisations as it is to those who simply wish to study how they work. Some careful attention to how we conceptualise organisations is therefore vital.

The nature of work organisations

The concept of 'organisation', used in a general sense, is fundamental to sociological analysis. A basic insight of sociology is that the whole of life is socially organised in various ways: it displays certain patterns and exhibits regularities. Indeed the occupational aspect of working life and the social division of labour are as much a part of this patterning of societies as is the organisational component that we are examining in this chapter and which is often referred to as *formal organisation*. It therefore needs to be made clear that in the ensuing discussion the concept of organisation is being applied to just one aspect of the wider *social organisation* of society. We are focusing on patterns of activity which have been deliberately set up at some historically distinguishable point in time to carry out certain tasks and which, to do this, make use of various administrative or bureaucratic techniques. Organisations thus include such things as manufacturing and service-providing enterprises, banks, hospitals, prisons but exclude families, tribes, social classes and spontaneous friendship groups.

However ramshackle formal organisations may become and however diverse and confused may be the interests and concerns of their members, what ultimately distinguishes them from other aspects of social organisation is some initially inspiring purposiveness. Important in this is the existence, at least in the organisation's early history, of some kind of relatively explicit charter or programme of action. Organisations are pieces of human social structure that are much more deliberately or consciously designed than other forms of human association. And the increasing pervasiveness of organisations in modern history is to be understood as part of the wider trend of increasing rationalisation looked at in Chapter 3 which underlies the development of industrial capitalism – the process identified by Max Weber whereby deliberately calculated means are adopted in the pursuit of consciously selected ends. Organisations are thus, in a sense, expressions of some of the basic cultural characteristics of modern societies. This is emphasised in *institutional theories* of organisations (Scott 1995; Tolbert and Zucker 1996; Hatch 1997) where it is argued that organisations take the shape they do because people draw from the culture around them value-based notions of how things should be organised. And this societal pattern of expectations is not to be seen as a politically neutral matter. Meyer and Rowan (1977) point to the significance in the modern world of the *rational myth* of the organisation, whereby rules in organisations are institutionalised in a form where they appear to be neutral technical matters. Their connection to values or interests is thus obscured.

This 'institutional approach' in organisation theory emphasises the extent to which common understandings in the culture outside the organisation come to be 'culturally embedded' within the organisation (Zucker 1988). The meanings and expectations which prevail in *any given organisational setting* are partly imposed upon organisational members by those holding power and are partly negotiated between the variety of parties involved in that situation. Those with power, and especially the organisation's management, attempt to create definitions of situations among the employees which make the prevailing pattern of power, and distribution of scarce and valued resources, acceptable. In Weber's terms, power is made legitimate and thus converted to 'authority'. Hence, managerial work is very much involved in the creation of meanings for organisational members, although these are not meanings which can ever be unilaterally imposed.

Organisations are specifically purposive and characteristically rational constructs. But purposiveness and 'rationality' is massively compromised by two things: first, by the tendency within social life towards human conflict and, second, by the tendency towards structural contradictions and unintended consequences. Social structures reflect the institutionalising by dominant social groups of the advantages which they have with regard to scarce and valued resources. The stability of social structures – seen as a 'pattern of advantage' in this way – is constantly threatened by social conflict, where less advantaged groups and individuals resist or challenge the current order. This occurs in formal organisations as much as in society as a whole as does the second tendency, that towards structural contradiction. In this, the institutionalised means chosen to achieve certain purposes tends to develop unintended consequences which may undermine the achievement of the ends for which they were designed. As we shall see later in this chapter, this tendency is central to the functioning of organisations.

The fact that organisations are more purposively conceived than other social forms has led to a degree of emphasis on their 'rationality' which has seriously exaggerated the extent to which, in practice, they operate as machines or systems efficiently pursuing specific purposes. Such an exaggeration has permeated business and management thinking but has also been present in much organisational sociology. This is revealed by the tendency of many writers on organisations to define organisations in terms of organisational goals. An informal survey of organisational textbooks (Watson 2002) showed the popularity of definitions of organisations such as

- 'consciously created arrangement to achieve goals by collective means',
- 'systems of roles oriented towards securing a goal',
- 'goal-centred systems of co-ordinated human and technological activity'.

The danger with focusing on goals in this way when defining organisations is that attention is drawn away from the sociological fact that organisations, in practice and despite any clarity of purpose of those in charge of them, involve a wide range of people who have different goals or purposes. As well as the co-operation which must occur for an organisation to survive there will be considerable differences and conflicts of interest. What common purpose there is in the typical modern work organisation is as likely to be the outcome of the power behaviour of those in charge and of compromises reached between differing interest groups as it is of any consensual recognition of 'neutral' or collective organisational goals.

A definition of organisations is required which recognises the existence of a multiplicity of interests and of a power structure in the typical organisation whilst nevertheless accepting that organisations are purposive or task-based arrangements. Thus,

WORK ORGANISATIONS

Social and technical arrangements and understandings in which a number of people come together in a formalised and contractual relationship where the actions of some are directed by others towards the achievement of work tasks carried out in the organisation's name.

This definition encourages a view of the organisation less as a pre-given structure into which people are 'slotted' and more as an ongoing and ever-changing coalition of people with quite different and often conflicting interests and purposes who are willing, within rather closely defined limits, to carry out tasks which help to meet the requirements of those in charge. And those people in charge are paid to achieve a level of *productive co-operation* in the carrying out of tasks which will enable the organisation to continue in existence under its formal identity and legal corporate status or 'name' as a furniture maker, a software company, a hospital or a university.

PRODUCTIVE CO-OPERATION

The achievement, in the light of the tendency of people involved in organisations to have their own projects, interests and priorities, of a degree of working together that ensures that tasks carried out in the organisation's name are fulfilled to sufficient a level to enable the organisation to continue in existence.

To look at organisations in this way – as patterns of activity in which the effective production of goods and services is something that the 'organisers' have to strive for in the face of the multiplicity of interests and purposes that organisational actors bring to the enterprise – is consistent with the turning away from systems thinking in the sociology of organisations. The strengths and the considerable weaknesses of this perspective were considered in Chapter 2 where the tendency of systems models to over-emphasise integration and consensus was noted as well as the tendency to make human individuals secondary or derivative of the systems in which they are located. Not only does systems thinking play down the conflicts of interest which are inherent in organisations, it also under-estimates the role of human initiative and the part that meanings, interpretations and understandings play in the shaping of organisational activities. Recognition of the importance of these matters in organisational sociology was significantly boosted by Silverman (1970, 1994). The basic insight of the 'social action' or interpretive tradition which this work brought to the centre of organisational analysis was that social arrangements – be they societies, groups or organisations – are not best understood as pre-given structures into which people are slotted but as the outcome of the interactive patterns of human activity. Organisations are often experienced as if they are 'things' which exist outside and prior to human activity, but what are really being experienced are institutional processes. And human actors as makers of meanings are always implicated in those processes rather than existing merely as a passive object upon which the process works.

The organisation can be seen as something which is continually being negotiated and re-negotiated by the inter-subjective relating of its members to each other. It is, in Silverman's (1970) words, 'the outcome of motivated people attempting to resolve their own problems'. This is consistent with the notion explained in Chapter 2 of the organisation as a *negotiated order*: a pattern of activities which emerges over time from the interplay of the variety of interests, understandings, initiatives and reactions of individuals and groups within originations. And it accords with some of the insights that the ethnomethodological tradition brings to the study of organisations. As we saw in Chapter 2 (p. 36), Bittner (1965) argued for treating the very notion of 'organisation' as a commonsense construct of ordinary people rather than as a scientific concept to be used unproblematically by the social scientist. According to this position, the social scientist has to be careful about confusing topic and resource. What ought to be studied are the human processes whereby organisational meanings are created rather than organisations as solid entities. Thus, for example, organisational rules or procedures are not simply followed by people because 'the organisation' requires it. Rather, people more or less comply with rules because they recognise a set of expectations that they should, with a greater or lesser degree of willingness, obey them. But they typically do this in a way which, as far as possible, suits their own current purposes or projects.

Official and unofficial aspects of organisations

A pair of concepts that has been used throughout the history of industrial and organisational sociology has been that of *formal* and *informal* organisation. It emerged in the 1930s as a way in which both social scientists and some management writers engaged with what we might call the 'two-sidedness of organisational life' (Watson 2001b). One side of every work organisation is the set of bureaucratic roles, rules and procedures that we see represented in rule books, organisation charts and formalised sets of operating procedures. This is the aspect of organisations that encourages us to conceive of them as entities that remain in existence even when the individuals who take particular organisational roles are completely replaced by another set of individuals. However, this first side of the work organisation can only come into being when human individuals enter the set of roles indicated on the organisation chart. When they enter the organisational scene they bring with them their own interests, purposes and understandings. And they are likely soon to want to shape certain aspects of their working lives for themselves, regardless of what the managerial blueprint dictates. Thus a second side of organisational life comes into being as people form relationships and coalitions of interests with others, play games, develop 'short cuts', create 'pecking orders' and generally seek ways of expressing and defending their humanity and pursuing personal priorities.

This second side of organisational life was given the label of *informal organisation* by writers and researchers associated with human relations thinking (Chapter 2, pp. 29–30). The bank wiring observation room experiment at the Hawthorne plant is one of the best-known illustrations of how informal organisation develops (the setting of informal output norms by the work groups members) in opposition to the formal organisation (the incentive system designed to encourage workers each to produce the level of output fitting their personally desired level of financial reward). Roethlisberger and Dickson (1939) in reporting this research emphasised that informal organisation does not necessarily undermine the formal in this way – it sometimes operates to support the formal system. This point is emphasised in Barnard's (1938) analysis of executive activities and the extent to which the 'informal society' that develops among managers is vital to the effectiveness of the executive process. Similar arguments emerged from later research on managerial processes with Mangham and Pye (1991) reporting that senior managers often stressed to them that 'informal organising' was as important, or more important, to their work than the 'articulation of a formal organisation'.

Aspects of this second or 'informal' side of organisation will be considered later in this chapter when we look at organisational micropolitics and will be important again when we look at a range of 'oppositional' activities in Chapter 8. At this point, however, it is necessary to recognise that industrial and organisational sociologists have tended in recent times to turn away from the use of the formal/informal distinction to deal with the phenomenon. In large part this has been because of the association of the pair of concepts with human relations thinking and with the systems thinking that, to a certain extent, developed out of it. The distinction became associated with analyses that were seen as too 'unitary' – as insufficiently locating workplace activities within wider patterns of conflict and inequality beyond the formal and informal arrangements of the workplace. A further, and perhaps more significant, reason for moving away from the formal/informal distinction is in recognition of a trend for organisational managers (in line with the recommendations of Barnard 1938, in effect) to integrate what was once separable into the 'formal' and the 'informal' into a single 'strong culture' organisation (Chapter 2, p. 32 and Chapter 5, pp. 129–31) in which, for example, 'empowered' workgroups or 'teams' are encouraged to develop their own 'informal' norms and practice – as long as, of course, these support and further formally stated corporate values and objectives.

The rejection of the formal/informal dichotomy does not mean that we have to abandon any distinction between the 'two sides' of organisational life identified earlier. But to overcome the ideological associations of the formal/informal dichotomy, we can adopt, instead, a slightly different distinction: that between *official* and *unofficial* aspects of organisations.

OFFICIAL AND UNOFFICIAL ASPECTS OF ORGANISATIONS

Official aspects of organisations are the rules, values and activities that are part of the formally managerial-sanctioned policies and procedures. Unofficial aspects are the rules, values and activities that people at all levels in the organisation develop but which do not have formal managerial sanction.

What this concept pair encourage us to do is to distinguish between – and examine the interplay between – the managerial aspirations expressed in official management statements, policies and claims and the observable patterns of belief and behaviour that prevail across the organisation in practice.

The official and unofficial aspects of organisation structures are best seen as only conceptually or analytically distinct aspects of what is really one overall organisational structure. The two are dialectically related. They are influenced by each other with activities in one often encouraging activities in the other. We might, for example, see managers devising a payment system in the hope of increasing work output. The officially stated purpose of this might be 'to share with employees the rewards of the high performance production system that we all want to see'. The introduction of the scheme might, however, invite unofficial strategies among workgroups, along the lines of those observed in the Hawthorne experiments, whereby workers resist managerial pressures to work harder than, as a group, they decide is reasonable. And, in turn, this might lead managers to introduce a new, and official, workshop layout which tends to segregate workers from each other, thus breaking up the unofficial relationship and communication patterns existing under the old arrangement.

This illustration of how official and unofficial aspects of organisations interrelate also illustrates the very important point that all of these facets of life within the organisation relate to patterns prevailing in the society outside organisational boundaries. There is a clear difference of priorities between those managing the workshop and those working the machines, these differences relating to the broader economic, social status and social class positions of these people. And Figure 4.1 represents both the interplay between official and unofficial aspects of organisations and the interplay between organisational patterns as a whole and the social order within which the organisation is located. The model presented here complies with the key criterion of a distinctly sociological perspective which was introduced at the beginning of this book; that whatever is studied is ultimately related back to the way society as a whole is organised. Hence the pattern of relationships in the wider society is represented in the outer circle in Figure 4.1 and the arrows pointing into and out of the inner circles represent the ways in which organisations are simultaneously outcomes of the wider pattern of advantage in society and contributors to it.

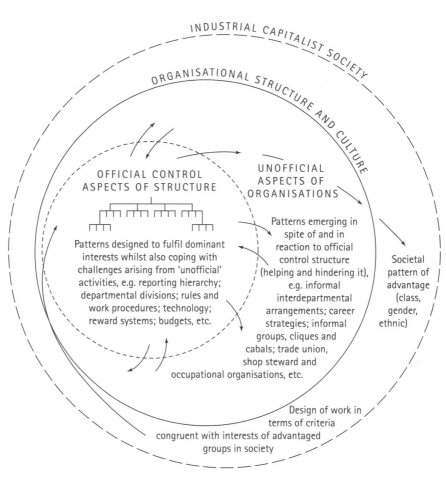

Figure 4.1 Official and unofficial aspects of organisations in their societal context

Organisations are generally designed to function in ways that are supportive of the interests of those who are better placed in society, if only because these tend to be the people with sufficient resources to establish and develop organisations. In this way they tend to reflect the wider social structure. But once they are in operation, organisations tend to support or 'reproduce' this structure through rewarding on a differential basis those who contribute to them, so contributing to the allocation of people to different positions in the class, gender and ethnic patterns of inequality 'in society'. And this pattern, in turn, helps reproduce the organisational form because the 'inputs' of investment, on the one hand, and labour on the other come from this structure of advantage and disadvantage.

Organisational structures and cultures

Organisational structures, seen sociologically, are part of the wider social structure of the society in which they are located. But if we wish to look at organisational structures in their own terms we need to conceptualise them in a way that ensures both official and unofficial aspects of organisational activities are covered.

ORGANISATIONAL STRUCTURE

The regular or persisting patterns of action that give shape and a degree of predictability to an organisation.

The structure of any organisation, seen in this way, will partly be the outcome of the efforts of managers and other organisational designers to structure tasks, activities and establish a controlling hierarchy of command. And it will partly be an outcome of the efforts of members of the organisation to find their own way of doing things, to establish their own coalitions of interest and, to some extent, to develop their own power hierarchies. Alongside official roles, like that of 'office team leader', will be unofficial roles, like that of 'office clown'. Alongside official rules like that which insists that members of staff always wear a tie when dealing with customers will be unofficial rules such as one insisting that staff leave their ties undone whenever a manager is not watching them. Alongside official procedures such as that whereby all letters sent out from the office should be signed by the manager will be unofficial procedures such as one whereby office workers use a rubber stamp of the manager's signature on letters they write, both to get the mail despatched more quickly than they would if they waited for the manager to sign each letter and to make life easier for everyone concerned.

When we look at organisational structures we are focusing on regular activities and behaviours. And when we turn our attention to the meanings that people attach to these activities we tend to use a concept of organisational culture.

ORGANISATIONAL CULTURE

The set of meanings and values shared by members of an organisation that defines the appropriate ways for people to think and behave with regard to the organisation.

In so far as we can identify a distinctive culture in any organisation (remembering that, as with structures, cultural patterns we see within an organisation are to a large extent facets of the culture of the society of which the organisation is a part), it will in part be shaped by managerial attempts to devise official 'corporate cultures' with sets of managerially propagated 'values', mission statements and the like (a topic of Chapter 5, pp. 129–31). Managerial talk about corporate cultures tends to treat cultures as things that organisations 'have'. But it is probably more helpful to talk about the cultural dimension of organisations rather than of 'organisational cultures' as such. And this dimension of organisational life has significant unofficial aspects. Officially, for example, 'the culture' of an organisation might be said to be one in which every employee is guided by the moral rule or 'value' that 'the customer is always right'. But unofficially the cultural pattern might be one in which complaining customers tend to be treated with contempt and only treated politely when it is deemed likely that they will take their complaint to a supervisor or manager.

To understand the cultural dimension of an organisation it is helpful to analyse a variety of expressions of culture, remembering that each of these can support either the official or the unofficial aspect of culture:

- *artefacts*, such as the tools, documents, building layouts, logos, badges and furnishing,
- *jargon* – the linguistic terms that are peculiar to that organisational setting,
- *stories* about how people have acted within the organisation, and with what effect,
- jokes and *humour* generally,
- *legends* about events that might or might not actually have happened but that have a sense of wonder about them and which point to activities that organisational members are encouraged to admire or deplore,
- *myths* about events that are unlikely ever to have happened but which illustrate some important 'truth' about the organisation,
- *sagas* about the organisation's history and how it has become 'what it is',
- *heroes* and *villains* that people speak of – inspirational figures that organisational members are encouraged to emulate and 'bad people' illustrating types of behaviour to be avoided,
- *norms of behaviour* – regularly occurring pieces of behaviour that become accepted as 'the way things are done' in the organisation,
- *rituals* – patterns of behaviour that regularly occur in particular circumstances and at particular times in an organisation,
- *rites* – more formalised rituals that tend to be pre-planned and organised,
- actions leading to *rewards* or *punishments* – behaviours that lead to positive or negative sanctions because they accord with or clash with cultural values.

The distinction between organisation structure and organisation culture which we have been using so far, with the former focusing on activities and the latter on meanings and values, is a useful one. But it can only be taken so far. Many aspects of organisational life can as readily be regarded as structural and they can be treated as cultural. A good example of this would be *rules*. An organisational rule can be seen as an element of an organisation's structure. But it can equally be seen as an expression of an organisation's culture. We need to recognise, in fact, that organisational structures and cultures are not really separate phenomena at all. The two concepts derive from two different metaphors that we use to try to give some solidity to the abstract phenomenon of 'organisation'. When we talk of an organisational structure we are utilising a metaphor of the organisation as 'something built' and when we talk of an organisational culture we are using an agricultural metaphor rather than a construction one and applying a metaphor of organisation as 'something cultivated'. The way in which we tend to switch about between these metaphors can be illustrated by the fact that we sometimes talk of 'the bureaucratic structure' of an organisation whilst, at other times, we talk about that organisation's 'bureaucratic *culture*'. This suggests that it might be wise to move away from the traditional sociological practice of treating such matters as bureaucracy as structural phenomena and recognise that they are both structural and cultural.

It is thus helpful when examining how modern work organisations have developed in the way that they have to consider the efforts of 'organisers' simultaneously to design official structures *and* cultures. There are certain key principles which have been applied in the shaping of modern organisations, 'bureaucracy' being a central one.

Official structure and culture: basic organisational design principles

Although, to understand organisations sociologically, we need to see them as involving both official and unofficial practices, at the core of any work organisation will be the *official control apparatus* which is designed and continuously redesigned by those 'managing' the enterprise.

THE OFFICIAL CONTROL APPARATUS OF AN ORGANISATION

The set of roles, rules, structures, value statements, cultural symbols, rituals and procedures managerially designed to co-ordinate and control work activities.

In designing the organisation, the managers seek to establish such things as:

- how the tasks to be done within the chosen technologies are to be split into various jobs,
- how these jobs are to be grouped into sections, divisions and departments,
- how many levels of authority there are to be,
- the nature of communication channels and reward structures,
- the balance of centralisation to decentralisation and authority to delegation,
- the degree of formalisation and standardisation of procedures and instructions,
- the values or principles that organisational members should be guided by in their behaviour,
- the beliefs about the organisation and the legitimacy of managerial authority that organisational members should hold.

The most basic set of principles underlying modern structural and cultural organisation design efforts are those of *bureaucracy*. We can consider what this entails first, and then go on to look at two prescriptive 'schools' of organisational thinking, classical administrative principles and Taylorism/ Fordism, which have provided managements with design guidance, respectively, for the organisation as a whole and for the part of the organisation most directly involved with productive tasks.

Bureaucracy

> **BUREAUCRACY**
>
> The control and co-ordination of work tasks through a hierarchy of appropriately qualified office holders, whose authority derives from their expertise and who rationally devise a system of rules and procedures that are calculated to provide the most appropriate means of achieving specified ends.

As we saw in Chapter 3 (p. 59), the bureaucratisation of work has to be seen as part of a wider set of historical processes in Western industrial capitalist societies whereby more and more aspects of life were being subjected to more instrumental or calculative styles of thinking. This rationalisation process involved the rapid development of scientific and technological thinking and, with regard to work organisation, it was increasingly felt that by carefully calculating the most appropriate way of achieving tasks and then basing on this formalised roles, procedures and arrangements within which people would be rewarded only in terms of their contribution to officially-set tasks, the efforts of large numbers of people could be co-ordinated and controlled and large and complex jobs done.

The appeal of bureaucracy was two-fold to those pushing the modernisation of the world. Bureaucracy could bring about:

- *fairness* in the distribution of posts and rewards, particularly in the sphere of public administration, this increasingly being expected in the democratising societies of Europe and America. By the following of procedural neutrality and impartiality, the old evils of favouritism, nepotism and capriciousness would be removed;
- *efficiency* both in state administration and in industrial enterprises. Great promise was seen in terms of output and quality if large organisations could be administered on the basis of clear procedures, expertise and co-ordinated human efforts.

To help analyse the process of bureaucratisation, which he saw as central to modern societies, Weber in *Wirtschaft und Gesellschaft*, published after his death in 1921, presents a model of what a bureaucracy would look like if it existed in a pure form. In doing this he used the device of the *ideal type*. Weber's ideal type of bureaucracy is often taken to be the conceptual starting point in organisation theory and much of the effort expended by sociologists and other social scientists to understand organisations has been an attempt to refine or take issue with what Weber was taken to be implying in its use.

In an ideal-type bureaucracy (that is, in an imagined pure case of the phenomenon):

- all operating rules and procedures are formally recorded;
- tasks are divided up and allocated to people with formally certified expertise to carry them out;
- activities are controlled and co-ordinated by officials organised in a hierarchy of authority;
- communications and commands pass up or down the hierarchy without missing out steps;
- posts are filled and promotions achieved by the best qualified people;

- office-holder posts constitute their only employment and the level of their salary reflects their level in the hierarchy;
- posts cannot become the property or private territory of the office-holder, the officer's authority derives from their appointed office and not from their person;
- all decisions and judgements are made impersonally and neutrally, without emotion, personal preference or prejudice.

Weber's ideal type of bureaucracy is in no sense a model of what he thought *ought* to be the case administratively. It is a device to help us analytically by providing us with a sketch of an impossibly pure and unachievable structure against which reality can be compared. Weber was concerned to contrast characteristically modern forms of administration (which he saw based on a legal-rational form of authority in which orders are obeyed because they are seen to be in accord with generally acceptable rules or laws) with earlier forms (based on traditional or charismatic authority). He was in no way advocating bureaucracy and he was not addressing himself to the managers of organisations. The bureaucratic principle which he was analysing in his historically based political sociology was, however, put into prescriptive form by a number of writers who were probably quite unaware of Weber's existence and who can be grouped together as the advocates of classical administrative principles.

Classical administrative principles

CLASSICAL ADMINISTRATIVE PRINCIPLES

Universally applicable rules of organisational design – structural and cultural – widely taught and applied, especially in the first half of the twentieth century.

Largely drawing on their own experiences and reflections, writers such as Fayol (1916), Mooney and Riley (1931) and Gulick and Urwick (1937) attempted to establish universally applicable principles upon which organisational and management arrangements should be based. Fayol can be seen as the main inspirer of this approach and the following suggestions for practice can be found among the mixture of exhortations, moral precepts and design principles that make up his writings. He said, for example, that:

- there should always be a 'unity of command' whereby no employee should have to take orders from more than one superior;
- there should be a 'unity of direction' whereby there should be one head and one plan for a group of activities having the same objective;
- there should be regular efforts to maintain the harmony and unity of the enterprise through the encouragement of an 'esprit de corps'.

The advocates of principles like these for the designers and managers of work enterprises vary in their sophistication and in the extent to which they see their principles as relevant to all conditions. However, there is a pervasive underlying principle of there being a 'one best way'. This can be seen in the suggestion that there should always be a differentiating of 'line' and 'staff' departments (those directly concerned with producing the main output of the organisation and those who support this process) and in the various attempts to fix a correct 'span of control' (the number of subordinates any superior can effectively supervise). This kind of universalist prescribing is of importance because it influenced a great deal of twentieth-century organisational design. Yet, as we shall see later (pp. 92–5), more recent research and practice has shown the limits of such a search for rules which can be applied to all organisational circumstances.

Taylorism and Fordism

Whilst the classical administrative writers were advocating what amounts to a set of basic bureaucratic design principles for work organisations as a whole, F.W. Taylor and his associates were putting forward principles for job and workshop design which would apply to the 'lower parts' of these organisations (Taylor 1911a, 1911b). Details of the Taylorist 'scientific management' approach are provided in Chapter 2 (pp. 23–4) and it is easy to understand how Weber came to see in these principles the most extreme manifestation of the process of work rationalisation and the 'greatest triumphs in the rational conditioning and training of work performances' – 'triumphs' he anything but admired but which he saw as fulfilling its 'dehumanising' potential.

Although Taylorist principles of work organisation can be understood as part of the general rationalising process hastening the bureaucratisation of work organisations after the turn of the present century, it is very important to note that these principles are only partly to be understood as bureaucratic. This was pointed out by Littler (1982) who noted that the 'minimum interaction model' of the employment relationship implied in Taylorism contrasts with the career aspect of the principle of bureaucracy. An official in a bureaucracy has the potential to advance up the career hierarchy but a shop floor worker, under scientific management, has no such potential. Different conditions therefore apply to people employed in the lower half of the industrial organisation's hierarchy than apply to those located in the upper part – which is therefore more fully bureaucratic. And this has considerable implications for the way in which formal organisations are implicated in the social class structure of society as a whole, as we saw earlier (p. 82).

Taylorism or 'scientific management' is a phenomenon that we encounter time and again when studying work and work organisation both historically and sociologically. It can be looked at as a contribution to intellectual and theoretical thinking about work organisation and was, accordingly, treated as part of the managerial-psychologistic strand in the sociology of work and industry (see Chapter 2, pp. 23–4). But, as was noted in Chapter 2 and is stressed later in Chapter 5 (p. 120), understanding Taylorism and its legacy is vital to an appreciation of how job design practices have changed over time and, especially, to understanding what the various attempts to rethink the way work tasks were shaped and allocated over the past half century were reacting against. If we look back to the account provided in Chapter 2 (p. 24), Taylor can be seen as a thinker and managerial innovator who combined a 'psychologistic' style of analysis (one which focuses on the psychological characteristics of human individuals) with a socio-political concern to influence the organisation of the work-related aspects of early twentieth-century industrial society. But when it comes to our understanding of patterns at the level of the work organisation, we can see the principles of the scientific management that Taylor initiated as significantly shaping the particular bureaucratic forms that work organisations came to take on as the twentieth century unfolded. Especially important here, and continuing to be significant in the twenty-first century, is the notion that scientifically-orientated managerial experts should take control over task peformance in work organisations, thus reinforcing the strength of hierarchical power in those organisations.

To some observers, the growing twentieth-century significance of the assembly line alongside the spreading influence of Taylorism is sufficient to warrant the recognition of a set of work design and management principles which came to exist in their own right. This is *Fordism*. Although Fordism has a significance way beyond the workplace, as we saw in Chapter 3 (pp. 66–7), an important aspect of the innovations that Henry Ford made in his car factories was an extension of scientific management principles of a detailed division of labour, intensive management work-planning and close supervision. Fordism, with its assembly line, creates an even closer attachment of the individual to their work station and increases the mechanising of work handling. On the cultural side, however, it departs from Taylorism – which tends to treat labour strictly as a commodity – by making a connection between labour management policy and attention to markets. Fordism is essentially a mass production process which recognises that the people it employs are part of the market for its products. It therefore recognises the necessity of taking an interest in the lives of workers as consumers as well as producers. A mass consumption market has to be created and stabilised to fit the mass production organisation of the factory. It is in this context that we can understand Ford's particular innovation of the Five Dollar Day – a relatively high wage level which could be obtained once the worker had a minimum of six months continuous service and as long as they complied with certain standards of personal behaviour. Fordism accepts that the workforce should be treated as more than a commodity to be dealt with at arm's length whilst, nevertheless, keeping them under the close control and instructions of the management in a machine-paced environment.

We noted in Chapter 3 (p. 66–7) how certain observers of changes in industrial capitalist societies see Fordism being replaced by 'post-Fordism'. At the organisational level, significant limitations to scientific management and Fordist practices became apparent, at least in certain circumstances. This was reflected in the psychological humanism that was reviewed in Chapter 2 (pp. 24–6) and has led to various practices of 'work redesign' that will be looked at in Chapter 5 (pp. 119–24). But it is to the serious limitations in the viability of the basic principles of bureaucracy that we now turn.

The limits of bureaucracy and the paradox of consequences

Modern employing organisations, all of which are more or less based on the bureaucratic principle, use rational calculative techniques of various kinds as means towards the ends pursued by their controllers. They also use the work efforts of human beings as resources, as devices, as means-to-ends. However, human beings are assertive, creative and initiating animals with a tendency to resist being the means to other people's ends. This potential means that they are always problematic when used as instruments – as the means to other people's ends. Every organisation is thus confronted by a basic paradox.

A BASIC PARADOX OF ORGANISING

The tendency for the means adopted by organisational managers to achieve particular goals to fail to achieve these goals since these 'means' involve human beings who have goals of their own which may not be congruent with those of the managers.

This paradoxical reality not only accounts for many of the 'motivational' and 'industrial relations' problems which organisational managements continually experience in their work; it also provides the starting point for explaining many structural features of organisations themselves. It provides the key to explaining the growth of quality and auditing functions and aspects of the human resourcing and employee relations structures within organisations. It also accounts in part for the existence of government and quasi-government agencies involved in regulating the activities of employing organisations. All of these are involved in coping with potentially destructive contradictions.

This view of organisations caught up in a paradox is very much in the spirit of Weber's view of modern society and is developed from his key distinction between formal and material rationality, explained in Chapter 2 (p. 40). Yet, ironically, many writers on organisations – who frequently look back to Weber as some kind of founder of organisation theory – completely miss the point of Weber's view of bureaucracy. They assume that when he wrote of the high degree of formal rationality achievable by bureaucratic organisation he was claiming that it is necessarily 'efficient' in its meeting of goals. As Albrow's (1970) important reappraisal of Weber's position showed, Weber did indeed recognise, in pointing to the high formal rationality of bureaucracies, their 'technical superiority' and their virtues of calculability, predictability and stability. But he was nevertheless well aware that, although these were necessary conditions for 'efficient' achievement of goals, they in no way constituted a sufficient guarantee of such success. Formal rationality (choice of technically appropriate means), as was argued earlier (p. 40), does not guarantee material rationality (achievement of the original value-based goal). In the light of this argument it is indeed ironic that attempts to refute Weber's imputed belief in the efficiency of bureaucratic organisations have provided a key motivation behind much organisational sociology. At this point we can introduce some of the key studies which have been done in this tradition, noting that their mistaken intention of 'correcting Weber' does not in itself invalidate their findings. In a sense they are extensions of the Weberian view rather than refutations of it. The basic mistake made by many writers on organisations is to take Weber's ideal type of bureaucracy as if it were some kind of prescription of what an efficient organisation should be.

One of the first sociologists to point to negative aspects of bureaucratic administration was Merton, who concentrated on what he termed *dysfunctions of bureaucracy* – a dysfunctional aspect of any system being some aspect of it which undermines the overall functioning of that system. Merton (1957) argued that the pressure put upon the individual official by bureaucracy, which encourages accountability and predictability through the use of rules, could encourage a counter-productive inflexibility on the part of the officials themselves. Rules and operating procedures thus become ends in themselves rather than means towards organisational goal achievement. Here may develop the 'bureaucratic personality' who inhabits contemporary folklore as the 'jobsworth' – the petty official who if asked to interpret any rule flexibility (such as unlocking a door half a minute before the appointed opening time of a building) characteristically responds with the words 'it's more than my job's worth'.

Selznick (1949) observed an equivalent form of *goal displacement* arising from a different source. The sub-units or departments resulting from delegation of authority within organisations may set up goals of their own which may come to conflict with those organisational purposes behind the setting up of that sub-unit. Responses to such problems involving the setting up of further departments to cope with these difficulties only exacerbate the situation as further sectional interests or goals are created.

Gouldner's classic factory study *Patterns of Industrial Bureaucracy* (1964) illustrates in a corresponding way how attempts to cope with contradictory tendencies within the organisation may merely set up a kind of vicious circle of increasing organisational dysfunctions. Impersonal rules in the workplace contribute to control and predictability in task-performance and they also function to reduce the visibility of the power relations between supervisors and workers. But the tendency of rules to be interpreted as minimum standards of performance may in certain circumstances reduce all activity to an apathetic conformity to this 'official' minimum. Should this happen there is likely to be a managerial response whereby rules are tightened or direct supervision increased – with the effect that power relations become more visible and overt conflict between managers and managed is increased. Through this the achievement of management's overall goals is increasingly threatened as their control is challenged.

The rules, procedures and administrative devices shown in these studies to create problems for those in charge of organisations, are all means by which power is exercised. The so-called 'dysfunctions' arising within organisations are, in effect, limitations on the successful exercise of power within the organisation. However, the problems which arise with bureaucracy have not just been a concern of sociologists wishing to deepen an analytical understanding of bureaucracy. An attack upon bureaucracy has been central to newer managerial discourses which place an emphasis on innovation and enterprise. Du Gay (2000) observes that bureaucratic modes of organisational governance are frequently seen as inefficient and ineffective because they fail to draw upon people's personal involvement and ideas. The assumptions behind this are questioned by du Gay with particular regard to the administrative aspects of democratic societies. He draws on Weber's observation that the 'impersonality' of the bureaucratic role is an alternative to the pre-bureaucratic situation in which office-holders could readily do their work in a way which prioritised their private advantage. Bureaucracy is thus defended by du Gay as an important ethical and political resource in liberal democratic regimes because it separates the administration of public life from 'private moral absolutisms'. Bureaucracy's 'indifference to certain moral ends' is its strength and not its weakness. This is not to deny the advantages of reducing the size and costs of certain bureaucratic bodies but to remember that in part bureaucracy is a 'positive political and ethical achievement'.

Contingency and choice in the shaping of organisational structures and cultures

Sociologists like Merton, Selznick and Gouldner raised problems about the practical functioning of bureaucracies in general. Other researchers have raised doubts about the universally relevant prescriptions of the kind suggested by Fayol and others. The classical administrative writers offered universally applicable guiding principles on the best vertical and horizontal span of hierarchies, the best degree of specialisation, formalisation, centralisation, delegation and the like. However, the *contingency approach* to the design of the official control aspects of organisational structures, which has grown in popularity in organisation theory since the late 1950s, suggests, instead, that managements tend to seek the most *appropriate* shape of organisation to achieve their purposes given prevailing situational *contingencies*.

CONTINGENCIES

Circumstances which influence the ways in which organisations are structured.

Two studies which were particularly important in establishing this new flexibility in thinking were those of Woodward (1994, originally 1965) and Burns and Stalker (1994, originally 1961).

Woodward's study of a hundred manufacturing firms in Essex started with an interest in seeking relationships between successful business performance and organisational structure. However, it was only when the variable of technology was introduced into the researchers' thinking that sense could be made of the variations which were found in such features as the spans of control within firms, the number of levels in the hierarchy, and the extent to which communications were verbal or written. When firms were examined in terms of their place on a scale of complexity of production technology (a scale ranging from unit and small batch production, through large batch and mass production to process production) it became clear that different structural configurations were appropriate to different technologies. Thus it would be appropriate for, say, a petrochemical company to have a relatively tall and narrow hierarchical shape whilst a firm turning out custom-built perambulators might be better suited to a short and wide configuration.

Burns and Stalker's study can also be taken to show the importance of technology as a contingent factor, although technology itself is emphasised here less than is the environment to which the technology relates. The authors observed that a different organisational pattern is likely to be appropriate in an industry like textiles where the environment is relatively stable compared to the pattern appropriate to an industry like electronics where the environment produces a constant pressure for innovation. To cope with pressures for innovation an *organic* type of structure will be appropriate. The structure here will be loose and flexible with a relatively low degree of formalisation and task prescription. Where conditions are more stable, however, *mechanistic* structures may be more appropriate, these approximating far more to the ideal type of bureaucracy and the prescriptions of the classical administrative writers.

Contingent factors of *technology* and *environment* are stressed in these now classic studies but other contingencies are emphasised by later contributors. Researchers at Aston University (Pugh and Hickson, 1976; Pugh and Hinings, 1976; Pugh and Payne, 1977), for instance, argue that Woodward's analysis does not sufficiently take into account the *size of the organisation*. The Aston studies are interpreted by their authors as indicating that Woodward's generalisations about organisational shape and technological complexity may only apply in smaller organisations and in those areas of larger organisations close to the production process itself. Generally valid organisational principles may well be applicable, it was argued, at the higher levels of management. Thus, once you move away from the 'shopfloor' or operating level of any organisation the structural pattern will be more influenced by the organisation's size and its degree of independence from other organisations (within and without a parent group).

Lawrence and Lorsch's (1967) work concentrated on environmental contingencies, stressing the influence of the degree of certainty and diversity in the environment on ways in which organisations are structured in terms of *differentiation* and the *integrating* mechanisms used to cope with problems arising from the operation of differentiated units. Perrow (1970b), on the other hand, argued for the centrality of technology, something which he conceptualised in a much wider way than have other writers. Perrow concentrates on the nature of the 'raw material' processed by the organisation, whether this be a living material as in an educational organisation, a symbolic material as in a financial institution, or an inanimate material as in manufacturing. These raw materials clearly differ in their variability and hence their processing will create different problems to be faced by the organisational structure. The more routine such materials processing is the more a formal centralised structure is appropriate, and vice versa.

There are important insights to be derived from these various studies. However, there are a number of difficulties that arise, not the least of which is the tendency for the studies to rival each other in the particular contingency which they emphasise. An overview of the contingency literature strongly suggests that a variety of contingencies are likely to be relevant to any given organisation. But if we accept this, we are still left with the problem of incorporating the insights of this literature into a general sociological theory of organisations which sees organisational structure as arising out of the interplay between official and unofficial activities within what is an essentially humanly initiated and political competitive process. In his influential critique and refinement of the contingency approach Child (1972) stressed the dangers of seeing organisational structures as automatically reacting to or being determined by contingent factors like environment, size or technology. He pointed out that those effectively managing the organisation, whom (following Cyert and March 1963) he calls the *dominant coalition*, do have a certain leeway in the structures which they choose to adopt in their strategic directing of the organisation. A range of contingent factors will always limit the decision-making of senior managements but their strategic choices are not limited to establishing structural forms. They also include the manipulation of environmental and the choice of relevant performance standards. In pointing to the *strategic choices* made by a concrete group of motivated actors as part of an essentially political process, Child provided a 'corrective to the view that the way in which organisations are designed and structured has to be determined largely by their operational contingencies' (Child 1997), and in applying the perspective in research on a major organisational change process developed it to demonstrate the significance of corporate ideologies and organisational learning processes in the shaping and reshaping of organisations (Child and Smith 1987).

Donaldson (1996b) says that the core assumption of 'contingency theory' is that whilst 'low uncertainty tasks are most effectively performed by centralised hierarchy since this is simple, quick and allows close coordination cheaply', higher 'task uncertainty' makes it necessary for the hierarchy to loosen control and 'be overlain by participatory, communicative structures'. This insight can be incorporated into a more fully sociological model of how organisations come to be shaped as they are by treating contingent factors as ones which managers, to a greater or a lesser extent, *take into account* when choosing organisational structures and cultures.

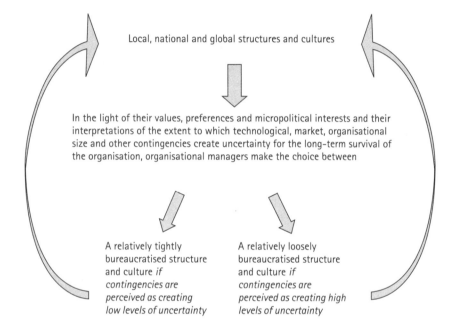

Local, national and global structures and cultures

In the light of their values, preferences and micropolitical interests and their interpretations of the extent to which technological, market, organisational size and other contingencies create uncertainty for the long-term survival of the organisation, organisational managers make the choice between

A relatively tightly bureaucratised structure and culture *if contingencies are perceived as creating low levels of uncertainty*

A relatively loosely bureaucratised structure and culture *if contingencies are perceived as creating high levels of uncertainty*

Figure 4.2 Contingencies and managerial choices in shaping organisational structures and cultures

The model represented in Figure 4.2 takes the contingency insight out of the systems-thinking tradition of organisation theory and incorporates it into a more political-economic and sociological type of theorising which recognises that:

- organisational structures and cultures are the outcomes of human initiatives and choices (as opposed to relatively automatic reactions to system needs);
- these choices are influenced by (and themselves influence) the broad institutional context of the organisation, that is by societal patterns of social structure and culture;
- organisational design choices are influenced by the preferences, values and interests of the managers who make them as well as by the interpretations which those managers make of the organisation's circumstances ('contingencies' like the volatility

of its markets, the complexity of its technologies, the size of the enterprise, etc.) and the degree of uncertainty about the future that those circumstances create.

In this conception of how organisations are shaped, managers are not seen as technical experts making politically neutral decisions about their organisations. They are seen as people with a variety of personal and group interests who, inevitably, act in a 'micropolitical' way as they simultaneously carry out the tasks they are paid to perform and manage their organisational and 'life' careers.

Micropolitics, careers and unofficial management practices

In turning to organisational *micropolitics* we are focusing on the 'upper' part of organ- isations. And we are looking at everyday aspects of how *power* is exerted and experienced within the bureaucratic hierarchy. 'Politics', Buchanan and Badham (1999) suggest, can be seen as 'power in action' with power itself being viewed as a 'latent capacity, as a resource, or a possession'. But power is a multi-dimensioned phenomenon:

- at an interpersonal level, some individuals have power over others to the extent that they can get those others to do things they would not otherwise do;
- at a societal level, power is more a matter of a pattern of relationships and under- standings – a 'structure' which enables certain social groups to exert pressures on others (through the wealth or the armaments they possess or through the authority that the culture vests in them);
- and, at an organisational level, power structures involve rules, hierarchies and cultural norms that people agree to comply with by joining the organisation and which make it 'reasonable' and normal for some people to get others to do what they would not otherwise do.

But what runs through all these three dimensions of power is the capacity of groups or individuals to affect *outcomes* of situations to their advantage.

POWER

The capacity of an individual or group to affect the outcome of any situation so that access is achieved to whatever resources are scarce and desired within a society or part of a society.

Micropolitics are the processes whereby competition occurs for the 'good things' of life in any particular organisation at a particular time: salaries, promotions, company cars, smart offices, status or simply opportunities to influence other people. Studies of micropolitics tend to see organisations as political arenas in which people both co-operate and compete with each other to further and defend their interests. Micropolitics are part of the unofficial 'side' of the organisation and involve individuals, groups and members of organisational 'sub-units' (departments, functions, divisions and so on) forming coalitions and alliances, helping friends and defeating rivals and bringing about the organisation's *negotiated order* (Chapter 2, pp. 35–6).

> ## MICROPOLITICS
>
> The political processes that occur within organisations as individuals, groups and organisational 'sub-units' compete for access to scarce and valued material and symbolic resources.

Vertical aspects

Noting that 'interests, influence and the resulting politics . . . are the very stuff of decision-making in organisations', Hickson (1999) asks, 'How else could it be when organisations are made up of so many people with diverse viewpoints and are surrounded by so many people who have a stake in what they do?' But organisational politics do not come about simply as a result of the diversity of human interests in an organisation, and organisational power is more than a matter of what von Zugbach (1995) calls 'deciding what you want and making sure that you get it'. A sociological analysis of politicking looks at how it is related to the broader structures and processes of which it is a part. It can be seen as an inevitable outcome of the way organisations are designed.

The bureaucratic structure of organisations, as a reading of Weber's ideal-type of bureaucracy would reveal, provides not only a control mechanism but a potential career ladder and thus a reward mechanism for individuals. Burns (1961) in early and influential work on micropolitics pointed out that organisational members are 'at one and the same time co-operators in a common enterprise and rivals for the material and intangible rewards of successful competition with each other'. The bureaucratic structure thus has both an integrative and a disintegrative aspect. The fact that the career rewards available to individuals are necessarily scarce ones means that those who are officially intended to work co-operatively are likely to find themselves in conflict with each other. Although a certain amount of competition between individuals may be 'functional' for the organisation, it equally may create organisational problems. And individuals' political behaviour readily takes a group form as coalitions, cliques and cabals arise. Sectional interests may be served at the expense of those of senior management. Burns (1955) notes the tendency for two types of group to arise:

- *Cliques* which develop norms and values contrary to the dominant organisational ones, especially among older managers who lack promotion prospects and feel a need to act defensively.
- *Cabals* which develop among younger managers whose individual interests may be better served by compliance with dominant norms and values.

The managers working in modern organisations are seen by Jackall (1988) as the 'paradigm of the white-collared salaried employee' and in his study of managers in several American corporations he portrays them as experiencing the corporation as 'an intricate matrix of rival and often intersecting managerial circles'. He says that 'the principal role of each group is its own survival, of each person his own advancement'. Individuals are forced to surrender their personal moralities when they enter the world of the bureaucratic career and the meaning of their work – especially if they are ambitious – 'becomes keeping one's eye on the main chance, maintaining and furthering one's own position and career'. In this pessimistic view of organisational politics all higher moral principles retreat in the face of a logic of bureaucratic priorities and the self-interests of those who seek careers in them. Such a view can be contrasted with the points made earlier about the ethical basis of bureaucracy as a form of governance. It is also challenged by evidence that managers may be able to bring personal ethical values to bear on managerial decisions as long as they can successfully argue that the decision they are arguing for will benefit the organisation (be 'good for business', in effect), in the longer run (Watson 2003a).

The provision by organisations of career advancement as a motivational inducement is frequently systematised in administrative procedures such as 'career development' programmes, annual assessments, promotion boards and the like. Yet again Weber's 'paradox of consequences' manifests itself since such systems may well create unrealistic expectations of advancement with consequential demotivating results when these expectations are not met. The potentially disruptive effects of internal promotion procedures were well illustrated in Burns's (1977) study of the BBC where promotion procedures were so highly stressed that the corporation appeared to put a 'positive value on careerism, on the energetic pursuit of promotion' with the effect that performing well at appointment boards become more important than actually being successful in one's job.

Officially, the criteria for career advancement are ones of merit but since there are often no clear technical criteria to make unambiguously achievement-based appointments possible, unofficial factors inevitably come into play. Advancement is likely to be based in part on what Offe (1976) called 'peripheral' characteristics. Dalton (1951) showed the importance of extrafunctional promotion criteria in the organisations he studied where particular importance was attached to membership of the Masonic Order, not being a Roman Catholic, being Anglo-Saxon or Germanic in ethnic origin, belonging to the local yacht club and being affiliated to the Republican Party – in this order of importance. Coates and Pellegrin's (1962) investigation of factors relating to the promotion of managers and supervisors indicates the importance not of 'native ability', hard work or the 'demonstration of ability' in the explanations given by interviewed individuals of their career success or failure, but of what the authors recognise as varying normative orientations. Such things as cultural and educational background together with early career experiences lead individuals to 'adopt attitudes, values and behaviour patterns which function as important positive or negative influences in subsequent career progress and occupational mobility'. Burns (1977) again provides research illustrations of this. He showed how individuals attempted to appear as 'BBC types' through carefully managed impressions of self, thus contributing to 'a latent system of approved conduct and demeanour'. Although this was by no means uniform, it was nevertheless 'always consonant with the prevailing code by which individuals . . . were selected and gained approval and promotion'.

Horizontal aspects

We have to take care here not to stress the interpersonal career competitions and the striving for individual power outside the context of the departmental structures in which people are located. Research on the horizontal dimension of organisational power activity has attempted to explain how it comes about that departments or organisational 'sub-units' are rarely equally powerful – in the sense of the access they allow to scarce and valued resources. In eleven of the twelve industrial firms studied by Perrow (1970a), managers felt the sales department to be the most powerful. Perrow explained this in terms of the 'strategic position with respect to the environment' of these sales departments. In line with this argument we find various authors arguing that coping with organisational uncertainties may be the key to power within organisations.

UNCERTAINTY

A state in which the understanding of a future situation or event is unclear or confused and is therefore open to a variety of interpretations.

The importance of uncertainty was stressed by Thompson (1967) who sees leadership within organisations going to those who deal with the sources of greatest uncertainty for the organisation and by Crozier (1964) who identifies power with the ability to resist the removal by others of uncertainty in one's sphere of activities. Thus, in this sense, maintenance workers in a factory will have more power than those who operate the machines they maintain. Similarly, the personnel manager in an organisation where labour is in short supply or where trade unions are well organised will be more powerful than the personnel specialist in an organisation where the resource of labour is less problematic.

The above type of insight has been developed and applied by Hickson and his colleagues (1971) to produce a *strategic contingency theory of power*. This theory suggests that as long as a sub-unit is central enough to an organisation's activities and non-substitutable enough for others to be dependent upon it, its influence over decision-making is significantly enhanced if it can show that it can deal with *strategically important uncertainties*. In other words, the 'ability to manage uncertainty on behalf of others provides a vital power base' (Miller *et al.* 1996). Thus, if any individual or departmental grouping within an organisation wishes to increase their access to the material and qualitative rewards available within the organisation, a successful claim must be made to being independent of other parties, irreplaceable by other parties, and capable of dealing with uncertainties that potentially threaten the survival of the enterprise.

The location of individuals within the administrative structure clearly influences their relative autonomy and their access to rewards, but it is important to note that these structures are not pre-given patterns into which people are simply slotted. Organisational structures are the outcomes of an interplay between official and unofficial influences. The organisational structures within which individuals both contribute to organisational performance and pursue sectional interests are in part the outcome of their own initiatives. Pettigrew (1973) showed in his study of organisational decision-making, 'by their ability to exert power over others, individuals can change or maintain structures as well as the norms and expectations upon which these structures rest'. Pettigrew's study shows how the head of a management services department is particularly able to influence key organisational decisions on computerisation through being in a 'gatekeeper' role – one which enabled him to bias the information which reached the formal decision-makers. The effective converting of 'potential power into actual influence' involves a great deal more than being in the right place at the right time, however. It requires considerable skills of 'matching power sources' to the various different situations that arise and the 'drawing on the right mixture of analysis, persuasion, persistence, tact, timing, and charm' (Pettigrew and McNulty 1995).

One of the power sources some organisational actors are able to deploy is specialist functional or professional expertise, making it possible for such specialists simultaneously to enhance the influence of their sub-unit and improve their personal careers. A study of industrial relations specialists by Goldner (1970) looked at how labour relations departments in American companies developed to cope with uncertainties facing those companies with regard to employment issues. This was not an automatic process, he observed – individuals sought out uncertainties and thus created roles for themselves. It is, he says, 'advantageous to an individual's career to find such activities if they are not already apparent'. Research in the British personnel management field also observed how it is possible to watch personnel departments 'expand ("empire build") as career advantages and structural uncertainties are brought together by individual personnel specialists who see the need for a job evaluation manager today and a remunerations manager the next' (Watson 1977). Similar issues have been tackled by Armstrong (1986, 1993) in a series of studies of 'professional' functional groups such as engineers, accountants and personnel managers. Armstrong makes the 'structural uncertainties' which provide these groups with opportunities to increase their influence more specific than other theorists and ties them into the interests of 'capital'. He interprets his own and others' research in this area as suggesting that 'there is a link between certain aspects of organisational politics, the process of professionalisation of managerial occupations and changes in the nature and intensity of the crises confronting capitalist enterprises'. That link, he says, is 'the need for capital to control the labour process' (Armstrong 1986).

Unofficial practices and bureaucratic dysfunctions

Not all unofficial or informal managerial behaviour is primarily concerned with sectional interests. Because of the contradictions and dysfunctions of bureaucratic structures (see above, pp. 89–91) managers often depart from formal or official procedures to help fulfil rather than compromise the overall goals of the interest dominant in the organisation. To illustrate this we can again refer to Gouldner's (1964) classic study which was used earlier to illustrate the dysfunctional aspects of rule-conformity. The same study illustrates how, conversely, unofficial rule-breaking may in fact help meet the ends which those rules were originally intended to serve. Gouldner noted the existence of an *indulgency pattern*.

INDULGENCY PATTERN

The ignoring of selected rule infringements by supervisors in return for those being supervised allowing supervisors to call for co-operation in matters which, strictly speaking, they could refuse.

Here supervisors avoided the potentially negative effects of workers taking certain rules as minimal performance standards by their own demonstrating of flexibility in conniving at the breaking of certain other rules by subordinates. Such a pattern is very common and industrial supervisors frequently find that one of the few devices left to them to obtain flexible and more than grudging co-operation from those they supervise is to be willing to turn a blind eye to illegally extended tea-breaks, late arrivals at work and various other minor rule infringements.

A study of two government agencies by Blau (1963) revealed what he called the *dynamics of bureaucracy* through observing the various ways in which employees avoid what could become 'dysfunctional' aspects of official procedures. 'Procedural adjustments' constitute one form of adaptation in which the officials, when faced with alternative courses of action choose the one more congenial to themselves, typically justifying this choice as the one more in the interests of successful organisational performance. Law enforcement agents, for instance, justified their preference not to obey the rule of officially reporting bribes which were offered to them on the grounds that keeping the offer to themselves gave them a psychological advantage over the offender which would help them complete their investigations. Another tactic is to redefine a rule or procedure in a way which 'deliberately sacrifices the original objective of a procedure in order to achieve another organisational objective more effectively' as in the case of the employment agents who more or less abandoned counselling clients in order to concentrate on getting them speedily placed in jobs. In reaction to this type of unofficial activity, Blau observes, managerial attempts are made to elaborate or 'amplify' procedures. These, in turn, lead to further unofficial adjustments. Here we see an ongoing dialectical relationship between the official and the unofficial aspects of the organisation. In the end all this helps the functioning of the organisation through accommodating the interests and preferences of employees to the wider purposes of those in charge of the organisation.

Ambiguity and decision processes

It is increasingly being recognised by organisation theorists that social scientists are prone to seeing far more rationality in organisational activities and arrangements, in the sense of fully calculated goal-oriented and purposive thinking, than is justified. As Perrow (1977) put it, 'a great deal of organisational life is influenced by sheer chance, accident and luck'; that most decisions are ambiguous and 'preference orderings incoherent'; that sub-systems are very loosely connected and that 'most attempts at social control are clumsy and unpredictable'.

A theoretical starting point for this kind of thinking is often found in the suggestion of Simon (1957) that human rationality is bounded.

BOUNDED RATIONALITY

Human reasoning and decision-making is restricted in its scope by the fact that human beings have both perceptual and information-processing limits.

Human beings can only 'take in' so many data and can only mentally manipulate them to a limited extent. As Weick (1979) expresses it, there is little viewing of all possible circumstances and a criterion of 'sufficiency' is applied with people dealing with the 'here and now in a way which involves least possible effort'. This kind of insight was incorporated into the 'behavioural economics' of Cyert and March (1963) where 'search procedures' are shown to be essentially 'simple-minded' (in that the search for a new solution to a problem stays close to the old solution) and as taking place within the overall process of coalition-manoeuvring which constitutes the norm in organisations.

Ambiguity is significant here.

AMBIGUITY

A state in which the meaning of a situation or an event is unclear or confused and is therefore open to a variety of interpretations.

March and Olsen (1976) argue that in organisational situations, there is typically ambiguity about what objectives are meant to be set; the nature of the technologies used; the state of the environment; people's knowledge about the past; the involvement of the individuals working in the organisation – given that their attention to what is going on varies and the pattern of participation is uncertain and ever-changing. And, because individuals have a range of interests of their own, they come to use decision-making situations or 'choice opportunities' as occasions for doing a lot more than simply making decisions, say March and Olsen. Decision processes are occasions in which people:

- fulfil duties
- meet commitments
- justify themselves
- distribute glory and blame
- exercise, challenge and reaffirm friendships
- seek power and status
- further personal or group interests
- simply have a good time and take pleasure in the decision-making process.

On the basis of their study of American universities, which they describe as 'organised anarchies', Cohen *et al.* (1972) developed their 'garbage can model of organisational choice'. The decision opportunity operates like a dustbin because the eventual outcome is a result of what happens to have been thrown into the bin. The 'garbage' includes problems which are around at the time, solutions which are available and might be attached to those problems, the people who happen to be around and the amount of time those people have available. On decision-making occasions we therefore get choices looking for problems, issues and feelings looking for decision situations, solutions looking for issues and decision-makers looking for work. Because there are so many types of garbage being thrown in, conventional rational and analytical processes will have difficulty in coping. Hence, March and Olsen (1976) advocate supplementing the 'technology of reason' with a 'technology of foolishness'. In this, organisational participants relax the normal rules and 'playfully' experiment.

Conceptual work of this kind can be seen to fit with the findings of those who have empirically examined the nature of the work which is done by managers in organisations. Carlson (1951) showed that his sample of managing directors were rarely alone and uninterrupted for periods long enough to engage in systematic analysis and thought. On the basis of a review of this kind of study, including a series of his own, Mintzberg (1973) argued that the manager's job is not one which 'breeds reflective planners'. Instead it produces 'adaptive information manipulators who favour a stimulus-response milieu'. Hence, managers gravitate towards the current, the specific and the well-defined and they prefer 'gossip, hearsay, speculation to routine reports'. Managerial work is thus seen as opportunistic, habitual and almost 'instinctual'. However, as the research of Kotter (1982) suggests, this may not reflect an inappropriate fondness for simply muddling-along but indicates a managerial recognition that their key concern has to be with developing and maintaining a network of relationships with other people in order to obtain the level of co-operation needed to get the job done. Managerial work is essentially social and political rather than fundamentally analytical (Watson 2001a). And managerial initiatives, as we shall see in Chapter 5, play a central role in the way work and work organisation is changing in the contemporary world.

5 The changing organisation and management of work

Work restructuring and the logic of corporate management

In the previous two chapters we have looked at the basic logic of, first, a changing social world in which industrial capitalist principles are dominant, and second, of modern work organisations in which industrial capitalist and bureaucratic principles are applied to shape work arrangements and practices. These two logics are now brought together to recognise a third logic, as we focus on the way the 'officers' of these bureaucratic corporations – their managers – initiate changes in how work is carried out as they strive to exert control over task performance in order to assist the survival of the enterprise that employs them. And this striving to achieve a level of *productive co-operation* (see Chapter 4, p. 79) which enables corporate entities to survive takes place in a context of competition and power struggle, at every level, across the world.

Industrial capitalist economies are essentially dynamic ones. Their mainspring is one of technical and organisational innovation in a context of both the general pursuit of material human improvement across the world and the competitive activities of particular interest groups in that same world. Because of the enormous promise of industrialisation, society after society followed the industrial lead taken by Britain in the late eighteenth century. France, Germany and America industrialised in the nineteenth century and in the twentieth century avowedly socialist societies followed the industrial path and aggressively capitalist nations emerged as major industrial forces in the Far East in the latter decades of that century. At the same time, oil-supplying nations showed their capacity to shake the foundations of economies throughout the world. All of this presented major challenges to established economies whose institutions and practices had become more settled with the new industrial capitalist economies that emerged in the second half of the twentieth century having the advantage of being able to learn from what they would see as both the achievements and mistakes of Western economies, organisations and technologies. They were therefore able to develop social institutions and priorities, at state and organisational levels, which gave them a commercial and technological thrust which powerfully challenged Western economies. But Western economic interests did not simply reorganise on their own territory to handle these changes in other nations. They took part in the broad development of the multinational and global corporations that, as we saw in Chapter 3, is often seen as part of a trend toward 'globalisation'. A part of this has been the practice of the moving of resources and production efforts from one part of the world to another where cheaper or more flexible labour is available.

The effect of these broad international economic trends, together with problems of economic recession and changing political ideologies at the state level, on work and employment in Western societies, has been considerable. International competitiveness and trade threats have forced employing organisations and states to seek ways of not only increasing the cost-effectiveness of labour *per se* but of increasing the overall capacity of the organisations within which that labour is used to innovate at a rate which will enable them to produce goods and services that are competitive in the international context. Work and work experience are widely seen as caught up in processes of restructuring.

THE RESTRUCTURING OF WORK

The changing patterns of work experience, organisational and occupational activity both resulting from and contributing to economic, political and cultural changes unfolding across the world.

Restructuring within the older economies has involved a move away from traditional heavy industry activities such as steel-making, textiles, mining and heavy industry towards, on the one hand, service industries and, on the other, the production of both consumer goods and capital products using advanced electronic technologies. Employment has shifted with this and white-collar employment has grown as manual work has decreased. Central to the growth of service work has been the expansion of financial services work and major changes in patterns of retailing, these two trends being made visible by the dominance of banks and building societies in British high streets and the way the superstores, away from city centres, have 'done much to rearrange the shopping and leisure habits of large proportions of the population' (Beynon *et al.* 2002). Increasing numbers of jobs are part-time or short-term, and governments, whether nominally of the political left or right, tend towards tight control of public spending and the freeing of labour markets from tight controls. A 'mood of austerity' has affected private and public organisations alike (Burke 2002). Industries previously controlled by the state have been privatised, deregulated or 'put into the market', especially in central and eastern Europe and in Britain. There has nevertheless been considerable variation in the policies of different nation states with Britain, for example, pursuing a distinctively more deregulatory approach than other nations within Europe. Nation states and blocs such as the European Union necessarily operate, however, within the broader patterns of global change.

The logic of corporate management

It is in this changing global context of competition and innovation that those managing work organisations struggle to control work activities and arrangements in such a way that the corporations employing them continue in existence. And 'struggle' is indeed the appropriate word to use here. In their case studies of seven employing organisations, Beynon and his colleagues (2002) show that the managers implementing changes neither had a clear sense of direction about the changes they were bringing about nor a ready capacity to 'meet their desired ends'. They were, rather, 'buffeted this way and that, dealing with uncertainty and risk by displacing it down the organisation – most normally through adjustment of employment policies'. Managers are working day-to-day in a context where the survival of the organisation, whether it be a profit-oriented business corporation or a state welfare agency, can never be taken for granted. This stress on organisational survival has been increasingly recognised by organisation theorists. One way in which this has been done has been to see the relationships between organisations and their 'environment' as a matter of natural selection: a fight for survival within the ecological system of which they are a part. This line is taken as part of the *population ecology* approach to organisational analysis (Hannan and Freeman 1989; Morgan 1990). Here, organisations are seen as adapting and evolving in order to survive within the organisational population of which they are a part. They go through both planned and unplanned 'variations' in their form, and, largely through processes of competition, the environment 'selects' the form which best suits the organisation. Organisations then 'retain' the form which best suits their particular 'niche' or domain', this retention process including all those normal organisational practices – from the use of operating manuals to socialisation activities – which organisations follow to maintain stability.

Although ecological theories of organisation offer useful insights, they suffer from the problem of giving little attention to the role of human agency in the way organisations come into being and go out of operation. The important insight that organisations tend to be managed within a strategic logic of fighting for corporate survival in a turbulent, competitive and otherwise challenging social, political and economic context can be retained without treating organisations as if they were biological entities like plants or animals. But why is this logic of survival insight so important? Why can it be argued that the logic of corporate management is one of seeking long-term organisational survival? One answer to this is to point out that it avoids all the difficulties of debating whether the primary goal of businesses is one of maximising profit, growth, return on capital or the creation of human welfare. All of these criteria of corporate effectiveness are likely to be relevant to organisational managers operating a business but, instead of seeing them as alternative criteria that managers apply, we can see them all as means towards the more general criterion of survival. Thus instead of arguing over whether, say, profitability or share of the market is the focus of managerial efforts, we can see both or either of them as important, to varying extents at different times, as *means to* survival (i.e. not as means in themselves). A similar argument can be applied to a non-business organisation like a hospital: we do not debate whether hospitals are run to cure patients, provide healthy workers for the economy, or please the politicians who fund them. Instead, we look at the range of pressures on those in charge of hospitals – of which the above are just a few – and which they have to handle to keep that hospital operating into the future.

The *resource dependence* approach in organisation theory (Pfeffer and Salancik 1978; Watson 1986; Morgan 1990) stresses the role played in the survival of the organisation by the *exchanges* or 'trades' in which it has to engage with all of those parties upon whom it is dependent for survival. Organisations are not seen here as simply competing with others but as depending on a whole series of other organisations (state, client bodies, pressure groups, trade unions and so on) as well as on various managerial and employee internal constituencies for the supply of resources upon which their continued life depends. Internal micropolitical and industrial relations processes are thus intertwined with market and other macropolitical ones. And in the development of this approach into a *strategic exchange perspective* on organisations (Watson 2002a), we identify the logic of corporate management as one of dealing with resource dependence relationships.

THE LOGIC OF CORPORATE MANAGEMENT

The logic of corporate management is one of shaping exchange relationships to satisfy the demands of the various constituencies, inside and outside the organisation, so that continued support in terms of resources such as labour, custom, investment, supplies and legal approval is obtained and the organisation enabled to survive into the long term.

It is this exchange and survival-based criterion of corporate 'effectiveness' that guides the practices of organisational managers: the logic of strategic managerial work is one of setting up and maintaining exchange relationships in such a way that the organisation continues into the future. And a further answer to the earlier question about why it is helpful to conceptualise corporate managerial priorities in terms of long-term survival lies in the vital recognition that it is simply not a feasible option to run an organisation of any reasonable size as a short-term operation. Little support for or commitment to an organisation, in its day-to-day or short-term task performance, is likely to be given by either investors or workers if they perceive that the enterprise with which they are involved lacks a secure future. This means that it is better to see the logic of corporate action, not as the making of profits, the curing of patients, the educating of pupils *per se*, but as the satisfying of the demands of resource-supplying constituencies to the level below which the constituencies would withdraw resources from the organisation and thus threaten its survival. Thus a manufacturing organisation located in an economy in which investors demanded profits of a certain level before they would continue their investment would only be effective if it produced those profits, although it would also need to pay employees enough to get the required level of performance, comply with the state and local laws, and so on. Corporate effectiveness is thus a contingent matter and not an essential quality which an organisation either possesses or lacks. And at particular times certain groups would have more pull than others so that managements have to deal first with the most 'strategic constituency' – with the one that is currently perceived as creating the highest level of strategic uncertainty. And, as we shall now see, the extent to which the various employee constituencies within an organisation are managerially perceived to be sources of greater or lesser uncertainty, is a major factor influencing the type of employment or 'human resourcing' strategy that is followed.

Choice and circumstance in the shaping of employment practices

It was pointed out in Chapter 4 (pp. 92–5) when we examined the dual role of contingencies and strategic choice in the shaping of work organisations that the level of uncertainty that managers see arising in their organisation's circumstances is an important factor in pushing them towards the adoption of either a *tightly* bureaucratised structure and culture (when uncertainties are perceived as low) or a *loosely* bureaucratised structure and culture (when uncertainties are perceived as high). A corresponding analysis can be applied to the approach that is taken to managerial relationships with employee groups. Before we do this, however, it is necessary to note how there has been increasing recognition with industrial sociology and industrial relations analysis of the variations in approach to employment relations that are possible.

Variations in employment relations style

Researchers looking at employment practices have utilised various typologies of styles of employee relations to recognise the extent to which there are managerial alternatives when it comes to how manager–worker relationships are to be shaped. Purcell and Ahlstrand (1994) for example identify six different management styles of employee relations. These vary in the extent to which they emphasise direct relationships with employees as individuals (*individualism*) or relationships with collective groups of employees (*collectivism*). Individualist styles may stress cost minimisation (giving a *traditional* style), paternalism (giving a *paternalist* style) or employee development (giving a *sophisticated human relations* style). A collectivist style which recognises the adversarial aspect of employment relations is characterised as a *bargained constitutional* style, whilst collectivism which emphasises the co-operative aspect of employment relations can give either a *modern paternalist* style or a *sophisticated consultative* one.

Labour processes and employment practice options

Having recognised that managements may follow different control strategies with regard to their employees, we are left with the question of which circumstances lead to the adoption of which general type of strategy. One approach to answering this question has been that developed by theorists in the labour process tradition who wanted to develop a more subtle and 'dialectical' approach to analysing capitalist labour processes which affords much greater recognition of the challenge offered to employers by organised labour than was the case in Braverman's (1974) seminal work. It is argued that managerial activity should be understood not as straightforwardly imposing upon employees the work tasks 'required by capital' but as engaging in a competition for control with employees, albeit in the same long-term interests of the owner of capital. Friedman (1977) showed how some employees are better able than others to resist managerial controls, and hence deskilling. Here the emphasis is on the longer-term aspect of the capitalist profit motive and it is stressed that the managerial treatment of labour and the way jobs are designed may vary according to the circumstances. Working on the assumption that managements operate in the ultimate interests of long-term profitability, he introduces what, in Chapter 4 (p. 94), we called the 'contingency insight' and suggests that management may choose either:

- a *direct-control strategy* which is consistent with Taylorist deskilling policies, or a
- *responsible autonomy strategy* in which employees are allowed a degree of discretion and responsibility in their work.

This latter approach is followed where management fear that the introduction of Taylorist controls would risk a loss of what they see as necessary goodwill. Workers who are *central* to long-term profitability, in that they have skills, knowledge or union power which renders their opposition dangerous, have to be treated carefully and are therefore candidates for responsible-autonomy treatment. *Peripheral* workers, on the other hand, who are less critical to longer-term profitability, can be more directly controlled. Their work is much more vulnerable to deskilling and 'degradation'.

This type of analysis was developed by Edwards (1979) who suggested that the simple employee control strategies of early competitive capitalism were gradually found wanting as the trend towards modern monopoly capitalism developed. As class resistance towards 'simple' managerial controls grew and as the centralisation of capitalist organisation increased, various alternative approaches to control were tried. However, as experiments with scientific management, welfare policies and company unionism proved less success-ful than was expected, there was a shift towards more 'structural' approaches to control in which there would be less dependence on the personal power of employers and managers and more on the effects of the physical and social structure of the enterprise. There are two types of more 'structural' strategy:

- A *technical control strategy* depending on the discipline of assembly line and similar types of technology,
- *Bureaucratic control strategies* which emerged as problems arose with the technical control approach. Central to this strategy is the role of internal labour markets within organisations.

These latter strategies involve career structures and relatively high levels of job security are offered to privileged sections of the labour force. The effect of this is to gain commitment of employees to employer purposes and to encourage 'reasonable' and predictable levels of performance. Again, there are elements of a contingency approach in Edwards' analysis and this is particularly visible when he points out that the three forms of control strategy (simple, technical and bureaucratic) exist at the same time. Simple control, for example, can be found in small businesses and 'core' sectors of the economy use strategies different from 'peripheral' ones.

HRM and the choice between 'high commitment' and 'low commitment' human resourcing strategies

The concept of HRM as a distinctive way of approaching the employment aspects of work organisation which differed from traditional personnel management originated with various American academic commentators (Tichy *et al.* 1982; Beer and Spector 1985; Walton 1985) and was later taken up by British academic researchers (Storey 1989, 1992; Hendry and Pettigrew 1990; Guest 1991, Legge 1995). Sisson (1993) suggested that the 'simple message' behind the advocacy of HRM was that Western employers should 'copy the Japanese' by integrating Japanese styles of flexible production and quality management practices with employment management practices aiming at:

- the 'development of a highly committed and adaptable workforce willing and able to learn new skills and take on new tasks';
- the elevation of 'the management of people' to a strategic level of organisational decision-making;
- an emphasis on trust rather than rules and procedures;
- the encouragement of managers to become leaders and facilitators of cultural change by 'harnessing the co-operation and commitment of others';
- the move away from hierarchical organisations with a number of tiers of management, separate functions and tightly defined job descriptions to much 'flatter' and more 'federal' organisations;
- an emphasis on the flexibility of function, task, time and reward and on teamworking and 'single status' terms and conditions of employment.

The HRM phenomenon is, as Storey (2001) puts it, 'an amalgam of description, prescription, and logical deduction' and it is based on the assumption that 'it is human capability and commitment which in the final analysis distinguishes successful organisations from the rest' and that, therefore 'the human resource ought to be nurtured as a valued asset'. But the single feature that distinguishes what are called HRM management approaches from non-HRM ones is its concern with developing a high level of psychological and social commitment towards the employing organisation on the behalf of the workforce. To avoid all the difficulties that arise with the notion of HRM as some kind of new managerial paradigm (Watson 1995b, 1997; Watson and Watson 1999), it is useful to bring a focus to the issue of choice of managerial strategy in the employment area by utilising this distinction between high and low commitment approaches and identifying two ideal types of human resourcing strategy, as we see in Table 5.1.

Which of these two broad directions is followed in any given organisation is likely to be influenced by the values and preferences of strategic managers but, as we saw in

Table 5.1 Two ideal type human resourcing strategy

High commitment human resourcing strategies	Low commitment human resourcing strategies
Employers seek a close relationship with workers who become psychologically or emotionally involved with the enterprise. Opportunities for personal and career development are built into people's employment, which is expected to continue over a longer-term period and potentially to cover a variety of different tasks.	Employers acquire it at the point when it is immediately needed. Workers are allocated to tasks for which they need very little training, with the employment being terminated as soon as those tasks have been completed. The organisation–worker relationship is an 'arm's-length' and calculatingly instrumental one.
Workers are given discretion about how tasks are carried out.	Work tasks are closely supervised and monitored.

Chapter 4 with regard to organisational design choices, these choices are very much constrained by circumstances and organisational 'contingencies'. In the final analysis, what encourages managers to move in one strategic direction rather than the other is the fact that a low commitment type of human resourcing strategy is probably more appropriate to a situation where employees are not a major source of strategic uncertainty for the employing organisation and a high commitment strategy is likely to be more helpful in dealing with employees if those employees do create uncertainties for corporate management. If, for example, an organisation has a simple technology and a relatively straightforward business environment that makes workers easily obtainable and replaceable, that organisation will not require a highly participative set of working practices. However, if the future of an organisation appears to managers to be at risk if they do not meet the much higher demands that might follow from employing a highly skilled or educated workforce to operate a complex technology or deal with an especially tricky business environment they are more likely to lean towards a high commitment employ-ment strategy. In this type of situation, workers are not easy to obtain or replace and thus relatively sophisticated employment practices are needed to attract them to the organ-isation and encourage them to stay and work creatively and flexibly towards corporate purposes. Figure 5.1 adapts the model introduced in Chapter 4 for analysing broad organisational shapes and practices to focus on the employment strategy dimension. It recognises that managerial discretion and micropolitical debate occurring in the context of political-economic, cultural and organisational contingency factors influence organisational human resourcing strategies.

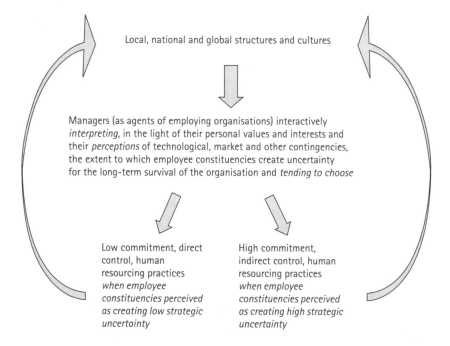

Figure 5.1 Choices and constraints in the shaping of organisational human resourcing practices

In Figure 5.1, the choice between low and high commitment human resourcing strategies is linked to a choice between what are identified as 'direct' and 'indirect' controls. This latter choice is central to issues of flexibility and managerial control generally, as we shall now see.

The pursuit of flexibility and direct and indirect managerial control options

Given the international dynamics of modern industrial capitalism, the shifting patterns of demand for goods and services and the innovative potential of information technologies, it can be argued that those economies and those work organisations which are going to perform relatively well in terms of generally accepted industrial capitalist criteria will be those whose work and employment institutions are the more responsive or *flexible* and are thus better able than their rivals to innovate. However, the concept of flexibility has been so widely used, applied to such a wide range of different phenomena and used to give ideological legitimacy to certain employer practices that there has been a backlash against its use. A key critic of the concept has been Pollert (1991) who writes of the 'fetish of flexibility'. Her main case is that the concept 'obscures' a variety of changes in the management of labour, such as job enlargement, effort intensification and cost controls by 'conflating them into flexibility'. Criticisms are also made of the tendency to oppose 'flexibility' of work and employment practices to the inflexibilities of Fordism on the grounds that Fordism clearly had its own elements of flexibility. It is pointed out that flexibility was indeed central to the basic principles of Taylorism.

However, many of these problems are avoided if we recognise that there are two types of flexibility which have been emphasised in different ways and in different settings at different times.

FLEXIBILITY FOR SHORT-TERM PREDICTABILITY

The ability to make rapid changes through the use of job designs and employment policies that allow staff to be easily recruited and trained or easily laid off – as circumstances require.
This fits with direct control managerial practices.

FLEXIBILITY FOR LONG-TERM ADAPTABILITY

The ability to make rapid and effective innovations through the use of job designs and employment policies that encourage people to use their discretion, innovate and work in new ways for the sake of the organisation – as circumstances require.

This fits with indirect control managerial practices.

This distinction recognises that the type of flexibility sought under Taylorist or Fordist regimes may not be the same as that being sought in the spirit of post-Fordism, for example. And the emphasis on one type of flexibility or the other, and the balance of the mix which will be attempted in many organisations, will vary with the circumstances and policies of each employing organisation. And this variation can be understood in terms of a leaning towards either direct control or indirect control managerial practices – two alternative emphases in the ways managers attempt to maintain control over work activities, represented as two ideal types in Table 5.2.

Table 5.2 Direct and indirect approaches in the pursuit of managerial control

Direct control attempts	Indirect control attempts
• Close supervision and monitoring of activities	• 'Empowerment' and discretion applied to activities
• Tight rules	• Loose rules
• Highly prescribed procedures	• Flexible procedures
• Centralised structures	• Decentralised structures
• Low commitment culture	• High commitment culture
• Low trust culture	• High trust culture
• Adversarial culture	• Culture of mutual interests
• A tightly bureaucratic structure and culture	• A loosely bureaucratic structure and culture

The factors which influence managerial choice of one approach to gaining control or the other are the same ones identified in Chapter 4 (Figure 4.2, p. 94) as 'fitting' with relatively tightly bureaucratised structures and cultures or relatively loosely bureaucratised structures and cultures, respectively. They are also the same factors identified earlier in this chapter as 'fitting' either a low commitment or a high commitment human resourcing strategy. Thus, for example, an organisation with a simple technology, a stable market and a steady supply of labour, would be more likely to seek flexibility for predictability. If, however, the nature of the product, technology, market situation and the rest were such that long-term survival depended much more on the active commitment and initiative-taking of employees then the emphasis would be on flexibility for adaptability.

In practice, most organisations are likely to experience pressures for both types of flexibility and their managers would have to handle the tension between them. This tension can be very significant. In a study of a telecommunications company (Watson 2001a), for example, the high-tech nature of the business and its need for significant innovation to achieve long-term survival was seen as encouraging managers to pursue a whole series of measures to achieve 'flexibility for adaptability' through gaining the long-term commitment and creative enthusiasm of employees. However, the corporation owning the business closely monitored costs and regularly insisted on reducing the numbers of employees to achieve certain accounting ratios. The effect of this imposition of a pursuit of 'flexibility for predictability' was to undermine the pursuit of flexibility for adaptability because it created a sense of insecurity across the workforce and undermined the type of high trust relations upon which flexibility for adaptability depends.

Combining two types of flexibility: the flexible firm

One way in which managers can be seen to handle the tension between the two types of flexibility without the strains seen in the above study is to move towards a structure of employment relationships that researchers have identified as *the flexible firm*.

THE FLEXIBLE FIRM

A pattern of employment in which an organisation divides its workforce into core elements who are given security and high rewards in return for a willingness to adapt, innovate and take on new skills, and peripheral elements who are given more specific tasks and less commitment of continuing employment and skill enhancement.

This pattern makes possible the adoption of measures to achieve 'flexibility for adaptability' in one part of an organisation whilst labour flexibility to achieve 'flexibility for predictability' is pursued in other segments of the enterprise. Studies by the Institute of Manpower Studies in the 1980s (Atkinson 1985, 1987) suggested that a new employment model reflecting such trends was emerging. This *flexible firm* maintains:

- A core group of permanently employed primary labour market staff of skilled workers, managers, designers, technical sales staff and the like. These share a single status (abolishing the old works–staff distinction) and, in return for their relatively advantageous work, reward and career conditions, are flexible in the work they do and are willing to retrain and shift their careers within an internal labour market as required.
- A first peripheral group of secondary labour market type also consisting of full-time employees, but with less security and career potential. They do clerical, assembly, supervisory or testing jobs which can more easily be filled from external labour markets.
- A second peripheral group of part-timers, public-subsidy trainees and people on short-term contracts or job-sharing arrangements.
- A supply of 'outsourced' labour whereby a range of specialised tasks like systems analysis and simple tasks like cleaning are supplied by agency temporaries, sub-contractors and 'teleworkers' (see Chapter 6, pp. 156–7).

This model is perhaps best seen as an attempt to identify a pattern within changes that are occurring in a piecemeal way across employing organisations. If we see strategic change in employment practices *as a pattern in outcomes* rather than as a deliberate and concerted plan, then 'the evidence, though not overwhelming' can be seen, as Procter *et al.* (1994) suggested, 'as indicating that important changes are taking place'. Research on the emerging pattern suggested that specific initiatives being followed were opportunistic, pragmatic, derived from 'higher level' business pressures, and in accord with traditional attitudes to labour (Hunter and McInnes 1992). This does not mean, however, that the sociological observer of trends and patterns in the structuring and managing of work should not perceive a continuing and clear direction, or strategic pattern, in the attempts of employers to increase the flexibility of their operations.

The pursuit of flexibility and new work management practices

Much of the pressure on work managements to increase the flexibility of their organisations in the 1980s came from perceived competitive threats from Japan, primarily to enterprises involved in manufacturing. The competition presented to established manufacturing enterprises by Japanese corporations came to provide a symbolic focus for many of the changes coming about both within the private manufacturing sector and beyond it. To understand changing work management practices it is necessary to look back to how the notion of 'Japanisation' has been used. But many of the restructuring and 're-engineering' practices that have emerged as part of the trends associated with that notion came also to be applied to the growing numbers of 'customer facing' service jobs where, as Poynter (2002) puts it, people are 'subjected to performance measurement and forms of work monitoring that obtain a level of management control and authority over the conduct of work that even Henry Ford would have envied'. Call centres are the most obvious example of this kind of work and we will return to these later.

To make sense of changing management practices, as they began to become significant in manufacturing enterprises, *Japanisation* was widely used as a label for several interrelated trends and Ackroyd *et al.* (1988) helpfully distinguished between 'direct Japanisation' whereby Japanese firms move into the economy of another society, and 'mediated Japanisation'. The latter includes two variants: one where there are 'attempts to incorporate the best of Japanese practice and to integrate the new with the old in appropriate ways' and another where an 'appeal to Japanese efficiency' is made as a way of 'legitimating the introduction of indigenous changes that are seen as necessary or desirable'. Although he questioned the concept of Japanisation itself, Mair's (1994) study of Honda showed how one particular Japanese corporation played a significant role in world level change by introducing what he calls the *global local corporation*. This involves a 'Westernisation' of Japanese management techniques, rather than the other way round as Honda adapts for plants around the world the principles it uses in Japan. All of these 'local' organisations are linked together through a worldwide learning network involving the sharing of experiences derived from local initiatives.

The key principle underlying the new approach to manufacturing, rightly or wrongly identified with Japan, which marks a move away from Fordist mass production, is, according to Kenney and Florida (1993), a new form of labour process involving the use of team commitment and effort to achieve *innovation mediated production*. Team pressure not only encourages people to work harder but continuously to improve both products and processes, as well as develop new ones. And Oliver and Wilkinson (1988) stress the centrality of 'high dependency relationships' to new ways of organising and managing manufacturing – approaches that incorporate just-in-time (JIT) and total quality management (TQM).

JUST-IN-TIME (JIT) PRODUCTION PROCESSES

A way of organising production processes so that no buffer stocks are held in the factory, with materials and components only being delivered immediately before they are required.

JIT arrangements mean that production is vulnerable to disruption and this makes necessary the maintenance of stable employment relations and flexible and co-operative behaviour on the part of workers. TQM requires the building of a commitment to continuous improvement of processes and the quality of the product. This makes the manufacturing system further dependent on employees' positive attachment to the employer.

TOTAL QUALITY MANAGEMENT (TQM)

An approach to the production of goods and services in which employees at all levels focus on 'satisfying customers', use statistical and other techniques to monitor their work and seek continuous improvement in the processes used and the quality of what is produced.

This innovation, according to Hill (1991), was embraced to enable companies to respond more rapidly to change and become more innovative by anticipating and creating new market opportunities and devising new products and better ways of producing at the same time as both increasing their cost efficiency and improving product quality. Hill's research led him to argue that quality management addresses the 'twin issues of how large corporations may increase the entrepreneurial propensity of their managers and debureaucratise their organisations'. However, many of the innovations in the area of quality improvement have been primarily associated with detailed changes of practice at the level of production processes – with what Wilkinson *et al.* (1992) call the 'hard' or 'systems and tools' side of TQM. Their full implications only emerge, as these authors point out, when they are linked to broader changes in organisational cultures and human resourcing practices. This relates to the point made above that TQM, like JIT, creates a higher level of dependence on employee constituencies than more traditional approaches to manufacturing. Successful implementation of these practices is thus dependent on a shift towards the more 'high commitment' style of human resource strategy looked at earlier (see pp. 108–11). In practice, the fulfilment of the espoused TQM values of 'autonomy, participation, responsibility and trust' are precluded by being introduced within an employment context 'characterised by job insecurity, hierarchical power relations, attempts by management to secure control, reduce costs and enhance short-term profitability' (Knights and McCabe 1998).

All of these trends were brought together in Storey's (1994) notion of *new wave manufacturing* (more recently called 'world class manufacturing'). This covers what is portrayed as a 'systemic break with conventional mass Fordist production' involving key characteristics of 'flexibility, teamworking, continual improvement and adaptation, and integration'. Practices covered by the new set of keywords – flexibility, quality, teamworking, just-in-time delivery, right-first-time production, elimination of waste and non-value-added activity, zero defect and continual improvement – are arguably not new, taken separately. What is different, according to Storey, is the way principles are brought together into 'a new, mutually reinforcing, whole'. Hence, JIT 'places a premium on right-first-time' and the continuous improvement theme of TQM 'requires involvement from everyone and some form of teamworking'. Teamworking, in turn, 'implies a need for flexibility, while flexibility means a better trained and more competent workforce'.

Teamworking is something that has existed as long as there have been situations in which people have worked together in a co-operative manner to complete work tasks. The concept covers a range of possibilities. The concept has what Buchanan (2000) calls 'plasticity' so that, as Procter and Mueller (2000) put it, 'teamwork is intrinsically indefinable, adopting different expressions over time and in different contexts'. In spite of this, one can attempt a conceptualisation which recognises that whilst work 'teams' do indeed range from ones in which the choices left to team members are very circumscribed to ones in which there is a considerable degree of freedom about how to act, there is always implicit in the notion a degree of freedom of co-operative choice-making.

> **TEAMWORKING**
>
> A form of group-based work activity in which a degree of discretion is left to group members, acting in a co-operative manner, about how they perform the tasks allocated to them.

A 'team' could thus be a group of senior managers in charge of a large enterprise (a 'top team' as some management writers would have it) or it could be half a dozen retail workers who are left by a shop manager to take a joint responsibility for ensuring that customers are served according to who is available at the time, without the manager having to direct particular workers towards particular customers.

The principle of people working in teams, within this variety of levels of autonomy or independence from direct management control, has come increasingly to the fore in recent decades especially since its 'rediscovery' by researchers from the Tavistock Institute (see below, pp. 121–2). It continues to take a variety of forms. The Japanese practice of forming teams to act as 'quality circles' or 'problem solving teams' is different from the 'semi-autonomous' type of team which carries out basic work operations within the organisation and is given a degree of discretion about how tasks are shared and carried out (Buchanan 1994). Perhaps the most significant use of teamworking is within the principle of modular or cellular work organisation, in which people and machines are grouped around information or product flows and in which these 'cells' are, to a greater or less extent, integrated with statistical quality controls and strategic manufacturing management accounting. In this approach, sometimes labelled MSE (manufacturing systems engineering), cells have a degree of independence from each other and from the organisation as a whole which not only reinforces identification of the team with their own product or service but also increases the flexibility of the whole organisation.

For some time there has been a polarisation in the literature on modern teamworking innovations, as Geary and Dobbins (2001) note, with managerially oriented 'optimistic' writers pointing to the ways in which workers would benefit from becoming empowered team workers and more pessimistic critical observers arguing that managerial motivations were essentially directed towards the 'intensification' of workers' efforts. Geary and Dobbins then identify a trend towards a 'more nuanced and context-sensitive under-standing' of these matters which recognises both the costs and the benefits of team-working and other innovations to all the parties involved, the balance which these benefits take varying from circumstance to circumstance (Wilkinson *et al.* 1998 and Edwards *et al.* 2001, for example). This is labelled a 'reregulation' point of view and the authors' own case study is interpreted within this perspective, it being observed in the case study company that whilst there was clear evidence of 'considerable intensification of effort and pressure levels', many workers actually welcomed the new pressures placed upon them. This corresponds with the findings of a study of TQM innovations by Collinson *et al.* (1997) in which workers were observed to appreciate the experience of working harder, given that it was occurring in a context of a welcome sense of order and direction in the workplace that had come about with the reorganisation of work. How changes in work management regimes are experienced by workers is something that has to be analysed in the light of the complex set of factors that influence the meanings that people attach to their work. The importance of these orientations to work is something that we will return to at the end of this chapter. Nevertheless, as Harley (2001) stresses after noting the limited survey evidence of any clear link between the adoption of teamworking and 'positive' employee experiences, 'unless teams entail a fundamental reconfiguration of dominant patterns of work organisation' (challenging, that is, hierarchical structures of power and influence in organisations and society) then 'they are unlikely to make a difference to employee discretion and via this to orientations to work'.

What is clear from the range of research available to us is that although many of the newer approaches to the organising of work clearly incorporate elements of indirect controls and high commitment employment practices to bring about 'flexibility for adaptability', they nevertheless also have built-in elements of tight and direct control to ensure the degree of 'flexibility for predictability' – these being most obvious in the task schedules arising from the pressures of just-in-time logistics. This mixture of direct and indirect controls is most obviously a characteristic of the *lean production* approach to car assembly (Womack *et al.* 1990).

LEAN PRODUCTION

A combining of teamworking with automated technologies. Workers are required both to initiate 'continual improvements' in quality and to ensure that every task is got 'right first time' and completed to a demanding 'just-in-time' schedule.

Here a ruthlessly tight managerial regime achieves a 'leanness' in which no time, resource or effort is allowed to be wasted. But workers are required to give a positive psychological commitment to this regime and enthusiastically to use their discretion *within the spaces where this is allowed* to act in a way that they will best 'benefit the customer'. As Danford (1998a, 1998b) illustrates in his detailed case study, the contradiction between an increased level of labour exploitation through directly controlled teamworking and nurturing a committed and 'co-operative' workforce 'creates as many new potential conflicts and management problems as it resolves'. Yet, as Storey and Harrison (1999) show, there is evidence of the adoption of 'world class manufacturing' practices enabling companies to become internationally competitive with this sometimes leading to the 'degradation' of the worker experience and sometimes to its 'liberalisation' – the general direction followed being an outcome of a range of factors varying from labour market conditions, level of unionisation, organisational and technological factors and 'the underlying intent of management'. Milkman's (1997) study of a General Motors plant reveals a tendency within 'new' production regimes towards a polarisation of skilling and experience within the workforce, with skilled male workers improving their position and production line workers experiencing a worsening. But, as Delbridge's (1998) ethnography shows, whilst workers in these situations may not directly and overtly challenge heightened managerial controls, they nevertheless develop their own localised workplace controls as part of a low-key resistance to intensified labour exploitation.

A mixture of ruthless managerial intervention in work arrangements and the encouraging of worker discretion within the space identified by management is also seen in *business process re-engineering* (Hammer and Champy 1993).

BUSINESS PROCESS RE-ENGINEERING (BPR)

The restructuring of an organisation to focus on business processes rather than on business functions. Advanced management control information technologies are used together with team working and employee 'empowerment'.

A range of organisations, within and beyond manufacturing, have been restructured to focus on business processes. All employees are encouraged to give prime attention to processes such as designing, manufacturing and selling a product and turning attention away from business *functions* whereby, say, a design function focuses on design, a manufacturing function focuses on production and a sales function concentrates on selling. Advanced information technologies are used to ensure a clear and integrated flow of processes and employees are *empowered* and given new degrees of freedom to manage themselves in teams. Because organisational members are no longer working in the separate 'silos' of functional organisation, managers, planners and schedulers no longer have to spend time and effort directing and co-ordinating people's efforts to ensure that all the separate tasks and operations 'add up' to the provision of a successful product or service.

It is questionable what degree of novelty there is in these ambitious aspirations, with the popularity of (rarely successful) attempts to 're-engineer' enterprises being primarily a matter of managements wishing to demonstrate that they are alert to the needs of the modern 'globalised marketplace' (Grint 1994). Not only does BPR contain significant internal contradictions (Grey and Mitev 1995; Willmott 1994) but its implementation faces the powerful barrier of resistance by middle managers (Grint and Willcocks 1995), people whose careers and functional identities are fundamentally threatened by BPR principles. From the point of view of other workers experiencing re-engineering, there is the massive 'downside of work intensification, stress, excessive control and employment insecurity' which Knights and McCabe (1998) note whilst, at the same time and on the basis of careful case-study research, observing that if managers take this downside into account they can make it possible for the workers who remain in employment after 'downsizing' changes to experience 'positive effects . . . in the form of empowerment and creativity' that BPR supporters espouse.

Changing patterns of job design and job redesign

All the changes we reviewed above involve issues of both organisational and work design. To examine patterns or trends at the level of *job design* – the level of the bundle of tasks that individual workers and groups of workers do in particular working settings – it is helpful to develop the direct/indirect control distinction which was applied earlier to management control attempts generally for application to job design specifically.

Fluctuation between an emphasis on direct and indirect management controls applied at the level of people's jobs and represented by the two ideal types in Table 5.3 has been occurring since the beginning of the Industrial Revolution. We tend to think of the shift towards indirect controls and 'whole jobs', as opposed to fragmented deskilled ones, as something new. But it can equally be seen, in part, as a return to earlier pre-industrial patterns of job design when a *social division* of labour prevailed.

The occupational principles of work structuring that underpinned the social division of labour saw individual workers playing their part in society as, say, a butcher or a shoemaker, and each of these possessed the cluster of skills that went with their particular occupation or craft. They would undertake what later 'job redesign' thinkers came to call 'whole tasks' – the killing, preparing and selling of meat or the design, production and selling of a pair of shoes, for example. Although there were undoubtedly people who worked simply as labourers or unskilled servants, something similar to what we have characterised as *indirect* work design thinking formed key principles of the pre-industrial working order. With the rise of industrial capitalism, the rationalising force of bureaucratisation and the growth of the institution of formal employment came the splitting down into deskilled jobs of the old occupational roles of the declining social division of labour. Industrialisation brought about

Table 5.3 Direct and indirect job design principles

Direct control work design principles	Indirect control work design principles
• Deskilled, fragmented jobs	• Whole, skilled, 'rich' jobs
• 'Doing' is split off from 'thinking', the latter being done elsewhere	• 'Doing and thinking' is combined in the job
• The worker has a single skill	• The worker has a range of skills
• The worker does the same task most of the time	• The worker does different tasks at different times
• The worker has little choice over pace or order of task completion	• The worker has choice over the pace and order of task completion
• The worker is closely supervised	• Workers supervise themselves
• The quality of work is checked by an 'inspector'	• Workers are responsible for their own quality
• If there is a group dimension to the work, the supervisor allocates roles and monitors the workgroup's performance	• If there is a group dimension to the work, the workers operate as a team with members allocating roles and monitoring team performance

the *technical division of labour* which saw the creation of jobs in which individuals did only one specialised part of what had previously been an occupational 'whole task'.

The logic of work deskilling which is central to Taylorism is by no means an invention of the 'scientific managers', then. They were only developing in a particularly systematic way principles of work organisation which were first written about by Adam Smith in his *Wealth of Nations* in 1776. Smith recognised that part of what was later to be seen as the Industrial Revolution was a move beyond the principle of the social division of labour into crafts and occupations into the detailed or 'technical division of labour'. Smith recognised that enormous gains in efficiency were to be obtained if what might be seen as a 'whole' task such as the making of tacks (or 'pins' as he called them) could be split up into a number of smaller scale and less skilled tasks or jobs. Each job would be easy to learn and each operation readily repeatable. The employer would benefit enormously from the increased dexterity of the worker, the reduction of time spent in preparation and changeover from one operation to another and from the possibilities which were opened up for further mechanisation. But it was Charles Babbage, in 1832, who pointed out that this kind of deskilling also reduced the cost of labour. If 'whole' tasks were carried out then you had to pay each worker a rate which was appropriate to the most skilful or physically demanding element of the task. You could, however, 'by dividing the work . . . into different degrees of skill and force . . . purchase the precise quantity of both that is necessary for each purpose'.

The way in which Taylorism or 'scientific management' systematised these principles was examined in Chapter 2 and, as we also noted in that chapter, the Human Relations thinking of the 1920s represented an important questioning of many of the assumptions of scientific management. This movement not only produced a theoretical approach to understanding work behaviour but provided a managerial ideology more fitted to the American inter-war period when trade union representation of employees was increasing (Bendix 1963). The common tendency to describe the Human Relations approach as rediscovering the social aspects of work which scientific management is said to ignore is quite mistaken. Taylor understood well work-group behaviour and, in place of his attempts to destroy work-group solidarity, the Human Relations approach prescribes an alternative tactic; that of integrating the work-group so as to control it better.

Human Relations ideas played a role in countering trade unionism in America and were especially influential in their encouragement of the use of personnel counselling (Madge 1963). Despite the systems element of the Human Relations stance (above, pp. 129–30), the prescriptions provided by it tend not to involve structural redesign within organisations. The most important manifestation of human relations thinking within organisations has perhaps been in the form of supervisory and junior management training schemes. These schemes, which are very popular across a range of contemporary organisations, tend to emphasise the importance of 'communications' and the careful 'handling of people'. Instead of altering work organisation, existing structures are marginally humanised through more sensitive 'people management'. There is no real interest in changing jobs in an indirect control direction within Human Relations thinking.

An interest in redesigning jobs does appear, however, with the *democratic humanists*. This approach, as with parts of Human Relations thinking, is also popular in contemporary management training. But its concern to create workplace conditions in which employees can achieve 'self-actualisation' does suggest a need for structural modification. Thus, for example, we find advocacy of *job enrichment* following from Herzberg's (1966) 'motivation-hygiene' theory of motivation.

JOB ENRICHMENT

The expansion of the scope of jobs by such means as the re-integration of maintenance or inspection tasks; an extension of the work cycle; an increased degree of delegation of decision-making by job holders.

Structural implications are also found in the work of Likert, another proponent of so-called participative styles of management. Likert (1967) advocates integration of individuals into the organisation through groups which are, in turn, integrated into the organisation's official structure of decision-making by their being made to overlap by means of their continuing 'linking pin' members who belong to more than one group.

Among the variety of approaches to job redesign one of the more theoretically sophisticated is that developed by the Tavistock Institute of Human Relations in London. This approach encourages a view of the organisation as a *socio-technical system*.

SOCIO-TECHNICAL SYSTEMS

An approach to work design in which the technical and the social/psychological aspects of the overall workplace are given equal weight and are designed at the same time to take each other into account.

Socio-technical systems thinking discourages managers from designing a technology and then fitting a social organisation to it and, instead, encourages them to devise each of these alongside the other in order jointly to optimise the two. It is assumed that the precise technical form required to achieve tasks is variable, as is the social structure to accompany it. Both can therefore be chosen to get the best fit, one with the other. Trist *et al.* (1963) showed how technical innovations introduced in post-war British coal mines failed to give either the social and psychological satisfactions traditionally expected by miners or the levels of productivity and uninterrupted working sought by management. This was because the technical pattern of such things as new occupational roles and the shift arrangements associated with new machinery took away the relative autonomy of work-groups and removed the opportunity for the coal miner to use a variety of skills. The researchers devised a different approach to the use of new machinery which allowed retention of some of the traditional features of the social and cultural arrangements preferred by miners. A better *fit* having been obtained between the social and technical arrangements, there was said to be a marked improvement in productivity, worker–management co-operation and absenteeism levels.

Probably the most important single innovation of the Tavistock researchers is that of the semi-autonomous work-group.

SEMI-AUTONOMOUS WORK-GROUPS

A work–group or 'team' in which individual jobs are grouped to focus work activities on an overall 'whole task', with group members being fully trained and equipped so that they can be given discretion over how the task is completed.

Work tasks are grouped together to form a logical 'whole task' which can be performed with minimal interference. The work designer attempts to devise 'a group consisting of the smallest number that can perform a whole task and can satisfy the social and psychological needs of its members', this being 'alike from the point of view of task performance and of those performing it, the most satisfactory and efficient group' (Rice 1958). A parallel movement towards devising work-groups organised around 'whole tasks' which can be carried out relatively autonomously was a 'group technology' approach increasingly initiated by work engineers. Typically, workplaces were rearranged so that machines (or desks) are grouped together not on the basis of their doing similar work (drilling, grinding, invoicing or whatever) but on the basis of a contribution to a certain product or service. Thus a group of people all involved in making, say, small turbine blades or dealing with house insurance are brought together in such a way that greater integration is obtained and a greater degree of job satisfaction is facilitated by members' greater relative autonomy and through their productive co-operation with colleagues.

In the 1970s and early 1980s there was a tendency to consolidate many of the work redesign ideas which had emerged over previous decades and present them as part of a social movement which would improve the 'Quality of Working Life' of people in industrial societies (Rose 1988). Littler and Salaman (1984) identified five principles of 'good' job design which they believed typified the QWL movement's alternative to scientific management. These principles helpfully bring together the challenges which have been presented to traditional industrial approaches to work design by reformers working with a variety of different purposes.

MAJOR JOB REDESIGN PRINCIPLES

1 The principle of closure whereby the scope of the job is such that it includes all the tasks necessary to complete a product or process, thus giving the individual a sense of achievement.
2 The incorporation of control and monitoring tasks whereby the individual or group assume responsibility for their own quality and reliability.
3 Task variety whereby the worker understands a range of tasks so as to be able to vary their daily work experience.
4 Self–regulation of work speed and the allowing of some choice over work methods and sequence.
5 A job structure which allows some social interaction and the possibility of co–operation among workers.

Practical interest in job redesign by some employers has developed less perhaps from a social concern with the quality of employees' lives than from more pragmatic worries about the *costs* of standard job design principles in terms of, for example:

- the willingness of employees to be reliable in their attendance at work;
- the degree of care shown by employees towards service and product quality;
- the amount of task flexibility employees are willing to undertake;
- the extent to which employees are prepared to show necessary initiative;
- the growing costs of a control, monitoring and trouble-shooting apparatus of quality, production planning and control, industrial relations departments.

However, it can be argued that the reasons for employer interest in job redesign have changed over recent decades. A 1970s survey suggested that the key motives for job redesign were shown to be ones of improving quality or reducing labour turnover and absenteeism (Wild and Birchall 1975). And a 1980s study of job redesign experiments suggested that managements were generally gaining from redesign through an improvement in the overall time and effort devoted to production, this often involving a loss of jobs at the same time as leading to improvements both in work experience and extrinsic rewards for those who kept their jobs (Kelly 1982). Kelly interpreted this research to argue that these job redesign efforts did not represent a major departure from the basic principles of work design which had been applied throughout the twentieth century. He claimed that job specialisation was less important to Taylorism than was the general intensification of effort through increasing the managerial control over labour. This could, at times, involve making tasks less specialised rather than more so. Consequently, Kelly divided job redesign efforts into three main types and was able to claim that a large proportion of these are quite compatible with Taylorism:

- In flow line reorganisation, the individualisation of tasks or the breaking up of a sequence of work interdependencies fits perfectly with Taylor's interest in replacing the stress on the group with one on the individual and the trend towards vertical role integration.
- Where workers take over tasks previously done by the more senior inspectors, supervisors and the like (as long as these are not 'managerial' tasks), accords with Taylor's principle of giving as much work as possible to the cheapest category of labour.
- Only a third type of job redesign, that involving the introduction of flexible work-groups (on the socio-technical and 'group technology' lines discussed earlier) represents a move away from Taylorist principles. And this is done because the flexible work-group enables managements to 'cope more effectively with production variations'.

In the 1990s and into the twenty-first century there has been a rethinking of the significance of many of these innovations. Although various commentators in the 1970s argued that these changes needed to be related to broader organisational design and cultural changes, if they were to have a significant impact, they were 'expressed at a time when their implications were seen as inappropriate, unrealistic or unacceptable by many managers' (Buchanan 1992). However, the arguments for a more comprehensive approach to work design were 'set in a new context, by developments in product markets, changing trading conditions and new technological possibilities' that came about in the 1980s and 1990s. Huczynski and Buchanan (2001) draw out the distinctiveness of the new, more comprehensive, approach to work design by contrasting the QWL techniques of the 1970s with the 'high performance' approach of more recent times:

- Whereas the earlier concern was with reducing costs of absenteeism and labour turnover and increasing productivity, the contemporary concern is with improving organisational flexibility and product quality for competitive advantage.
- Where the older 'quality of working life' advocates argued that increased autonomy improves quality of work experience and employee job satisfaction, the contemporary argument is that increased autonomy improves skills, decision-making, adaptability and use of new technology.
- Where changes in the 1970s had little impact on the management function beyond first line supervision, contemporary changes involve attention to organisation cultures and the redefinition of management functions at all levels.

Information and communication technologies (ICTs), work design and organisational shaping

Technological factors play a role within social processes which make them seem at times as if they are a determining force. But technology in itself can make no difference to human history. It is what human beings do with the technologies they develop that has the potential to transform the ways in which they live and work. In sociological terms, it is inappropriate to speak of computers and communication technologies bringing about a *revolution* in human life or work experience. For such a term to be appropriate there would need to be a movement beyond the industrial capitalist ways of organising work. Information and Communication Technologies (ICTs) nevertheless have the potential to modify significantly the ways in which we live and work, albeit within the same set of basic principles which underpin our present society and economy.

INFORMATION AND COMMUNICATION TECHNOLOGIES (ICTS)

The combination of microelectronic and computing technologies with telecommunications to manipulate human information.

In fact, some of the basic characteristics of ICTs make them an ideal 'engine' for the future development of industrial capitalism. There is a fit between the basic dynamics of industrial capitalism and the potential that information technologies have for:

- reducing production costs;
- accelerating innovation in products and services and in the ways these are produced and delivered;
- increasing flexibility in production and service-provision methods.

The key characteristic of modern information technology is the linking of advances in microelectronics with innovations in telecommunications and, with its associated developments in computer science, software engineering and systems analysis, it 'dramatically increases the ability to record, store, analyse, and transmit information in ways that permit flexibility, accuracy, immediacy, geographic independence, volume, and complexity' (Zuboff 1988). IT has a unique capability, as Zuboff says, to 'restructure operations that depend upon information for the purposes of transaction, record keeping, analysis, control, or communication'.

The idea of computerising and automating tasks is, of course, not new. What is new about the microprocessor-based innovations, however, is the potential impact they can have as a result of their cheapness, speed, reliability, smallness and, above all, breadth of application. Information technology is having an increasing impact on the various aspects of work and its administration. It has an impact on:

- *the products* people can buy, from home computers through to 'chip-controlled' car engines or domestic appliances;
- *how goods are developed*, since products can be speedily designed on computers and rapidly tested by electronic simulations;
- *how things are made*, through the use of robots and computer-controlled machine tools and transfer devices;
- *how work is administered*, through its applications in word-processing, information storage and retrieval, electronic mail and computerised data analysis;
- *how goods and services are distributed*, where, in retailing, for example, barcoded products are priced at the 'point of sale' and are stock-controlled and monitored by computers. Other service applications are seen in financial institutions where innovations ranging from cash dispensers to 'electronic funds transfer' are appearing and in legal and medical work where 'expert systems' can help the practitioner rapidly tap vast electronic banks of information and the accumulated recordable judgements and diagnoses of countless human experts.

Perhaps the greatest impact of ICTs is coming not so much from discrete developments of this kind as from the *integrating of what have previously been treated as separate areas*. Electronic networks (and, later, optical-fibre networks) are able to connect together different organisations and link their component parts so that processes of learning, research, design, manufacturing, administration, product and service-delivery can be closely linked. This makes possible the abolition of old distinctions between office and factory, works and staff, training and doing and even home and work, through the development of electronic 'outworking'. It can also, in certain fields, undermine the distinction between worker and manager. In fact, a large proportion of currently existing managerial and administrative jobs could disappear as machines are used for the co-ordination and the monitoring of tasks and the processing of information. Zuboff (1988) explains how information technology can be used to do far more than 'routinise, fragment, or eliminate jobs'; it can be used to 'increase the intellectual content of work at virtually every organisation' level and, hence, 'challenge the distinction between manual and mental work as it has evolved in the industrial bureaucracy'. This potential exists because ICTs can do far more than automate. They also *informate* work.

ICTS AND THE POTENTIAL TO INFORMATE WORK

ICTs can 'record' and hence can 'play back' or make visible the processes behind the operations that were once deep in the minds of the people doing that work.

As Zuboff expresses it, ICT-based automation 'extends the body' as machines have always done, but it is different in that it 'simultaneously generates information about the underlying productive and administrative processes through which an organisation accomplishes its work' and thus provides 'a deeper level of transparency to activities that had been either partially or completely opaque'.

The informating potential of ICTs clearly has major significance for job design. As a form of indirect control, it can enhance flexibility for adaptability within an organisation, enabling employees to think for themselves and to take initiatives to cope with crises or technical problems which cannot be designed out of the work context. Alternatively, the use of ICTs in a non-informating way can enhance *flexibility for predictability* by applying direct controls and reducing the work efforts of employees to ones involving machine-minding and machine-feeding. Predictability and tight control becomes possible with the bulk of discretion being given to the managers who programme the machines and tightly control a limited workforce which can be cheaply employed, easily trained, readily recruited or dispensed with and who have limited bargaining power. Evidence has been put forward of circumstances which are associated with movement in one direction or the other. In the area of computer numerically controlled (CNC) machines we find Noble (1984), in his social history of this form of automation, claiming that its development at the Massachusetts Institute of Technology was closely tied to a desire to produce a technique which would suit its military customers and was less influenced by a cost-minded business logic than by one of avoiding methods of production being left in the hands of skilled workers rather than in the hands of management or programmers. On the other hand, there has been a long tradition of studies of this CNC technology by people such as Jones (1982), Rosenbrock (1982) and Wilkinson (1983) showing that the removing of the control over machine processes from the hands of the workers is not the only possibility. Managements may alternatively choose to involve the operators in the implementation of the new system and can choose to retrain and re-skill them so that they play a part in programming the machines which they use.

Research in a variety of technological contexts by Boddy and Buchanan (1986) showed that new technology decisions can either 'distance' employees from their tasks and limit the positive contribution which they make or can bring about 'complementarity' between the employee and their job. In the latter case, much fuller use is made of both technical capabilities and human skills. But what comes about is unlikely to follow directly from what is pre-planned. For example, negotiations and accommodations which accompany the introduction of changes may lead to actual outcomes which differ from those originally intended by management (Rose and Jones 1984). Certain circumstances, however, may be more conducive to deskilling and others to reskilling. Child (1984b) showed for example how a greater degree of initiative appears to be left to workers in circumstances where there are frequent batch changes, a high incidence of new work and where variability in materials or physical conditions creates a 'requirement for flexibility at the point of production'. And, in the politics of real organisational life, the relative power which the workforce enjoys prior to their work being changed is an important factor operating alongside managerial choices. A study of various service sector contexts (Child *et al.* 1984) showed how some workers are better able than others to resist degradation of their work through their being collectively organised, through their scarcity on the labour market and through their key position in the production process.

The interests and motives of managers themselves are also inevitably relevant to directions followed in the up-skilling of employees and the 'pushing down the hierarchy' of responsibilities and decision-making. Zuboff's (1988) studies in a number of American organisations showed major resistance to the realisation of this potential coming from managerial staffs. Her case studies revealed no instance of an organisation 'fully succeeding in exploiting the opportunity to informate' work and hence significantly increase workers' understanding of processes and the amount of discretion they exercise. The main force resisting such change she takes to be the anxieties and insecurities of managers whom she portrays as unnerved by the concept of workers taking initiatives and engaging in creative thinking. The managers thus lean more towards the automating potential of ICT, the promise of which 'seemed to exert a magnetic force, a seduction that promised to fulfil a dream of perfect control and heal egos wounded by their needs of certainty'. Organisations that use ICT to automate work – which implies a deskilling of remaining workers – are, according to Zuboff, 'likely to find themselves crippled by antagonisms from the work force and the depletion of knowledge that would be needed in value-adding activities'.

Call centres have been an increasingly common form of knowledge-oriented workplaces where serious issues of how the discretion often associated with knowledge-based work (implying a need for *indirect* managerial controls) can be balanced with the use of machine-based work controls (typically associated with *direct control* regimes).

CALL CENTRE WORK

Work in which operators utilise computer terminals to process information relating to telephone calls which are made and/or received, these calls being mediated by various computer–based filtering, allocational and monitoring devices.

It is increasingly recognised that early analyses of call centres which saw them as essentially factory-like but with all-powerful electronic surveillance (Fernie and Metcalf 1998) were over simplistic (Bain and Taylor 2000; Hutchinson *et al.* 2000) with a range of possibilities emerging as the nature of the calls dealt with were seen to vary from ones that were relatively complex (therefore demanding discretion and a degree of indirect control) to ones where calls were routine, repetitive, simple and undemanding of workers and could be dealt with in a direct-control sweatshop manner. Whilst recognising this range of possibilities, Taylor *et al.* (2002) conclude from their research that in call centre operations 'routinisation, repetitiveness and a general absence of employee control are the dominant, although not universal, features of work organisation'. These findings are used to qualify the claims of the important analysis of the broad rise of 'front line' service work by Frenkel *et al.* (1999) and their attention to work, ranging from call centre employment to highly knowledge-intensive professional jobs, in which workers have regular contact with actual or prospective customers. Frenkel and colleagues suggest that both theorists of knowledge-based work (Bell 1974) and ICT (Castells 1996) ignored the significant tendency of 'the rise of customer sovereignty in the context of a more competitive, globalised economy'. The implication of this trend for the work which people do is that the competitive importance to the employing enterprise of a high *quality* of interaction with customers necessarily pushes them towards an 'info-normative' type of control which emphasises worker discretion rather than direct or technical control. Their overall analysis is an optimistic one in which the combination of the growth of knowledge work, the use of ICTs and the emphasis on pleasing customers means that 'work is becoming more complex, in part because of customisation and in part because high labour costs and IT in combination are reducing the demand for lower-skilled jobs and increasing the demand for jobs with higher-level competences'.

In the same way that it is apparent that ICTs have the potential to enhance both direct and indirect managerial controls, it is apparent at the level of the broader shape of work organisations that ICTs are compatible with both recentralisation and decentralisation of organisations. They have the potential, on the one hand, to help centralisation through getting comprehensive and current information directly to senior management and through an ability to simplify management structures and so reduce senior managers' span of control. On the other hand, as Child (1984b) observes, it has the potential for decentralisation through more effective delegation whereby sub-units are put into an information network with other sub-units, so enabling them to make acceptable decisions without checking with the centre. Decentralisation is also assisted by the opportunities which computerised analytical tools offer for the enhancement of the capacity of local units to make 'sound' judgements. In practice it is likely that the need of organisational managements to balance *flexibility for predictability* with *flexibility for adaptability* (p. 111) will lead to the development of 'decentralised' structures which retain a strong degree of 'centralisation' in certain key respects. This possibility was stressed in the influential analysis of Peters and Waterman (1982) who suggested that 'simultaneous loose–tight controls' will increasingly be developed whereby a basic simple structure (probably divisional) and a strong organisational culture will be combined with a tendency to 'chunk' the organisation into 'small-is-beautiful' units, 'cabals' and other problem-solving and implementation groups. ICTs would inevitably be central to such arrangements and can play a major part in the trend which Deal and Kennedy (1982) envisaged for the future in which small task-focused work units are bonded like molecules into a 'strong corporate whole'. The need to achieve this bonding through integrated business and manufacturing *systems design* is also central to Drucker's (1992) analysis of management in the future and of the *postmodern factory*. Where the traditional factory was seen as a battleship, says Drucker, the new enterprise will be more like a *flotilla* – 'a set of modules centred around stages in the production process or a set of closely related operations'. Castells (1996) writes in a similar vein about the *network enterprise* which not only uses flexible rather than mass production and emphasises horizontal rather than vertical relationships but also becomes intertwined with other corporations within a pattern of strategic alliances.

The term *virtual organisation* has become popular as a way of referring to work enterprises made up of networked relationships in which people tend not to be physically located in the same place or relate to each other as co-employees. In the virtual workplace, 'employees operate remotely from each other and from managers' (Cascio 2002).

VIRTUAL OR NETWORKED ORGANISATIONS

Sets of work arrangement in which those undertaking tasks carried under a corporate name largely relate to each other through electronic communications rather than through face-to-face interaction.

Snow *et al.* (1999) associate the growth of virtual organisations with the 'disaggregating' of 'hierarchical organisations through outsourcing and partnering' as alliances and partnerships are made with suppliers, major customers and other companies – to obtain necessary expertise, access to distribution channels and markets, or to lower costs. There has been a tendency to view the developments associated with the notion of the virtual organisation as representing a 'new paradigm' of work organisation and, although, as Harris (1998) recognises, this does not stand up to scrutiny in the light of the clear continuities with earlier principles of work organisation, we must nevertheless avoid under-estimating the extent of the changes that are possible if the technological possibilities are shrewdly combined with social and organisational innovation. These various reflections on the future of organisational forms are clearly based on the potential that ICTs offer. Their realisation is quite another matter and would involve all the challenges and difficulties that we earlier saw arising with lean production, business process re-engineering innovations and the like. There is also the question of the type of organisational culture that managements would need to bring about.

Culture management and worker subjectivity

In the review of the systems emphasis in industrial sociology in Chapter 2, it was noted that sociological recognition of the importance of the cultural dimension of organisations has encouraged a managerial interest in developing 'strong' cultures that serve managerial interests. The theorising that encouraged this interest can be traced back to Selznick's (1949, 1957) contrast between the mechanical idea of an 'organisation' and the more culturally developed notion of an 'institution' (an idea which also influenced the institutional theorists discussed in Chapter 4). Organisations are set up to act as tools to meet certain purposes, Selznick argued, but a process of *institutionalisation* occurs whereby the organisation becomes a more responsive and adaptive social organism with an identity and a set of values. These integrate the organisation in such a way that it has significance for its members which is far greater than one of simply being involved in fulfilling the tasks for which it was originally designed. The management is centrally involved in moulding what Selznick calls the 'character' of the organisation. Although Selznick does not formally use the concept of 'culture', his thinking was taken up by the authors of one of the most widely read management books of all time, Peters and Waterman (1982), who argued that the American business organisations which they identified as outstanding or 'excellent' were characterised by several key features. These were not, as many might have expected, the rigorous use of techniques of organisational design, of financial planning, or of computerised control systems. Outstanding business success came, they argue, from reliance on simple structures, simple strategies, simple goals and simple communication.

The key to managing in a basically simple way in what are often large and potentially complex organisations is the use of a clear and 'tight' culture. The stronger was the culture, in which shared values would be communicated through 'rich tapestries of anecdote, myth and fairy tale', and the more it was directed towards the marketplace, the 'less need there was for policy manuals, organisation charts, or detailed procedures and rules'.

These ideas had a major impact upon management thinking and it has became almost normal for the managements of the larger organisations in Britain and America to frame their restructuring activities in terms of 'changing culture' or 'managing through values'. Where close research on organisations adopting such approaches has emerged, the picture looks far more complex than the widely read prescriptive managerial texts would suggest, however. An ethnographic study of a case of attempted culture change showed how a 'discourse' of culture change, personal development and employee 'development' came to clash with alternative discourses which reflected corporate interests in cost controls and tight corporate control (Watson 2001a). The 'progressive' culture-based ideas in fact became counter-productive as the expectations they created were undermined by corporate policies leading, for example, to regular redundancies among employees. These tensions clearly relate to differences of interest *within* an organisation's management, and McCabe (2000) illustrates from his case study the ways in which managers whilst 'imbibing' new managerial discourses nevertheless tend to slip back into an 'older language' of 'industrialism' which reflected their 'lived reality' – one of working within an organisation which, like all organisations, is 'replete with political intrigue, hierarchical divisions, inequality, power struggles and conflict'.

Parker's (2000) three ethnographic case studies show the variety of ways in which managerial attempts to develop an organisational culture to which all employees can subscribe are undermined by the range of spatial, functional, generational and occupational divisions that manifest themselves in different ways in different organisations with, for example, doctors, managers and information technology specialists competing for control over new IT systems in a hospital and, in a foundry, tensions and distrust developing between progressive 'new engineers' and mass-production-oriented 'old engineers'.

In a further ethnographic study of an organisation attempting to 'mould' its culture and its employee, Kunda (1992) looked in detail at processes of 'normative control' through which attempts are made to win the deep commitment of technical workers to corporate goals and values. The author expresses strong concern about what he sees as managerial attempts to channel people's feelings, thoughts and ways of seeing the world. Yet he does show how individuals tend to balance an absorbing of some of this with a degree of personal distancing from the corporate embrace. Casey (1995) shows a degree of this too in her study of another American company which she calls Hephaestus, one which promoted an 'official discourse' defining an 'ideal Hephaestus person' who worked within 'values of diligence, dedication, loyalty, commitment and the ability to be a good team-player, to be adaptive and flexible, and to be a good, somewhat conservative, citizen'. However, in spite of limited evidence of resistance and 'defence of self' among employees, Casey notes a 'homogeneity of view and values and a conformity of self-presentation as the language practices and values 'become everyday parlance and employees act out the desired characteristics most come to own these practices and roles of the ideal Hephaestus employee'.

Employers and managers engaging in these ways with issues of employees' self-identities and the values through which they judge the rights and wrongs of their daily lives has led some sociologists to raise value questions about such trends. To attempt to mould cultures – given that culture in its broad sense provides the roots of human morality, social identity and existential security – is indeed to enter 'deep and dangerous waters' (Watson 2001a). The 'guiding aim and abiding concern' of what Willmott (1995) calls *corporate culturism* (and Parker 2000, calls *culturalism*) is to win the 'hearts and minds' of employees, and Willmott expresses deep anxiety about corporate attempts to 'colonise the affective domain' and to attempt to achieve 'the governance of the employee's soul'. The American research of Kunda and Casey perhaps gives grounds for this pessimism. The British evidence, which is still limited, however, suggests a greater degree of scepticism. The employees of ZTC were cautious about, although not universally dismissive of, the management's 'winning culture' (Watson 2001a) and the workers in a British company taken over by an American organisation dismissed the new management's corporate culture campaign as 'yankee bullshit' and 'propaganda' (Collinson 1994).

Managerial attempts to 'engineer' cultures may well connect to what Webster and Robbins (1993) call 'social Taylorism' (where empowerment and close surveillance of individuals are combined) and they may be understood in part as attempts to produce 'a culture of self-gratificatory narcissistic individualism' which is consistent with 'more generalist consumerist social relations', as Ezzy (2001) argues. But it is vital to recognise two things. First, recognition of the power of discursive and cultural attempts at the subjective 'incorporation' workers must be balanced with a recognition that, as Taylor and Tylor (2000) put it after studying the 'discursive effects of quality management' and emotional labour in the airline industry, 'structural and material power must also be taken into account'. And, second, the potential for worker resistance to managerial attempts to harness workers' emotions, subjectivities and identities must be fully taken into account. This will be looked at in Chapter 8.

6 Occupations and society

The occupational principle of work structuring

If we look for patterns in the work which people do in modern societies we can observe two basic principles giving structure to these activities. These principles are partly complementary and partly in a relationship of conflict and rivalry. They are:

- *The organisational principle of work structuring* – this has been the focus of the previous two chapters and involves the structuring of work on a bureaucratic, administrative or 'formal organisation' basis. Emphasis is on the ways in which work tasks are designed by the managerial agents of the owners of work organisations who then recruit, pay, co-ordinate and control the efforts of others to carry out tasks in a way which enables the organisation to continue into a future existence.
- *The occupational principle of work structuring* – the structuring of work on the basis of the type of work that people do. Emphasis is on the patterns which emerge when we concentrate on the way specific work tasks are done. Here we take as our starting point the carrying out of a specific type of work operation, say driving a lorry, cleaning a house, catching fish or running a business. We then concentrate on the social implications of there existing within society groups of people regularly doing similar tasks.

The implications of the existence of occupational groupings arise at various levels, as we shall see in this chapter. Occupations have implications for the way a society as a whole is structured and for the way this structuring changes over time. They have implications for the members of occupational groups, especially when there is the possibility of the people engaged in a particular occupation acting jointly or *collectively*, through trade union or 'professional' mobilisation, in order to defend or further shared interests. And there are implications for the individual engaged in a particular type of work, implications relating, for example, to how they enter that kind of work, learn how to do the tasks associated with it and advance their careers within their selected type of work activity.

It is important in defining an occupation to recognise that the notion is not simply a sociologist's conceptual tool of analysis but is also used by the people whom the sociologist studies. A working concept of occupation therefore has to take into account the fact that whether or not any given work activity is to be regarded as an occupation depends both on the decisions made by those doing the tasks and the inclination by the wider public to bestow such an identity on that type of work activity.

OCCUPATION

Membership of an occupation involves engagement on a regular basis in a part or the whole of a range of work tasks which are identified under a particular heading or title by both those carrying out these tasks and by a wider public.

This conception of an occupation is one which is wider than simply paid employment. Membership of an occupation may involve total independence of an employer, as in the case of a freelance writer, say, and it may mean that there is no direct financial reward from the work. In this latter case the individual would have to be supported by some-one else. This would apply to a commercially unsuccessful poet or to a student for example.

Most people who carry out work tasks can be assigned to an occupation. But for many individuals, their location in a work organisation may be more salient than their occupational membership. In trying to learn where a stranger 'fits into society' we may ask either 'what do they do?' or 'who do they work for?' Traditionally, we located people in society by their occupation – tinker, tailor, soldier, sailor – but with the growth of bureaucratised work organisations the specific tasks in which a person is engaged and the skills which go with it have become less relevant for many people than the organisation in which they are employed. It is not uncommon for one person to say of another 'I don't know exactly what he does but it's something with the council', and the nearest to any occupational specification which is often achieved with regard to the work of friends, acquaintances or relatives may well be along the lines that 'she does something in the offices' or 'it's some kind of factory job'.

For many people, then, the way they are seen by others and often the way they regard their own work is less in terms of the occupational principle than the organisational or administrative one. There are, however, two special cases where the *study* of people's work has tended to concentrate on the occupational principle:

1 Where the tasks associated with a job are particularly distinctive. This may be through (a) their work having a degree of public visibility – as with police officers, teachers, or actors, say, or (b) their work being somewhat peculiar or deviant, as with prostitutes, undertakers, or criminals, say.
2 Where the tasks involved in a certain kind of work are such that control over the carrying out of those tasks can be sought by members of the occupation itself at the expense

of control by an employer, government or clients. These will tend to be highly skilled 'trades' or, more especially, the 'professions'.

The twentieth-century study of particular occupations by sociologists has tended to veer between a near obsession with high-status professionals and a fascination with various low-status or deviant work activities. The history of Western occupations has, however, been very much one of the rise and fall of the degree of occupational self-control maintained by various groups. The occupational principle is seen very clearly in the occupational guilds which were at their height in the thirteenth century. The guilds developed as part of the urban world which was growing within the feudal structure. They originally served as protective societies for merchants trading in Europe but were then taken up by groups of artisans within the cities as an organisational form to provide them in a similar way with mutual aid and protection.

With the guilds, we see an example of the common tendency in social life and social change for people to form coalitions of interest. The guilds, as such coalitions, helped mediate between the trades people and the city authorities, thus providing in part a defensive role for the group. But they also acted in a more assertively self-interested manner by maintaining a tightly controlled monopoly in their trade. They not only controlled raw materials, and restricted entry to trades, but laid down work procedures which, whilst maintaining quality of the product or service, ensured that any job took the longest possible course with the effect that technical change and any move toward an increased technical division of labour was ruled out. The guild gave the occupation a stratified structure of master craftsman, journeyman and apprentice, thus providing in theory a career structure for the individual. However, groups tend to exist *within* interest groups and those who find themselves with relative material advantages tend to operate so as to maintain that advantage. Thus the master craftsmen began to operate as an elite within the guilds, often preferring to pass on their advantaged positions to their own children rather than to aspiring journeymen.

With the growth of the more competitive and market-orientated capitalism which developed within and threatened the feudal order, master craftsmen were strongly tempted to break their guild monopolies and associate more with the growing class of merchant capitalists. These individuals helped break down the occupational principle of work organisation as they began to use former guild members as wage labour and as they made use of the former peasantry within the putting-out or domestic system of production. Later, of course, the development of factory production accelerated the dominance of the administrative principle, leaving the occupational form of organisation as a residual principle – a principle to be defended by groups whose trade skills were a resource sufficiently exclusive to allow them to maintain some autonomy.

The survival of the occupational principle among the growing working class was carried over into workshop and factory production in the first half of the nineteenth century in the form of a 'labour aristocracy' which retained an elite position 'through the force of custom, or combination and apprenticeship restriction, or because the craft remained highly skilled and specialised' (Thompson 1968). The growth of the new skills accompanying the rise of engineering created a potentially new occupational elite or labour aristocracy, but by the late nineteenth century the growing predominance of the organisational or bureaucratic principle of work structuring was such that the more important bodies formed by groups like the engineers were the more *defensively orientated* trade unions. Throughout the twentieth century the trade or occupational basis of unions increasingly became undermined as occupational groups amalgamated with each other to help in the primary union task of representing *employee* interests rather than occupational ones. The occupational principle of work organisation did not survive the growth of industrial capitalism only in the vestigial form represented by skilled trade unions, however. It has survived and indeed flourished in parts of the middle-class sphere of work in the guise of professionalism, as we shall see later (pp. 168–72).

Occupational structure

In contrast to the term 'organisational structure', which refers to the internal patterning in work organisations, the concept of occupational structure is used by sociologists not to look at the shape of occupations themselves but to look at patterns of occupational activity at a societal level.

> ### OCCUPATIONAL STRUCTURE
>
> The pattern in a society which is created by the distribution of the labour force across the range of existing types of work or occupation.

Horizontal aspects of occupational structure

Patterning may be sought, for example, by looking for both *hierarchical* and *horizontal* differentiating factors. A traditional way of showing horizontal differentiation is to divide a workforce into three sectors: such as a primary sector of agricultural and extractive industries, a secondary sector of manufacturing, and a tertiary sector of services. This type of distribution, widely used by economists, has been used sociologically to study industrialisation processes. However, sociologists also developed the alternative 'horizontal' notion of *occupational situs*. This refers to a grouping of occupations which is differentiated from other groupings according to various criteria other than or in addition to ones which imply status or reward-yielding capacity. Morris and Murphy (1959) took up this concept (which had first been applied to the occupational sphere by Hatt 1950) using the criterion of 'societal function'. Hopper and Pearce (1973), who point out that the particular criterion used may vary with the purpose of the research being undertaken, classify occupations for their own purposes on the basis of economic function. They thus develop nine situs categories:

- distribution
- manufacturing
- finance and insurance
- agriculture
- building and transport and communications

- civil service
- church, military and government
- education
- medicine and health.

The concept of occupational situs has been used as a tool of analysis far less than that of occupational *status*. This is perhaps unsurprising, given that an individual's occupation is the key indicator of their social class and social status – as those concepts are generally used, inside and outside of sociology. As well as the prestige which one derives from a job, one's market position and relationship to the means of production is generally dependent upon the job which is held. Also, as we recognise in Chapter 7, the hierarchy of jobs based on material rewards tends to coincide with that based on intrinsic rewards which contribute to job satisfaction, and both of these factors influence the general life-chances not just of the workers themselves but also of their dependants.

Vertical and social class aspects of occupational structure

Sociological researchers often develop their own set of socioeconomic categories or classes to help in their investigations, one particularly influential scheme being the 'Goldthorpe class schema' (Goldthorpe 1987) which locates occupations in the class structure according to where people fit into the societal system of employment relations. Such principles were used by the sociologists to whom the UK government statistics office turned to devise a scheme for use in the first national census of the twenty-first century. This locates different occupational groups in a hierarchical classification according to criteria relating to the quality of the overall employment contract that members of any given occupation might expect to achieve – especially the working conditions, the prospects for future advancement and the degree of security of employment (Rose and O'Reilly 1997). The seven groupings are:

1 Higher managerial (employers of more than twenty-five staff and senior managers) and higher professional (doctors, dentists, lawyers, university teachers).
2 Lower managerial and professional (junior managers, police sergeants, teachers, social workers, journalists).
3 Intermediate (police constables, fire brigade workers, junior prison officers).
4 Small employers and own account workers (non-professionals employing fewer than twenty-five people).
5 Lower supervisory and technical (supervisors, train drivers).
6 Semi-routine (shop assistants, call centre workers).
7 Routine (drivers, cleaners).

CLASS

An individual's class position is a matter of the part which they play (or the person upon whom they are dependent plays) within the division of labour of a society and the implications which this has for their access to those experiences, goods and services which are scarce and valued in that society.

The concept of class links people's occupational position and their position in the overall societal structure of advantage.

Within sociology, there is a variety of different approaches to class analysis. In the basic Marxian model (see pp. 42–6) we have an image of capitalism relentlessly pushing towards what would eventually be just two classes; the property-owning bourgeoisie and the proletariat. The proletariat can only subsist, given their lack of sufficient property, through selling their labour power to those with property or capital. Marx recognised the existence of various other classes but he saw their status as a transitional one. This notion has been very influential in sociology, even among non-Marxist sociologists who have refused to accept the two-class model. Perhaps most important in Marxian thinking is the emphasis on the fact that one's class position is not so much defined by one's income as by the part one plays in the way wealth is created in society. Weber followed a similar approach to this in so far as he regarded property or the lack of it as a basic feature. But he differed from Marx in that he gave an emphasis to both markets and production where Marx had concentrated on production. He also insisted on there usually existing a variety of classes.

Weber (1978) sees a class arising when a number of people share similar *life-chances* in the market.

LIFE-CHANCES

The ability to gain access to scarce and valued goods and services such as a home, food and education.

This ability to gain access to these benefits derives from the 'amount and kind of power, or a lack of such, to dispose of goods or skills for the sake of income in a given economic order'. The Weberian approach thus encourages us to differentiate between, say, a class of people who basically live off capital, senior and junior classes which manage, administer or provide professional services, a clerical and a shopkeeper class and a manual working class. But precisely which classes exist at any one time in any one society are a matter for empirical investigation and not simply for abstract analysis alone. And Weber recognised that alongside the objective aspect of social inequality which can be understood as 'class' is a subjective aspect whereby people are located hierarchically in society in terms of prestige or status.

STATUS

That aspect of social inequality whereby different positions are awarded different degrees of prestige or honour.

People belong to both classes and 'status groups', membership of the latter giving a certain amount of socially estimated honour or prestige. In practice, says Weber, class and status positions tend to coincide, but he insists that this need not necessarily be the case and we can indeed see cases where some disjuncture occurs in the ethnic or religious status groupings that exist within industrial capitalist societies. For example, a successful entrepreneur of visibly different ethnic background from the main population may well not be placed in the same subjective or 'status' ranking as a member of the majority population who, by virtue of their being similarly placed in economic terms, has an identical class position. Class, then, whilst a key element in the 'stratification' of modern societies has to be seen in conjunction with and interlinked with other issues such as gender and ethnicity, and changes in patterns of inequality need to be understood not just in terms of technological and managerial changes but also in terms of challenges to ruling interests that come from struggles by women, ethnic minorities and other socially excluded groups (Crompton 1998).

In both Marx and Weber, social class is seen in terms of power rivalries and conflict. Weber has traditionally been read as identifying a three-fold shape to inequalities; class, status and 'party'. But Scott (1996) valuably re-reads 'party' as *command* and uses this to emphasise the influence on people's life-chances of 'the differentials of power that are inherent in structures of authority'. There is, then, a dynamic dimension to social and economic inequality as a result of the struggles which go on between different groupings in production and in markets. This contrasts with a popular 'common-sense' view of inequality which sees the different types of reward which are attached to different occupations as being simply a matter of what is needed to motivate people to do socially important kinds of work. Such an explanation of social stratification took an influential academic form in the *functionalist theory of social stratification* (Davis and Moore 1945). This suggested that occupational roles vary in terms of their importance to the overall functioning of society (or to the 'common good', if you prefer) and those which require of their members greater individual application, motivation and willingness to undergo long training are more highly rewarded, materially and in terms of satisfactions, comforts, and status. Among the numerous problems with this theory is the basic one that it ignores the issue of power and the way occupations, 'professions' and trade unions struggle to achieve the level of status and reward their members enjoy. It also ignores the extent to which efforts by these groups may be contested and resisted by other groups.

Overall, the study of occupational structure involves classifying occupations horizontally, vertically, or in a way which mixes both of these. The categories developed are used to do various things, including examining the numbers of people covered by certain sectors or socioeconomic groups, the mobility of people between different categories, the characteristics of people in various positions in terms of such criteria of gender, race and age and, especially, the way these patterns change over time. All of these factors are central to understanding the social structure and processes of change occurring in society at large. We shall now look at some of the major changes that have been suggested.

Labour market segmentation, contingent, atypical or non-standard work

As we observed in Chapter 3 one of the main distinguishing features of an industrial capitalist society is that labour, or 'labour power', is treated as a commodity to be bought and sold on the market. This makes it vital to relate matters of occupational structure to the principles that underlie the operation of labour markets. It is also necessary to recognise the economic and political difficulties faced in industrialised societies generally that put pressures on how work is organised and how the overall division of labour is 'managed'.

When Fordist principles of organising employment practices and state welfare and economic policies were at their height in the middle period of the twentieth century, there was a tendency for solutions to tensions arising over labour market inequalities and competitive actions of organised labour to be sought by governments following *corporatist* principles.

CORPORATISM

A political system in which major decisions, especially with regard to the economy, are made by the state in close association with employer, trade union and other pressure group organisations.

As Goldthorpe (1985) observed, a variety of factors including inflationary pressures, saw a move of emphasis away from corporatism towards *dualism*.

DUALISM

The effective division of an economy into two major parts; typically a prosperous and stable 'core' sector of enterprises and jobs and a 'peripheral' sector which is relatively and systematically disadvantaged.

Whereas corporatism deals with the problems posed by major economic interest groups, and organised labour in particular, in an 'inclusionary' way – by involving them in forming and implementing economic policy – dualism works on 'exclusionary' lines. Here, the increased power of organised interests is offset by the creating or expanding of groups of workers (and potential workers) who lack effective organisation or the potential to mobilise themselves. A major source of dualism would be that of migrant labour which can provide employers with a flexible, tractable and generally quiescent source of labour supply (e.g. Doeringer and Piore 1971). This acts not only as an 'industrial reserve army' but as a labour force susceptible both to market forces and the changing needs of employers and managers. Goldthorpe saw the trend towards dualism going further than this, however, and related it to the general trend in Western societies – very closely connected to the managerial pursuit of *flexibility* that was examined in Chapter 5 (pp. 111–9) – whereby production is subcontracted and various types of temporary and part-time labour are employed on terms which push them towards a 'secondary' category within the overall labour market.

The logic of a division between *core* and *peripheral* work was clear in the analysis in Chapter 5 of pressures on employers' attempts to increase the flexibility of their operations. However, the patterns of employment that become apparent when the overall occupational pattern is examined show that matters are more complex than a simple core/periphery distinction would imply – a distinction which has been associated with one between *standard* and *non-standard* employment.

STANDARD EMPLOYMENT

Employment in which the contract between the employer and employee is understood to be one in which the employee is likely to stay with the employer over the long term at a particular location, putting in a working day and week which is normal for that industry and receiving regular pay and the protection of pension and sick pay benefits.

NON-STANDARD EMPLOYMENT

Employment in which the contract between employer and employee is short-term and unstable with the worker taking part-time, temporary and, sometimes, multiple jobs – the work sometimes being at home rather than in an organisationally located workplace and there being little by way of employment benefits.

Sometimes the term 'contingent work' is used for non-standard work, to recognise that the availability of short-term and unstable employment, in which there is a minimal attachment between employer and worker, is dependent or 'contingent' on employers' need for labour at a particular time (Kalleberg 2000; Gallagher 2002).

In spite of broad expectations that standard forms of employment would decline with the inexorable pressure for increased flexibility, research evidence suggests a considerably greater degree of continuity than might have been expected. Gallie *et al.* (1998) showed that the British temporary workforce expanded in only a limited way above the 5 per cent level of the previous decade and a half, and they observed that many of the part-time jobs in the economy (which indeed increased by 25 per cent between 1984 and 1995) could be seen as relatively permanent and hence not be carelessly put into the 'temporary' category. This analysis warns us to be careful about assuming that work that does not follow the standard full-time model is homogeneous. And statistical evidence also questions the assumption that there is a significant trend towards polarisation of standard and non-standard jobs. Dex and McCulloch (1997), for example, showed that although by the mid-1990s half of working women and a quarter of working men were in non-standard jobs, the pace of change in employment practices (the most significant shifts in this having taken place in the 1980s) was slowing down and the standard type of employment growing rather than declining. Later surveys confirm this, and although there is a significant expansion in various forms of homeworking (see below, pp. 156–7), emerging evidence from the British 'Change in Employer Practices' survey suggests that the 'overwhelming majority of paid jobs remain full-time and permanent and physically located in a specific place of work' (Taylor 2002).

Although the survival of the 'standard' job can be related to the pressures of tightening labour markets (Taylor 2002) it can also be related to the fact that the 'flexibility' that employers increasingly require is not just the type of *flexibility for short-term predictability* that might encourage an increase in non-standard employment. As we saw in Chapter 5 employers are also pressured to seek *flexibility for long-term adaptability* – this clearly fitting better with secure and 'standard' employment arrangements. And the evidence from case studies of changing employment practices *within* work organisations suggests that the flexibility 'gains' sought by employers are significantly being achieved from within their apparently 'standard' workforces, this involving, for example, work intensification, longer or more varied working hours and the need to multi-task and become multi-skilled (Burchell *et al*. 1999).

The demise of occupation?

There is clearly a trend for workers with security of employment and a relatively high level of rewards to work flexibly, not just in the tasks they take on, but in the skills which they acquire and use. One implication of such a trend, combined as it is likely to be with the growth of teamworking and a commitment to philosophies of 'continuous improvement' and involvement in the values of a corporate culture (Chapter 5, pp. 129–31), is what Casey (1995) calls the demise of occupation. In her study of the Hephaestus corporation she shows how its former specialists in mechanical and electrical engineering, in computing science, in chemistry and maths were 'crossing former professional demarcations and performing a range of duties in the team structure that promotes team responsibility for product development'. Casey claims that there has not yet been a full recognition of the social and self-identity implications of the decline of specialist occupations as 'persons from expert professions along with those from trade and service occupations are being transformed into multifaceted, pan-occupational team players in the new corporate organisation'. The social bonding which was provided by occupational status is being taken over by 'the identificatory processes of the new corporation'.

This trend takes increasing numbers away from having a job in what is clearly becoming an especially historically specific sense of the term 'job' – a sense in which the individual has an ongoing relationship with an employer who pays a wage or salary for the performance of tasks which utilise a set of occupational skills which more or less remain constant over the period of employment. Bridges (1995) sees this as a trend towards the dejobbed organisation and those who, in the changing patterns of work organisation, remain in employment will increasingly 'work full-time under arrangements too idiosyncratic to be called jobs'. A 'redeployment manager' of a company producing microprocessors is quoted as saying that they 'no longer look at a job as a function or a certain kind of work [but] as a set of skills and competencies'. This is similar to what was observed in a study of a British telecommunications company in which the very word 'job' was deliberately being removed from the corporate vocabulary (Watson 2001a). According to what Bridges calls the 'new rules' of work organisation, everyone is a contingent worker, not just the part-timers and contract workers; everyone's employment 'is contingent on the results that the organisation can achieve' and individuals will tend to work in project teams made up of people with different backgrounds. This experience is one in which 'workers must be able to switch their focus rapidly from one task to another, to work with people with very different mindsets, to work in situations where the group is the responsible party and the manager is only a co-ordinator, to work without a clear job description, and to work on several projects at the same time'.

Just how these patterns of employment and changing occupational activity are experienced and interpreted by the workers involved in them – like the trends and patterns themselves – is less straightforward than they might seem. Interpretations and experiences must be understood within the work orientations of particular groups and individuals (Chapter 7, pp. 186–94). However, we do not completely turn away in the present chapter from issues connected with the part-time dimension of 'non-standard' work: it is very relevant to the gender issues to which we now turn and, especially, to the question of the extent to which women in particular 'choose' or are pressured into part-time work.

Women and men in the division of labour

Changing historical patterns

The distinction between male and female roles in both the working and the non-working spheres of life is generally understood to have been much less stark in pre-industrial and pre-capitalist Europe before the modern separation of home life and working life came about. In the feudal period the home and work spheres were generally one, with both men and women contributing to furtherance of the family's economic interests, whether these were simply a matter of economic survival in the case of the peasantry or one of the maintenance of superiority and honour among the nobility. But this unity of home and work and of production and consumption was eroded as the economic basis of social life changed (Kanter 1989). The steady conversion of the peasantry into wage labour meant that female tasks of bearing and suckling children could less easily be combined with the productive work which was increasingly being performed in a setting away from the home. Where women could obtain work, their vulnerability to exploitation was much greater than that of men who were, in effect, 'biologically freer'.

These general trends took place at different rates in different industries and in different areas (Tilly and Scott 1978). In certain contexts, women employees were preferred to men and in some areas there was a pattern of employing family units (Joyce 1980). Nevertheless, the trend was towards women becoming increasingly dependent on men and, at times, when the wages of male manual workers became too low to support wives and children, these became a charge on the community. In middle-class circles, the women were not being left at home as domestic drudges as were working-class women but as 'useless' domestic decorations or bearers of male property-inheritors. In the more recent stages of industrial capitalist development where middle-class homes largely lost their ability to employ servants and where working-class wages made it more possible for males to support non-employed wives and children, it more or less became the cultural norm for women to play the domestic role whilst men 'went out to work' and earned the basic family income. We will return to contemporary patterns of relationships between home and working lives, but, at this stage, we need to recognise the extent to which the idea that only men 'go out to work' has changed in recent decades.

Contemporary patterns

Women play a very major part in the employed workforces of industrial societies with a considerable increase in the extent of women in paid work having come about over the past century. Yet, as Hakim's (1993, 2000) statistical analysis shows, there has been considerable continuity in the proportion of women in full-time work. She observes a decrease in both the proportion of women 'staying at home' and those pursuing full-time work careers as more and more part-time jobs have become available with the increasing flexibility of labour markets. Approaching half of the workforce is now female in Britain (Walby 1997; Crompton 1997) and in other advanced industrial capitalist societies (Drew *et al.* 1998) with married women, including those with children, forming a considerable proportion of this. In addition to increased employment flexibility leading to many more part-time jobs, disproportionately taken up by women, there has been growth in service jobs of the type with which women have traditionally been associated. This has been accompanied by the decline in manufacturing jobs, with which men have typically been associated, this not being unrelated to the increase in male unemployment – a situation that has seen a significant move away from the 'male breadwinner' pattern of family economy and the rise of the dual earning pattern. Bradley's (1999) study of the north east of England found two-thirds of the women covered reporting that their incomes were essential for the household and over a quarter assessing them as 'important'.

Despite this considerable change in the extent of work activities of women in advanced societies, patterns of occupational segregation have changed to a much lesser degree – men, broadly speaking, tending to do 'men's work' and women tending to do 'women's work'.

OCCUPATIONAL SEGREGATION

A pattern of occupations in which some are predominantly male and others female. Horizontal segregation describes the tendency for male and female work to be separated into types of occupational activity whilst vertical segregation sees gender differentiation in who takes the higher level and who takes the lower level jobs within an occupation.

Although basic patterns of segregation have not changed, there has been significant change in certain high status occupations such as law, accountancy and medicine – and to some extent management – with women's increased participation in higher education providing a new supply of qualified female workers (Walby 1997; Crompton 1997). However, when it comes to who fills the most senior posts in these occupational areas, we see the force of vertical segregation coming into play, with few women reaching the top jobs in the professional areas where they have increasingly played a part at the lower and middle levels (Wilson 1999a). As Evetts (1996) observes, in scientific and engineering occupations, women's advancement faces the problem that senior positions within such occupations are likely to involve an emphasis on managerial work rather than strictly 'professional' activities. Such managerial work was very much defined as a masculine activity, with those women who did become managers still being identified as 'women managers' rather than simply as 'managers'.

If we note the traditional association of women with the less pleasant and the more onerous work tasks in the home and we put this alongside the fact that men in employment are more or less in control of the better rewarded and higher status jobs, we can see why men might be expected to want to 'keep women in their place'. Research among male managers, for example, shows a tendency for men to 'work late' not just to demonstrate how committed and important they are to the company, but also to avoid arriving home before the children have been fed, bathed and got ready for bed (Watson 2001a). Casey noted the importance to men who wished to demonstrate their commitment to her case study organisation of their cars being seen in the car park at the weekend and early in the morning, as well as in the evening. We can readily link this behavioural pattern to structural aspects of society if we remember that the people making the employment decisions within industrial capitalist societies are men – with many of these 'organisation men' showing 'extreme devotion to company and career', a commitment 'facilitated by the servicing work of secretaries and wives' (Roper 1994). And this servicing work includes emotional support given by wives and secretaries to help men maintain the appropriate masculine image of a character 'driven by intellect' rather than by emotion. As Wajcman's (1998) study shows, women striving to succeed in managerial work are not only pressured to work the hours that only men with supportive wives, or women without families, can devote to work, they have to 'act like men' in a whole variety of formal and informal ways, ranging from the clothes they wear to the topics they chat about. All of this creates a social atmosphere that helps constitute the 'glass ceiling' present in many organisations – one that encourages women to leave jobs for ones where a less male-dominated culture prevails (Marshall 1995). If women managers are also members of a minority ethnic group, it is more a concrete rather than a 'glass ceiling' upon which they find themselves hitting their heads (Davidson 1997).

The complex interplay between domestic identities and working patterns is not only seen at senior levels, it is important to note. A study which skilfully illustrates this point is that of the development, manufacture, marketing and use of the microwave oven carried out by Cockburn and Ormerod (1993):

• In the microwave factory, the female 'home economists' have different inputs from male designers and, indeed, a degree of tension exists between these groups.
• In the shops, women shop assistants sell functional 'white goods' like microwaves whilst the entertainment-oriented 'brown goods' (hi-fi's, etc.) are sold by male assistants, this being based on the alleged affinities of women and men salespersons to the gendered interests of the respective purchasers of these two types of product.
• In the home, there is the gender politics of food preparation in which men tend to make use of the oven but only within understandings that leave the main food-providing responsibilities to women.

Managers are keen to recruit what Jenkins (1986) calls 'predictable manageable workers' thereby both creating and being influenced by general patterns of gender discrimination. Detailed case study research by Collinson *et al.* (1990) shows the considerable extent to which private sector managers, often in defiance of legal and organisational equal opportunities policies, blatantly excluded women from what they saw as 'men's jobs' and seemingly shamelessly utilised rationalisations for this which focused on the allegedly greater reliability and ability of men. Women's biology, their temperaments and their unreliability in the face of domestic commitments all rendered them less desirable for certain jobs – regardless of evidence which might have indicated to them otherwise. All of these assumptions about masculinity and femininity play their parts in the everyday interactions that occur in workplaces and help achieve what Collinson and Hearn (1996) call the 'gendering of organisations'. The discourses used both draw upon and contribute to the social construction of masculinities and femininities in the broadly gendered way in which the whole of work and social life is organised (Alvesson and Du Billing 1997). Patterns of gender relations with regard to work therefore go beyond what occurs in employing organisations.

Work occurs in the home as well as in the workplace, and we will look at this below (pp. 156–8). But significant findings on gender roles have also emerged from research on those involved with small businesses. Scase and Goffee (1982) showed that wives of men who had established and were running such businesses tended to be economically, socially and psychologically subordinated to the needs of their husbands and that, without the largely unrecognised contributions of wives, many small businesses 'would not even get off the ground'. Not only do the wives contribute unpaid time and effort to the business, they are left to cope single-handedly with domestic work, often with limited financial resources, as their husband devotes himself to the fledgling business. And Baines and Wheelock (2000) show in their study of 'micro businesses' how spouses typically work together to run the enterprise but rarely do so on the basis of equality. When women entrepreneurs themselves are studied, they do not appear to get anything like the degree of support from their husbands that entrepreneurial men get from their wives. Stoner *et al.* (1990) suggest that husbands are generally 'unhelpful' in this context and that work–home conflicts are common. Goffee and Scase (1985) said that their interviews with such women suggest that husbands rarely contribute to the running of either homes or businesses. The women are nevertheless forced to be dependent on men for financial and technical assistance. This is a pattern that is socially reinforced by such experiences as those, which Vokins (1993) reported, of successful women entrepreneurs approaching banks for assistance: '"Where is your husband" was a frequent question, as were the condescending and sexist comments like "Well, do your best dear"'. Businesswomen are liable to be reminded in such ways of their subordination in the sexual division of labour, as are the women married to men in occupations varying from the church or medicine to farming, military service or fishing where wives are often incorporated into their husbands' careers (Finch 1983).

The relationship between the work aspects and the domestic or personal aspects of the lives of men and women, and the way both of these play a part in how they shape their identities and make whatever choices are available to them, are complex and vary across class situations and occupational settings. Whether the focus is on large employing organisations or upon smaller businesses, it is necessary to note how relations between women and men in work contexts are 'embedded in a broader social context' (Fletcher

2000). A useful way of pulling many of these factors together is the *total social organisation of labour* concept developed by Glucksmann (1995, 2000). To understand gender aspects of social and employment change it is suggested that the starting point should not be one of focusing separately on the division of tasks in the different spheres of home and work but of considering all the work done in a society whether it be paid, unpaid, permanent, casual, part-time, full-time, productive, 'reproductive' and whether it be carried out in domestic, organisational spheres, or wherever. Only when we adopt this position, and reject the automatic assumption of two 'separate spheres', will we come fully to understand the ways in which work meanings and personal identities are shaped – and the part that gender relations play in all of this.

Explaining patterns

To understand the differences between the work activities or experiences of women and men in society we have to recognise the interplay that occurs between factors that relate to the prevailing type of economic system and the more universal factors relating to relationships between men and women. To put it very simply, it could be said that the patterns currently prevailing in industrial capitalist societies serve both the interests of the employers as employers and the interests of men as men. The maintenance of women's relatively disadvantaged market position can be seen as functioning in three ways.

1 it provides employers with a relatively cheap and malleable labour force;
2 it reduces the number of potential competitors which aspiring males face in their work careers;
3 it avoids attracting too many women away from the domestic setting which would either leave men without wives or would require them to take on the dirtier and more boring household tasks.

This kind of explanatory framework for looking at how the sexual division of labour operates in industrial capitalist societies usefully relates occupational patterns back to the wider pattern of inequality which prevails between the sexes in society at large. What it does not do, however, is to help us understand how male members of society came to achieve the kinds of advantage which it sees them having over women in the first place. To understand this is a much more challenging matter.

The first difficulty we have to overcome with regard to the problem of explanation is that of separating the particular pattern of male–female relations which exists in any one society or time from the more general patterns which run through all kinds of society. The importance of considering the particularities of the basic form of economic organisation, in ways like this, is effectively illustrated by the case of the !Kung bush people of Africa. Draper (1975) observed that, as these people changed from a nomadic foraging type of economy to a more settled pattern in which the women engaged in agriculture and the men in herding, so could women be seen to lose the high degree of power and autonomy which they had held in the bush life. Whereas they had been mobile and independent workers in the bush, they were now less mobile and soon became tied to the home. There was an increase in domestic tasks to be done in the more settled existence and this became designated as the province of the women. The men, however, developed an 'aura of authority' and distanced themselves from the domestic world. In the place of the egalitarian pattern of childrearing followed in the bush came a more gender-differentiated pattern in which the lives of girls were more narrowly defined than those of the boys. The girls' world was to be the domestic one.

Underlying this kind of 'particular' process we have to find some general factor, or set of factors, which encouraged these tribes-people to adopt this type of sexual division of labour or encouraged the corresponding pattern to be followed historically in Europe with the growth of industrial capitalism. An important starting point for understanding these matters can be found in the observation of the anthropologist, Margaret Mead (1962), that a problem which faces all men, in all civilisations, is that of defining their role in a way which they feel is satisfactory to them. Women have a key role which is defined by nature: that of childbearing. Men, on the other hand, have to create a role for themselves through culture in order to differentiate themselves from women. It is almost as if men have to compensate for the fact that they have no natural role as significant as that of bearing children and therefore feel the need to give themselves prestige and status through cultural institutions which award them a superior status. Explanations of the tendency of males to want to assert dominance in most societies and in most social settings within any society can also be found in accounts of the psychology of childrearing. Chodorow (1978), for example, has argued that the social and psychological differences between men and women go back to the fact that male children, unlike female children, have to achieve their identity by breaking away from the mother who has nurtured them and by building an identity which is distinctive. This involves a rejection of feminine patterns of behaviour but also a fear of regressing to their earlier state. Masculinity has to be worked at and, as Chodorow says, because masculine identity is so 'elusive', it becomes important that certain activities are defined as masculine and superior. Control of these activities and 'the insistence that these realms are superior to the maternal world of youth, become crucial both to the definition of masculinity and to a particular boy's own masculine gender identity'.

It follows from this phenomenon that, although societies vary in the particular details of gender relations, there tends to be a general pattern whereby men take up certain occupational roles from which they exclude women – most typically roles in government, warfare and religion. And, typically associated with this, will be an awarding of high status to these exclusively male occupations and a tendency to downgrade the domestic tasks of women. These two tendencies are often linked by a 'superstructure of myths' (Pickford 1985) in which women's prime place in social life is seen as that of protecting, nurturing and fostering the growth of others and in which it is suggested that women's biology somehow makes them unfit to perform as, say, politicians, priests or generals. The concept of patriarchy is helpful here, this stressing the interrelating of the variety of aspects of relationships between men and women – paid work, domestic work, male sexuality, male violence, state power – and how they amount to a fundamental pattern of inequality (Walby 1986).

PATRIARCHY

The system of interrelated social structures and cultural practices through which men exploit women.

Cultural support and legitimation of patterns of sexual division of labour developed historically with the growth of certain 'patriarchal ideologies'. Hamilton (1978) noted the effect of Protestant thinking in giving 'unprecedented ideological importance' to the home and the family and in establishing the ideal for women of the faithful and supportive 'proper wife'. By the nineteenth century this had evolved into a powerful 'domestic ideology' which enabled working wives and mothers to be presented as unnatural and immoral (Hall 1979).

Male interests and supporting ideologies have undoubtedly pressured women to think and act in particular ways with regard to work at all stages of history. But it is vital to avoid developing sociological explanations which emphasise determining structural factors at the expense of attention to human choices and, in this case, the meanings and orientation that women themselves bring to their lives. This is examined in Chapter 7 (pp. 192–4).

Occupational analysis

So far in this chapter the emphasis has been on the way we can analyse societies and how they are changing through examining occupational patterns and the division of labour. This continues to be a concern but the emphasis moves more towards looking at specific occupations or groups of occupations. The following questions can be asked when analysing any occupation:

1 How does the occupation fit into the broader structure of society?
2 How are people recruited to the occupation?
3 How are people socialised into the occupation?
4 What career paths are typically associated with the occupation?
5 What culture and ideologies are associated with the occupation?
6 Does engagement with the occupation involve members in a broader occupational community?
7 What strategies, if any, have been followed by members of the occupation; have there been attempts to acquire the label of a 'profession'?

The rest of this chapter is structured around this set of questions and the ways in which such questions have shaped research and theorising in the sociology of occupations. We turn, first, to the question of how occupations can be related to broader social, political and economic patterns.

The structural location of occupations

Locating an occupation in the class structure

We looked earlier at how researchers relate occupational and class positions in modern societies. But sociologists have also attempted to understand the processes whereby changes occur in this relationship. To do this, Giddens (1973) encourages us to follow Weber's preference for combining conceptual analysis with attention to the observable behaviour and the perceptions of the members of society at a particular time in his emphasis on processes of *class structuration*. In this he accepts that class consciousness and action do not automatically follow from the existence of economic divisions; the actual degree of structuration or 'classness' of a group depends on cultural and status factors as well as on economic structure. In this spirit, Roberts *et al.* (1977) interpreted their study of British class imagery in the latter decades of the twentieth century as showing that the class structure of Britain was fragmenting; and Marshall *et al.* (1988) argued that growing ambiguity, ambivalence and contradiction in people's class images were reflecting objective characteristics of an increasingly 'opaque' class structure.

Marshall *et al.* follow Weber in viewing the operation of the 'capitalist market' as the primary mechanism determining class processes and see three consequences for the class structure in changing patterns of investment and division of labour:

1   The ownership and control of capital is becoming more complex as family proprietorship gives way to pension funds, multinational companies, cartels and the like.
2   The differences between workers in various economic sectors is increasing as both the industrial structure and the labour force structure change.
3   The shedding of surplus labour during the recession has reinforced labour market segregation and in particular the boundary between those in relatively secure occupational or company careers and the unemployed and subemployed. As a result of all this, the owners and controllers of capital are less concrete and more distant, the occupational structure is more complex and manual/non-manual distinction is becoming less salient both sociologically and among the population at large.

In spite of this kind of complexity and growing 'opaqueness', it is still possible to locate occupations within the overall social structure, not least as a way of understanding the major structural changes which are occurring. It is possible to take insights from the various approaches to analysing social class to suggest that three basic factors influence how an occupation fits into the societal division of labour and to the general pattern of rewards which is associated with it. These three factors, which are closely interrelated in practice, are:

1   The contribution which an occupation makes to the carrying out of tasks which, if neglected, would undermine the general social order and, especially, the distribution of power and 'structure of advantage' associated with the overall social and economic system. This takes account of 'functionalist' arguments but replaces the social consensus emphasis of functionalist sociology with the important recognition of the part played by occupations in maintaining a specific structure of advantage. This factor has to be related to the next one.
2   The possession by the members of the occupation of a skill or other attribute which is scarce and marketable and which is more or less exclusive to the members of that occupation, or at least is believed to be exclusive in the relevant market. The way in which the occupation is controlled, through a professional body or a trade union, will be important here, not only in controlling and restricting supply but in persuading clients, employers or even the state that only the members of the occupation can or should apply the relevant skill or expertise. Associated with the latter aspect may be the third factor.

3 The existence of some traditional criterion of status or 'mystique' within the society's culture. This can be utilised by an occupation as in the case of undertakers or, especially, by the so-called professions where a great deal is made of tradition by such groups as lawyers or clerics.

With these various principles and these three specific factors in mind, we can now go on to look briefly at the societal location of several occupational groups and at some of the issues which face them with respect to this. In doing this, however, it is important to remember that the occupational principle, as was explained earlier, is only one of the two main principles of work structuring which operate in contemporary societies. It has to be seen alongside the 'organisational' principle considered in the previous two chapters. The future division of labour and the fortunes of occupation will continue to be profoundly influenced by the strategies of employing organisations and the technological changes associated with these.

Managerial and administrative occupations

Managerial, administrative and associated 'expert' occupations have been seen by many commentators as forming part of a new 'technocracy' and as playing an increasingly significant role in the control of enterprises as the *separation of ownership and control* has allegedly increased following the appearance of the joint stock company in the nineteenth century (Galbraith 1972). In the words of Burnham (1945), a *managerial revolution* is said to have come about. It is argued that the specialist knowledge and skills of managerial experts have become crucial to the successful running of the increasingly large and complex business corporations and public bureaucracies. The dominance of the owners of wealth is therefore undermined and a new class of professional salaried managers is said to be exercising significant control. Enteman (1993) goes as far as to argue that modern societies are, in effect, constituted by the decisions of those who 'manage' governments, corporations and other organisations.

The 'managerialist' thesis, as it is sometimes called, has tended to claim a fundamental change in the division of labour and the structure of advantage.

THE MANAGERIALIST THESIS

The claim that the people who manage or 'direct' the corporations of modern societies have taken control away from those allegedly separate interests who own wealth.

Research evidence from America and other countries was effectively used by Zeitlin (1989) to dismiss the thesis of the managerial revolution and to establish that the claim of a separation of ownership and control is a 'pseudo fact'. He pointed out that 'growth, sales, technical efficiency, a strong competitive position are at once inseparable managerial goals and the determinants of high corporate profits'. These corporate profits are the prerequisites of high managerial income and status. The high status and material rewards which can be achieved by membership of a managerial occupation are dependent on the contribution made to profit achievement or at least to the continued survival of the corporation in a context where too great a deviation from profitable performance would lead to collapse or takeover. The ownership of wealth and the control of work organisations are closely related, on the basis of this kind of evidence. It is the case, however, that ownership of enterprises is far more dispersed than it was in the past with, as Scott (1997) puts it, a transition having occurred in industrial capitalist societies 'from personal to impersonal forms of ownership and control'. Institutions such as banks, insurance companies and pension funds own companies rather than individuals or families. Yet this does not mean that control has shifted to managers. Although there are variations across different societies, family interests and broader 'constellations of interest' tend to ensure that the interests of owners generally tend to take priority over those of managers.

The growth of managerial and administrative occupations has not, then, had the degree of impact on the structure of industrial capitalist societies as some have claimed. Although managers do play their parts in, and benefit from, the 'constellations of interest' that hold sway, it would be wrong to suggest that all managers, at all levels, simply share the interests of the owners of capital or that they are simply and unequivocally the agents of capital. Managers simultaneously carry out certain functions on behalf of capitalist interests whilst having to defend themselves against corporate capital (Carter 1985). This can be illustrated by Smith's (1990) study of middle managers in an American bank. A significant number of these managers clashed with the top management of the bank over organisational issues and implemented different measures from those which they were directed to take. Their defiance was not however anything to do with questioning basic corporate goals. Instead, their actions were 'shaped by an alternative sense of the corporate interest'. Watson (2001a) shows, similarly, how managers in a British company disputed the particular decisions and styles of their corporate headquarters on the grounds both of their own interests (a desire to be more involved in strategic decisions) and those of the 'business as a whole'. Managers are *agents* of the owners of capital and this kind of research suggests that they seek ways of operating which recognise an affinity between their personal or group interests and the interests of those who employ them. This means that managerial and administrative occupations have to be seen as holding a distinctive position in the division of labour and in the class structure which distinguishes them from both ownership interests and working-class ones.

The notion of a 'service class' is one way of recognising this sociological principle (Goldthorpe 1982, 1995). This heterogeneous class contains several 'situses' (see pp. 136–7) and includes public service employees such as civil servants, managerial, administrative and technical experts in private businesses and employees in the social services. These people exercise power and expertise on the behalf of corporate authority yet they are 'proletarian' in that they are employees selling their services on the market. But their salaried employment is distinctively different from that of the wage-earning working class in three respects; they have relative security, they have prospects for material and status advancement, and their work involves a measure of trust and a 'code of service'. The role of this class in future social and political development is likely to be a significant one given that they are unlikely to ally with the manual groups (over whom they will tend to defend their advantage) whilst they will have no 'necessary preference for capitalism'

– they will only go along with it as long as it is a means to their maintaining their lot. Middle-class groups such as this are, however, becoming increasingly heterogeneous. Savage *et al.* (1992) identify three factors which influence the class circumstances of individuals within this broad category:

- Bureaucracy – their position within organisations, this varying with their positions as managers or 'professional' workers and whether they are in the public or private sectors.
- Property – with position in the housing market being important.
- Culture – where different lifestyles, values and political orientations are found among different segments of the middle class.

And Hanlon (1998) sees growing divisions and competition within the 'service class' category, these arising especially as a result of 'the struggle to redefine professionalism' in which different groups, ranging from health service to accountancy 'professionals', compete to legitimise the different types of cultural capital with which they are associated.

This mention of 'professionalism' takes us on to consider the position of non-managerial middle-class workers of varying status levels.

Professional, supervisory and clerical occupations

It may seem extravagant to bring together such a broad range of occupational types into a single category, especially given that the notion of 'professionalism' is to be dealt with later in its own right. The rationale for the present grouping is that these three occupational categories are often discussed sociologically to ascertain whether any particular section of this broad occupational category is moving 'up', 'down' or staying steady in the overall class structure. The alleged growth of 'post-industrial' or 'knowledge' societies led various writers to see society as becoming increasingly 'professionalised' as the locus of power moves from commercial organisations to those occupations upon whom society is more and more dependent for specialised knowledge and its application. This would enable members of knowledge-oriented occupations to improve their class and status position. Freidson (1994) recognised the potential for this to occur. He also observes tendencies towards polarisation, whereby certain occupational groups gain and others lose within processes of organisational, technological and economic restructuring. He does not accept the 'proletarianisation thesis' associated with writers like Braverman (1974) and Oppenheimer (1973).

PROLETARIANISATION

A trend whereby members of a 'middle-class' occupational group move downwards in the class and status hierarchy, finding themselves located in a position more like that of working-class rather than middle-class people.

The 'proletarianisation thesis' argues that professional work is becoming devalued as increasing fragmentation of work associated with an extensive division of labour brings 'experts' more under administrative control and hence treats them more like the traditional wage worker. But as Johnson (1977) valuably pointed out, both of these trends can occur simultaneously. Which way an occupation, or a part of one, goes is a matter of whether the knowledge or skills associated with it can be routinised, split down or taken over by machines and thus become identified with the 'collective labourer' or, alternatively, are such that the degree of uncertainty or 'indetermination' in the knowledge or skills is of a kind which cannot be routinised and devalued without interfering with the contribution it makes to the 'global functions' of capital.

Divergences within a previously common occupational position are a possibility which can arise in all kinds of administrative, technical and 'professional' work with the occurrence of technological change. It would be possible, for example, for certain branches of the accountancy occupation to be downgraded through, say, the computerising of routine operations whilst other branches might retain traditional advantages through their continued exercise of discretion and expert judgement at a strategic level in the management of capital. Similarly, in the spirit of science fiction, we might imagine the invention of a wonder medicine-machine which could cure all physical human diseases, disorders and injuries. This we can envisage leading to the rapid social and economic down-grading of medical practitioners whose expertise-dependent and critical role in the maintaining of the nation's health (and the health, therefore, of the labour force) had been severely curtailed. At the same time, it might be that the psychiatric branch of the medical profession, whose skills and mystique had not succumbed to technological change, continue to retain the prestige, income and occupational autonomy allowed them through their role in the maintenance of a 'sane' population of producers and consumers of goods and services.

The possibility of movements in either direction, in terms of class location, have been significant in sociologists' studies of clerical workers. The seminal analysis of the class situation of clerical workers was Lockwood's (1958) study of the 'blackcoated worker'. Accompanying a re-issue of the book, Lockwood (1989) reviewed the changes which occurred in the intervening decades. The most significant shift has been that clerical work has moved away from being a predominantly male occupation to being three-quarters female. He shows that rewards and working conditions for women clerks are superior to those of manual women workers and argues that the increasing coverage of routine tasks by women leads to a situation where young male clerical workers are experiencing very good promotion opportunities. There is a high degree of occupational mobility – through promotion or (women) leaving to start families – and little evidence of an overall lowering of skill levels. A simple proletarianisation thesis is not therefore supported. Nevertheless, Crompton and Jones (1984) concluded that white-collar work generally is seen as liable to proletarianisation in two ways: (1) as it gets more involved in the actual processes of production rather than the purchasing of labour-power to carry out that production; (2) as involvement in buying labour-power itself becomes routinised, deskilled and restricted by bureaucratic controls.

Supervisors or 'foremen' are a further group whose location has often been seen as problematic sociologically. The industrial foreman emerged out of the role of the labour contractor or piecemaster in the late nineteenth and early twentieth centuries (Littler 1982). Their emergence was not a straightforward one, however; some contractors became integrated into the organisation as a directly employed foreman, whilst others simply became workers or ended up as chargemen or leading hands. In spite of being a paid employee rather than a contractor, the traditional foreman hired, fired, set wages, planned and allocated work. This made him, says Littler, 'the undisputed master of his own shop', yet the role's 'power started to be eroded almost as soon as it had emerged from the decay of internal contract'. Incursions were soon made by various technical experts, inspectors and rate-fixers. This was followed by erosion by production engineers, personnel managers and the rest so that supervisors became reduced to a role as 'the man in the middle' (Roethlisberger 1945) in which they owe locality to both management and workers and yet are part of neither. Alternatively, the supervisor has been seen as the 'marginal man' of industry (Wray 1949) – the one who is held accountable for work carried out but who is excluded from managerial decision-making. One might expect all this to have changed with the growth of teamworking, a change in which control is allegedly moved downwards from supervisors to group members themselves. Yet comparative research in Britain, Germany and the USA suggests the change is not, as might be expected, predominantly one in which supervisors disappear from the scene. Instead, such innovations as 'lean production' and teamworking have the potential to free supervisors from having to deal with the day-to-day details of the workplace and 'help to restore the influence of supervisors in strategic decision-making which was lost in the early transition from craft to mass production' (Mason 2000).

Dirty and deviant occupations

In any society there are various jobs which have a clear and often necessary function within the overall division of labour but which are seen by the public as 'dirty' – either in a literal way or figuratively in that they are regarded as somehow morally dubious by the public (Hughes 1958).

> **DIRTY WORK**
>
> An occupational activity which plays a necessary role in a society but which is regarded in some respects as morally doubtful.

Thus the work of people like mortuary attendants, sewerage workers, prison guards or even police officers, can create problems for their members with regard to how they are received and accepted socially. Their position is a paradoxical one, in that they play a part in servicing the social order generally approved of by the same people who often prefer to avert their eyes from such occupations – or from their members. And the same could be said of other pursuits of a more dubious or even illegal nature, with pornographers, prostitutes and 'exotic dancers' helping to cope with sexual tensions which might otherwise threaten the respectable institution of marriage. These are often termed *deviant occupations*.

155

Many of the anxieties which arise for members of marginal occupations such as these may be seen as weaker versions of those which are experienced by people in more mainstream or 'respectable' occupations. It is not unknown, for example, for an estate agent, an undertaker or even an accountant to be as coy about their occupation in a social gathering as a lavatory cleaner or sewage farm worker. In the following sections of this chapter the lead of the Chicago school in the sociology of work (Chapter 2, pp. 34–5) will be followed by taking a number of illustrations from marginal or deviant occupations to illustrate principles applying to occupations in general, recognising that, as Hughes (1958) puts it, 'processes which are hidden in other occupations come more readily to view in these lowly ones'.

Self-employment, home and teleworking

Associated with the notion of 'standard employment' is the idea of people leaving their home each day to work for an employer in the workplace owned and managed by that employer. However, a growing proportion of workers in contemporary societies work in a home-based way without being formally employed by a single employer. In spite of surface similarities between such workers it is vital not to regard people in this category as occupying a broadly similar occupational position: lumping together, say, a woman assembling children's garments from sections delivered to their front door by a business which pays them by the piece, a painter and decorator whose home is their office and paint store, a regional sales manager who co-ordinates sales workers from an office in their house, and a computer specialist developing software applications for one or two companies with which they have long-term contracts. When we speak of 'homeworkers' we need to distinguish between people who are working 'at home' or 'from home', for example, and, especially important, we need to distinguish between those who are self-employed in the sense of having a product or service to sell on the market and those who, although formally designated as 'self-employed' have, in effect, a waged work relationship with the businesses with which they are employed (Felstead et al. 1996). Felstead and Jewson (2000) note the increase in both what they call 'industrial homeworking' and 'teleworking' in the last quarter of the twentieth century, estimating that about a quarter of the British workforce was working at home for some or all of the time towards the end of the century, with this expected to increase to 50 per cent in the subsequent decade.

Many of those in the industrial homeworking category and who are in a quasi waged-based relationship with an organisation tend to have regular relationships with the businesses which bring work to their houses, lack the legal protection and benefits of the formally employed, yet still experience the pressure of deadlines, productivity rates, piece work systems, and fragmented work tasks. As Allen and Wolkowitz (1987) observe, such arrangements not only reinforce gender patterns of inequality (given the predominance of women homeworkers) but lower both labour and capital costs of firms who adopt such a labour strategy. Such businesses have an advantage over ones conventionally employing people, and these competitive pressures, in turn, reinforce the tendency to casualise the work of those they employ as in-workers.

The industrial type of homeworking can be seen as close to the 'outworking' tradition which existed before the Industrial Revolution and the spread of the factory system. However, the use of computers and information technology to enable people to work at home or from home introduces a new variant of the old theme with clerical and 'professional' workers increasingly engaging in 'teleworking', 'telecommuting' or 'networking', where computers are used to link the home and the client organisation.

TELEWORKING

Work which is carried out away from the location of an employer or work contractor using electronic information and computing technology in either or both (a) carrying out the work tasks, (b) communicating with the employing or contracting organisation with regard to those tasks.

It would appear that teleworking involves a high proportion of people in 'senior' work, half of those identified in the British Labour Force Survey (IES 2000) being managers or professionals. However, the technology is such that it would be as amenable to use by routine clerical workers as it is to those doing more complex tasks. Teleworking, again, is not a homogeneous occupational category. And it is extremely important to remember that with all kinds of homeworking, work is not an individual activity that can simply be switched from a structured and organised workplace to a domestic setting. The workplace, as Jackson and Van der Wielen (1998) point out, is 'not primarily a *physical* location but the locus of *collective endeavour*', and that when telework has been introduced simply because it is technically feasible and economically desirable as a means of reducing office space and commuting costs, results have often been poor. With all types of homeworking, as Felstead and Jewson (2000) show, a great deal of what was formally 'managerial' responsibility falls on the homeworkers themselves and they can find it a considerable struggle to decide how and when to work, how to manage quality or health and safety standards, and so on, as well as to maintain the relationship both with people in the organisations to which they relate and the other people living in the household (see also Phizacklea and Wolkowitz 1995).

Domestic work

As we saw earlier, the separating of home and 'workplace' is a relatively recent historical development associated with the rise of industrialism. Nevertheless, work is still carried out in the home, as the evidence of most people's home lives readily demonstrates.

DOMESTIC LABOUR

Household tasks such as cooking, cleaning, shopping and looking after dependent young, old or sick members of the household.

The majority of full-time domestic workers are women who are located in the social division of labour with the title of 'housewife' and, as Williams (1988) observed, the definition of 'domestic labour' which dominates the literature is one of the 'unpaid work undertaken by women in their own households'. Since this is not a paid or employee occupation and since housewives experience widely varying social and material conditions in line with the varying economic positions of their spouses, it is far more difficult to locate economically and sociologically than most occupations. Feminists have nevertheless been concerned to come to terms with this problem, and considerable use has been made of Marxian concepts within what has come to be known as the 'domestic labour debate'.

Most of the protagonists in the debate agreed that housewives not only work for the sake of their husband and family but also work to contribute to the maintenance of the capitalist economic system by 'reproducing' the labour force through childbearing and by 'maintaining' the labour force through caring for husbands and children. However, the danger which arises if too much attention is paid to the contribution made by women's work in the home to 'capitalism' is that the crucial sexual politics of housework are played down. To deal with this, Delphy and Leonard (1992) argued that a distinction should be made between the industrial mode of production within which capitalist exploitation occurs and the domestic mode of production which provides the basis for patriarchal exploitation. Marriage is equivalent to the labour contract within employment and the husband can be seen as appropriating the labour-power of his wife just as the employer appropriates that of the worker. This kind of conceptualisation assumes the validity of Marxist assumptions about work and exploitation whilst expanding the category of 'work' to include emotional, cultural and sexual/reproductive work as well as directly economically productive work. But recognition of the problems which arise in the experiences and meanings of those engaged in full-time housework is not dependent on an acceptance of such assumptions. The work of housewives was analysed by Oakley (1974) as if it were an occupation like any other. She reported three-quarters of her sample of women as dissatisfied with their role and noted its loneliness, its monotony, its repetitiveness, its long hours, its low status, and the fact that tasks never seemed to be complete. Bonney and Reinach (1993), however, found a majority of houseworkers 'endorsing' the role. Women with young children experienced more of the negative features of the role than others. As these researchers say, their research stresses the need 'to appreciate the diverse, as well as the common, experiences of incumbents of the role of full-time houseworker'.

With the considerable increase in the proportion of women working outside the home which we noted earlier, it would be reasonable to expect that there would be a shift towards men and women sharing domestic tasks. Wheelock (1990), on the basis of a study in which the women were employed and the men were unemployed, suggested that the shifting pattern of paid work roles among men and women might indicate a trend towards a more egalitarian approach to domestic work. However, Morris (1988) reported her 'general impression . . . that within working-class culture there are strong feelings against male involvement in tasks commonly regarded to be essentially female'. Inevitably, the differing pictures emerging here are in part the outcome of different research designs. This was recognised by Warde and Hetherington (1993) who attempted in their investigation to produce evidence which could, as effectively as possible, be compared to material from the 1960s. This suggested that, with some qualification, 'gender stereotyping of specific work tasks and unequal contributions between men and women cannot have changed much in the last twenty years'. And Bond and Sales (2001) interpret survey evidence as showing that women carry a 'dual burden' of paid and unpaid work which 'disadvantages them in terms of employment, income and welfare'.

Such patterns appear to apply across social class boundaries. Edgell (1980) showed that the majority of the middle-class families he studied had a pattern of role segregation in which the wife 'typically performed a distinct range of domestic and child-rearing tasks considerably more often than the husband, and generally deferred to the husband's authority in the "more important" areas of decision-making'. The major influence on the pattern of role allocation was not the work or the family career cycles but the husband's orientation to paid work and the wife's orientation to domestic work. Again, the importance is demonstrated of the meaning which individuals attach to their work roles, whether these be employment or domestic. And this continues to apply, it would appear, when families are able to afford to employ domestic labour. The late 1980s in Britain saw a dramatic expansion in the use of waged domestic labour by high income dual-career households, according to Gregson and Lowe (1994a), whose research indicates that the employment of cleaners and nannies does not create a more egalitarian pattern of role allocation between men and women. What are emerging here are 'new domestic divisions of labour which involve just women' (Gregson and Lowe 1994b).

It remains to be seen how the activity of domestic labour, and how it is seen in society, will adjust to the increase in the numbers of 'house husband' domestic workers and the numbers of people brought into homes as paid domestic workers (Gregson and Lowe 1994a). Yet the evidence available so far is that whatever changes might be appearing are 'slow a-coming' with women continuing to 'perform a disproportionate amount of domestic and parenting work, even when they also undertake paid work' (Pilcher 2000). And Baxter (2000), on the basis of her Australian research evidence, suggests that it is helpful in trying to understand the 'slow pace of change' to look at women's 'subjective interpretations of the division of household tasks'. Although women in the study reported spending 24 hours per week on domestic work compared to men's reported 9 hours (and women spending twice as much time on childcare as men), 59 per cent of them said they felt this division to be a 'fair' one (compared to 68 per cent of men).

Work in the informal economy

When people are not formally employed or self-employed they do not necessarily cease to engage in working activities that might ameliorate material aspects of their unemployed status. And people who are formally employed might choose to supplement their incomes by working informally in their 'spare' time. Both groups are sometimes said to be working in the *informal economy* (also known as the 'black', 'hidden', 'subterranean' or 'irregular' economy).

THE INFORMAL ECONOMY

An area of economic exchange in which work, legal or illegal, is done for gain but is not officially 'declared' for such purposes as taxation.

There has been much argument about the extent and nature of the 'hidden economy', and the level of confusion which exists led Harding and Jenkins (1989) to question the very basis of the distinction between the formal and the informal. In so far as these both exist, however, they are interdependent as well as separate. This is illustrated in Pahl's (1984) studies in the Isle of Sheppey which showed that the benefits gained from the various kinds of informal economic activity occurring in this not untypical part of Britain accrued to those households in which there were already incomes from formal employment. This is clearly seen in 'self-provisioning' activities where the employed were much better able to brew their own beer or do their own decorating than the unemployed – who were less able to afford the materials. As in the formal business world, money is needed for investment before work is created, whether this be 'do-it-yourself' work or 'moonlighting' activities where tools, transport and raw materials are often needed to enable one to earn extra money 'on the side'. If this evidence is right, and it is supported by French evidence as Gallie (1985) mentions, then the informal economy is to be seen as functioning to reinforce a polarised pattern of 'haves' and 'have nots' in society rather than promising to undermine it.

Occupational recruitment and socialisation

The effect of occupational socialisation and the ways in which people 'learn the ropes' of particular occupations has been a key theme of writers in the interactionist tradition, and Becker *et al.* (1961) in their classic study of medical students showed how groups facing common problems and situational pressures tend to develop certain common perspectives or 'modes of thought and action'. A peer group pressure on the individual's orientation to work is thus created.

OCCUPATIONAL SOCIALISATION

The process whereby individuals learn about the norms, values, customs and beliefs associated with an occupation which they have joined so that they are able to act as a full member of that occupation.

Most people's work socialisation is not as specifically 'occupational' as that of medical students, however. A large proportion of people are recruited into work and trained by an employing organisation. Although this may emphasise a 'trade' or a type of 'professional work' it is much more likely to concentrate on the specific organisational tasks in which they will engage rather than on occupational characteristics of the work. The occupational principle nevertheless retains sufficient force for us to recognise the existence of various patterns of recruitment and socialisation which are essentially occupational rather than organisational.

OCCUPATIONAL RECRUITMENT

The typical processes and routes of entry followed by members of an occupation.

Certain occupations will restrict their entry in terms of the recruit's age. This often came about in the past through trade stipulations with regard to apprenticeships – something which served as a protection for members of that occupation by presenting a barrier to sudden or uncontrolled recruitment into the occupation. The stipulation of youth may also help with the problem of socialising new members of the occupation, not only in terms of learning skills but in order to aid the acquisition of appropriate attitudes and values. This is as likely to apply to a professionally oriented occupation as much as to a trade-based one. In some cases the age requirement may relate to the physical attributes necessary in the occupation as would be the case with professional sportsmen, dancers, models or air hostesses (Hochschild 1985).

Associated with age requirements may be certain educational or qualification barriers to occupational entry. This may be specific to the skills to be developed in the occupation – the requirement of some certification of mathematical ability in the case of engineering apprentices for example – or it may have far less specific functions. Dalton (1959), in his study of industrial managers, for example, pointed out that the 'total experience of going to college' may be more relevant to occupational success than the technical content of what is learned. The future executive learns, as a student, how to analyse their teacher's expectations and manoeuvres, how to utilise social contacts, how to cope with competition, meet deadlines, co-operate with others, cope with intangibles and ambiguities and make rapid adjustments to frequently encountered new personalities and situations. There equally may be a degree of occupational *pre-socialisation* in this sphere. This is suggested by Marceau's (1989) study which observed how common it was for her European business graduates to have been infused with business values and aspirations and inspired by the examples of their successful relatives. The majority of these graduates of a leading and prestigious European business school had fathers or grandfathers who had held senior business positions. The relevance of educational background for entry to elite occupations and the social class and family implications of attendance at prestigious schools and universities has been widely demonstrated. Salaman and Thompson (1978) closely examined the behaviour of officers engaging in recruitment for commissions in the British Army and noted the 'inevitable residue of flexible ad hoc practices' which takes place within what is claimed to be an objective and scientific selection procedure. These practices ensure that class and cultural factors intrude into the apparently 'neutral' procedure so helping the 'legitimised perpetuation of a social elite' in this occupational elite.

It is clear that a variety of patterns of occupational recruitment exist, ranging from the very formal to the very casual. The casual nature of the recruitment process is stressed, for example, in the case of striptease dancers by Skipper and McCaghy (1970). Occupational entry here is 'spontaneous, nonrational, fortuitous, and based on situational pressure and contingencies'. The appeal of monetary reward urged upon them by agents, friends and others encourages them to move on from work as singers, dancers, models and the like, to stripping. People may well 'end up' in an occupational setting simply because they have found no alternative. Gabriel (1988) shows this to be the case for most of the workers in his study of catering; they had 'an instrumental orientation *thrust upon* them by unrewarding jobs and the lack of alternatives due to the economic slump'. Few had systematically looked for alternatives; 'Age, lack of qualifications and training, poor command of the language, the chores of housekeeping and the need to look after children outside school hours, all compounded the feeling that "there is no alternative".'

Once the typical pattern of recruitment to a given occupation has been noted attention can be turned towards the way in which people acquire occupationally relevant knowledge (Coffey and Atkinson 1994) and generally 'learn the ropes' (Geer *et al.* 1968) of the particular milieu which has been entered. Richman (1983) showed how traffic wardens only really learn the ropes once their formal training is over and they begin to collect 'a repository of information and collective wisdom' by means of an accumulation of 'stories from the street'. The more coherent and socially self-conscious the occupation the more likely is there to be an initiation ceremony at some turning point in this socialisation process and the more pressing will be the need to learning the special language, formal and informal rules, and attitudes of the group as well as the technical skills involved in the work. The informal rules, values and attitudes associated with an occupation are of great importance in helping the newcomer to adjust to the exigencies of the occupation which has been entered. Becker and Geer (1958), for example, observed the way in which the low status of the medical student within the hospital setting was adjusted to by the students through their suspension of the idealism with which they entered their training and its replacement by a relative cynicism which pervaded the student culture. The idealism which re-asserted itself later as the students moved closer to graduation and professional practice is consequently a more realistic one than had previously existed – an idealism which would not have helped the practitioner cope with difficulties to be confronted in the real world of medical practice.

A significant element of cynicism developed by the socialisation process is also suggested by Bryan's (1965) study of the 'apprenticeship' of call girls – an apprenticeship which has little to do with skills and is aimed at developing appropriate values and rules. Central to these values are those which stress the maximisation of gain for a minimum of effort and which evaluate people in general and men in particular as corrupt (the prostitute thus becoming defined as no more reprehensible than the public at large). Rules which follow from this include the regarding of each customer as a 'mark' and avoiding emotional involvement or pleasure with the client. In addition to learning relatively practical matters such as strategies to avoid violence (McKeganey and Barnard 1996), the prostitute learns to take on what Phoenix (1999) calls a 'prostitute identity' and see themselves as workers or 'rational-economic agents' as well as 'commodified bodies'. We see here a significant *emotional* element to the socialisation process and this is also stressed in Hill's (1992) study of people becoming managers. This, she says, is 'both an intellectual and emotional exercise' with the managers being as 'desperate for help in managing the new position's emotions and stresses' as for help in solving business problems. Managers' interlinked personal and occupational identities are continually *emergent* and the 'managerial learning' that occurs once in a managerial occupation often relates back to learning experiences occurring throughout their earlier lives (Watson and Harris 1999).

The socialisation process which the occupational entrant both undergoes and participates in will contribute to the extent to which the individual identifies with and becomes committed to the occupation. Becker (1960) uses the term *investment* to conceptualise the processes by which commitment can come about. This can refer to the investment in time, effort and self-esteem which the individual makes in his job and in acquiring the relevant skills but it also covers a series of 'side bets' which are external to the occupation itself but which discourage movement out of the job which might break up friendship networks, disturb children's schooling, and so on. A factor which may either encourage or discourage individuals' commitment to an occupation is the career structure which they find associated with it.

Occupational careers

As we shall see in Chapter 7, we can understand the way in which people achieve a sense of coherence in their working lives through the use of the idea of the 'subjective career'. However, the structural context which influences that processual self-view may be the objective career pattern provided by either an occupation or an organisation. These two are frequently related but, here, we are concerned with the occupational dimension.

OCCUPATIONAL CAREER

The sequence of positions through which the member of an occupation typically passes during the part of their life which they spend in that occupation.

Different positions within an occupation generally involve different levels of prestige and give varying levels of reward of various other material and psychological kinds. We therefore tend to see careers in terms of the upward, downward or horizontal movement which they imply for the individual. It is commonplace to observe that many professional and administrative occupations provide career structures of a 'ladder' type; a series of positions of improving status and reward through which the successful individual can expect to move. But other occupations involve quite different career patterns. For many manual workers there may be little change in the work done over the whole of a working career and, although a certain status may accrue from 'seniority' in later years, it is just as likely that rewards may decrease as physical strength falls off.

It is an important part of the analysis of any given occupation to note just what shape the typical career, or variety of careers, may take. We may note, for example:

- the relative shortness of the typical career of the sportsperson, dancer, soldier or policeman;
- the insecurity of the typical career of the actor;
- the risks involved in certain entrepreneurial careers.

These are all factors which must seriously influence the orientation to work of the occupational member. Involvement in the occupation of lorry driver, for example, holds promise of advancement from initial shunting work to tramping and then to trunking but is later likely to return to the earlier lower-status shunting work (Hollowell 1968). Of course, any one occupation can offer more than one typical career pattern, depending on certain characteristics of the individual and various other career contingencies. The high-class call-girl, for instance, may progress to work as a madam, given the appropriate abilities and opportunities, or she may be reduced to the status of a street-walker – the difference between these two 'career grades' of prostitution being graphically illustrated by a prostitute interviewed by Terkel (1977) as equivalent to the distinction between an executive secretary and somebody in the typing pool. In the former role 'you really identify with your boss' whereas in the latter 'you're a body, you're hired labour, a set of hands on the typewriter. You have nothing to do with whoever is passing the work down to you. You do it as quickly as you can.' Brewis and Linstead (2000b) note the variety of career patterns that sex workers can be seen to follow, varying from older prostitutes prolonging their business lives by offering 'domination' or sado-masochist specialisms, to street workers moving 'up' from street to parlour work, to a prostitute taking a business course to help her establish a business of her own.

Occupational culture and ideology

Throughout social life we see human beings forming coalitions of interest, and to justify or legitimate shared interests to both members and relevant outsiders, a set of ideas is frequently developed and propagated, thus creating a *group ideology* (Watson 1982). An occupational ideology is an example of this.

> ### OCCUPATIONAL IDEOLOGY
>
> A set of ideas developed by an occupational group, and especially by its leaders, to legitimate the pursuit of the group members' common occupationally related interests.

The ideology associated with an occupation is a component of the wider occupational culture.

> ### OCCUPATIONAL CULTURE
>
> The set of ideas, values, attitudes, norms, procedures and artefacts characteristically associated with an occupation.

The tasks in which an occupation is involved, the occupational culture and the ideological component of that culture are all closely interconnected. Bensman and Lilienfeld (1973) argued, for example, that the specialisation of occupational members in handling certain materials creates 'habits of mind, attitudes and loyalties' and that these craft attitudes interlock with interests and attitudes which are based on the historical success of the occupation in developing its professional acceptance and claims in the society at large.

Occupational cultures and ideologies are to be found in occupations of varying status levels. Among the higher status occupations (and many other less prestigious but aspiring ones) the symbol of professionalism is frequently drawn on. It is an invaluable ideological resource which typically assists occupational members and spokesmen in seeking legitimacy for their claim to exclusive involvement in certain tasks and in justifying the high rewards which are felt to be appropriate. This is done by pointing out how it is in the interest of clients and, especially, of society at large for the tasks to be carried out on the occupation's terms. An occupational claim is 'ideological' regardless of the truth of the claim. Doctors may or may not have been right in arguing on the grounds of patients' interests against the licensing of rival osteopaths to carry out treatments, and solicitors may or may not have been justified on similar grounds in their insistence on an exclusive right to do conveyancing work. Either way, the claim made is an illustration of professional ideology in action. Self-interest and altruism may often clash in the politics of work but this is by no means necessarily the case. The best way for a group to serve its self-interest may well be to do the best for others.

At the lower status levels the occupational culture is less likely to be expressed in ideological form by any official group 'leader' as is frequently the case with professionally organised types of occupation. Any occupational member (as in all groups) is likely to articulate the culture when talking about his or her work in a way which will vary with the audience (again, as with all groups). With the more lowly type of occupation, however, the content is more likely to function in a defensive way – helping occupational members cope with problems created for them by the disadvantageous or threatening environment in which they operate. Pringle's (1989) Australian study of secretaries illustrates this, showing how women have managed to move definitions of their occupational role away from that of the 'office wife' of the pre-1960s and 'sexy secretary' of the 1960s and 1970s towards some recognition of their being a member of the management team in their own right (and not as an appendage of a man). To understand the varieties of function and emphasis found in different occupational cultures we can look at further examples found in studies of both 'professional' and deviant occupations.

A study of two occupational groups involved with the treatment of cancer (Elliot 1973), observed how different positions are taken up by doctors on the one hand and scientific researchers on the other with regard to how the disease is to be approached. The two major positions are related to and bound up with the occupational situation of each group. The occupational and organisational positions and problems of the doctors are reflected in their adherence to a 'therapy ideology' whilst the different situation and career interests of the scientists influence their adherence to a 'basic science' ideology. This research illustrates the need for the public, as consumers of occupationally created goods and services, to be sensitive to the ideological accounts given by occupational members. It is an important question of public policy as to how resources should be allocated to dealing with diseases like cancer. In relying on the experts to whom lay persons must turn for advice it may be vital to take note of the occupational interests behind the advice which is given as to how resources should best be allocated. However sincere occupationally related advice or actions may be, they are unlikely to take a form which undermines the major career investments which practitioners have made in their occupation.

Certain features of the occupational culture of prostitutes were discussed earlier when we considered some of the values and associated rules which are met in the process of occupational socialisation. Occupational members face the problem of retaining self-respect and overcoming what O'Connell Davidson (1998) identifies as the denial of personhood implicit in a type of work that amounts to an 'eroticisation of social death'. But purely personal or psychological defence mechanisms would not be enough to handle this. They have to relate to wider societal norms because 'prostitutes and clients alike are socialised into a world where particular meanings are attached to human sexuality . . . a world in which it is widely held that the only legitimate sex is between men and women who love each other and that "money can't buy you love"' (O'Connell Davidson 1995). For this reason, occupational cultural devices need to be available to handle the sex worker's 'deviance' from these norms. The legitimatory function of certain ideas upon which prostitutes typically draw is also illustrated in the ways in which prostitutes sometimes present themselves as skilled educators guiding people towards safe sex practices or as social workers providing services to disadvantaged clients (Brewis and Linstead 2000b).

The echoes of professionalism here in what is often ironically called the 'oldest profession' are quite apparent. Similar attempts at rationalisation and enhancement of the occupational image are reported in studies of strippers who may alternatively stress the quality of their work as entertainment, sex education or therapy for men who would otherwise be lonely and sexually frustrated (e.g. Salutin 1971).

Occupational communities

We can expect an occupational culture to be especially strong and to spill over into areas of members' lives outside the work sphere itself in occupations where the work and non-work lives of its members are closely related. This tends to be particularly the case with what some sociologists have described as occupational communities.

> **OCCUPATIONAL COMMUNITY**
>
> A form of local social organisation in which people's work and non-working lives are both closely identified with members of the occupation in which they work.

The notion of the occupational community is implicit in the analysis of Kerr and Siegal (1954) who suggested that the high propensity to strike of such groups as miners, longshoremen, sailors and loggers could be related to their living in an 'isolated mass'; the communities found in the 'coal patch, the ship, the waterfront district, the logging camp, the textile town' are all seen to have 'their own codes, myths, heroes and social standards'. The notion was further developed by Lipset *et al.* (1956) to characterise the interlinked work and non-work life of printers, and Blauner (1960) followed up their arguments in his discussion of factors which can contribute to job satisfaction. Blauner suggests that the essential feature of the occupational community is that workers socialise more with persons of their own occupation in non-work hours than they do with members of other occupations. To this he adds that participants tend to 'talk shop' in their off-hours and that the occupational community constitutes a little world in itself. It follows from this that its members regard it as their key reference group in such a way that 'its standards of behaviour, its system of status and rank, guide conduct'. Blauner suggests that occupational communities arise either where there is spatial isolation or where communal identity is encouraged by the kind of shifts worked by some printers, by steel workers, fire brigade workers and railway workers.

It is clear from the above discussion that the concept of occupational community implies more than the geographical proximity of members' homes. The concept of community in sociology implies a type of relationship between people which need not, in a society with relatively developed means of communication, necessarily involve geographical identity. The essence of community is an integrated set of social relationships, a system which provides its members with a sense of common identity and a shared values system. Goode (1957) suggested that professions constitute communities in this sense, an argument which encouraged Salaman (1974) to propose that we can usefully talk of two types of occupational community:

- one based on the occupation as a whole,
- one based on a common geographical location.

Salaman suggested that both the architects and the railwaymen he studied can be seen as members of occupational communities, and he noted that both were strongly and positively involved in the work they did, gaining satisfaction from carrying out their work tasks, using their valued skills or from such things as the responsibility or autonomy intrinsic to the work they do.

The suggestion that occupational communities may be important sources of job satisfaction, as Blauner and Salaman argue, is one important reason why occupations should be examined in such terms. The presence or otherwise of a sense of occupational community is also relevant to understanding certain dynamics of political and industrial conflict behaviour as well as occupational and professionalisation strategies. Filby (1987) observes how the 'independence in relations with employers' is sustained by racing lads working in the Newmarket stables by a 'vibrant occupational culture'. In spite of 'disagreements, competition, divisions and contradictions' among the lads, 'the occupation of the racing lad provides a basis of a community of shared forms of discourse, understanding, experience and affectiveness'. Membership of an occupational community need not, however, necessarily lead to an oppositional 'them and us' class conflict view on the part of manual workers. Moore (1975) has pointed out that coalminers have on various occasions recognised market situations shared with supervisors and employers in their particular industry. Elements of this became very relevant in attempts to resist state rundown of the British mining industry in the 1980s and early 1990s with events during and after the mining dispute in 1984–5 showing a powerful mixture of class-related oppositional action and community oriented solidarity in the face of attacks on a whole occupational identity (Beynon *et al.* 1991; Warwick and Littlejohn 1992).

Occupational communities tend to be associated with more 'traditional' occupation activities. Care needs to be taken over this, however, as any examination of the very modern technologies used in contemporary coalmines would show. A study of the fishing industry by Thompson (1983) shows how that industry is not, and never has been, a 'traditional' one – in spite of the fact that it is often carried on by people living in seemingly traditional communities. It was, in fact, one of the first industries to be developed within an international capitalist market. Recent developments in the British fishing industry have shown, however, that the distinctively capitalist institution of labour-employment can undermine the effectiveness of the industry. The 'modern' capitalist trawler fleets of the big ports – which depend on wage labour and therefore suffer from all the problems that go with standard industrial employment practices – have been failing. In contrast, and working within a set of values which combine egalitarianism, social independence and individuality, the northern Scottish fishermen, in their co-operatively owned boats which may be worth more than half-a-million pounds, flourished. It is, says Thompson, to the community oriented, co-operative and family based approach of the fisher people of the Moray Firth and the Scottish islands that we can look for ideas on work organisation and patterns of ownership for the future. This may, however, be over-optimistic and the community orientation of these areas may be more significant, as they were in mining areas, as sites for resistance to state-mediated (or state-initiated) occupational decline.

Professionalisation and occupational strategies

The work people do is, as we have seen, bound up with the distribution of power and resources of society at large. Most individuals are not in a position to defend or improve their location in the wider structure of advantage on their own. Some form of collective action to defend or further individuals' interests is inevitable. A variety of ways in which people attempt to control the extent of their autonomy in work will be looked at in Chapter 8, but our present concern is with the way the members of any identifiable occupation form an association for such purposes *by virtue of their membership of that occupation* rather than on the basis of commonly experienced problems arising from their position as employees.

As was suggested earlier, the trade union as an *occupational* association is of decreasing significance as former trade groups increasingly amalgamate to deal with the more crucial problems experienced by people as employees or organisational members rather than as holders of specific skills and knowledge. The trade union strategy, traditionally associated with working-class values and interests, is essentially defensive. It is a coalition of interest arising from the recognition of a common problem of defending individuals' implicit contracts in a situation where the other party to that contract, the employer, tends to treat the rewards offered to employees as a cost to be minimised. But where the members of an occupation recognise in their skills, expertise or knowledge a potential basis for their own monopolistic control over their work they may look towards an alternative strategy; one which draws their eyes towards the traditionally middle-class symbol of *professionalism*. This, in contrast to the trade union strategy of seeking power through an amalgamation of occupational groups (following what Parkin, 1974, has called a *solidaristic* attempt at social closure), is a move towards *exclusivity*, involving, in Weber's (1978) terms 'the closure of social and economic opportunities to outsiders'. It is the members of the occupational group, not a group of employees, who define who is an outsider.

Those occupations, like law and medicine, widely recognised as professions, can be seen as forms of work organisation which gave a place within industrial capitalism to people doing high status work whilst keeping them in part outside and above those processes which were bringing the work lives of so many people under the administrative control of employers.

PROFESSIONS

Occupations which have been relatively successful in gaining high status and autonomy in certain societies on the basis of a claimed specialist expertise over which they have gained a degree of monopoly control.

The increasing influence of the work ethic in the developing industrial capitalist society meant that those upper-class practitioners in such areas as medicine, law and university teaching, who had formerly seen their efforts as gentlemanly pursuits rather than as labour needed to redefine their position. We thus see the decline of what Elliot (1972) calls status professionalism and the rise of occupational professionalism. Those who had previously been 'above' having an occupation (the upper class being in many ways a leisure class in principle if not always in practice) now embraced the occupational principle as a way of engaging in work without becoming contaminated by industrialism and commercialism. The ideology developed by such high status groups existed beyond these specific occupations, however, being found among the military and senior civil servants and propagated in the universities and new public schools. This ideology of liberal education, public service and gentlemanly professionalism was elaborated, as Elliot (1972) stresses, in opposition to the growth of industrialism and commercialism: 'it incorporated such values as personal service, a dislike of competition, advertising and profit, a belief in the principle of payment in order to work rather than working for pay and in the superiority of the motive of service'.

The essence of the idea of a profession is *autonomy* – the maintenance of the control over work tasks by those doing these tasks. It should not be surprising therefore to find groups of people who operate within formal organisations or within other restricted settings looking to the traditional high status 'free' professions to find ways of developing strategies to oppose control over them by others. The concern of so many sociologists with the occupational strategy of professionalisation is a justifiable one because it represents one of the major ways in which the prevailing mode of work organisation and control has been and will perhaps continue to be challenged. The possibilities of the occupational principle developing so as to reduce the conflicts and excesses of capitalism have been suggested by both classical and modern sociologists (Durkheim 1984; Halmos 1970). In recent years there has been a powerful and sceptical reaction to this approach. Crompton (1990), however, points to the danger of an 'either or' approach to assessing 'professional' occupations; seeing them on the one hand in G.B. Shaw's famous phrase as 'conspiracies against the laity' or, on the other, as 'islands of occupational altruism in a sea of self-interested commerce'. She suggests, instead, that we see these occupations as incorporating elements which 'reflect the contradictory tendencies underlying the division of labour' in modern societies. They are clearly involved in furthering the projects of 'dominant interests' in a capitalist market context. At the same time, they still express certain norms of what Merton termed *institutionalised altruism*; 'experts and professionals have protected the weak as well as the strong, sought to restrain and moderate the excesses of the market'. Crompton relates this to the fact that market capitalism is 'simply not viable in its own terms'. Without accompanying norms of trust and reciprocity and the same defence of what Durkheim calls the 'non-contractual aspects of contract' the system would collapse. Consistently with this, Freidson (2001) argues that proponents of professionalism need to justify the considerable privilege that it offers those who embrace it and suggests that this can be done by mediating between the state and private capital by sounding 'an effective third voice for choosing social policies that provide benefit to all'.

It is clear that in a society where the great majority of people work as employees rather than as independent fee-paid practitioners, any given group strategy – involving whatever mixture of self-interest and concern for others may be the case in particular circumstances – is likely to involve some mixture of elements from both the trade union and the professional ideal types of strategy. Hence we see the high-status medical profession using, from time to time, trade union tactics in its relations with the government which, in Britain, mediates between the professional and the client. Sociological analysis of occupations has often sought to identify the extent to which any given occupational group is able to act as an occupational collectivity, on the 'professionalisation' model. This has involved identifying the conditions which influence the capacity of any group to act in this way. Before we do this, however, we must clarify what we mean by the process of professionalisation.

> ### PROFESSIONALISATION
>
> A process followed by certain occupations to increase its members' status, relative autonomy and rewards and influence through such activities as setting up a professional body to control entry and practice, establishing codes of conduct, making claims of altruism and a key role in serving the community.

Traditionally, professions have been identified by the extent to which they have certain features, the six most commonly cited (Millerson 1964) being:

- skill based on theoretical knowledge
- the provision of education and training
- the testing of member competence
- the existence of a professional body
- adherence to a code of conduct
- emphasis on altruistic service.

However, the position taken here is that there is no clearly definable category of occupations which can be recognised by their possession of a series of traits or elements of professionalism. There is, however, what Becker (1971) has called a *symbol of professionalism*. This is a 'folk concept' or image based on traditionally independent occupations like law and medicine and, as Becker puts it, the 'professions' are 'simply those occupations which have been fortunate enough in the politics of today's work world to gain and maintain possession of that honorific title'. To acquire the professional label and the prestige and economic benefits associated with it, any given occupation will, *to the degree to which its material situation allows it*, organise itself on a basis resembling the traditional elite occupations. An occupation following the professionalisation strategy will therefore tend to stress a claim to esoteric competence, the quality of which it will argue must be maintained for the sake of client and society, and will accordingly seek for its licensed members the exclusive right to do work in its sphere of competence whilst controlling who enters the work, how they are trained, how they perform their work tasks and how this performance is checked and evaluated. The fact that many occupations by their very nature can never approach the level of autonomy traditionally associated with lawyers and physicians does not prevent occupations as varied as industrial managers, estate agents and embalmers getting together and pursuing some elements of the professionalisation strategy.

A view of professionalising processes as a form of occupational market strategy which seeks monopoly control over an area of activity so guaranteeing an advantaged position within the class structure was central to the influential analysis of Larson (1977). Larson (1991) subsequently said that her earlier work, in concentrating on Anglo-American cases, gave undue emphasis to the *market* aspect of professionalisation. In Britain and America it may have been the distinctive 'inaction of the state' which prompted 'professional leaders to take the initiative in organising mechanisms of closure and protection around their fields'. Alternative processes of mobilisation around expert knowledge can occur in other circumstances. She argues, therefore, that we should move away from trying to develop a general theory of the professions and focus instead on the more important theme of 'the construction and social consequences of expert knowledge'. The concept of profession or professionalisation, however, is still pertinent, she argues, to the 'relatively high levels of formal education and relatively desirable positions and/or rewards in the social division of labour'. Education is thus the linking mechanism between occupational 'expertise' and social class advantage.

In spite of his 'defence' of professionalism as a force mediating between institutions of stage and capital, Freidson (2001) identifies professionalisation as a process of occupational closure and control and he emphasises how attempts are made to 'institutionalise' specialist skill and expertise in occupational and organisational forms so that they become a *resource* to be used to the social and economic advantage of those engaged in the professionalisation strategy. Abbott (1988), however, attempted to change the direction of analysis away from professional structures and onto the *work* undertaken by professionals. He observes that there is a *system of professions* operating in any given society. Professions evolve through their interactions with each other; they compete with each other for *jurisdiction* over *abstract knowledge*. It is not control over technique which gives a group professional advantage (that can be delegated) but it is control over a 'knowledge system governed by abstractions' that allows members of an occupation to defend themselves from interlopers or 'seize new problems' (as medicine has seized alcoholism, according to Abbott). For his purposes, he says, motor mechanics would be a profession if they were able to develop a form of abstract knowledge about the repair of internal combustion engines. Were they to do this, they would assert their role within the 'competitive system' of professions and would take over or 'contain' what are currently sections of the engineering profession.

The value of this emphasis on competition between members of occupational groups for jurisdiction over abstract knowledge is that it brings together issues about the power and advantage of people's labour market position with the changing nature of knowledge, technology, markets and political contexts. As global markets change, new technologies emerge and governments react to or attempt to shape these shifts, so certain groups within the division of labour will mobilise themselves to defend or further their interests. In all of this, the notions of 'profession' and 'professionalism' are likely to be powerful *discursive resources* that spokespersons of almost any knowledge-related occupation are likely to deploy to protect and advance their shared interests, even if this means deploying a degree of 'discursive ingenuity' to bend them to particular occupational purposes – with human resource managers and 'competitive intelligence' consultants alike claiming to be members of professions (Watson 2002b, 2002c) and 'eco-auditors' emerging as an outcome of a 'new form of Euro-professionalisation' (Neal and Morgan 2000).

7 Work experiences, opportunities and meanings

Work, meaning and culture

Work is something we associate with human beings – unless we are thinking of animals that are given working roles by humans, as sheep dogs or dray horses, say. Yet all living creatures expend some kind of 'working' effort in the process of acting upon and taking from their environment whatever they need for survival. Human beings are no different from other animals in this general respect. Members of the human species are, however, different in three respects:

- they have devised an infinitely greater variety of ways of dealing with their material situation,
- they are unique in the extent to which they have divided up and allocated particular tasks to individuals and groups within the overall and general task of subsisting,
- they apply value-based judgements to the problem of maintaining life – distinguishing between 'good' and 'bad' or 'honourable' and 'dishonourable' ways of earning a living, for instance.

The human capacity to make choices on the basis of values means that neither the methods of work which human beings adopt nor the social organisation which accompanies it can be explained by reference to any clearly definable set of instincts. Human agency, choice, values and interpretations are essential factors to be appreciated in any examination of work forms and experiences.

Work is basic to the ways in which human beings deal with the problems arising from the scarcity of resources available in the environment. The scarcity of resources in the world influences the patterns of conflict and competition which arise between social groups. It follows from this that the social organisation of work will reflect the basic power relationships of any particular society. But patterns of social relationships do not relate to

CHAPTER SEVEN

power structures alone. They are also closely connected to the patterns of meaning created within human cultures. And this means that the ways in which people think and feel about work will closely relate to their wider political and religious doctrines and to the culture of the society within which they live.

> ## CULTURE
>
> The system of meanings which are shared by members of a society, organisation or other human grouping, and which define what is good and bad, right and wrong and what are the appropriate ways for members of that grouping to think and behave.

All cultures have to deal with the same basic problems of human existence – of life, death, social obligation and so on – and they all give guidance on how to solve these problems. But cultures vary in the particular way these problems are tackled. And since the problems of how 'properly' to go about working and 'making a living' face all human groups, we would expect every society, through its culture, to have its distinctive way of making sense of the question of work and a distinctive set of values and priorities giving guidance on how its members should proceed with it. We can see some clear differences of emphasis historically:

- The ancient Greeks regarded the most desirable and the only 'good' life as one of leisure. Work, in the sense of supplying the basic necessities of life, was a degrading activity which was to be allocated to the lowest groups within the social order and, especially, to slaves. Slavery was the social device which enabled the Greeks to maintain their view of work as something to be avoided by a full human being: what human beings 'shared with all other forms of animal life was not considered to be human' (Arendt 1959).
- The Romans tended to follow the Greek view, whilst the Hebrews had a view of work as unpleasant drudgery which could nevertheless play a role of expiating sin and recovering a degree of spiritual dignity (Tilgher 1930).
- Early Christianity also modified the relatively extreme Greek view and recognised that work might make one healthy and divert one from sinful thoughts and habits. Leading thinkers of the Catholic Church, such as Aquinas, were influenced by the Greek view but a doctrine emerged which gave a role for work in the Christian scheme of things as a penance arising from the fall and original sin. It also contributed to the virtue of obedience but was by no means seen as noble, rewarding or satisfying; 'its very endlessness and tedium were spiritually valuable in that it contributed to Christian resignation' (Anthony 1977).
- The Reformation and the emergence of Protestant Christianity saw work coming to be treated positively within Western cultures. With Luther we see the suggestion that work can itself be a way of serving God. This is the origins of the Western or Protestant work ethic.

The historical implications of this Protestant work ethic were considered in Chapter 3, but what we must note here is that it established the all-important idea that one's work was a 'calling' of equivalent value to that of a religious vocation – something which had previously involved a turning of one's back on the mundane and a movement 'upwards' towards virtue and other-worldliness. Where living a life of leisure, rather than working, had once been an indicator of prestige and a 'good life' it now became associated with failure and even disgrace.

WORK ETHIC

A set of values which stresses the importance of work to the identity and sense of worth of the individual and which encourages an attitude of diligence, duty and a striving for success in the mind of the worker.

With the growth of modern industrial capitalism we see the work ethic spreading further and wider with work becoming the essential prerequisite of personal and social advancement, of prestige, of virtue and of self-fulfilment. The modern pattern of working life in which 'jobs' and 'careers' are central to people's identities as well as sources of income is supported as the work ethic encourages people to seek and sustain involvement in this institutional pattern. Although in modern times the work ethic may not be formally underpinned by religious faith, it still has religious undertones. The ideas of a duty to work and to be dutiful in work are essentially moral and go deeper than our rational attachment to a particular way of making a living. As Max Weber (1965) put it, 'the idea of duty in one's calling prowls about in our lives like the ghost of dead religious beliefs'.

It began to be suspected by some commentators in the latter half of the twentieth century that the 'work ethic' was losing its force. However, Rose (1985, 1988) rejected the thesis that the work ethic was being abandoned. He nevertheless argued that a process was under way whereby the more educated and highly trained were 'modifying the interpretation' of the work ethic whilst not 'repudiating it as a scheme of values'. A new pattern of work meanings was observed among the more educated and trained which contains elements of the traditional work ethic combined with a concern with self-fulfilment, the obtaining of 'just treatment' and the developing of 'more humanly rational economic organisation and technology'. This also involves an anti-authoritarianism in which people are systematically suspicious of those giving orders. The adoption of these 'post-bourgeois values' is likely to be encouraged, says Rose, by such structural changes as the growth of service work (where employers will experience a tension between wanting tight control and avoiding the danger of disaffected employees alienating clients) and the attraction to public service work of those more educated people who believe that they can here better follow a 'service ethic'. The new values are also supported by 'commercial hedonism' (taking the waiting out of wanting, as the advertisers put it) and, potentially, by the, as yet limited, re-negotiation of family and gender roles.

Alienation and the corrosion of character

Associated with the notion that people can achieve self-fulfilment or self-actualisation in their work and their careers is its opposite: that of work alienation. This notion, as we saw in Chapter 2, is central to Marx's analysis of capitalist society, and his view that the essence of human existence is found in people's capacity to labour and transform the material world has been very influential in sociology. It has been widely used by those wishing to understand the dehumanising potential of industrial or capitalist ways of organising work.

> ### ALIENATION
>
> A state of existence in which human beings are not fulfilling their humanity.

The basic notion underlying the concept of alienation is one of 'separation' (Schacht 1970) and, in Marx's usage, various forms of 'separation' within human experience under capitalism are identified. The fragmenting of experience which Marx discusses is the result of the capitalist organisation of work activity and not, as it is sometimes wrongly taken to be (see below p. 182), an outcome of the use of any particular kind of machinery or work method.

Individuals were seen by Marx as alienated in various ways in capitalist society:

- They become alienated or estranged from other people as relationships become merely calculative, self-interested and untrusting.
- They become alienated from the product of their efforts since what is produced is expropriated from them and was not, anyway, conceived by the workers themselves to meet their own ends or needs.
- They are alienated or separated from their own labour in that they do not derive the satisfactions or the delight that is possible in labour since that labour is forced upon them as a means of meeting other needs and because they put themselves under the control of other people in the work situation.
- They experience work as an alien thing which oppresses them.

Potentially, however, work could be a source of human fulfilment, and here we come to the essential element of the Marxian notion of alienation: people can be alienated from themselves. Marx's conception of human nature is one in which it is assumed that people realise their essential nature, as a species, through productive work which is carried out for their own purposes and not under the control and exploitation of others. What this implies – and many users of the concept of alienation forget this – is that alienation is basically an objective state. Alienation is not necessarily reflected in felt job dissatisfaction or in frustration. A person may be very happy sitting at a desk in someone else's factory five days per week sorting pieces of paper which mean little to them, in return for a wage. This person is nevertheless alienated: they are not fulfilling themselves in the way they might be were they working under different conditions. People are alienated when they are not being what they possibly could be, and for people to become what they could be

– to fulfil themselves or achieve 'self-actualisation' – they would need to create a wholly new type of society which would treat work as a source of fulfilment in its own right.

A tendency can be seen in modern societies to encourage a level of expectations that people are then prevented from fulfilling – thus potentially creating a state of 'alienation'. In a classic industrial sociology study, Chinoy (1992, originally 1955) showed the extent of the gap between the ambitions for personal and family fulfilment instilled in American automobile workers and the realities of a class and employment system which denied the realisation of these ambitions. Milkman, in noting the continuing relevance of the Chinoy study half a century later (in Chinoy 1992), says such work 'remains deeply alienating' and adds that any 'reduction in the degradation of the labour process is counteracted by the continual fear of job loss' that pervades the major car producers. Sennett (1998) provides in his notion of *corrosion of character* a variant of the classic concept of 'alienation' to fit the 'new capitalism' of flexibility, market domination, quick financial returns and impermanence. Under these conditions, and the associated corroding of loyalties, trust relations and mutual commitments in work contexts, people are no longer able to maintain a sense of character – a coherent personal narrative of who they are and where they have come from.

Because work is still seen as central to human self-fulfilment, apparently radical critiques of capitalist work forms can, ironically, be criticised as functioning as a conservative work ideology: 'the essential paradox of alienation is that it emerges with any meaning only as a result of an over-emphasis on a work ethic and work-based values' (Anthony 1977). People can only be seen as alienated from their work when they have been subjected to an ideology of work which requires them to be devoted to it. Anthony sees alienation as a 'managerial conception' functioning within an ideology of work which, like all ideologies of work, is essentially a defence of subordination. He argues that a stress on the importance of work which goes beyond the necessary part which it must play in meeting other needs is only required when some groups require the labour of others to meet economic ends other than those of the people in whose mind the required work has to be justified. Thus Marxist stress on the problem of alienation is precisely equivalent to the stress on self-actualisation in the work of the 'psychological humanist' management theorists discussed earlier (pp. 24–5). Both of the ideas, or rather how they are used, serve to close off human options. They imply that, whatever we do in the future, our work must be central to our lives, psychologically as well as materially.

Whatever the possibilities for the future may be, we have to recognise that work currently takes up a large proportion of many people's lives and that the satisfactions and deprivations which it – or the lack of it – involve are not equally shared across the social structure.

Work and satisfaction

Whatever it is that constitutes a 'good job', as Tilly and Tilly (1998) emphasise, 'is hard to define' and can differ radically over 'time, place, culture and class'. Yet no research on job quality, it is pointed out, has found people giving priority to 'expressive values' over 'material measures of success'. In spite of this, there has been a long tradition in the psychological and the sociological study of work to focus on the expressive side of work involvement and, in particular, on people's 'satisfaction' with their work experiences. At first sight, we might expect this to be a very personal matter, varying from one unique human individual to another. However, satisfaction is not a totally individualistic notion. In any given society there will be certain basic notions of what is desirable and we can expect people with different degrees of access to these satisfactions at work to recognise this. Some indication of the distribution of these satisfactions can be derived if only in a very general way, by looking at the variations in response to questions about 'satisfaction' between people working in different settings.

In a classic review of work satisfaction studies, Blauner (1960) found that professionals and businessmen claimed relatively high levels of satisfaction, that clerical workers claimed higher levels than manual workers, whilst skilled manual workers appeared more satisfied than unskilled workers or assembly line operators. We may well observe that these accounts fall into a pattern closely relating to the social class hierarchy – itself a patterning of the way those resources most valued in society at large are distributed. But this does not invalidate our seeking factors in the work itself which appear to relate to these differences. Blauner suggests four major areas:

- the importance or the relative prestige of the occupation;
- the degree of independence and control over the conditions of work – this covering the freedom from hierarchical control, the freedom to move about, the opportunity to vary the pace of work and allocate one's time;
- the extent to which social satisfactions are gained from working within an integrated group;
- the degree to which people who work together share non-work activities – perhaps in something approaching an occupational community (Chapter 6, pp. 166–7).

In a later review of work satisfaction surveys, Parker (1983) noted some additional factors, such as opportunities:

- to 'create something';
- to 'use skill';
- to 'work wholeheartedly'; and
- to work together with people who 'know their job'.

Dissatisfactions are likely to involve formulations which simply oppose these but Parker also usefully locates specific factors like:

- doing repetitive work;
- making only a small part of something;
- doing useless tasks;
- feeling a sense of insecurity;
- being too closely supervised.

All the factors connected to 'satisfaction' emerging in these studies relate to ones often characterised as intrinsic satisfactions in Figure 7.1 – that is, those relating to factors inherent in the work itself rather than the extrinsic rewards which may be obtained.

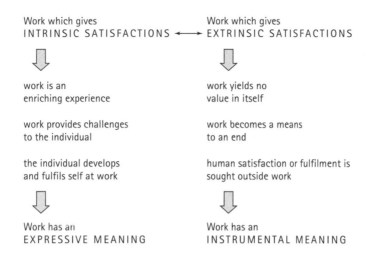

Figure 7.1 Intrinsic and extrinsic work satisfactions: a continuum

Different researchers have used different methods to elicit information about the nature of people's involvement in their work and hence the rewards and satisfactions which are sought or expected. Morse and Weiss (1955), for example, asked respondents whether they would continue to work if they had sufficient money to live comfortably. People in middle-class occupations pointed to the loss which would result with regard to the interest which they found in their jobs and the sense of accomplishment to which they were used. The type of loss mentioned by those in working-class jobs, however, was typically more in terms of the lack of activity with which to keep themselves occupied. Another classic study in this area is that of Friedmann and Havighurst (1954). Here the lower status workers were those most likely to stress the importance of money as the major reward. The relationship between the nature of rewards and satisfactions and job level is also suggested by studies which have followed Dubin's method of attempting to elicit whether the individual's *central life interest* lies inside or outside the work sphere. Dubin (1956) himself, in his original study based on a large sample of industrial workers, found that three out of four individuals in this manual work had central life interests *outside* their work. Yet Orzack (1959) found that four out of five of the professional nurses whom he studied, using a procedure similar to Dubin's, indicated a central life interest *within* their work. More recent international studies using the central life interest notion, among others, suggest that there are occupational similarities in work meanings across different countries, this implying that national cultural factors might be less influential than structural matters such as the market situation of the occupational activity (MOW Research Team, 1987). Nevertheless, Hirschfield and Field (2000) demonstrate a connection between people's work centrality and their attachment to values associated with a Protestant work ethic, this suggesting that work centrality is tied into 'a person's value system and self-identity'.

It is important to bear in mind that most of the 'data' about work satisfaction upon which generalisations tend to be made derive from the accounts given to researchers. The evidence is such, however, that at the very least, we can take it that those in higher level work expect more by way of intrinsic satisfactions than do those in more routine manual work. Using Daniel's (1973) distinction between satisfaction *in* work and satisfaction *with* work, we might say that workers in routine jobs both find and seek satisfaction *in work* less than do those in managerial, professional or highly skilled work. But this does not mean that they are not *satisfied with* their job. The 'affluent' car workers studied by Goldthorpe *et al.* (1968) appeared to be *satisfied with* jobs in which they achieved little or no intrinsic job satisfaction. They did not seek or expect such satisfactions. As Mann (1973) points out in his study of workers moving with a relocated factory, the fact that the instrumentally involved worker sets little store by intrinsic work activities is, paradoxically, all the more reason for their staying firmly attached to their job. One stays in a job in order to increase its stability and predictability, thereby lowering one's 'emotional investment' in work.

Technology and work experience

Technology, for the majority of employees, is central to their work experience, and for many it is something which is chosen, is designed and its mode of use dictated by persons other than those applying it. In addition, these persons are frequently ones with higher status, higher level of material rewards and, especially important, greater apparent autonomy in their own work experience than those directly applying the technology. Given cultural norms which encourage the valuing of personal autonomy, individuality and self-expression, we can see why technology is such a source of potential resentment, conflict and opposition in workplaces.

Industrial sociology in the 1960s paid considerable attention to the ways in which workers applying different types of technology were likely both to think and to act differently. Such an approach has been given the label of *technological implications*.

> ## TECHNOLOGICAL IMPLICATIONS
>
> A way of thinking about technology which sees it as determining, or at least closely constraining, the way in which tasks are organised with this, in turn, significantly influencing the attitudes and behaviour of workers.

Following this approach, investigators like Woodward (1965), Blauner (1964) and Sayles (1958) argued that workers' social relationships with each other, the quality of their work experience and their propensity to engage in conflict with management would be heavily dependent on technology. To make this clearer, let us compare a situation where the technology is a craft-based one like printing with the very different technology of the car assembly line:

- *Printers* would be closely bound up with their workmates through the craft group which they will have joined as youths and, because of the nature of the tasks which they carry out, they will be relatively free to interact with their colleagues.

- *Car workers'* social experiences would be quite different. The lack of skill required by the work will mean that there is not the craft tradition and resulting cohesiveness and the fact that the workers are paced by the machines, rather than the other way round, will mean that they are less free to interact with others even if they wished to.

These differences affect the social satisfactions which can be derived from the two types of work and also have implications for the type and amount of industrial conflict engaged in. The nature of the tasks themselves – potentially interesting and fulfilling in the craft case and typically boring and frustrating in the assembly-line case – will strongly influence the feelings, thoughts and hence preparedness to act in certain ways on the part of the two groups. Other technological situations will each have their own particular determining influence. More advanced technologies, like automated process production for example, could be expected to bring about attitudes and behaviour more in line with those of the traditional craft worker and away from those of the alienated and resentful mass production operative.

The individual will tend to be aware of, and take into account, the general nature of the technology they are likely to use when they shape their prior orientation to work. Once in work, their subsequent attitudes and behaviour may be conditioned by more specific factors such as the extent to which the technology enables them to mix with others, the freedom it allows them to use discretion, and so on. Wedderburn and Crompton (1972) found that, although they were studying 'a group of workers with primarily instrumental attitudes to work', there were nevertheless distinct differences of attitude and behaviour between different parts of the plants examined, and technology was taken to be the key variable in this. The degree of interest expressed in the job, the attitude to supervision and the level of grievance activity were all found to be more 'favourable', for instance, in the continuous flow plant than in the batch production plant (even though pay levels were higher in the latter area). These authors stress the importance of two factors which relate to technology:

- the structuring of the job itself,
- the way in which the relationship between the supervisors and the operators was shaped.

It is thus not the technology itself which operates on the individual. It is the opportunity which the technology allows for personal discretion and the part it plays in the power relationships between the managers and the managed.

Blauner's influential classic study, *Alienation and Freedom* (1964), attempted to bring together several of the major factors thought to influence work satisfactions and to relate those to work experience in different technological settings. He used the overall concept of alienation to bring together those factors influencing satisfaction. These four 'dimensions of alienation', as he termed them, were

- *powerlessness*, or lack of opportunity for control;
- *meaninglessness* or lack of opportunity to feel a sense of purpose by linking one's job with the overall production process;
- *isolation* or an inability to relate closely to others at work;
- *self-estrangement* or a lack of opportunity to achieve self-involvement or personal fulfilment at work.

Blauner used a variety of research materials to measure alienation defined in this way in four types of industry: printing, textiles, car assembly and chemicals. There were four distinct types of technology here: craft, machine-tending, assembly line and process technology and Blauner found that alienation was relatively low in the craft printing industry and the process chemical industry, higher in the machine-tending textile setting and highest on the car assembly line. We thus get the famous 'inverted U-curve' shown in Figure 7.2.

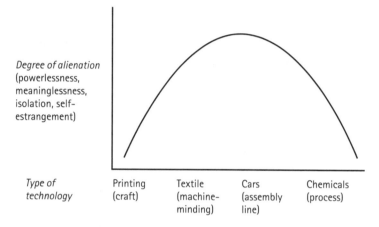

Figure 7.2 Blauner's 'inverted U curve' relating alienation and technology
Source: Based on Blauner (1964)

Critics of Blauner's thesis suggested that it trivialised Marx's notion of alienation by conceptualising it in subjective terms, that its inferences from attitude survey data can be questioned, and that the representativeness of the areas surveyed can be doubted (Eldridge 1971a). Although the study has important things to say about the relationship between certain technical settings and sources of work satisfaction, its greatest inadequacy lies in its failure to locate technology within its *political* context. Blauner suggested that as technology becomes more automated in the future so will the opportunity for people to experience control, purpose, meaning and self-realisation at work increase. What this does not recognise is that technology is a means to the ends of those who employ labour rather than those who are employed. The 'deskilling' of work is as great a possibility arising from the employer's introduction of new technologies to increase their control over work effort as is the evolution of a workforce of autonomous skilled, integrated and satisfied control room workers and maintenance engineers. Automation is merely one way of increasing control over work process on the part of the owner or manager and its combination with other methods of achieving control such as partial automation combined with deskilling is just as feasible.

Justifications for the type of reservations expressed here were found in a study done in the British chemical industry more than a decade after Blauner. Nichols and Beynon (1977) found that in six out of the seven plants of a major British chemical company which they visited, control room operatives – the archetypal non-alienated worker of automated industry – were a minority: 'for every man who watched dials another maintained the plants, another was a lorry driver and another two humped bags or shovelled muck'. This study has, however, been criticised for selecting evidence which fitted with the ideological preconceptions of the researchers and, especially, for completely ignoring the category of workers in the plant who were classified as skilled – the maintenance workers (Harris 1987).

Care has to be taken not to make generalisations about the effect of technological change on work experience on the basis of quite real differences of experience within specific and limited work settings and without recognising that any given technology is typically a mediating factor between those who control work and those whose efforts are controlled. Since the managers of work are typically under constant pressure to maintain and increase this control we can expect their efforts to introduce technical change to be a constant influence on the changing work orientations of the employee, that is, on their ongoing definition of their situation and their preparedness to act in certain ways.

Technology, then, is a major factor in people's work experience and their orientations to work. As was stressed in Chapter 3, technology involves a great deal more than simply the tools and machines which people use at work. What Hill (1988) called the 'technology text' pervades every aspect of work and its organisation. It is often difficult to separate out at all the technological from the organisational. As Scarborough and Corbett (1992) put it, it is increasingly difficult because of 'the fluidity and interpenetration of technological and organisational forms to know the dancer from the dance'.

Entering work

Choice and opportunity structures

A successful sociology is one which does full justice to the interplay botwoon individual characteristics and initiatives on the one hand and structural factors and contingencies on the other. But in spite of the growing *sociological* emphasis on the interplay of agency and structure, there has been a tendency in much of the literature on how people enter work for a stress *either* on the individual's *choice* of occupation or on the *determining* influence of external factors. Much of the literature on the so-called process of occupational choice is psychologically based and examines the way in which the individual develops and passes through a series of stages during which the self-concept grows as abilities, aptitudes and interests develop. Two very influential theories of this type were those of Ginzberg *et al.* (1951) and that of Super (1957), the latter giving relatively more attention to the situational factors that condition the eventual occupation chosen. Musgrave (1967) attempted to be more sociological by concentrating on the series of roles through which the individual passes at home, in education and early work experience. These roles provide the settings in which the individual is socialised and learns to select the work role in which they eventually settle. However, the problem that arises with this kind of approach is that the structural limitations on choice are underplayed.

In reaction to approaches which exaggerated the degree of free 'choice' which people have about the work they enter, Roberts (1975) stressed that, for many individuals, entry to work is a matter of fitting oneself into whatever jobs are available given the qualifications which one's class and educational background has enabled one to attain. Roberts argued that it is careers which tend to determine ambition rather than the other way round. Careers can be regarded as developing into patterns dictated by the *opportunity structures* to which individuals are exposed, first in education and subsequently in employment, whilst individuals' ambitions, in turn, can be treated as reflecting the influence of the structures through which they pass.

In an attempt to do equal justice to both individual choice factors and structural circumstances, Layder *et al.* (1991) make use of the notion of *structuration* (Giddens 1984) to show that 'structure and action are inextricably interwoven and should be given equal analytical weighting'. Their research on the transition from school to work shows that structural variables (ones over which they had no control) such as the social class of their parents, their sex and the local opportunity structure (measured by their place of residence and the level of unemployment at the time they entered the labour market) played a more significant role for people entering the middle and lower level jobs in the youth labour market than they did for those entering the higher levels. In the upper segments of the job market it was found that 'the factors which individuals perceive as being a product of their own efforts and achievements are indeed the most significant factors in determining the level at which they enter the labour market'. Individuals here had a greater ability to control their circumstances through strategic activities of job search and behaviour informed by values and attitudes. Research by Banks *et al.* (1992) reveals a similar picture and their findings trace the subtle interplay which occurs between young people's self-identities and the structural circumstances in which they grow up.

This kind of research indicates that if we wish to produce a model which identifies the various factors that influence how individuals approach work, we must consider both objective and subjective factors. Objectively, the individual has certain resources such as cash, skills, knowledge or physique. Subjectively, the individual has certain motives, interests and expectations such as to make a living, achieve power or gain job satisfaction. Both of these sets of factors are, in turn, strongly influenced by structural factors. These are, on the one side, the structural settings of the individual's family, class, ethnic and educational background and, on the other side, the occupational structure and the prevailing job market. All these factors are interlinked as indicated in Figure 7.3 with the structure of opportunities acting as an influence alongside the various non-work influences on the individual's approach to work.

Class, family and educational influences

The life career of the individual is influenced to a very considerable extent by the class-family-education cluster of structural factors. As we saw in Chapter 6, the occupational structure of society which people enter is structured and segregated on a basis of class, status, gender and ethnic factors and people do not enter that structure with equal opportunities. Both the resources they take into the labour market and the aspirations they hold will be influenced by their class, family and educational background together with the

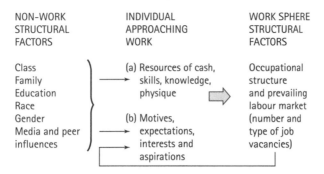

Figure 7.3 Factors influencing the individual's approach to work

way this affects their perception of themselves as members of a particular gender or an ethnic group or as male or female.

Parental occupational and class background is likely to make a significant difference to the individual's life-chances both through the material advantages which can be given (providing books or computers in the home, for example) and through the kind of encouragement or discouragement which is provided. There may be direct pressure on the child's job preferences, with the parents either encouraging or discouraging them from entering work like their own ('I would like my daughter to follow me and go into medicine'; 'I do not want to see a son of mine going down the pit') or a desire to see a child succeed where a parent failed ('I always wanted to be a lawyer and I hope to see one of my children fulfilling my dream'). Family networks can play a significant role in individuals' work opportunities, not just in cases where middle-class parents have contacts which can provide entry to careers for their children but also where manual workers may 'sponsor' members of their own families in the organisation which employs them. Grieco (1987) shows how this can be helpful both to the employee, who gains support from family members both inside and outside work and is sustained in steady employment, and for employers, whose recruitment costs are kept low and who can look to employees' relatives to help train them and teach them to 'fit in'. Whipp (1990) in a study which shows the very significant role played by family networks in the British pottery industry notes that potters frequently 'employed' their own relatives in subcontracting relationships. And in the contemporary Asian small businesses studied by Ram (1994) the employing of family members is shown to have:

- a practical rationale in which family labour is cheaper and easier to supervise (Ward 1987);
- an ideological rationale in which there was a concern to develop a 'family culture' for the organisation, one intended to promote trust and to align the goals of managers and employees (though what came about in practice was a form of 'negotiated paternalism', arising as family members resisted impositions).

More generally, socialisation in the home and in society at large, especially through the images to be seen in the communication media, not only provides information about and evaluations of different occupations, it suggests what kind of work might be appropriate for members of each gender. And formal schooling operates alongside the general cultural and family socialisation processes. Devine (1992b), for example, shows how the 'gendered' nature of subject choices within the education system 'accounts for the small number of women who embark on technical degree courses in pursuit of high-level careers in industry'. Even the ways in which certain school pupils resist authority at school is seen by Willis (1977) as a form of preparation for the way those particular individuals will need to live with their subservient roles once they enter paid employment. The research on youth career entry carried out by Banks *et al.* (1992) is taken by the researchers to 'confirm the centrality of educational career in the reproduction of social inequality'.

Work orientations: variations, dynamics and the negotiation of implicit contracts

As we saw in Chapter 2 (pp. 40–1), the notion of orientation to work – the meaning attached by people to their work which predisposes them to think and act in particular ways with regard to that work – entered industrial sociology in the mid-1960s and the perspective associated with it is one which, as its originators put it, takes the employee's own definition of the situation as an 'initial basis for the explanation of their social behaviour and relationships' (Goldthorpe *et al.* 1968). Perhaps its greatest value for general discussions of 'work motivations' is that it overcomes the popular tendency to engage in 'either-or' types of debate about what people 'look for in their work'. So much everyday discussion of work attitudes and work motivation centres, in effect, upon the question of whether people generally are intrinsically or extrinsically oriented towards their work. It is frequently debated, for example, whether people 'go to work for the money' or 'are looking for job satisfaction'. Sometimes such discussions are about people in general and sometimes they are about a particular type of worker, or a particular individual. But this is too simplistic; the concept of work orientation goes beyond this and shows that the ways in which people approach their work typically includes mixtures of these basic inclinations whilst nevertheless containing specific leanings in one or other of these general directions. And the concept has been employed to help explain the factors, both individual and structural, which influence people's attitudes and behaviour with regard to their work.

The research study which first introduced the notion of 'orientation to work' looked at workers in the car industry. As part of their wider study of social class in Britain in the mid-twentieth century, Goldthorpe *et al.* (1968) examined the attitudes and behaviour of various types of worker. The car assembly line workers in the Vauxhall plant in Luton were particularly interesting. These workers did not appear to be deriving any intrinsic or social satisfactions from their work experience. Yet they did not express dissatisfaction with the jobs they were doing. The possible paradox here was removed by the authors' explanation that these workers had knowingly chosen work with these deprivations, regarding such work as a means to a relatively good standard of living which could be achieved with the income made on the assembly line. The workers were said to have an *instrumental orientation* to work. The sources of this orientation were in the class, community and family backgrounds of the employees and not in the workplace itself. The technological implications approach (pp. 180–3) was strongly questioned by the finding that workers in other technological situations investigated (a chemical plant and a batch-production engineering plant) had similar work orientations with consequently corresponding patterns of behaviour and attitude. Technology thus appears to be less important a variable than had previously been suggested. The motives, interests and outside-work background of the worker had to be taken into account if not given central emphasis. These authors accepted that technology does have an influence but argued that this influence has to be put into the context of what it is people are looking for in their work.

Whilst accepting that all work in industrial societies has an instrumental basis, Goldthorpe *et al.* suggest that a variety of ideal type work orientations are possible. We could contrast, for example, the work meanings of:

- an 'instrumentally oriented' worker who sees their work as a means to an end or a way of earning income; has a 'calculative' involvement in the employing organisation; does not treat work as a central life interest or source of self-interest, and who separates their working lives from their home life – both mentally and in terms of the people with whom they socialise;
- a 'bureaucratically oriented' or 'career' worker who sees their work in terms of their providing a service to an organisation in return for career progress; has a sense of moral obligation towards the organisation; regards their work position and career prospects as sources of social identity, and allows an overlap between their working and their non-working lives.

Researchers who have revisited the Luton setting of this pioneering industrial sociology study suggest that the original researcher exaggerated the amount of choice being exercised by the 'instrumental workers'. Devine (1992a) and Grieco (1987) say that pressures of avoiding unemployment and the need to find better housing were as relevant to their behaviour as a desire to maximise earnings. The study can also be criticised for going too far in stressing the factors which influence workers' initial choice of their job and for failing to recognise that the individual's work orientation, once in that job, is constantly liable to change both as a result of factors operating within and factors located outside the workplace. Subsequent work in this area has suggested that attention to 'prior orientation' to work has to be balanced by a greater recognition of the structural conditions in which these orientations subsequently operate and a recognition that orientations or definitions of the situation are not necessarily fixed but are dynamic. Later studies did precisely this.

Dynamic work orientations and changing worker priorities

In interpreting their research in a luxury foods factory, Beynon and Blackburn (1972) argued that although employees tend, as far as possible, to select employment in keeping with their priorities in what they want from work, they nevertheless make important accommodations and adjustments once in work, as their experience is influenced by such workplace factors as work processes, pay levels and power structures. Orientations are also shown to be influenced by biographical factors in the worker's life outside the factory. The authors argued that the rejection of the adequacy of explanations based on technological determinacy and systems needs should not lead us to adopt one which replaces an analysis of the work situation with one based on prior orientations. They felt that the Luton study came 'dangerously near to being stuck the other side of the factory gates'. Wedderburn and Crompton (1972), who studied three chemical plants, make a similar point. They found that the workers whom they studied generally displayed the instrumental orientations to work described in the Luton study. However, they found that within specific work settings different workers displayed different attitudes and behaviour which 'emerged in response to the specific constraints imposed by the technology and the control setting'. As Bechhofer (1973) put it, we should not ignore the influence of factors such as technology on work orientations but might most usefully regard these as non-social *conditions* of action rather than actual *sources* of action.

In a significant critique of their work, Daniel (1973) accused Goldthorpe *et al.* of failing to recognise the complexities of what it is workers look for in their jobs. He argued that the researchers paid too much attention to the job choice situation and thus failed to recognise that, once in work, employees display varying priorities, attitudes and interests – depending on the context in which we look at them. Daniel suggested that different attitudes will prevail, for instance, in what he calls the *bargaining context* from those which are indicated in the *work context*:

- In the *bargaining context* priority is given to the material rewards accruing from the job. The negative aspects of the job are stressed (these justifying appropriate compensation) and the management are seen as being the 'opposite side'.
- In the *work context*, where the work content itself is the focus of interest, we find that there is more concern with the quality of work experience and with the social rewards of contact and communication with others and that the relationship with management is 'more characterised by a sense of common interests'.

The importance of Daniel's contribution here is considerable. It suggests that every employee is likely to have different priorities at different times and in different contexts. Definitions of the situation vary with the aspect of the situation which is of major concern at any particular time. The employee acting to improve his or her pay packet or salary is not likely to show much interest in job satisfaction at that point in time. However, once the individual returns to the machine or desk, the intrinsic satisfactions to be gained in that specific context may come to the fore. The study of ICI's attempt to introduce 'participation' among a semi-skilled workforce in a nylon-spinning plant illustrates this tendency. The improved quality of working experience was recognised and appreciated by the workforce yet, as the authors comment: 'this does not extend to any radical change when it comes to pay and effort-bargain. On this there are still two sides facing each other over a table in collective bargaining' (Cotgrove *et al.* 1971).

What is becoming clear is that to understand work behaviour we must recognise the importance of dynamic orientations and that, instead of relating work attitudes and behaviour in a direct way to either fixed psychological needs or technological constraints, we must recognise that individuals see things differently and act accordingly in different situations and at different times. This may seem fairly obvious but, as with so many generalisations which emerge from sociological study, this insight is not always present in our everyday thinking. We can illustrate this by looking at the common practice in industry of labelling individuals in specific ways, as 'an ambitious career woman' or as a 'poor team member', say. Let us consider several examples of the ways in which the appropriateness of such labels might change as an individual's orientation changes. These are all examples from the present author's participant observation research in the engineering industry:

- An apprentice was widely regarded by supervisors as a 'poor worker' and as something of a trouble-maker. The apprentice's girlfriend became pregnant, they got married and he not only settled to his training but applied himself rigorously to his work in a way which he hoped would help him achieve eventual promotion.
- A long-established foreman was regarded by managers as the epitome of the 'loyal company man'. But, like many other 'loyal company men' in the organisation, he became increasingly angry at the erosion of supervisory authority in a period of rapid organisational and technical change. He encouraged his colleagues to unionise and present a militant opposition to the management, the ferocity of which had previously been unimaginable.
- A graduate trainee was assessed as 'having little interest in the firm'. He then found himself in a training placement which he saw as giving him access to the type of advancement he had previously felt unlikely to occur. He became a devoted and ambitious 'company servant'.
- A shop steward who was perceived by managers and workers alike as especially 'militant' and anti-management effectively defeated a set of managerial proposals to which his shop were strongly opposed. After this success and his decision that he had 'proved my point about management respecting shop floor views' he became, in the eyes of the management and his colleagues alike, one of the most 'reasonable' and co-operative of all the stewards.

These characterisations or labels that were attached to each of these people in the first place were significant since they influenced how each of them was treated by others. The common tendency is to assume that such characterisations are fixed qualities of the individuals involved. But these four cases show how changed circumstances can be associated with changed orientations which, in turn, lead to changed perceptions on the part of others and hence to changed behaviour and relationships.

Dynamic work orientations and the negotiation of implicit contracts

The notion of work orientation can be linked with the notion of *implicit contract* – a concept that emerged at the same time as the work orientation one (Levinson *et al.* 1966) and is related to the concepts of *effort bargain* (Behrend 1957; Baldamus 1961).

IMPLICIT CONTRACT

The tacit agreement between an employed individual and an employing organisation about what the employee will 'put in' to their job and the rewards and benefits for which this will be exchanged.

The implicit employment contract is the largely tacit agreement made between the two parties with regard to what will be given by each and what each will take from the relationship. The employee's priorities, the resources which they take to the labour market and their personal circumstances all influence what kind of bargain they can make. This model is similar to Schein's (1978) notion of a *psychological contract*. The contract is formed as a result of 'various kinds of symbolic and actual events' which define what the employee will 'give in the way of effort and contribution in exchange for challenging or rewarding work, acceptable working conditions, organisational rewards in the form of pay and benefits, and an organisational future in the form of a promise of promotion or other forms of career advancement'. Schein says that this contract is 'psychological' in that the 'actual terms remain implicit; they are not written down anywhere'. However, 'the mutual expectations formed between the employee and the employer function like a contract in that if either party fails to meet the expectations, serious consequences will follow – de-motivation, turnover, lack of advancement, or termination'. In Table 7.1 we see the major elements that make up the implicit contract which can be seen to be at the core of every employment relationship.

Table 7.1 The individual worker's perceived implicit contract at the centre of their work orientation

Orientation to work	
Worker's perceived input	**Worker's perceived reward**
• Physical effort	• Money
• Mental effort	• Job satisfaction
• Initiative	• Personal 'growth'
• Responsibility	• Social reward
• Impairment – *fatigue, risk of injury, etc.*	• Security
• Compliance – *acceptance of a degree of managerial control*	• Power
	• Status
	• Career potential

Within the individual's personal priorities – conditioned as these are by personal resources brought to the labour market and by the knowledge and the reality of the jobs available – a certain degree of calculation is involved in the taking of any job. The individual will balance the likely personal costs in the shape of the amount of physical and mental effort to be expended, together with the likely deprivations of fatigue and the loss of freedom involved in accepting the instructions of others, against the available rewards. For certain employees cash may be a priority, for others there may be more concern with the career advancement possible in the future, whereas yet another person may be more interested in intrinsic job satisfaction, the status of a given job, the chance to control other people or simply the opportunity to fulfil personal values afforded by a job which, say, involves 'helping people'.

Whatever the individual's priority is, the various factors indicated in Table 7.1 will have to be balanced against each other. The schoolteacher giving up the satisfaction to be gained in the classroom to earn a higher level of income by selling financial services, for example, will make particular calculations as will the individual entering a theological college to train for a calling which is likely to involve little by way of future material advantage. In each case the calculations made prior to the decision to enter into a particular type of implicit contract will orient the subsequent attitudes and behaviour of the individual once engaged in a work career within that organisation.

The implicit contract is never fixed, nor is it ever fully stable, and a key factor tending to threaten its stability is the push towards increased efficiency on the part of the employer. In fact it is possible to consider managerial efforts to 'motivate' workers, to design and redesign jobs and to engineer organisational cultures as attempts to *manipulate worker implicit contracts.*

THE MANAGERIAL MANIPULATION OF WORKER IMPLICIT CONTRACTS

The attempts by managers to 'motivate' workers not by 'meeting needs' as in classic 'motivation theory' but by negotiating with and persuading workers that a particular bundle of rewards that is on offer is a fair and reasonable return for the bundle of 'efforts' that the management is asking them to put in.

The relationship between the organisational management and the worker, unequal as the two parties typically are in terms of power and resources, is essentially one of *exchange* within the 'negotiated order' that is the work organisation (see Chapter 2, pp. 35–6). And how people behave or 'perform' in their employment situation is significantly influenced by how they perceive the 'employment deal' that is currently in existence between them and the organisation. Managers, in 'motivating' workers, structuring their tasks or shaping workplace 'values' are necessarily involved in complex processes of negotiation. They do not, however, necessarily straightforwardly negotiate with workers what tasks they are to undertake or how much they are to be paid for doing those tasks. In effect, they negotiate over the basic 'realities' of the employment relationship. Within the basic and unequal power balance of the employment relationship, managers work to establish and maintain a pattern of workplace relations and understandings. As part of this, the workers have to be persuaded that there is a fair and reasonable return for the efforts and initiatives that they make, the risks to health and mental well-being taken, and the degree of managerial authority over them that they accept. That 'return' will be a complex mix of monetary, psychological and social rewards. The mix of reward will involve a certain amount of pay, a certain amount of security, a certain degree of opportunity for career advancement, a certain element of 'social standing' and so on. And managers will strive to ensure that this will be perceived by the employee as a fair balance with what is being asked of those employees by the employing organisation.

Patterns of work orientation and experience within the organisational hierarchy

Because of the different resources that they take into the labour market, the quality of the implicit contract which a worker at a senior organisational level – occupying the associated middle- or upper-class position – is very different to the one that a worker at the bottom end of the organisational and class hierarchy can make. In this way we can link work orientations and work experiences of individuals to the broad structural patterns of modern societies – patterns having interlinked corporate and societal dimensions:

- Those in the higher positions in the class structure, typically in managerial or professional positions, tend to have a relatively *diffuse implicit contract* which means, as Fox (1974) shows, that they will be required to use discretion in their work and experience a high trust relationship with their superiors. The high trust which is put in this type of staff and the relatively high level of rewards (in the form of cash, status, opportunity for intrinsic satisfaction and career advancement offered) are reciprocated on the part of the employees with a willingness to comply with organisational requirements on their own initiative. The type of control to which they are submitted is *indirect* (Chapter 5, p. 112). Organisational norms are 'internalised' and individuals, in effect, control themselves (as well as their subordinates) on behalf of their superordinates.
- Those in lower class positions, typically in less skilled routine work, are more likely to experience a *restricted type of implicit contract*. The generally lower level of rewards is associated with what Fox (1974) describes as institutionalised low-trust relationships with superiors. Work tasks are much more closely prescribed and these are executed (their conception occurring elsewhere) on the basis of a contractual commitment which is specific rather than diffuse. This specificity is represented by there typically being an hourly or weekly wage as opposed to an annual salary, by the much tighter specification of what is required of them and, especially, by the lack of the inducement of potential career promotion. The control mechanism will tend to be of a *direct control* type – one tending to minimise worker responsibility and submitting workers to close supervision.

The broad pattern here is represented in Figure 7.4. It shows general structural tendencies within which individuals each have their own unique experience of work and satisfaction.

Women's preferences, choices and work orientations

The work orientations of women in paid employment are inevitably influenced by the implications of their gender and all that this implies for their life career. A study of over 5,500 women of working age in Britain indicated that girls at that time tended to base their educational, training and job decisions on the assumption that they will be wives and mothers (Martin and Roberts 1984). Whereas boys expected to be the primary wage-earner and to have employment as their main lifetime occupation, girls looked forward to a working life 'interrupted by childbirth and childrearing, usually characterised by partial employment so as to enable them to do the domestic work involved in looking after a husband, children and a home'. Indeed, even where they worked full-time, only a minority of the women in the study said that they shared housework equally with their husbands.

Studies show that economic factors are highly significant within the work orientations of women workers. But, as the implicit contract model would suggest, there is a range of other 'rewards' pertinent to work orientations. Sharpe (1984), for example, suggested that

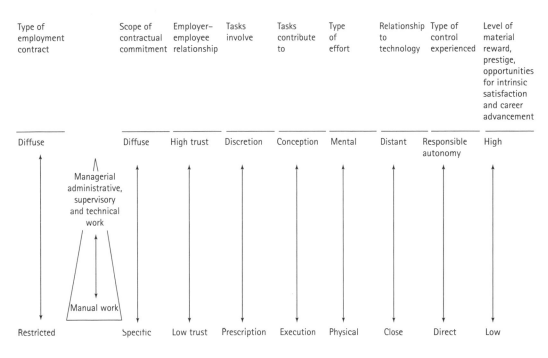

Figure 7.4 Two ideal types of relationship between individual and employing organisation (seen as two ends of various continua related to the hierarchical structure of organisation)

it was the 'social characteristics' of working which gave most meaning to the jobs of the wives and mothers she interviewed and that this was especially the case after a period of not working. Pollert (1981) talked of the 'ray of light' provided in the factory she studied by the company of others for women with children who were experiencing the double burden of home and work. Cavendish (1982) added to this the point that her participant observation study of factory life gave her a feeling of being 'more rooted in social life', enabling her to becoming more outgoing and socially relaxed than she had previously been. On the basis of her sharing this life, 'it seemed only sensible to get married and benefit from the economics of scale of two wage packets'. To consider role reversal would have been 'economic suicide'.

Women's attitudes to work and family do not, however, simply follow labour market opportunities and Dex (1988) provides historical evidence to show that between the 1940s and 1965, attitudes 'changed independently of women's employment experience . . . that is, attitudes appeared to change before women's employment experience had grown'. Subsequently, Dex argued, the structures of employment in Britain had been 'changing to accommodate to women's availability and attitudes towards work'. It is not a matter of women simply reacting to changes in demand: 'the fact that women are prepared to accept primary responsibility for child care, and then structure their employment participation around the availability of their husband to fill in the child care gaps, has its roots, in part, in attitudes'.

Women's 'attitudes' cannot be separated from 'reflexive modernisation' trends in late modern societies for individuals generally to be concerned with expressing their identities and questioning traditional limitations on their desire to express or fulfil themselves (Beck *et al.* 1994). This is recognised by Hakim (2000) in her stress on the part played by choice or 'personal preference' in how women shape their lives. Structural circumstances are seen as freeing women to make such choices, these including the contraceptive and equal opportunities 'revolutions', the increase in white-collar work, the availability of jobs for secondary earners, as well as the cultural emphasis on personal preferences in lifestyles. As a result of these choices, three ideal type work–life preference groups are identified in contemporary European and American societies:

- home-centred,
- work-centred,
- adaptive – where women seek both to work and lead a full family life.

Hakim estimates that around half of British and American women can be allocated to the adaptive category.

Hakim's emphasis on choice and her desire to question the 'feminist myth' that part-time work is forced on women as a result of their domestic responsibilities (Hakim 1995) has been controversial. Ginn *et al.* (1996) insist that the choices women make in these respects are often *constrained* ones, with the contentment they express explainable as an accommodation to their 'lack of alternatives and weak bargaining position', given the pressures of their domestic situation. Walsh's (1999) study of the work orientations of part-time working women showed more than half of her sample having made such constrained choices – choosing part-time work in order to cope with dependent children. Yet there was a significant proportion of women in the study who had chosen part-time work for a variety of 'lifestyle' reasons other than ones relating to domestic pressures. It is clearly vital to take into account both 'agency' and 'structure' (Chapter 1, pp. 4–5) when trying to under-stand how and why women are balancing their working and home lives. And this must mean recognising the opportunity structures that women meet once they are in a particular kind of work. Evetts' (1996) study of women in science and engineering shows the importance of this in her analysis of the pattern of 'promotion accommodation' whereby women would opt out of their career for a period to have children and then accept as organisationally reasonable – gender-neutral that is – the consequential limits that this put on their career opportunities. Crompton and Harris (1998) show something similar in the case of women doctors who 'satisficed', moderating that is, both their occupational and their family ambitions in order to reconcile the two. However, the researchers contrast this picture with the one they found with senior women in banking who had, unlike the women doctors, insisted on more sharing of domestic responsibilities with their spouses and refused to compromise their work careers. This finding is taken to show that occupations vary in the pressures they put on women to seek accommodations in their family relationships to avoid compromising occupational advancement.

Career, identity and experience at work

To recognise that people's work orientations may change over time, sometimes in quite significant ways, as we saw illustrated earlier (pp. 187–9), is to raise the question of the extent to which the human individual is a fixed entity with a given 'personality' that changes little over time. Both the interactionist and the discursive strands of sociology (Chapter 2, pp. 33–7 and 47–51) encourage us to see individuals as having *emergent identities* rather than fixed and relatively unchanging personalities.

IDENTITY

The conception which each individual develops, in relation to others, of who and what they are.

SELF-IDENTITY AND SOCIAL IDENTITY

The two components of a person's identity: self–identity being an individual's own notion of self; and social identity being the notion others have of who and what that individual is.

As we move through different situations and circumstances and interact with different 'others' so we adjust ourselves to achieve a sense of selfhood – our self-identities and social identities (the ways in which we see ourselves and the ways others see us) shape and reinforce each other.

The life of the individual can be seen as a process of continuous emergence (Watson and Harris 1999). But there will nevertheless be a pattern to this emergence, whether this is one viewed by the observer or by the social actor themselves. This process is referred to in the interactionist tradition as *career* – a vital concept in linking the subjective aspects of life with its objective circumstances.

CAREER

A sequence of social positions filled by a person throughout their life or through an aspect of their life such as their involvement in work.

Looking at the individual's work life objectively, for instance, we see them moving through various structural 'statuses' which may be viewed as making up *occupational careers* (each occupation involves various typical stages through which a member may pass, as we saw in Chapter 6, pp. 163–4) or *organisational careers* (each organisation has a series of positions through which individuals may move in typical sequences). However, individuals also have their own view of the process which their life is following. Hughes (1937) refers to the 'moving perspective in which the person sees his life as a whole and interprets the meaning of his various attributes, actions, and the things which happen to him'. This is the individual's *subjective career*.

> **SUBJECTIVE CAREER**
>
> The way an individual understands or makes sense of the way they have moved or are moving through various social positions or stages in the course of their life, or part of their life.

The concept of subjective career is a necessary one if we accept the proposition that 'people seek to achieve overall stability in the outward life and coherence in their inner world' (Collin 1986), a proposition which is central to the interactionist strand of the sociology of work. This further implies that if we wish to understand the work experience of individuals we have to look at their whole life-career. We have to trace through their upbringing and education to appreciate what might happen to them in their later work-career. Their work experience is likely to be fundamentally influenced by the wants and expectations of work which they derive from their upbringing as well as by the skills and abilities with which their physique, intellect and social milieu have endowed them.

Discourse and identity

In reviewing the discursive strand of thinking in Chapter 2, it was noted that various theorists stress the importance of role of discourse in shaping people's subjectivities. Discourses, as we saw, are sets of concepts, statements, terms and expression which provide a framework within which people come to understand and act towards whatever area of life any given discourse covers. They provide important *discursive* resources that the individual may utilise in shaping their notion of who they are. If, say, a discourse is current within a work organisation 'framing' that corporation and its employees as a 'family', we may find people drawing upon the notion to make sense to themselves and others of their involvement in work. Equally, though, we may find others utilising elements of the discourse to distance themselves from their employer – emphasising perhaps that their 'real family' is at home or celebrating their workplace rebellion with notions of their being the 'black sheep of the family'. As Alvesson and Willmott (2002) stress, corporate attempts to target and 'mould the human subject' are balanced with 'other elements of life history forged by a capacity reflexively to accomplish life projects out of various sources of influence and inspiration'. Either way, the corporate 'family discourse' is likely to influence in some way people's work meanings and their behaviours – their orientations to work. Occupational discourses, especially that of 'professionalism', can be a rich source of discursive resources to be used by specialist workers themselves or by spokespersons for their occupational associations. The degree of *discursive ingenuity* that can be deployed in these situations is illustrated in an analysis of managerial talk, part of which is that of the director general of an occupational association who almost redefines what a profession is in order to justify his human resource managers being recognised as belonging to a 'chartered profession', and another part of which is the talk of an HR manager who deploys the language of 'being professional' quite differently (Watson 2002b).

Discursive resources are not simply 'drawn upon' by people to shape their identities. As the Foucauldian tradition emphasises, discourse and power are deeply implicated in each other. How this works is shown by Grey (1994) in his linking of a whole series of 'discursive and non-discursive practices' associated with accounting careers. The idea of an accounting career 'provides a meaning and a rationale for the otherwise disillusioning grind of accountancy training'. Regulation of behaviour is thus achieved in the form of a self-discipline which follows from trainees' acceptance of a 'discourse of career'. Sturdy (1992) combines this kind of insight with interactionist notions of the individual striving to achieve a sense of self to throw light on the way the employers of the clerical workers he studied achieved the 'consent' of the workers to carry out managerial requirements. Collinson (1992) focuses on the subjective experience of shopfloor employment and the role of gender and class elements in employees' subjectivities and how these are linked to patterns of both conformity and resistance in the workplace. He shows, for example, how 'manual workers' socially skilled and culturally embedded practices of resistance, compliance and consent' were 'heavily "saturated" with specific masculine subjectivities'. Knights and McCabe (2001) demonstrate how a shifting discourse of masculinity was to be seen in a financial services call centre, one in which the practices and the language of managers reflected the contradiction whereby a discourse stressing trust, teamwork and creativity simultaneously retained masculine notions of competition, control and conquest.

With the growth of flexible working practices, and increasing numbers of people moving about between jobs, the ways in which people can 'discursively frame' their subjectivities becomes less straightforward than in situations when one was able to draw upon, say, a professional or 'trade' discourse to form the work component of one's identity. Garsten (1999) characterises the situation of temporary workers in terms of *liminality* – one in which they are 'betwixt and between more regular positions' and hence, in effect, have to fall back on their own resources to develop their subjectivities. But what we see if we look at different types of temporary work is the 'experiential ambiguity of liminality': on the one hand the worker may 'transcend the institutions of regular, full-time employment and . . . create a personalised work biography'. On the other hand they may have to settle for 'being disposable' and 'just a temp'. The optimism associated with this former possibility has influenced some observers to talk of a new type of portfolio or 'boundaryless' career.

Portfolio and 'boundaryless' careers or 'one dead end job after another'

Claims that there is a major replacement of 'standard' work with non-standard types of employment have often been exaggerated, as we noted in Chapter 6. It was long ago recognised that certain individuals prefer not to confine their whole career to one employing organisation. W. Watson (1964), for example, identified the *spiralist* – a particular type of aspiring middle-class employee who moves 'upwards' in career by moving from organisation to organisation and locality to locality. This type of person would fit Gouldner's (1957) category of the *cosmopolitan* latent role holder, as opposed to a *local* latent role holder, a person who is more inclined to seek advancement through a single employing organisation. With the increasing pursuit of flexibility by employing organisations and the declining use of internal labour markets (Beynon *et al.* 2002) it is argued that more and more people will build careers that take them beyond the boundaries of particular organisations or localities. Handy (1994) saw what he termed *portfolio careers* offering people opportunities for personal growth and enhanced choices in life. Individuals would combine a variety of work activities within their chosen bundle – some perhaps being primarily concerned with creating income, others aimed at achieving more extrinsic satisfactions.

Arthur and Rousseau (1996) see a general shift occurring from careers which are 'bounded' by relatively stable occupational and organisations structures to *boundaryless* careers where people move, over a lifetime, between occupations, organisations, localities and different types of work task. This is not said to be a move, however, to a state of 'career anarchy'. Instead, people with 'career capital', in the form of networks of contacts, a sense of self-assurance and a capacity to learn and develop new skills, are able creatively to 'enact' (Weick 1995) their careers by experimenting, improvising, adapting and then 'making sense' of their actions. Littleton *et al.* (2000) show how this can work in practice with studies of workers in California's Silicon Valley and people working in the independent film-making industry; and Arthur *et al.* (1999) examine the career history of seventy-five people working in jobs ranging from senior management to unskilled labouring in New Zealand to show that 84 per cent of these moved across jobs and localities in a way that could not be characterised as random. The authors demonstrate how individuals can be seen as experimenting and developing themselves as they move through these unplanned sequences, searching for novelty and fulfilment. Cohen and Mallon (1999) provide British evidence of people in portfolio work reporting a sense of freedom and feeling 'in control' in their work. But they produce a more ambiguous overall picture in which a proportion of the people studied were anxious to *reconstruct* boundaries, rather than break out of them, for example by seeking long-term contracts with organisations.

These shifts in the types of career that individuals are able to make for themselves have been connected to an alleged shift in the type of implicit or 'psychological' contract that employing organisations are offering workers. The old style *relational* contract involving a long-term mutual commitment is being replaced, according to Herriot and Pemberton (1995), by *transactional* contracts where an acceptance of greater instability, uncertainty and willingness to work flexibly is traded for higher material returns. Such a shift pushes the responsibility for career management away from the employer to the workers themselves, at least in circumstances where the employer sees this as to their advantage (Arnold 1997).

Perhaps inevitably, the crucial factor influencing the extent to which any given worker or type of worker can benefit from these trends in career patterning is that of the 'capital' that the individual takes into the labour market, in the sense mentioned above. Research on people lacking such capital and having to work at the 'low wage' end of modern labour markets suggests anything but a pattern of personal growth and fulfilment through experimentation and adaptation. Ehrenreich (2002) took six low-paid jobs in turn to discover first-hand what it is like to work in modern America as a care worker, cleaner, shop worker or waiter. The first thing she discovered was that none of these jobs was truly 'unskilled'. In each case she had to 'master new terms, new tools, and new skills – from placing orders on restaurant computers to wielding the backpack vacuum cleaner'. But what Ehrenreich found 'surprised and offended' her most was the extent to which the worker's self-respect had to be surrendered in the face of a series of humiliations ranging from having one's purse searched or the 'routine indignity' of being tested for drugs. Workers were regularly 'kept in their place' by rules such as ones forbidding 'gossip', or even talking, and by 'little explained punishments' such as having schedules or work assignments unilaterally changed.

In an analysis reminiscent of the classic Chinoy study referred to earlier (p. 177), Ehrenreich writes about hearing throughout one's upbringing that hard work was the 'secret of success'. She comments, however, 'No one ever said that you could work hard – harder even than you ever thought possible – and still find yourself sinking ever deeper into poverty and debt.' If we needed to characterise a 'dead end job', Ehrenreich has done it for us – and for the millions of people who work in jobs like those in the sequence of six that she sampled. Toynbee (2002), in a similar British investigation, powerfully illustrates the strains and the financial hardships of moving from one low paid, low status, job to another. There was no question of 'moving seamlessly from one job to another with no unpaid gap', let alone seeking the personal fulfilments associated with 'portfolio' or 'boundaryless' careers. Toynbee observes that such conditions apply to the 'third of people' who have missed out of the considerable improvements in life circumstances experienced by the other two-thirds of the population, ones which have come about since the 1970s when she previously sampled a variety of manual jobs. Most of the poor in contemporary Britain, she comments, are 'now in work and working as I have described, ferociously hard, often at two or more jobs'.

Managerial orientations and experiences

It may be possible, as we saw earlier (p. 187), to adopt an 'instrumental' orientation to work and lower the emotional involvement in it. This, however, is not so easily done for the worker in the professional or managerial sphere. The prior orientation to work of such people is likely to be quite different, and the absence of intrinsic satisfactions may lead to a greater degree of dissatisfaction and felt deprivation than among working-class employees operating in settings at first sight far more potentially depriving. A picture consistent with this point was painted of the work orientations of British managers in a study by Scase and Goffee (1989). The people they called the 'reluctant managers' were the ones who were 'less than fully committed to their jobs and who have great reservations about giving priority to their work, their careers and, indeed, their employing organisations'. They were warier than they had been in the past about becoming completely 'psychologically immersed in their occupations'.

Similar pressures on the work of managers were observed in a study by Dopson and Stewart (1990) but they found different orientations from those observed by Scase and Goffee on the part of the managers they interviewed. In large part because they believed that they had greater control and responsibility in the 'flatter' managerial hierarchies than they had experienced in the older taller ones, they felt that their jobs had become more challenging and they 'enjoyed the additional responsibilities and variety of their work'. A third study of managerial work in Britain (Watson 2001a) suggests that either of these patterns of orientation are possible in different circumstances within the broad changes occurring in work organisations. The managers closely studied in one industrial organisation were shown to display a strong ambivalence towards their work. It was common within the firm for managers to say they felt rewarded by the opportunities presented in their immediate jobs to achieve tasks, to be 'in control' and to have the respect of the people they worked with. But they were increasingly 'becoming concerned about whether their energies were being directed towards the sort of overall business success' that would give them the security and involvement that they had once experienced. McGovern *et al.* (1998) suggest that in 'leading edge' companies that have 'downsized' there has been an erosion of the old model of managerial employment, rather than a replacement of it. There are fewer opportunities for upward promotion with sideways moves and 'managing your own career' being more than norm (with less employment security, especially for older managers).

In light of the changing situation of managers, and especially the so-called 'middle managers', it would appear, according to Wajcman and Martin's (2001) evidence, that younger managers are moving away from an orientation based on loyalty to the organisation to one emphasising individual career projects. These men and women can be seen to draw upon a range of discourses to *construct their identities*. Thomas and Linstead (2002) show middle managers struggling to avoid 'losing the plot' in the relatively blurred career situations they find themselves in. To provide legitimacy and to justify their existence they make use of various sets of discursive resources such as those of 'professionalism and expertise, gender, performance and commitment, and the public sector ethic'. The researchers note tensions within the accounts that people construct of themselves, however, but overall conclude that managers facing all the pressures of modern organisational life are not becoming psychologically withdrawn in the way Scase and Goffee (1989) observed: rather they are making sense of their situation and their identities by 'drawing on contemporary discourse of management to secure a fixed rhetoric as an "effective manager"'.

Anxiety, emotion and sexuality at work

Angst in the human condition generally and in one type of work specifically

One outcome of the growing interest in human subjectivity within the sociology of work and work organisations is the attention beginning to be paid to the anxieties, fears and emotions which are part of the human condition. The human being, in order to survive psychologically, has to overcome 'the precariousness of identity implicit in the unpre-dictability of social relations' (Knights and Willmott 1985). The world is potentially an utterly ambiguous place and, without the set of meanings which is supplied by human culture, people would be unable to cope. Without a sense of order or *nomos* (which comes from culture) the individual would become 'submerged in a world of disorder, senselessness and madness' (Berger 1973). The anxiety or *existential angst*, which people can only handle with the help of culture, is more than a matter of specific fears. It has to be understood 'in relation to the overall security system the individual develops' as part of their self-identity (Giddens 1991). However, the human is not a simple creature of its culture in the same way that other animals are largely creatures of their instincts. Cultures are constantly being made by people and each individual has their own interaction with – their own pattern of giving to and taking from – the cultures within which they live. This means that, for all of us, a sense of order and self-identity is constantly in the process of being won from the social environment in which we find ourselves. Angst is an ever-present condition which we, each and every one, have to handle. The work context is one of the key arenas in which we experience and learn to handle, more or less effectively, the angst which is inherent to the human condition.

A study of managers in American corporations (Jackall 1988) suggested that managerial work of this kind is especially anxiety-making with managers constantly attempting to hide their daily fears, panics and anxieties behind a mask of self-control and amiability. Jackall shows his managers terrified by the unpredictability and capriciousness of their employment and work experience, a terror which they mask with a demeanour of enthusiasm. A different emphasis is to be found in a British study of managerial experience (Watson 2001a). Here anxiety is seen much more as the normal human condition but it is argued that the nature of managerial work and, especially, its expectation that the manager has to exert control over others (directly or indirectly) as well as over their own lives, can exacerbate this basic human condition. Managers having to face a 'double control problem' in this way leads them to seek comfort in managerial 'fads fashions and flavour of the month' (Watson 1994) as well as encouraging them to engage in all kinds of ill-tempered behaviour, threats of violence, interpersonal rudeness as well as more benign joking behaviour. Most of the classic texts on management, Taylor's and Mayo's most notably (see Chapter 2), portray managers as rational non-sentimental beings. This has been to deny the very humanity of those holding command roles in modern bureaucracies.

The rise of the stress discourse

An aspect of personal experience of work that relates to anxiety is that of 'stress'. The notion of stress and the popularity of its use is a historically recent phenomenon with what Newton *et al.* (1995) call 'the stress discourse' significantly coming to the fore in the 1970s and 1980s. At the heart of this discourse is a stretching of the simple and ancient notion of 'feeling distressed' to a near medical condition in which people's circumstances somehow render them incapable of performing in the way they would normally be expected to perform in those circumstances.

STRESS

A sense of distress arising because of pressures experienced in certain social or economic circumstances that render the sufferer emotionally, and sometimes physically, incapable of continuing to behave in the ways expected of them in those circumstances.

The increasing attention to stress at work beginning in the latter quarter of the twentieth century has been linked with growing concern about the intensification of work together with increased job insecurity and longer working hours. However, this link is questioned by Wainwright and Calnan (2002) who, whilst accepting that work may currently be more demanding than it was in the recent past, question whether, when put in an historical context, contemporary work can be seen as the 'psychologically scarring' experience presented in the work-stress discourse. Just as Newton *et al.* (1995) portray the stress discourse as reducing the social to the biological, Wainwright and Calnan suggest that it takes emotional problems that could be seen as normal responses to everyday life and redefines them as symptoms of mental illness. They relate the rise of the stress discourse to the increasing popularity of psychotherapy and counselling and suggest that problems and conflicts at work that were once handled through collective industrial action or political changes are increasingly converted into individualised threats to worker health – issues to be dealt with by therapeutic intervention rather than by industrial or political action.

Emotions and feelings

When we talk of anxiety and stress, we are clearly dealing with aspects of human feelings and emotions – topics that sociological analysis has not tended to examine closely until recently. To make it easier to get a 'sociological purchase' on these matters, it is useful to conceptualise 'emotion' in cultural terms.

EMOTIONS

Feelings are sensations relating to a psychological state that are felt bodily and emotions are the way these sensations are culturally interpreted.

A retail worker, for example, may find themselves confronted by a shopper who starts to shout at them and, as this happens, starts to *feel* agitated, perhaps as their hands begin to shake and their skin reddens. Where 'emotion' comes into this is when sense is made of those feelings by drawing on discursive resources available in that individual's culture – by relating them perhaps to 'anger', perhaps to 'embarrassment' or, yet again, perhaps to 'taking offence'. This is not to say, however, that emotions (the 'cultural' dimension of this experience) are what *follow* feelings (the 'animal' dimension of the experience): it could be that a cultural awareness of the appropriateness of being angry in the face of certain rude behaviour is what triggers the physical sensations or 'feelings' that manifest themselves in a particular situation.

The rediscovery of feelings and emotions in the sociology of work and organisation is often connected to the influence of Max Weber and his ideal type of bureaucracy in which there is 'no place for love, hatred and all purely personal, irrational and emotional elements which escape calculation' (Weber 1978). But this should not be read as assuming that Weber wished to discourage attention to matters of irrationality or affectivity. His interest in these was 'submerged by twentieth-century rationalistic models of organisation' says Albrow (1994). Albrow (1997) argues that Weber was pointing out that the bureaucratic ethos does not attempt to exclude *per se* emotional elements from organisations – it is concerned only to exclude those 'which escape calculation'. This means, in effect, that emotions, feelings, sentiments and the like are harnessed to corporate ends in the ideal-type bureaucratised organisation. This was indeed the logic followed in the human relations strand of industrial sociology (Chapter 2, pp. 29–30) when it was argued that the managers should pay attention to the 'sentiments' of workers (like their desire to 'belong') and not allow these sentiments to undermine corporate purposes.

It is now recognised that emotions and feelings pervade every aspect of working and organisational lives. As Fineman (2003) puts it, emotions are not an 'optional extra, or incidental to "real" work' but are part of the 'warp and weft of work experiences and practices as people take into the workplace our loves, hates, anxieties, envies, excitement, disappointments and pride' – all of these underpinning, consciously or unconsciously, 'the collations, conflicts and negotiations that emerge'.

Emotional labour

Issues of emotionality at work do not only arise because 'people are people' and are therefore continually at the mercy of their feelings. Certain types of work formally require people to engage in what Hochschild (1985) calls *emotional labour*.

> ### EMOTIONAL LABOUR
>
> An element of work activity in which the worker is required to display certain emotions in order to complete work tasks in the way required by an employer.

Hochschild shows how the emotional labour required of airline flight attendants who were expected continually to wear the 'mask' of a smile when in the presence of passengers took its toll of these workers – whether they were those who complied zealously with the requirement or were those who handled it self-consciously as a form of 'acting'. There was always the danger of feelings of anger or irritation breaking through the facade of pleasure and happiness. Taylor (1998) draws a parallel between the emotional labour he observed among telephone sales agents, who were required to create an atmosphere of friendliness and intimacy with external customers, and the emotional labour that was required of production workers operating within a Total Quality Management regime which required them to treat 'internal customers' – organisational co-workers – in a similar manner.

There is a danger with analyses like this, however. As Bolton (2000) points out, the notion of 'emotional labour' can become overstretched and conceptually imprecise. Hochschild (1989) differentiated between two types of 'emotion management' that people engage in: the 'emotion work' that we all do in our private lives and 'emotional labour' that we do in a commercial context for a wage. But this tends to push aside the ways in which people at work engage with others emotionally in ways that are not directly tied into the formal job requirements (most obviously, developing warm and supportive relationships with either co-workers or customers in the workplace out of personal choice). Bolton (2000) helps overcome this difficulty by developing four categories of emotion management: *presentational* (where one handles emotions according to general social rules); *philanthropic* (emotional management given as a gift); *prescriptive* (emotional management according to organisational or professional rules of conduct); and *pecuniary* (emotional management for commercial gain). Any particular worker may range across all of these categories in the course of their working day, and to look for the links, overlaps and contradictions that arise between these can help us to understand more fully the richness and complexity of the emotional dimension of work.

Sexuality and the workplace

There are sexual dimensions to almost every aspect of organisational life, as Hearn and Parkin (1987) show, even if these only become clearly manifest when formal complaints are made about sexual harassment or where events occur such as the hospital 'works do' observed by these authors where open sexual acts occurred with couples making 'blatant use of the premises, both cubby holes and semi-public "back regions"'. Burrell (1984, 1992) points out how managements in organisations ranging from monasteries, prisons and ships at sea to factories and commercial organisations, attempt to repress sexual relations and expel them from the organisation into the 'home'. Yet people's notion of themselves as 'sexual beings' is a vital part of their identities, and Brewis and Linstead (2000b) argue that this influences the 'particular sense of organisation' that people experience in specific work circumstances. The sexual harassment discourse that one associates with attempts to avoid sexually abusive behaviour in organisations, for example, can come to reinforce such behaviour – by identifying men as predators and women as victims.

In spite of a managerial interest in suppressing sexuality in the workplace, managements may also collude in a degree of expression of sexuality as part of the delivery of what is not formally seen as a kind of sexual service. This is effectively shown in Filby's (1992) research in off-course betting shops where there is an 'elision . . . of emotional labour and sexuality'. Filby shows how a 'minority undercurrent' of the conversations which go on between staff and between staff and customers involve 'sexy chat' – speech acts 'which themselves are experienced as pleasurable as well as sometimes discomforting and hurtful'. Sexuality is also 'embodied in gaze, deportment and clothing, and sometimes more obviously in expressive physical encounters'. In the light of certain unspoken assumptions which exist about 'what men and women are and what male punters want' there is an extent, says Filby, to which 'these moments are related to the milieu of service delivery as implicitly constructed by management, a milieu which is envisaged as an aid to business'. Put more simply, the management is more than happy for customers to receive a little light sexual amusement. But it might or it might not suit the employees who are expected to provide it. And, as Williams *et al.* (1999) observe, while service workers are sometimes paid to act in a 'sexy' manner or to engage in sexual innuendo with customers, in other jobs, in prisons or hospitals for example, 'mere rumors of sexual behaviour or desire can destroy a career'.

Work and non-working lives

The relationship between the work and non-work aspects of our lives is complex and two-way. At the highest level of generality the two spheres interrelate to form a particular type of society, the industrial capitalist type examined in Chapter 3 being the one with which we are concerned. Work arrangements are located in the power structures and cultural understandings of the wider society with social class, family, education and other social structural factors having a major influence on individuals' prior orientation to work as well as on their socially conditioned predisposition to act and think in a certain way once in work.

Work, leisure and work–life balance

Leisure is something we generally identify as 'not work'. It can be defined along such lines.

> **LEISURE**
>
> Those activities which people pursue for pleasure and which are not a necessary part of their business, employment or domestic management obligations.

Ways of taking leisure clearly vary with personal taste. But they may also vary with different types of employment. The hours left free for leisure by different kinds of work and the money available to spend on leisure are factors which clearly relate work and leisure forms. However, other factors are also relevant and, to help indicate a pattern in these, Parker (1982) identified three types of relationship between work and leisure: extension, opposition and neutrality.

- Leisure is likely to be experienced as an *extension* of work where a relatively high degree of autonomy and intrinsic satisfaction is experienced in work. The academic's work and leisure reading may well shade one into the other and engineers may well apply their expertise to hobbies and read professional literature in their non-work time (Gerstl and Hutton 1966). Parker's research indicates that social workers tend not to see a sharp distinction between their working and non-working lives, and Evans and Bartolemé (1980) argue that for the majority of managers in their study the relationship between work and non-work was one of 'spillover', generally with the work experience influencing individuals' private lives much more than the other way round.
- Leisure is likely to have a neutral relationship to work where there is less autonomy and potential self-fulfilment. Those in jobs such as ones involving routine clerical work reflect their lack of involvement and passivity at work in their leisure pastimes.
- Leisure operates in *opposition* to work where the worker who is liable to be frustrated and unfulfilled at work concentrates on the fulfilling and comfortable pastimes of home and family (this privatised lifestyle fitting with the instrumental orientation to work considered earlier) or they may pursue the more gregarious and even riotous type of leisure associated with the coalminer or deep sea fisherman (Tunstall 1962).

Some writers have pointed to the opportunities which some workers may find to compensate for work experience in the exercise of skill and the obtaining of social satisfaction in activities like pigeon racing (Mott 1973). But the general likelihood of this type of compensatory effect has been strongly argued against by people such as Meissner (1971), who diagnosed what he calls 'the long arm of the job' and argues that the suppressing of the capacity for initiative in the work setting will tend to reduce the capacity for engaging in leisure activities which involve discretion, planning and co-ordination.

Leisure is only one way in which time is spent away from the formal workplace. As was implied in the definition of leisure set out above, domestic management responsibilities can be seen as a form of work. Hochschild in her influential book *The Time Bind* (2001) argued that the type of work carried out in the home was becoming seen as less desirable than the work done in the workplace, the latter being both more economically and psychologically rewarding. A vicious circle was observed in Hochschild's research whereby people were opting to work longer in the formal workplace with the effect that home and family tasks seemed even more burdensome, this pushing people further into long working hours, at a significant cost to the quality of family life and, especially, the well-being of children. The public concern created by this study came on top of the effect of an earlier book by Schor (1991) which popularised the notion of the 'overworked American'. In Britain, worry about a poor 'work–life balance' with negative effects both on family life and workplace effectiveness was taken up by the government, and a government-sponsored study (DfEE 2000) pointed to a 'long hours culture' in which one in nine employees, many of these with children, were working more than a sixty-hour week, with two-thirds of men arguing that to shift to lower or part-time hours would undermine their career prospects.

When systematic surveys are carried out of shifts in working patterns over time, a very different picture emerges. Sullivan and Gershuny (2001) suggest that time-use diaries from a range of industrialised societies showed 'relative stability in the balance between work and leisure time' between the 1960s and the 1990s. There are various reasons for this discrepancy between the statistical data and the notion of a 'time famine' that people are writing about and reporting to researchers. An important one may be a bias arising from a tendency to generalise too widely from evidence of what is being experienced by the sort of professional dual-earner couples with dependent children that writers like Hochschild focus upon. This view is supported by the research of Jacobs and Gerson (2001) who question the claim that there is a general pressure on people's time and that, instead, working time is becoming bifurcated with one segment of the labour market containing workers who are 'putting in more hours at work than ever before' whereas another segment 'are unable to find jobs that provide enough hours of work'. This suggests that it might be realistic to worry about the negative effects on working productivity, health and family life that, for example, the British survey of 1,223 executives by Worrall and Cooper (1999) reports – at the same time it is realistic to be concerned about the implications for other people of there not being enough work available to them. Either way, it is important always to remember, as Epstein and Kalleberg (2001) put it, that patterns of time use are socially constructed and that we must always 'differentiate perceptions of time pressures from the actuality'. It may also be helpful to question the use of the notion of a 'balance' of work and non-work activities since the metaphor suggests, as Thompson and Bunderson (2001) put it, that there is 'some appropriate distribution of hours that an individual should achieve among the various domains of their life'. To do this misrepresents the complex psychological processes by which people make sense of their time and manage multiple life domains.

Unemployment

The experience of being unemployed in a society in which there is a work ethic which puts considerable value on being 'in a job', and where a reasonable level of income can only come for most people from employment, is likely to be both psychologically and materially distressing. There can be 'an experiential gap that can exasperate the jobless' in the face of 'the sheer force of the effect of no longer being creditworthy in a society that builds so many of its transactions, in one way or another, on cash' (Fineman 1987). In her influential study of the experience of unemployment, Jahoda (1982) concentrated on what people tend to lose, in addition to a source of income, when they become unemployed. A person's job:

- imposes a time structure on the day;
- enlarges the scope of social relations beyond the often emotionally charged ones of family and neighbours;
- gives them a feeling of purpose and achievement through task involvement in a group setting;
- assigns social status and clarifies personal identity;
- requires one to engage in regular activity.

These socio-psychological functions of employment are not easily replaced when unemployment is experienced. However, a variety of other factors also influence how unemployment is experienced. Both the financial impact and the impact on work identity and identity within the family tend to vary with the 'previous location within the labour market' (Ashton 1985). Workers who have been in routine and repetitive jobs can experience short-term unemployment as a relief, for instance, and housewives who also work full-time may be able to use their domestic responsibilities to 'impose a temporal structure on their daily activities' if they become unemployed.

A considerable amount of evidence has been collected to show that there is a significant connection between the experience of unemployment and both physical and mental ill health. In reviewing the evidence gathered by a series of studies, Gallie and Vogler (1994) showed that the unemployed suffer from a process of cumulative disadvantage and that their 'weak labour market position is accompanied not only by much greater financial difficulty, but by disadvantage in both health and housing'. However, there are considerable differences in the way the 'welfare regimes' of different countries affect the experiences of the unemployed and, in addition to the level of support given by the state, factors such as the strength of family and community ties make a considerable difference to the level of 'social exclusion' experienced by unemployed people (Gallie and Paugam 2000).

It is widely believed that it is the fall in income which has the greatest impact on people's mental health followed by the removal of the socio-psychological factors identified by Jahoda. Burchell (1994), however, places particular stress on insecurity as a generator of psychological stress. His research showed little difference between the levels of stress among the unemployed and among those experiencing high levels of insecurity within work. He further showed that unemployed people who enter a secure job show much greater improvement in psychological well-being than those taking up insecure jobs.

The evidence which we have from those cases where people appear to cope well with the experience of unemployment strongly indicates the importance of psychological factors and personal values. Warr (1983), for example, reported that the 'good copers' whom he studied all had financial difficulties but maintained high levels of emotional well-being. This was associated with 'considerable personal activity, driven by strongly held religious, social or political values'. Nordenmark and Strandh (1999) use Swedish evidence to demonstrate that relatively good mental well-being can be achieved if *both* economic and psychosocial needs are met by means other than employment. Miles (1984) found that the psychological well-being of the sample of more than a hundred unemployed men he studied was better where there was involvement in such activities as voluntary work, team sport or part-time education. But he added that the large majority of men failed to get very much access to experiences which would meet socio-psychological needs; the signs of 'adaptation to unemployment' were 'very limited'. This is supported by the evidence gathered by Gershuny (1994) which shows that, once they are unemployed, people have far fewer opportunities of experiencing social interactions than the employed. This applies to men more than women, however.

The evidence indicates that the unemployed form, as Gallie and Marsh (1994) put it, 'a distinctive group at the bottom of the social heap'. This raises the question of whether members of this group possess or develop distinctive attitudes to work and employment in general. The studies gathered by Gallie, Marsh and Vogler (1994) show that only a minority of the unemployed studied were not seeking work or were inflexible about what work they were willing to undertake. There is little evidence of a 'culture of dependency' developing among the unemployed. Where there is inflexibility about opportunities it tends to be among those who are held back by their circumstances – age or being a single mother (Dawes 1993). A study of redundant steelworkers carried out by Westergaard, Noble and Walker (1989) suggests that it was much less worker attitudes and behaviour that led to success or otherwise in obtaining work as the qualifications of individuals and how this related to the level of demand for particular skills in the labour market. Commitment to the work ethic among these men was high and they were typically prepared to take jobs at a skill level lower than the one for which they were qualified. Young unemployed people are similarly shown to want to find jobs. Research by Banks and Ullah (1988) shows this but it also shows how continuing unemployment created a sense of discouragement and reduced efforts to find work.

8 Conflict, challenge and resistance in work

Conflict and co-operation at work

To do justice to the subtlety and the complexities of the phenomena which it studies, sociology has to take account of the interplay which occurs in social life between initiative and constraint. Attention has to be given to both structural factors and the experiences and intentions of individuals. Structural patterns were emphasised in earlier chapters of this book on the nature of industrialised societies, on organisations and on occupations. The accounts given of these tendencies towards a patterning in work life were not, however, ones which reified these structures, giving them a concrete existence over and above the human efforts which create them. These structural tendencies are to be seen, rather, as the outcomes of various human processes of initiative, power-seeking, negotiation and conflict. The concept of *conflict* is one that is sometimes used with a structural emphasis, emphasising differences of interests between social parties, and sometimes with an emphasis on activities or behaviours.

> **CONFLICT**
>
> A phenomenon that occurs at two levels. Conflict at the level of interests exists where there is a difference between different parties (employers and employees, say, or workers and customers) over desired outcomes; and conflict at the level of behaviour comes about when parties seeking different outcomes either directly clash over those differences and engage in open dispute or indirectly express their differences through such gestures as acting destructively or co-operating in a sullen or grudging manner.

Sociologists see conflicts existing and occurring in the context of societal, occupational and organisational structures. These structures reflect to a large degree the greater success of some social groups compared to others in the securing of control over their own lives and over parts of the lives of others and hence in their gaining of access to scarce and generally desirable rewards. The emphasis of this chapter will be on various reactions to these efforts to control and, inevitably – given the continuous dialectic which occurs between initiative and structuring – on the resulting institutionalisation of these reactions, giving us once again patterns or structures. We will not be so much looking at something different from the earlier concerns with occupational and organisational patterns as looking at a different aspect of the same things. Whereas, for example, the emphasis in our discussion of work organisations was on attempts of managerial interests to exert control over work and its products, we shall now give greater emphasis to the efforts and accommodations of the subordinate, the disadvantaged and the aspiring. The view from above, so to speak, will be complemented by the view from below. But efforts to control from above continue to play their part, as we see managerial efforts to manage conflict and to handle potentially rival challenges to control.

Part of the chapter will be concerned with the area of academic study which takes the title 'industrial relations'.

INDUSTRIAL RELATIONS

The activities and institutions associated with relationships between employers and groups of collectively organised employees.

However, a sociological interest in conflict at work goes beyond the territory of the typical industrial relations specialist in two respects:

1 it sets specific conflicts and activities in the wider context of the structure and dynamics of the type of society in which they occur;
2 it looks to the opposite end of the spectrum to consider the unofficial, the informal and the relatively spontaneous activities of conflict, challenge and defence in work.

Kelly (1998) has argued for a 'rethinking' of the subject of industrial relations consistent with the first of these more sociological emphases, in the light of the subject's tendency to avoid explicit theory construction and the way it has had to compete for attention with academic human resource management (Chapter 5, pp. 108–11). He argues for an emphasis on the dynamics of class mobilisation and the relating of these to patterns of labour history and long-wave patterns in capitalist economies. Ackers (2002), however, questions the emphasis on workplace-centred patterns of mobilisation and militancy, arguing for a 'neo-pluralist' focus on industrial relations which takes into account connections between work and other spheres of life, such as the family, and which is sensitive to ethical issues. In effect, this is to argue for a sociology of work focus rather than an 'industrial relations' or 'employment relations' one.

Since the experience of work for the majority of people in industrial capitalist societies occurs in an employment relationship, employer–employee conflicts inevitably remain central to the concerns of the sociology of work and industry. These conflicts are indeed the most crucial ones and they provide the context in which many other work conflicts occur. Edwards (1986) characterises the basic conflict of interests between capital and labour in terms of *structured antagonism*. Each side to the employment relationship 'depends on the other while also having divergent wants'. This means that 'conflict is intertwined with co-operation: the two are produced jointly within particular ways of organising labour processes'. However, employer–employee conflicts are by no means the only ones which occur, although the context for other divergences of interests will be the more basic patterns of 'structured antagonism'. Within this context, people at work not only come into conflict with their bosses and their subordinates but with their peers, their customers and their clients. Divergence of interest and orientation between individuals and groups in the course of their work experience is our concern here and justice must be done to the range of these divergences and to the variety of ways in which they are manifested in the different contexts and at the different levels at which people work.

For social life to proceed at work as in any other sphere, be it leisure activity or political life, there must be co-operation between people. Co-operation is not only vital for necessary tasks to be achieved, it also gives stability to daily life. The minimising or controlling of differences of interest between people required by it suggests some positive psychological significance for co-operative activity. Co-operation is comfortable, we might say. From this it is not difficult to make the leap to the suggestion that co-operation is 'good' and conflict 'bad'. But co-operation and conflict cannot really be opposed in this way, either ethically or theoretically. Conflict and co-operation are omnipresent and inevitably co-existent in social life. Given the scarcity of humanly valued goods in the world and the competition which tends to follow in order to obtain access to these, we find that co-operation with one interest group may automatically imply conflict with another. Conflictful activities are as much part of life therefore as 'co-operative' ones.

Conflict and co-operation are two sides of the same coin. Yet there is a common tendency in everyday thinking about social life to see examples of co-operation as healthy and conflicts as pathological. This no doubt relates back to the psychologically comforting overtones of the notion of co-operation. But it is none the less a nonsense. Co-operation cannot of itself be evaluated as good or healthy any more than can conflict per se be seen as bad or unhealthy. We can only judge it by the ends to which it is related. Co-operation with a murderer would be as widely deprecated, for example, as conflict with a rapist would be applauded. By the same token, to enter into conflict with one's employer (or one's employee) cannot of itself – without reference to the point at issue – be judged right or wrong, desirable or undesirable, healthy or unhealthy. Yet in our contemporary society such judgements do tend to be made. This probably results from ideological influences combined with the negative psychological overtones of the idea of 'conflict'. And such a tendency presents a major barrier to the understanding among academics and laymen alike of work conflicts and 'industrial relations' activity. For sociological analysis of these spheres to proceed, issue has to be taken with a formidable array of conventional wisdoms and everyday evaluative tendencies.

Analysing conflict at work

Frames of reference

To come to terms with some of the difficulties of analysing issues of work conflict and to deal with the frequent confusions of description and prescription which characterise this field, it is helpful to look at the various frames of reference which are typically used in discussions of industrial relations issues. Following the approach of Fox (1973, 1974) we can note the existence of three analytical frameworks which are available to us: the unitary, the pluralist and the radical. Each of these stresses particular aspects of work relations:

1 The *unitary* framework assumes a fundamentally common interest between all of those operating in the workplace or in society at large.
2 The *pluralist* view recognises a variety of interests but sees these as more or less balancing each other out in practice.
3 The *radical* perspective recognises the basic inequalities and power differentials characterising industrial capitalist society and relates work conflicts back to these structural patterns.

These three frames of reference are clearly rivals as tools for analysis. But our problem in evaluating them is made particularly complex by the fact that these three perspectives not only tend to describe the world differently but are frequently used to support arguments for how the world should or should not be. In other words, these analytical models also function as ideologies. Our consideration of these three approaches will primarily be concerned to judge their relative analytical utility.

Unitary thinking

In what Fox characterises as the unitary frame of reference (1966, 1973) the employing organisation is seen as being based on a community of interest. The management are the best qualified to decide how these common interests are to be pursued. Hence employee opposition is irrational and 'industrial action' on the part of the employee is generally misguided and frequently the outcome of the successful agitation of troublemakers or 'politically motivated' individuals. The ideological value of such a perspective to the owner or manager of the work organisation is clear to see; the employee who questions the authority of the manager can readily be compared to a disloyal family member or to a footballer who challenges the captain of his own team. In this way the employee challenge is rendered dishonourable or misguided.

At the national level, the unitary frame of reference makes much use of the concept of 'national interest', a notion which is popular with government representatives – whose task is not dissimilar at times to that of the manager in the work enterprise – in a way directly analogous to the industrial manager's talk of football teams, families and the like. The effectiveness of such appeals is questionable in practical terms. Nevertheless some general legitimacy given to them in the culture at large is suggested by the resorting from time to time to criticisms of trade unions or groups of workers for 'holding the country to ransom'. As Fox (1973) points out, the unitary framework offers a variety of ways of questioning the legitimacy of trade union activities suggesting, alternatively, that unions are historical carry-overs, no longer needed in an age of enlightened management; that they are outcomes of sectional greed; or that they are vehicles for subversive political interests.

There is no denying the sense behind the advocacy by leaders of enterprises or governments of 'team spirit' or community of interest. All leadership requires legitimacy and this involves ideological utterances. Where such utterances become a threat to the understanding of what is the case is where prescription and description become confused. Managers or politicians are as likely to be misled as are the rest of us if they come to believe their own propaganda. To attempt to run an organisation or a government on the assumption that there are no fundamental conflicts of interest between employers and employees, producers and consumers, and so on, would be folly indeed. Hence the increasing popularity, at least among academics, of viewing both industrial and political issues through a pluralistic frame of reference.

Pluralist analyses

Pluralism as both an ideology and an analytical perspective has been the subject of extensive debate among both political scientists and industrial relations analysts. At the level of the work organisation this perspective recognises the existence within the enterprise of various different and indeed conflicting interests. However, these differences are not such that they cannot be accommodated: the benefits of collaboration between these fairly evenly balanced interests are such that compromises can be achieved to enable collaborative activity to proceed – to the benefit of all parties. Employees do have to surrender autonomy at work and recognise certain managerial prerogatives. This should not be seen as unreasonable or as reflecting any basic inequality, since management has to accept corresponding constraints. These involve recognition of a right on the part of employees to organise themselves to 'loyally oppose' and bargain over rewards and procedures. In this view, trade unions and the mechanisms of collective bargaining are necessary for the 'managing' of the conflicts of interest which exist between employers and employed and whose existence it is naive and foolish to deny. At the national level the state tends to be seen becoming involved as only one among the range of different stakeholders or as the protector of the public interest where that may be threatened by any one interest group becoming too powerful. This pluralist doctrine was supported by the Donovan Commission on industrial relations in Britain which argued in 1968 for the continuation of the British voluntaristic tradition whereby managements and unions are left to settle their differences, as far as this is possible, on their own terms.

The pluralist frame of reference became almost an orthodoxy among British industrial relations experts in the 1960s, but for a variety of reasons it became increasingly subject to critical scrutiny in the 1970s. This was largely as a result of its being found to be inadequate *sociologically*. As has been pointed out by one of those who became a leading critic of the pluralist perspective, which he had once advocated, the pluralist framework offers a fairly appropriate set of working assumptions for those involved in the practical world of industry and politics, given that 'irrespective of personal philosophy, a working acceptance of the basic structure, objectives, and principles which characterise industry is usually a condition of being able to exert influence towards reform' (Fox 1973). Nevertheless, it is felt that the radical alternative, as well as offering what Fox sees as a 'necessary stimulus and guide to the pursuit of more fundamental change', also has 'greater intellectual validity'.

Radical perspectives

The sociological reaction to pluralist analyses of industrial conflict and 'industrial relations' helped shape industrial sociology more broadly and, says Brown (1992), provided a 'favourable context' for the new interest in labour processes (Chapter 2, pp. 44–6), which was to emerge. The reaction to pluralism was based upon the recognition of various 'crucial limitations' (Brown 1983):

- Pluralist analyses fail to recognise the extent and persistence of 'marked inequalities of condition and opportunity' in society at large. This means that there is a playing down of the extent to which settlements ultimately rest on the power of some groups to impose outcomes on others in a society which lacks what Goldthorpe (1974) called 'any principled basis for the distribution of income and wealth'.
- The extent to which the state has to become involved in industrial relations is underestimated.
- Too little attention is given to problems in the societal 'infrastructure' which is so diverse and differentiated that there is no basis for the growth of a formalised and centralised set of institutions for the regulation of industrial conflict.

Given that a basic characteristic of sociological thinking is that it ultimately relates whatever it is studying back to the way society as a whole is organised (Chapter 1, p. 3), it is not surprising that sociologists who have been sensitive to the structured inequalities of modern societies baulked at industrial-relations analyses which might imply some degree of power equality between the various parties in industrial conflicts. However, some of the radical critics of pluralist thinking may have exaggerated the extent to which pluralists have assumed such equality. Radical analyses of industrial conflict, in the sense of analyses which go beneath the surface phenomena to the underlying 'roots' of issues and stress the importance of basic inequalities, need not necessarily involve a rejection of pluralist values. Fox (1979) observed that one can argue that a country like Britain has deep social inequalities, and is not therefore adequately liberal and pluralist, whilst still believing in liberal pluralism as a means of action and a desirable goal. Because there is a tendency to question all forms of liberal pluralism within Marxism, as Fox pointed out, it may be helpful to use Crouch's (1982) distinction between Marxist analyses and radical (or, more properly, 'radical pluralist') ones.

> ### A RADICAL PLURALIST FRAME OF REFERENCE
>
> This recognises the plurality of groups and interests in society (and welcomes social pluralism in principle) whilst observing the more basic patterns of power and inequality which tend to shape, as well be shaped by it.

As Crouch says, in applying these frames of reference to questions about the nature and role of trade unions, the Marxists go a stage further than the radicals. Whereas the radicals differ from the pluralists in generally 'digging deeper into the social structure to find their explanatory variables', the Marxists are more specific in taking as the cornerstone of their analyses the class relationship between capital and labour as 'the major determinant of social relations'. The concept of contradiction, however, is one which is used by both Marxists and non-Marxists as a device for examining the structural patterns which underlie the surface phenomena of work conflicts.

Contradictions and conflicts

To talk of contradictions in social arrangements is to consider the ways in which the various principles that underlie social organisation are inconsistent or clash with each other. To analyse contradictions is to locate internal tensions or strains which exist within 'systems' and which may lead to either collapse of that system or some kind of adaptation of it by those wishing to retain the basic features of the system.

> **CONTRADICTIONS**
>
> Tendencies within a social or organisational structure for certain principles on which that structure is based to clash with each other in a way that undermines that structure.

Whereas Marxian usage of the term contradiction emphasises the ways in which contradictions lead to the collapse of particular 'modes of production', the concept can be used in a more 'open' way, accepting that constant adaptation is as likely a possibility as collapse or revolutionary supersession. Whilst it is true that the early industrial employers created a working class which had the potential to undermine employer interests, it is equally true that they adopted policies that coped with such a challenge, giving us, for example, the dynamic behind changing employment or 'human resourcing' strategies (Chapter 6, pp. 180–1).

The notion of contradiction, in one form or another, is widely used throughout sociology and it can be applied to some of the fundamental issues that arise within industrial capitalism. The close correspondence between the Marxian notion of contradiction and structural-functionalist ideas of 'strain' (structural-functionalism having been seen by many as the most conservative brand of sociological theory) was pointed out by Lipset (1976) who cited Eisenstadt's (1973) observation that 'both Durkheim and Weber saw many contradictions inherent in the very nature of the human condition in society in general, and saw them articulated with increasing sharpness in the developments of the modern order in particular'. These sociologists, said Eisenstadt, were far less optimistic than Marx about overcoming the ubiquitous and continuous 'tensions between the creative and restrictive aspects of modern life, of potential contradictions between liberty and rationality, between these on the one hand and justice and solidarity on the other'.

In stressing the idea of structural contradiction we are drawing attention away from the specific or 'surface' conflicts which may arise between different actors or groups in social life to the general or 'deeper' problems which give rise to these. For example, within the Marxian perspective it is not the particular conflicts which happen to take place between capitalists and workers that are crucial but the more basic contradiction between the collective production of wealth and its private appropriation. A basic sociological question is thus raised: are the organisational principles of collective production and private consumption compatible in the long run? Such questions correspond to ones raised by Weber's notion of a 'paradox of consequences' in social life (Chapter 4, pp. 189–91). In the long run can the formally rational means such as those of wage-labour, advanced technical division of labour, and instrumental motivation serve the materially rational ends of those who devised them?

The particular strain or contradiction with which Durkheim has commonly been associated is that whereby social inequalities lead to a situation in which certain goals are stressed by the culture but to which access for many is systematically denied. Durkheim's observation of industrial capitalism in action led him to an increasing awareness that persisting inequalities threatened the kind of social solidarity which he thought to be possible within the 'organic division of labour' which characterises modern economic life. For economic life to be regulated there needed to be some kind of moral basis underlying it, otherwise anomie would prevail, but he could not see how such a 'normative order' could be achieved whilst inherited inequalities of opportunity and condition existed. Industrial capitalist society, with its basic class inequalities, has to impose order, and, to the extent that this is so, 'fundamental discontent and unrest persist if only in latent form' (Goldthorpe 1974). From his reading of Durkheim, Goldthorpe infers the futility of trying to bring lasting 'order' to industrial relations activity, on the lines advocated by pluralist thinkers, whilst major inequalities of wealth and opportunity persist in society at large.

On the basis of the various discussions of structural contradictions, and the centrality to them of a concern with the implications of structured inequalities, we can draw together certain basic factors in the structure of industrial capitalist society which give rise to conflicts in work. Industrial capitalist society involves the buying and selling of people's labour capacity. These transactions are not made on a basis of equality between the parties. Inequality itself does not create a problem. The threat to the stability of industrial capitalism arises from it in two indirect ways:

1 Instability arises from the fact that industrial capitalism has been historically dependent on expressed values of social equality and of rewards based on achievement, values which conflict with the actual or effective distribution of rewards, and opportunities for advancement in society. This gap between claims and 'realities' is less likely to be visible during periods of economic growth and changing occupational structures than when growth slows down or stops. Inequalities of distribution, for example, are more likely to become contentious when there is a 'cake' of fixed size to share out, than when this cake is growing.
2 Instability arises from the fact that in a culture where individual freedom, choice, independence and autonomy are central values, the great majority of people in their work experience find themselves coming under the control and instruction of others to a degree which potentially clashes with cultural expectations.

Many of the conflicts which arise between employers and employees can be seen as paradoxical outcomes or unintended consequences of the actions and means which have been chosen by employing interests themselves in the course of the history of industrial capitalism. Collective resistance to employers could not have arisen had not employers brought together employees in single workplaces, for example. Further, the instrumental and calculative approach to work of many employees about which employers tend to complain reflects the logic of employers' own policies as much as anything else: 'the first generation of factory workers were taught by their masters the importance of time; the second generation formed their short-time committees in the ten-hour movement; the third generation struck for overtime or time-and-a-half' (Thompson 1967). The low level of moral involvement of junior employees can also be seen as reflecting the very way their work is designed. If employees are given narrowly restricted tasks to do, are closely and often coercively supervised by 'superiors' and are treated as dehumanised factors of production, managements can expect little more than grudging compliance.

Untrusting management policies and control techniques are likely to be reciprocated with low trust employee attitudes and behaviour. As Fox (1974) puts it, 'low trust industrial relations' result from this together with bargaining on a win–lose basis, attempts to bring the other side under closer prescription and control and a screening and distortion of communication between bargaining parties. Managements often recognise this danger and therefore attempt to build trust relationships. This reflects their involvement in the central contradiction that 'the function of labour control involves *both* the direction, surveillance and discipline of subordinates whose enthusiastic commitment to corporate objectives cannot be taken for granted; *and* the mobilisation of discretion, initiative and diligence which coercive supervision, far from guaranteeing, is likely to destroy'. But to build trust relations within employment is expensive, observes Armstrong (1989), and recognition of this takes them back to the pressure to substitute 'performance monitoring and control' for trust. This, in turn, creates a contradiction: 'because trust is expensive there arises a contradiction between its indispensability and employers' economic interest in substituting for it'. Out of this contradiction Armstrong sees arising a 'historical dynamic within capitalist organisations' whereby some managerial groups attempt to wrest from others a role in building trust on behalf of the employers for whom they are acting as agents. In this way the specific type of 'micropolitical' rivalry between managerial groups which we considered earlier (Chapter 4, pp. 95–9) is understood within the more structural dynamics of the basic employer–employee antagonism.

The logic of this type of analysis, with its radical concern to 'go to the roots', is fundamentally sociological. It not only questions the validity of many of the assumptions upon which the pluralist frame of reference is based, it also inevitably takes issue with many of the simplistic and psychologistic common-sense beliefs which are held about industrial conflict. Such phenomena as strikes, restrictions of output, sabotage and managerial politics are seen sociologically not so much as the outcomes of greed, bloody-mindedness or envy but as partly logical reactions and initiatives of people living in a certain type of society and economy.

The basic reason, beyond general issues of 'human nature', why conflicts arise within the work institutions of industrial capitalist societies is that employers in effect 'use' employees for various purposes of their own whilst employees, in turn (though from a weaker position) use their employment for their own various purposes. For the employment relationship to exist at all there is clearly a range of common interests, which provides the co-operative dimension to employment, whilst the remaining divergence of interests provides the considerable conflict dimension. Industrial capitalism, we can say, is dependent on the three intertwined institutions of *the employment and rational organisation of free labour* (Watson and Watson 1999):

- the institution of *formally free labour* – labour which is not 'unfree' like that in slavery or serfdom and which, in principle, involves choices on the parts of workers about where and how they are going to work;
- the institution of *employment* whereby some people sell their capacity to work (labour-power) to others;
- the institution of *rational organisation* which subjects work activities to processes of close calculation, a detailed division of labour, a bureaucratic hierarchical control structure.

A basic contradiction arises from the relationship between these three institutions, however. It is a contradiction between:

- the principle of *control* of human beings implicit in the institutions of employment and rational organisation; and
- the principles of *freedom and autonomy* implicit in the institution of formally free labour.

To handle these tensions, structures and institutions arise to regularise and cope with potentially disintegrative conflicts of interest. These institutions range from highly informal 'understandings' and accommodations in the workplace to more formal collective bargaining arrangements and to state involvements in employment relationships through methods as diverse as employment legislation, industrial policy and the placing of informal pressures on employers and trade unions. Although it is most often applied to institutions of collective bargaining, the notion of the *institutionalising of conflict* can usefully be applied to this very wide range of arrangements. All of these institutions function to help maintain and reproduce a particular type of social order that is associated with industrial capitalism. To locate the situation of the working individual to this broad structural context, it is helpful to return to focusing on the implicit contracts of people within employment relationships.

Effort bargains, fragile implicit contracts and the inevitability of grievances

Attention was drawn in Chapter 7 (pp. 189–91) to the role of managerial initiatives in attempting to manipulate the implicit contract between the employing organisation and the worker to persuade that worker that the exchange occurring between the parties was a fair and reasonable one, thus 'motivating' the worker and getting his or her compliance with managerial requirements. It was emphasised, however, that these processes of exchange, negotiation and persuasion occur in a context of unequal power relationships. There is always an underlying conflict of interests. This was emphasised in the classic analysis of Baldamus (1961) who pointed out that 'As wages are costs to the firm, and the deprivations inherent in effort mean "costs" to the employee, the interests of management and wage earner are diametrically opposed.' This conflict of interests is manifested in the struggle which takes place to achieve 'wage disparity' in the favour of either the employer or the employee. In certain circumstances the employee may achieve an improvement in the amount of reward which they gain for a certain effort but, more typically in a capitalist economy, the tendency is towards disparity in the favour of the employer. This is:

- partly because employees have been socialised into accepting a certain level of work obligation 'as a duty', thus conceding some effort to the employer 'free of compensation'; and
- probably more crucially, the employer, in the context of a capitalist market economy, simply cannot afford in the long run to concede wage disparity in the favour of employees. The capitalist context obliges the employer to intensify the work effort derived from the employee at a given cost.

Baldamus' concern with the ongoing conflict over what Behrend (1957) called the *effort bargain* tends to emphasise the material rewards available from work and concentrates on the factory shopfloor situation. The concept of the *implicit contract* developed in Chapter 7 and represented in Table 7.1 broadens these insights to recognise that something similar to shopfloor wage and effort bargaining goes on in all types of employment and over a wide range of issues, ranging from job satisfaction and social reward to matters of status and career potential. The contract, made up of a complex bundle of 'inputs' and 'rewards', is a fragile one, existing, as it does, in the context of the dynamic nature of the priorities of both work organisations and workers. The following framework, bringing together elements of our earlier analyses, sets this fragility in its broad sociological context and identifies how it makes inevitable the emergence of grievances in the workplace:

1 In a world where valued resources are scarce, people form coalitions of interest to help in the pursuit or defence of interests with regard to these resources.
2 Over time, some groups win out over others in the competition for scarce resources and attempt to consolidate their advantage through their control of institutions and through the propagation of ideologies.
3 Industrial capitalism emerged as 'bourgeois' groups which became successful in pursuing their interests in certain societies (Chapter 3, pp. 60–1), but the advantages which accrue from their use of such formally rational means as bureaucracy, technical division of labour, wage-labour, advanced technology and the rest, are constantly threatened. The threat comes not only from challenges on the part of less privileged groups but also as a result of various contradictory tendencies in the industrial capitalist system itself.
4 The relationship between the employer and the employee centres on an *implicit contract* (Chapter 7, p. 189). This is an agreement between unequal parties in which workers, in the light of their particular motives, expectations and interests, attempt to make the best deal possible, given their personal resources (skill, knowledge, physique, wealth, etc.). The bargain which is struck involves a certain relationship (in part explicit but largely, owing to its indeterminacy, implicit) between the employee inputs of effort, impairment and surrender of autonomy and employee rewards of cash payment and fringe benefits, job satisfactions, social rewards, security, power status, career potential.

5 The bargain is essentially unstable, especially as a result of the market context in which it is made. Market viability on the part of the employer creates a constant pressure to minimise costs – this in turn leading to a pressure to either cut the rewards or increase the efforts of the worker – either way to the worker's disadvantage. However, workers are bound to defend themselves, especially since they buy goods and services on the same market. Paradoxically, the advertising and marketing efforts of employing organisations create a pressure on their employees to increase, or at least hold stable, their rewards (employees and customers being ultimately the same people). The contradictory pressures operating on the employment relationship here are illustrated in Figure 8.1.

6 To increase efficiency or market viability, employers introduce various organisational and technological changes (Chapter 5), but any such change, however minor it may seem, potentially invites opposition from employees whose implicit contracts may be seen to be threatened. This may be because of a tendency to reduce 'rewards' like job satisfaction or the opportunity to use craft skills or because of a tendency to call for increased employee 'inputs' in the form of increased effort or a further reduction in the amount of autonomy which the employee has at work. Potential conflict, we can see, arises with practically any kind of managerial initiative in employment situations.

7 Both to improve their market position and to defend themselves, employees tend to form various coalitions of interest to present the kind of group challenge which is necessary to have any effect in the face of the greater power of the employer (the exception here being where the individual worker has unique skills or knowledge on which the employer is dependent). Thus we get, within employing organisations, trade union organisation, 'professional' group mobilisation and 'informal' office and shopfloor groupings. All of these present challenges to the managerial prerogative.

8 In every workplace there is a constantly negotiated and renegotiated agreement about what goes on and what rewards accrue. Only a fraction of the processes leading to this *negotiated order* (pp. 35–6) is formal and much of the agreement is tacit. External conditions are never constant and therefore there are always threats to the stability of arrangements. The underlying conflicts of interest between employer and employee may become overt and apparent at any time and will tend to centre on two main issues: the amount of material rewards available to the employee and the extent of control over employees conceded to the employer.

9 We can say that a grievance situation arises whenever a particular implicit contract is perceived to go out of balance. The grievance may lead to any of a range of worker reactions, from striking to absenteeism and from obstructive behaviour to resigning. A grievance can be settled or accommodated not only by a return to the prior status quo but by a rebalancing of the implicit contract in a new form; for example, an increase in cash being agreed to compensate for a loss in autonomy resulting from an organisational or technical change.

Here we have a frame of reference which can be used to analyse conflict in the widest possible range of employment situations. Having established this framework we can now turn to the variety of ways in which people adjust and defend their interests and their very selves in their work situation.

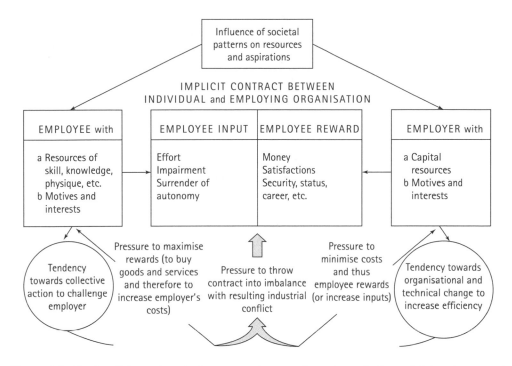

Figure 8.1 The implicit contract between employer and employee in its societal and economic context

The mobilisation of interests

Coalitions and interests

The typical worker in an industrial capitalist society, unless they have especially marketable personal skills or attributes, rarely has the capacity to defend themselves against attempts of employers to alter the balance of the implicit contract in the employer's favour – let alone improve the conditions or rewards of work. A concerted challenge coupled with the threat of a general withdrawal of effort can create such a possibility, however. We therefore see a general tendency within the world of work for groups to form around common interests and for collective action to be taken to defend or further those interests.

In the discussion of occupational strategies and cultures in Chapter 6 we saw how such mobilisation may occur around a common *occupational interest*, and particular attention was paid to the professionalisation process. Here we are concerned with situations where the common interest primarily arises, although not always exclusively, from the individuals' statuses as *employees*. Groups of employees located at all levels tend to form groups to defend or further their interests. Groups of employees, or their spokespersons, can be seen to make claims to professional status even when they are primarily managerial *employees* (Watson 2002b). We have seen how managers form themselves into defensive cliques or assertive cabals, depending on how they perceive their career interests within the organisation (Chapter 4, p. 96). However, it is at the lower levels, where autonomy and discretion is lower, that defensive groups are most necessary. It is here that we have traditionally seen the strategy of unionisation.

Trade unions and collective bargaining

Early trade unions were only marginally related to industrial relations, as Hyman (2003) notes, originating as local societies of skilled workers operating as 'a social club, a local labour exchange, and an insurance society'. Yet as industrialisation proceeded, with employers becoming larger and more assertive, technologies changing, labour markets widening and occupational differences becoming blurred, they expanded, took on non-craft members and developed their structures to engage effectively in collective bargaining with employers.

> **TRADE UNION**
>
> An association of employees formed to improve their ability to negotiate working conditions and rewards with employers and, sometimes, to represent common interests within the political sphere beyond the workplace.

Trade unions increased their significance in industrialising societies as the typical employment relationship changed from:

- a traditional one based on a *status contract* – a relatively diffuse master–servant relationship with an implication of longer-term mutual commitment, to
- one based on a *purposive contract* where 'the emphasis is on a transitory arrangement for limited and specific performances' (Fox 1974).

With the growing rationalisation of work organisations and the spread of low-discretion direct-control work tasks among white-collar groups unionism spread to groups higher and higher up the organisational and occupational hierarchy. The increasing application of what Baldamus (1961) called 'administrative instruments of effort intensification' on the part of employers later led to a shift from status to performance criteria and hence union-like initiatives among groups such as teachers and doctors (Eldridge 1975). Increasing stress on the cash nexus and the erosion of the 'moral obligations which are traditionally embedded in the idea of vocation' (Eldridge 1975) was reflected in the growth of the term 'instrumental collectivism' (Goldthorpe *et al.* 1968) and hence the spread of collective bargaining among non-working-class workers. There was still a social class dimension to these trends, however. One of the important factors in the expansion of white-collar trade unionism was 'the objective change in the class situation' of such workers (Crompton and Jones 1984). These resulted from pressures on labour costs which led to the rationalisation and deskilling of white-collar work and an accompanying decline in job security and in their conditions of employment relative to manual workers.

Given the low-trust type of economic exchange associated with this form of contract, collective defence of the employees' position becomes necessary. It would be wrong, however, to view the history of trade unionism simply in terms of necessary and inevitable reactions of a purely calculative kind. Trade unionism, particularly in Britain, has always been associated with the idea of a labour movement, something which has provided an ideology over and above the legitimation of sectional interests.

LABOUR MOVEMENT

A coming together of such bodies as trade unions and associated political parties to represent the interests which employed people as a whole are believed to hold in common.

The political potential of trade unions, varying from vehicles of revolutionary potential in association with revolutionary political groups to acting more pragmatically to improve the welfare of working-class people, has been a matter of radical political debate from the time of Marx (Moses 1990). It is unlikely, however, that a political dimension to trade union activity can arise separately from a concern with the daily circumstances of people's employment situations. To mobilise people to act collectively, a fairly clear and direct link has to be established in their minds between the proposed political action and the specific circumstances of their lives which may be changed by that action. And the specific circumstances to which group leaders and their representatives typically have to look are connected with the implicit contract with the employer. To appeal to generalised ideal interests in the absence of a clear link between these and specific local advantage is unlikely to be effective given the essentially calculative ethos of the industrial capitalist workplace. British trade unions have generally been ambivalent towards politics and the law, and Hyman (2003) connects this, together with their going along with a system of labour law based on immunities as opposed to 'positive rights', to their experience of 'the anti-collectivist bias of the legal system' with the effect that 'laissez-faire was in this respect as resonant a slogan for trade unionists as for early British capitalists'. Freedom to engage in free collective bargaining has thus been a trade union priority.

COLLECTIVE BARGAINING

A method of agreeing work conditions and rewards through a process of negotiation between employer representatives and the representatives of collectively organised employees.

The institution of collective bargaining did not arise solely as the result of pressures from employees. The organising of employees in trade unions in certain respects suited employers, not least because having an employee representative to negotiate for employees simplified the negotiating and communication channels which otherwise would have been necessary. This is not to suggest that employers always welcomed unionisation of employees – far from it. Union initiatives were only likely to be welcome to employers once the degree of organised employee opposition had reached a point where it was seen as needing to be contained and institutionalised. To a certain extent trade union leaders could be seen as 'managers of discontent' (Mills 1970). The historical rise of the shop steward movement has to be understood in the light of such tendencies. It was the joint creation of employees and managers and not something simply imposed on employers (Willman 1980). A similar pattern arose with regard to the institution of the closed shop, something which has now become of more historical than contemporary interest. This was an arrangement whereby work in a particular setting was exclusively carried out by members of a specified trade union. The closed shop – the demise of which came about as a result of state initiatives rather than employer ones – was something which managers encouraged to achieve 'order, cohesion, and a sense of authority in the workplace' (Taylor 1982).

When considering evidence such as this, it is vital to recognise that differences in national cultures and systems of political ideologies are important in understanding how trade unions and their members behave (Bean 1994). Fox (1985) showed how a series of features of British history lay behind the unrevolutionary nature of British trade unionism, for example. In addition to the role of a non-interventionist state, a period of economic growth and reluctance on the part of employers to engage in an all-out battle with trade unionism, there was an employer recognition of the part that 'respectable' trade unions could play as a safety valve for class conflict. On the employee side, the pre-industrial religious and political movements left a legacy of differentiated groupings which precluded the evolution of a general and united confrontational consciousness. Yet a low-trust adversarial approach to collective bargaining within enterprises did develop in Britain which Fox contrasts with the more consensual German approach, something which emerged from a different set of historical and cultural factors again. In contemporary circumstances, it is a matter of debate whether British industrial relations are becoming Europeanised (with an emphasis on 'social partnership') or Americanised, an approach which 'embraces the continuing decline of unions and the assertion of a market-driven model' (Edwards 2003).

Changing patterns of employer–union relations

In spite of international differences in patterns of employment relations broad changes in the occupational structures and the social compositions of labour forces across the world in the latter part of the twentieth century were 'largely detrimental to union organisation' and, in particular, 'the growth of new occupational groups with scarce skills' (leading to a preference for individual, rather than collective, labour market strategies) made it 'difficult for unions to recruit such workers, while the growing numbers of employees in private services with low-paid and insecure jobs' tended to 'lack the resources and cohesion to undertake collective action' (Bean 1994). British governments at this time were especially zealous in restricting the activities of trade unions, introducing a series of acts which, for example, first restricted and later removed all legal basis for closed shops, made secondary picketing illegal, made the sacking of strikers possible, required secret ballots before strikes and later for approval of political contributions, and required the regular re-election of main union leaders by secret ballot. The government strategy was not so much to bear down directly on unions but to pass enabling legislation that would be implemented by employers, union members or even customers (Undy *et al.* 1996). The effect of all of these shifts was, in Fairbrother's (2000) terms, to leave the British trade union movement 'in a parlous state'.

British survey evidence reveals a pattern of change whereby:

- In 1980 unions represented employees in a 'clear majority of workplaces' and through a variety of channels.
- In 1984 union bargaining power was severely reduced but unions were still a 'core element' of the industrial relations system.
- In 1990 much of this had changed and 'key elements of the system of collective bargaining had faded or been transformed' (Millward *et al.* 1992).
- In 1998 there was 'continuation of the widespread falls in trade union presence and aggregate membership density' and a 'general withering of enthusiasm for union membership within continuing workplaces, especially in the private sector, and a lack of recruitment among new workplaces in both private and public sectors' (Millward *et al.* 2000). Employees reported low levels of perceived *effectiveness* of trade union representation (Cully *et al.* 1999).
- In 1998, where there was collective workplace representation it predominantly involved consultation rather than negotiation (Brown *et al.* 2000).

Accompanying these trends has been a decline in the occurrence of strikes. This occurred across most of western Europe in the last two decades of the twentieth century, but the decline has been steepest in Britain and has reached the lowest level since statistics were first collected in 1891 (Waddington 2003). This decline has resulted in part from the changing occupational structure (with traditionally 'strike-prone' industries declining) and in part from the changing balance of power (supported by state initiatives) and in part because the 'entrenched adversarialism' that once characterised certain sectors of the economy has been weakened with the 'resort to the strike' being seen as less 'natural' than it once was – this not necessarily meaning that the absence of strikes reflects the achievement of 'higher quality' industrial relations (Waddington 2003).

Changes in the 'power' of trade unions or the frequency of strikes have not resulted from a rush by employers to derecognise unions. Rather, managements have preferred simply to take advantage of the weakness of union representation in changing circumstances. Claydon (1989) observed that where there were attempts to *exclude* unions this was not part of any concerted anti-union movement but a matter of an 'extreme reflection of a much wider shift in the frontier of control *within* collective bargaining'. Millward *et al.* (2000) did not find significant evidence of employers actively derecognising unions noting that, instead, it was the persistently lower rate of recognition among new workplaces (and those that grew from being very small) that fuelled the continuing decline in the proportion of workplaces with recognition. This did not mean that employees were necessarily being denied a 'voice' in their workplaces but channels of communication changed a great deal, from ones involving trade unions and trade union representatives to 'channels where employees communicated directly with management, largely on occasions and on terms set by management themselves' (Millward *et al.* 2000).

Alongside these changes, a shift in the relationship between trade unions and their members can be observed. This was seen as moving through three phases in Britain (Heery and Kelly 1994; Kelly and Heery 1994):

- Between the 1940s and the mid-1960s a 'largely passive membership was serviced by a cadre of professional negotiators'.
- After the mid-1960s this was partially displaced by a participative relationship in which 'the function of union officialdom was to facilitate self-serving and participation in decision-making by members'.
- From the mid-1980s this organisational model has given way to a new servicing relationship in which members are viewed as reactive consumers whose needs must be researched and responded to using the techniques of strategic management.

However, Waddington (2003) observes a later shift away from the *servicing* model, where members rely on union support and services from sources external to the workplace, to the *organising* model which emphasises the role of local representatives and members, these being trained, guided and supported by the trade union (Carter 2000; Gall 2003). The distinctions between the two models can be exaggerated (Boxall and Haynes 1997) and union leaders and full-time trade union officers are likely to mix both strategies as they continue to need to be sensitive to members' expectations and to the pragmatic circumstances in which they find themselves working (Watson, D.H. 1988).

Trade union leaders are, at the same time, being pressed to come to terms with what Towers (1997) calls the 'representation gap' in which there is an 'untapped demand' among workers for union protection against arbitrary managerial actions. Guest (1995) has noted the growth of workplaces which are 'black holes' in terms of employee representation – with workers benefiting neither from trade union representation nor the consultative opportunities associated with progressive human resource management. But even where unions have made 'partnership' deals with employers, a tendency can be seen for the 'pluralist' inclinations which this might imply on behalf of employers, to fall back to 'unitarist' ones (Ackers and Payne 1998) and for managements to benefit more from such arrangements than workers (Guest and Peccei 2001). In his review of the evidence on partnership arrangements, Bacon (2001) comments that trade union representatives in many workplaces appear to feel that they have little option 'but to accept management terms' and union support for partnership 'resembles a resigned compliance'.

It is easy to assume that in smaller firms there will be a much greater degree of informality in employment relationships with the closeness of contacts between managers and owners making formalised collective bargaining unnecessary. Research has shown that the potentially more 'intimate' and even family-like aspect of smaller enterprises does not avoid conflicts or preclude exploitative relationships (Holliday 1995) with external factors such as the influence of large firms over smaller ones pressuring managers to assert strong controls (Rainnie 1989) and patterns of internal relationships often involving continuous bargaining over shopfloor activities (Ram 1994; Moule 1998). Given the considerable variety of different technologies and markets with which small firms are involved, it is possible to see a variety of different mixes of formal and informal employment relations practices across small firms in a way corresponding to what we might see in larger enterprises (Ram *et al*. 2001; Scase 2003).

Shop stewards and workplace representation

A major tension which has long existed within the trade union movement has been one between the need for large-scale representation across a wide constituency and the need for the defence of interests of individuals and groups in specific or 'domestic' work settings. It was this tension which can be understood as lying behind the growth of the shop steward movement in Britain during the First World War. This movement was motivated in part by radical and syndicalist ideals (Hinton 1973) but the later importance of the workplace representative or shop steward had a more pragmatic basis. The spread of payment-by-results schemes, the high demand for labour, the inappropriateness of the district (rather than plant-based) organisation of union branches, and the decline of employer associations all contributed to the tendency for the workplace itself to become the point at which the implicit contract was to be protected or improved.

Shop stewards can usefully be regarded as semi-formal workgroup representatives.

SHOP STEWARD/UNION WORKPLACE REPRESENTATIVE

A worker representative and 'lay' trade union official who represents to management the interests of fellow employees who elect them as their workplace spokesperson.

This implies far more than their being a 'mouthpiece', however. It recognises the potential for them to articulate the common objective interests of the group, thereby creating subjective interests and willingness to mobilise. This equally may mean encouraging members to desist from immediate and spontaneous action as it might the opposite. Batstone *et al.* (1977) showed that the 'leader' type of steward, who tried actively to shape group activity, was more successful than the 'populist' steward who tended to follow group instructions. The stronger links of these 'leaders' with other stewards and the respect which they obtained from the management not only enabled the more effective defence of employee interests in the face of managerial control and the improvement in wages but also aided management by ensuring a greater predictability of shopfloor. The behaviour and level of effectiveness of union representatives has changed over the decades, however. Darlington (1994) observed how the approach of stewards changed from being relatively *conflictual* in the 1970s to being more *consensual* in the 1980s. A range of factors influenced this but Darlington's case study research points to the importance of the management's approach to stewards and their tendency to switch back and forth between a 'hard line approach' and a more co-operative 'soft line . . . aimed at incorporating them into accommodative relationships'. Although almost a quarter of a million workers in Britain were acting as workplace union representatives at the end of the century, shop stewards had become less effective in terms of outcomes than they previously were, often being 'ignored or sidelined by management' who are 'bypassing . . . shop stewards as communication channels to the workforce, and flouting . . . procedural presumptions of consultation or negotiation with trade union representatives before the implementation of change' (Terry 2003).

Job control strategies and 'making out'

Whether or not a role is played in them by workplace union representatives, we can observe a variety of different group strategies followed by employees to protect their relative autonomy *vis-à-vis* management and generally to defend their implicit contract with the employer. These are *job control strategies* or, more pejoratively, restrictive practices. A particularly significant activity here, given the constant pressure on employers to rationalise their methods and improve their efficiency, is the tendency towards resisting change.

Resistance to change on the part of lower status employees is frequently regarded as a kind of neurotic behaviour or an irrational conservatism. In practice, it can be seen as highly rational. This only becomes clear once we recognise that any change in work organisation, payment scheme, technology or whatever, contains a potential threat to the implicit contract between employer and employee. Unless the employee can clearly see that there is not going to be a disparity in the favour of the employer (and a consequent loss to the employee), the safest thing to do is to resist the change. The charge of irrationality often arises, however, because managers tend to see resistance occurring to changes which they believe will benefit the employee as well as the employer. In the low-trust atmosphere which characterises so much of contemporary industrial relations, it is most unlikely that employees will 'take the management's word for it'. When employees have any kind of countervailing power whatsoever they are likely to draw on it and insist on negotiating over any managerially initiated change which may threaten their current implicit contract. A case study in which a serious dispute almost occurred over management's attempt to stop factory workers making tea on the shopfloor shows that behind this seemingly trivial concern was a perception of the management's intention to interfere with established break-time practices as a very serious infringement of their general autonomy (Watson 1982). The workers' implicit contract was threatened by the management's apparent intention to increase the sphere in which it exerted control over employee behaviour. As many employees explicitly stated, this was a matter of principle. Ultimately this issue was conceded by the company and a number of other fairly costly concessions had to be made in the course of negotiations before union co-operation with the introduction of changes was secured. The whole shopfloor strategy was based on a sensible, rational and wisely sceptical approach to defending the existing implicit contracts of employees.

One form of job control strategy which has received a great deal of attention over the years has been the practice of work-groups paid on an incentive scheme to restrict their output to a level which they find acceptable. Taylor (Chapter 2, pp. 23–4) called this 'systematic soldiering' and saw it as an abuse which scientific management would remove. The Human Relations investigators (Chapter 2, pp. 29–30), noting such behaviour in the Bank Wiring Room, did not stress the rationality of the fixing of a norm of a 'fair day's work' and the defence of this norm by the sanctioning of 'ratebuster' and 'chiseller' behaviour (going above and below the norm, respectively) but interpreted the phenomenon in terms of an assumed social need and the necessary defence of a psychologically supportive group social system.

Later studies of the way incentive schemes are 'fiddled', especially those of Roy (1952, 1953, 1954) and Lupton (1963) have laid emphasis on the rationality behind them, however.

Lupton argued that the 'systematic manipulation of the incentive scheme' was an effective form of worker control over the job environment. The 'fiddle' not only gives a measure of control over the relationship between effort and reward but protects the workers against the effects of management shortcomings, defends them against rate cuttings and helps stabilise earnings. The widely followed practices of 'cross booking' and 'banking' of work helps hide high bonuses when these are earned and enables workers to carry over and spread earnings. This activity of 'making out', in American terminology, can also give workers an opportunity for self-expression and the enjoyment of an '"exciting game" played against the clock on the wall, a "game" in which the elements of control provided by the application of knowledge, skill, ingenuity, speed and stamina heightened interest and lent to the exhilaration of "winning" feelings of "accomplishment"' (Roy 1952). Burawoy (1979) who found himself doing research in the same factory that Roy had studied years earlier, observes however, that in developing these strategies of seeming independence, the workers were also accommodating to the established pattern of power and ownership in the factory, a pattern in which they were the relative losers – in political economy terms, they were 'manufacturing their own consent'.

In moving now towards acts of 'mischief' in work settings that often look more individualistic than group-based, it is important to recognise that effects can be achieved by such activities that undermine managerial goals as readily as concerted and formal worker sanctions. In the lean production and teamworking setting studied by Danford (1997), for instance, it is clear that the reduction in official disputes had not led to the removal of defiance to management. Instead, the various individual acts of resistance of team members such as personal 'go slows' and refusals to undertake overtime, all occurring within a collective shopfloor sense of resentment, add up to an effective challenge to managerial controls and undermine the achievement of managerial performance targets.

Adjustment, resistance and organisational mischief

When individuals take up employment, they inevitably surrender a certain amount of autonomy. In effect, all employees are *made use of* in some sense when they submit to the control of others in the work setting. We now consider how people adjust to the variety of ways in which they are made use of in the employment situation. We will also see that individuals adjust to being made use of in different but corresponding ways in service occupations where adjustment has to be made to being made use of by customers or clients as well as or instead of by employers.

A concept that brings together the considerable variety of behaviours that arise in this context is that of *organisational mischief*, a concept similar to that of 'organisational misbehaviour' developed by Ackroyd and Thompson (1999) but which is broader in its embracing behaviours at all levels in an organisation (the 'misbehaviour' concept focusing on forms of resistance and adjustment of workers at lower organisational levels). Although 'worker' acts of misbehaviour or 'deviance' might generally be more visible than managerial ones, there is no reason why we should not expect even senior managers to pursue personal rather than corporate interests or to resist 'threats to self' coming from even more senior managers. It is quite possible for managers at the very top of corporations to act in ways both contrary to the official norms of the corporation and detrimental to the broader dominant interests served by the corporation.

> ## ORGANISATIONAL MISCHIEF
>
> Activities occurring within the workplace that (a) according to the official structure, culture and rules of the organisation, 'should not happen', and (b) contain an element of challenge to the dominant modes of operating or to dominant interests in the organisation.

To understand many of the expressions of mischief that we are about to consider – from people making themselves absent from work, to people sabotaging equipment, bullying others or fiddling expenses – it is useful to take as a starting point the element of the organisational members' *implicit contract* that requires them to *surrender a degree of personal autonomy*. Not only does this mean that people have to put aside doing what it is that they might prefer to do (go to play golf rather than go to work, say, or slip cash into their own pockets rather than put into the till), they also have to give up a degree of control over their very 'selves'. Sometimes having to take instructions from others may be a matter of minor irritation. But, at other times, it may be felt as a major attack on one's personal pride, or on the shared sense of honour of a working or occupational group.

The forms of 'mischief' to be considered here all, in one way or another, involve a degree of resistance to the patterns of power in which people find themselves at work with this resistance often involving attempts to maintain individuals' sense of personal integrity. Yet, paradoxically, in so far as 'oppositional practices' involve *adjusting* to circumstances the effectiveness of resistance is undermined (Collinson 1992). Attention and effort is deflected from changing those circumstances, and existing patterns of power are, in effect, reproduced.

Accommodation, subjectivity and values

It is important to recognise that when we are talking about people defending their sense of self in the face of more powerful 'others', there is not a fixed 'self' which is wholly separate from its structural context. Self-identities 'are always in process' and power 'provides the conditions of possibility' for the self-formation of identities, 'a process involving perpetual tension between power and resistance or subjectivity and identity' (Jermier *et al.* 1994). Accommodation to managerial requirements is thus always partial and the concept of *subjectivity* is helpful in understanding why (see Chapter 2, pp. 48–9). Knights and McCabe (2000) apply a notion of subjectivity as 'the way in which individuals interpret and understand their circumstances [which is] bound up with the sense they have of themselves (identity)' to their research on work under a Total Quality Management regime. They conclude that however hard consultants and managers search for a 'perfect' technology for controlling labour, 'even in the most oppressive regimes, there will be spaces and opportunities for escape and perhaps even a bit of misbehaviour'.

An individual's self-identity involves them in holding values and beliefs which will always differ in part from those implicit in the 'subjectivities' which are pressed upon them in the discourses current in their employment setting. This is illustrated by O'Connell Davidson's (1994) research in a recently privatised public utility. Clerical workers' resistance to changes being made by the management to emphasise profitability at the expense of service to the public, as these employees saw it, related to the 'subjective state' of these workers and this, says O'Connell Davidson, was not simply shaped by their immediate work situation but also by 'their commitment to supplying a socially useful service'. Similarly, opposition to corporate policies by managers in ZTC was shown to be related not just to a sectional interest in keeping open the plant in which these managers worked but also to personal values and notions of personal integrity – these often being articulated in terms of 'the sort of person I am' (Watson 2001a).

Withdrawal, instrumentalism and the management of boredom

One of the most direct ways of reacting to the deprivations of a given work situation is to leave the job. Indeed, levels of 'labour turnover' in employing organisations are often taken to be useful indicators of the level of conflict within that organisation. It was shown in a study of navvies, for example, that 'jacking suddenly and for little or no reason was regarded as a demonstration of freedom and independence of the employer' (Sykes 1969). The importance of the idea of 'jacking' in the navvies' occupational ideology reflects the men's strong desire to feel and be seen as being independent of any particular employer and as indicating a basic hostility to employers in general.

The same grievances or dissatisfactions which are reacted to by people leaving their job may equally take the form of absence from work or the collective application of formal sanctions. Even accidents may reflect industrial discontent (Nichols 1997). But care has to be taken in regarding different manifestations of conflict as straightforward alternatives for employees. Edwards and Scullion (1982) stress that the different forms of conflict behaviour which they studied, ranging from absenteeism to strikes and effort bargaining, have to be understood in the context of the specific work control structures of which they are a part. They show, for example, how the absenteeism among a set of women workers was acceptable to their management. These same managers, however, would have found a similar level among male workers – who were much more directly and intensely controlled than the women – far less acceptable. Absenteeism itself is not an issue; the issue is what it means given the control structure context in which it occurs. As Turnbull and Sapsford (1992) observed in the case of the British docks, where there was a considerable conflict across the workplace 'frontier of control' then absenteeism is especially likely to be an 'expression of industrial conflict' rather than a matter of separate individuals choosing to take time off without reference to wider norms of that workplace. Here, absenteeism is more a social than an individual act as is seen elsewhere where there exists a 'subculture' of absenteeism (Edwards and Whitson 1989).

One very significant way in which the employee may come to terms with work deprivations is by taking his or her identity not so much from the occupation but from their home life. Thus, for the 'instrumental privatised worker' (Chapter 7, p. 187), it is the non-work life which forms the central life interest. Work deprivations are coped with by their being rationalised as necessary means to other ends. Here, for instance, we find workers accounting for their acceptance of the negative aspects of work by pointing to the way that their income is enabling them to give their children a better 'start in life'. In addition to or as alternatives to deriving vicarious satisfactions from children's advancement people may daydream at work about the material goods or the holidays which their work enables them to buy and this may be extended into fantasising about the delights of, say, winning the national lottery.

In their discussion of what they call the 'hidden injuries of class', Sennett and Cobb (1977) argued that for people to accept a circumstance whereby they are constantly given orders by others they may have to adjust by viewing themselves in a self-disparaging way and even by feeling secretly ashamed of what they are. Purcell (1982) suggested that a key reaction of the women factory workers whom she studied to such 'hidden injuries' was one of fatalism. This was manifested in their daily interest in horoscopes, fortune-telling and superstitions. She argued that this is stronger among women than among men. Women at work, as in their biological and domestic lives, have to adjust to 'things happening to them' more than do men. Gossip, among men as much as among women, can play a role in encouraging fatalism with it sometimes acting as a medium of 'emotional ventilation' (Ribeiro and Blakely 1995). However, gossip may function in different ways in different circumstances, sometimes helping workers adjust to insecurities and anxieties arising in the workplace (Noon and Delbridge 1993) and, at other times, especially when there is considerable change and disruption, heightening anxieties and insecurities (Tebbut and Marchington 1997).

Perhaps the simplest expedient for getting through an unfulfilling day's work is for the individual to allow themselves to be 'drawn along' by the technology which they are operating – what Baldamus (1961) calls 'traction'. Delbridge (1998) reports his participant-observer experience of assembly line work coming to 'hypnotising him so that he almost became entranced by it on occasions'. Nevertheless, a typical work shift represents a long period of time for the manual worker to pass in this way. For long periods of unchallenging work to be psychologically manageable, the experience has to be structured and broken down into manageable components. This type of structuring is illustrated in Roy's (1952) classic participant observation study of a group of machine operators who alleviated the monotony of their daily routine by creating games and rituals within the work-group and by devising a series of work-breaks: coffee time, peach time, banana time, window time, and so on. An alternative strategy is for workers to devise ways of imposing their own pacing on even the most mechanically paced of jobs. On the car assembly line, for example, the individuals may work 'back up the line' to 'build a bank' (by completing operations before the car reaches their station on the line) and hence buy time for themselves (Walker and Guest 1952).

Humour at work

Joking and humour is more than a peripheral or incidental aspect of work activities and cultures. It plays a major role in how people both adjust to and challenge work circumstances. Humour covers a variety of activities.

> ### WORKPLACE HUMOUR
>
> All forms of communication occurring in the work situation which create within people feelings of amusement and a predisposition to express that emotion through laughter.

At its simplest, workplace humour may be seen as a way of inserting a degree of fun or leisure into the working day. However, it has functions that go beyond this and a parallel can be drawn between joking at work and behaviour patterns noted by anthropologists in other settings. The classic discussion of the so-called joking relationship in social life is that of Radcliffe-Brown (1965). He points out how playful antagonism and teasing may help individuals in a potentially conflictful situation to accommodate to each other thus enabling them to co-operate and interact successfully. Such relationships are typically seen to develop in families between new spouses and their various 'in-laws'. Bradney (1973) showed how such relationships and associated humorous behaviour developed between sales assistants in a London department store. It was in the interest of each assistant to increase her own sales, something which put her in conflict with colleagues. To avoid hostility and strain, joking was regularly resorted to. For example, a new assistant soon to be working too hard and seriously was told by an old hand 'You want to sell up the shop today, don't you?' Bradney notes that this was said 'in a friendly joking manner even though it did conceal a reprimand'.

The two-sided nature of much humour was noted by Applebaum (1981) in his study of construction workers, and he observed that 'kidding and horseplay' simultaneously channel hostility and elicit feelings of friendship and solidarity. This corresponds to the suggestion in Boland and Hoffman's (1983) machine-shop study that humour serves a dual function – helping people accept a structure whilst avoiding their surrender of self. Thus, jokes are played on new members to teach them their 'place', but later jokes are allowed which reverse this 'place' – building them up again. Humour thus helps maintain an organisational culture. Again, subversion and resistance help existing structures reproduce themselves. As Linstead (1985) puts it, humour has the capacity both to 'resist a dominant formulation and also to accommodate to it'. But Ackroyd and Thompson (1999) nevertheless stress the subversive effects of workplace humour and the 'undercurrent of satirical debunking of management pretensions' that it entails.

In spite of the potential for humour to undermine managers, they frequently use it themselves to achieve their purposes. Far from sabotaging organisational purposes, humour can be 'instrumental in pursuing it' (Barsoux 1993). Managers, says Barsoux, sometimes use humour 'as a sword to influence and persuade, to motivate and unite, to say the unspeakable and to facilitate change', and sometimes 'as a shield, to deflect criticism, to cope with failure, to defuse tension and to make their working lives more bearable'. Humour is increasingly used as a deliberate and formal managerial device. To revitalise the damaged corporate cultures that resulted from the downsizing and fragmentation of organisations in the late twentieth century, say Deal and Kennedy (1999), managers can be seen 'putting the fun back into work' in such place as the airline where employees were rewarded for introducing joking into their working practices.

In the workplace the dominant mode of making sense of events is what Mulkay (1988) calls the 'serious mode'. Subordinate to this, but always likely to break through it, is a 'humorous mode', and Barsoux (1993) shows how the 'serious, structured, rational side of business provides a poignant backdrop' for humour. Humour is born out of incongruity and a key incongruity in organisations is that between this serious side of life and the 'pettiness, chaos, fallibility and uncertainty of any human endeavour'. We often laugh at work, then, as we attempt to come to terms with the contrast between the earnestness of the tasks we are meant to undertake and our human shortcomings. Laughter helps us 'cope emotionally with that which could frighten us into madness: the fragility of our identities and the contingency of our social locations' (Watson 2001a).

Much of the workplace joking which goes on can hardly be seen as riotously funny, and the humour indulged in by Roy's subjects (1952) in his 'banana time' article is funny only in its pathos. One of the men's standard themes, for example, was to ask each other 'how many times did you go poom-poom last night?' The perfunctory nature of much workplace communication was recognised by Meissner (1976) who portrayed workplace humour as a rather alienated form of activity in itself, as opposed to a brave resistance to alienation. Such a suggestion is clearly made when he claims that the kind of obscene joking frequently observed among female manual workers is participated in more 'as a matter of defence against male presumption and dominance than for fun'. If it is at all funny, he notes, it is only in a 'self-destructive sense'.

In contrast to this, Willis (1977) emphasised the ways in which manual workers 'thread through the dead experience of work a living culture which is far from a simple reflex of defeat'. He notes how in the shopfloor situation and in the classroom situation of boys destined for the shopfloor there is the same kind of informal groupings with the same counter-cultural 'complex of chauvinism, toughness and machismo'. He argued that the attempts of 'the lads' to control their own routines and life spaces at school parallel their fathers' informal control strategies at work. He also noted continuities between the attitudes to conformists and informers ('earoles' and 'grassers') in both situations as well as their common 'distinctive form of language and highly intimidating humour', where many of the verbal exchanges which occur are 'pisstakes', 'kiddings' or 'windups'. The way in which the working-class counter-culture can be seen as a reaction to middle-class culture is illustrated by the fact that the shopfloor 'abounds with apocryphal stories about the idiocy of purely theoretical knowledge'. A story is told, for example, of the book enthusiast who sent away for a book which he has yet to read – it arrived in a wooden box which he is unable to open.

The multiple purposes which humour may serve in the manual work situation is illustrated by Collinson's (1992) factory study which highlighted 'three aspects of the joking culture', first, as a medium to help develop 'collective solidarity to resist boredom, the organisational status system and managerial control'; second, to reinforce the central values of 'working class masculinity' so that workers were 'required to show a willingness, for example, to give and take a joke, to swear, to be dismissive of women, white-collar workers and managers' and to retain their domestic authority; and third, to control those perceived to be 'not pulling their weight'. But, as we saw earlier, humour is equally a concern of managers in organisations, and Collinson (2002) observes that in so far as humour is becoming involved in both resistance and control it is 'becoming incorporated into the contested terrain that is the contemporary workplace'. Collinson sees two historical and contemporary managerial strategies towards humour: a strategy of humour suppression and a strategy of humour manufacture with the former of these being akin to general managerial strategies of *direct control* or *responsible autonomy* or 'indirect control' (Chapter 5, p. 112). Put simply, organisational managers might choose to pursue worker compliance by stopping those workers joking and fooling about at work or, alternatively, they might choose to invite workers to joke and fool about with the managers – as long, of course, as those humorous activities contribute to the long-term success of the corporation.

Bullying and sexual harassment

The harassment or informal persecution of people at work is the last thing we might think of as funny. Yet studies show that sexual harassment, in particular, is often connected by its perpetrators with 'having a laugh' or 'just joking' (Wise and Stanley 1987). Sexual harassment may be perpetrated on men or women by people of the same or a different sex and it involves the expression of a sexual interest which may take either an apparently complimentary or an insulting form.

SEXUAL HARASSMENT

Unwanted and offensive expressions of sexual interest in a person or persons through words, gesture or touch.

Although men at work do experience sexual harassment (Lee 2000), the dominant form of the phenomenon is that in which men harass women and a key characteristic of such harassment at work is its treatment of women as primarily sexual beings rather than full persons (Pringle 1989) who can be treated in a derogatory and undermining fashion and, in effect, can be excluded from full participation in a male dominated workplace culture where men 'routinely act in concert' to 'mobilise masculinities at work' (Martin 2001). Such practices create considerable barriers to the movement of women into areas of work which were previously the preserve of men or into previously male dominated levels of authority in workplaces. The study by Collinson and Collinson (1996) of women in insurance sales shows how the 'exercise of gendered power by men' eventually led to the 're-exclusion of women' from this area of employment that women were beginning to penetrate. Women were harassed by managers, colleagues and clients and not only were these practices rationalised as 'rites of passage' or 'normalised' with comments to the effect that it was all 'a bit of fun', they involved blaming the victims for their own persecution – this giving harassment a 'vicious, self-justifying logic' whereby 'its reproduction was rationalised on the grounds that it already existed'. Women who cannot 'take the jokes' that men make are deemed unfit to work amongst those men.

Bullying at work may well contain a sexual element but it can be seen as a broader phenomenon, one in which the harassing of the worker has a deleterious psychological effect on them.

> ## BULLYING AT WORK
>
> Repeated actions towards people at work which have the effect of humiliating and mentally distressing them.

Bullying may be carried out on workers by co-workers but, as Fineman (2003) points out, it is something 'associated with differences in power and status' and it is 'superiors' who are the main culprits with work organisations more likely to be sites of bullying when their culture incorporates 'an exaggerated emphasis on winning, greed, privilege, power and management by fear'. But harassment and bullying is not only perpetrated by organisational members upon each other. It is also liable to enter the worker–client relationship in service work. Workers in restaurants and hotels, in particular, are made vulnerable to abuse by customers, given the quasi-servant role they have to play and given the fact that this is often a matter of women providing service to men (Hall 1993; Guiffre and Williams 1994; Leidner 1993; Guerrier and Adib 2000).

Cheating, fiddling and breaking things

The counter-cultures which grow up in work settings in part represent a challenge and an opposition to dominant interests and values, but in the end these cultures often enable the less privileged simply to adjust to their lack of freedom and privilege at work. To this extent they provide an integrative mechanism within work organisations. As was argued in Chapter 4, organisations are constituted by the interplay between official and unofficial practices of participants. Even those activities which are 'against the rules' or are illegal in the narrowest sense can often be seen as integral to the way work is organised rather than as aberrant and constituting an unambiguous threat to dominant interests.

If we look at the type of pilfering and fiddling which Mars and Nicod (1984) observed among hotel waiters, it is clear that the money made – which is seen as 'a part of wages' – is a form of theft from the employer. Yet we need to bear in mind that these losses by theft may constitute very reasonable 'costs' from the employers' point of view. This is not only because they enable wage rates to be kept low but also because they constitute a form of reward which is not conducive to official negotiation. Because of this, unionisation is unlikely. By maintaining a particularly individualistic form of activity, the potential for collective organisation and opposition to managerial control is effectively reduced. Ditton's (1977) participant study of bread salesmen also shows how illegal gains can become part of the implicit contract of the employee. Here it is the money 'fiddled' from customers which makes up the wage and Ditton (1974) interprets the way 'the firm's entry and training procedures are explicitly geared to teaching recruits how to rob the customer regularly and invisibly' as indicating how the fiddle helps solve certain managerial problems.

The officially deviant behaviour in the above cases is very much tied into the implicit contract between the individual and the employer. In other cases the illegal activity may be more clearly group-based as happens in the case of dockers (Mars 1974). Here the illegal activity and its control contributes to group solidarity, which may indeed contribute to its oppositional potential. Yet it is also likely, given the particular technology involved, to increase their technical efficiency, and hence the meeting of official goals. The social functions of illegal activity in the workplace have been strongly emphasised by Henry (1978), who argues that the general trading in pilfered goods which goes on in many workplaces and which constitutes a 'hidden economy' involves deals which 'often have less to do with the material worth of the goods and more to do with fulfilling the expectations and moral obligations of the friendly relationship'. To obtain for a colleague something which 'fell off the back of a lorry' is as much to 'do a favour' for that colleague as it is to make money, we might say.

The extent and variety of workplace fiddles is enormous. In a survey by Mars (1982) fiddling is shown to be 'woven into the fabrics of people's lives' but in ways which vary with their occupation:

- *hawks* are the entrepreneurs and professionals;
- *donkeys* are those highly constrained by rules at the cashier's desk or beside a machine;
- *wolves* operate in packs in places like the docks;
- *vultures* operate in highly individualistic and competitive ways as befits their work as we see, for example, with travelling sales representatives.

These fiddles represent activities designed primarily to benefit individuals and groups at work. They may or may not threaten the dominant interests in the work organisation but, if they do, this is not their key purpose. With sabotage, however, such a purpose is more central.

SABOTAGE

The deliberate disruption of work flows within an organisation or the undermining of the conditions whereby dominant management purposes are readily achieved.

Destructive physical workplace behaviour is perhaps the most obvious form of sabotage. Such acts should not, however, be seen as meaningless. Taylor and Walton (1971) identify three types of physical sabotage, each with a different degree of immediate disruptive intent:

- Attempts to reduce tension and frustration – for example, the ship builders who, about to be sacked on completion of a ship, got drunk and smashed the royal suite.
- Attempts to facilitate or ease the work process – for example, 'tapping' nuts into place in aircraft assembly.
- Attempts to assert control – for example, the 'collective bargaining by riot' indulged in by the Luddites.

Thus, even literally destructive behaviour can be seen as a part of the process whereby realities are negotiated, interests are defended, and the problems of 'getting through' the day at work are coped with. The most apparently senseless acts of vandalism have a rationale – a rationale which can only be appreciated as long as we note not only the conflicts but also the element of reciprocity between employer and employee expectations which develops in many 'low-trust' employment situations. This reciprocity is illustrated in the comments of a former shop steward in a car industry press shop who suggested that workers tend to feel that if they are treated like children they can act like children and hence behave irresponsibly (Brown 1977).

Sabotage should not be associated with low status work alone and may take forms other than that of engaging in physical destruction. Where managers and technocrats find themselves subjected to the types of control normally associated with manual workers, LaNuez and Jermier (1994) observe that we may find them:

- letting machines break down;
- allowing quality to fall;
- withholding critical information;
- revealing information to competitors;
- denigrating the product;
- speaking negatively about the organisation to employees;
- falsifying data;
- actually engaging in physical destruction; for example, destroying information.

LaNuez and Jermier suggest five macro-level forces which can lead to this:

1 mergers and organisational restructuring;
2 increased use of monitoring and other control strategies;
3 technological changes that have replaced highly skilled with less skilled labour;
4 deskilling and deprofessionalisation;
5 displacement due to technological obsolescence.

To understand sociologically deviant behaviour at work, we clearly need to locate it in the social structure and culture of the setting in which it occurs. Quinney (1963) also makes this point when he shows how the level of prescription violations committed by retail pharmacists depends on the way the individual deals with a particular 'role conflict' built into the occupation; that between an orientation to professional values on the one hand and business values on the other. In effect, the extent to which those activities which are labelled 'deviant' are ultimately oppositional in society at large is questionable. 'Fiddling' can be seen as sharing many features with business and legitimate commerce itself and, like selling, it can be said to epitomise the 'capitalist spirit' (Ditton 1977). In the jargon of the deviance theorists, much workplace deviance is sub-cultural rather than contra-cultural: it reflects dominant values and norms as much as or more than it opposes them.

Rule manipulation

Supervisors and managers are necessarily implicated in many of the manifestations of conflict at work which we have considered here. Conflict and co-operation are two sides of the same coin and, at all levels, the breaking of official rules designed to help achieve official goals may, paradoxically, be necessary to meet these goals. In Chapter 4 we saw how supervisors operate an 'indulgency pattern' whereby rule-breaking is connived at to achieve employee co-operation, and we noted how bureaucratic procedures are sometimes broken or modified to get the job done.

Writers who have used the insights of ethnomethodology in studying organisations have questioned the common assumption that rules determine behaviour. It is argued, instead, that individuals frequently use rules as *resources* or as means to be employed in dealing with whatever situations arise and have to be coped with. Thus, Bittner (1973) shows how the police officers operating on skid-row do not simply enforce the law – even when they invoke it. Instead they 'merely use it as a resource to solve certain pressing practical problems in keeping the peace'. Zimmerman (1973) has shown how reception personnel in a public assistance organisation similarly draw on official rules and procedures to explain or justify the way they happen to cope with the day-to-day pressures and circumstances of their jobs. People cope with the conflicts and contradictions of their work situation through what Zimmerman (1973) calls 'the practicalities of rule use'. This is illustrated in Manning's (1977) discussion of the contradiction between:

- the 'myth' of police work which sees it as controlling crime; and
- 'the reality' in which they maintain order (often without invoking the law) and help out people in trouble.

In the end, street-based police officers have to use their discretion and decide how they should apply general rules to particular situations. In this way, the individual working police officer finds a source of relative freedom from control by superiors. The 'fractional bargaining' indulged in by industrial supervisors (Kuhn 1961) and the condoning of prisoner rule-breaking by warders (Morris and Morris 1973) can be seen in a similar light.

Service work and defence of self

Given the strong cultural value put upon independence, autonomy and self-expression, problems are as likely to arise for many of those in work which involves taking instructions from customers or clients as they are for people who take orders from bosses. The strategies used by prostitutes to maintain their self-respect in such situations were noted earlier (Chapter 7, pp. 162, 166) and something similar can be seen across the range of service occupations. The more potentially demeaning the service given might be to the service worker, the more there is the tendency for contempt for the client to become an element of the particular work culture. Hence we get a variety of depersonalising titles used for the client: the mark, john, patsy, trick or punter. In all of these is an implication of naïveté on the part of the client and hence an implied superiority on the part of the worker, one which compensates for his or her superficial subservience.

Labelling of clients is not simply a mechanism used by service workers to maintain their self-respect in the face of implied servant status. The refining of the labelling process and the development of typologies of clients can play a useful technical role and help the individual cope with the exigencies of the job. Taxi-cab drivers, for instance, find that their livelihood depends on how accurately they can 'size up' the ability of potential customers to pay. Hence, as Davis (1959) observes, they may utilise a typology of customers which ranges from the generously-tipping 'sport' through the 'blowhard', the 'businessman' and the 'live ones' to the 'stiffs' who give no tips and are passionately disliked. Correspondingly, Spradley and Mann (1975) describe the complex typology of customers used by cocktail waitresses (jocks, animals, regulars, bitches, annies, zoos, pigs, johnnies, etc.) and note how, in particular, the most potentially antagonistic relationship which exists within the bar, that between waitresses and female customers, is reflected in the way 'bitches' almost become a synonym for 'women'.

Every service occupation has its own types of 'awkward customer' and develops strategies to deal with them, whether it be the handing out of large quantities of low value coins in the change of the shop assistant's over-choosy customer, or the adoption of ludicrously jargon-ridden language by the car-mechanic dealing with a know-all motorist. Sanctions play an important role in the achieving of client control; an integral element of service work, as Richman observes in noting how busmen tend to train their passengers into 'the correct attitude' (1969) and how traffic wardens accrue to themselves or lose honour through the 'street bargains' which they make with motorists (1983). The warden who bargains successfully with the motorist transforms them into a 'client', 'instilling a sense of social responsibility' towards the warden's purposes. And ride operators at Disneyland have a variety of ways of punishing customers who offend them, including adjusting their set belts so tight that the customer doubles over with pain (van Maanen 1991). Practices like this should not be seen, however, simply as acts of resistance against customers. They also represent a degree of protest against managerial control, in so far as the employing organisation is not one whose managers are likely to appreciate their workers hurting their customers. But, in a contrasting situation, Lankshear *et al.* (2001) observed call centre workers resisting managerial controls and applying their 'own definitions of professionalism and good performance' in order to give the customers better treatment that directly following managerial dictates would allow. Such are the complexities of the relationships and patterns of conflict and co-operation to be seen within the negotiated orders of all workplaces.

Concept guide and glossary

The main concepts used throughout the text are presented here together with a number of other sociological terms that the reader may come across in this and in other sociological works. The subject index can be used to link most entries to the main text.

Action research A form of combined research and consultancy in which the client receives help with problem-solving whilst the researcher/consultant is able to contribute the knowledge gained in the process to the academic community.

Alienation A state of existence in which human beings are not fulfilling their humanity.

Ambiguity See also **Uncertainty**. A state in which the meaning of a situation or an event is unclear or confused and is therefore open to a variety of interpretations.

Anomie A form of social breakdown in which the norms that would otherwise prevail in a given situation cease to operate.

Artefacts Objects that have been created by human hands. They often play a symbolic role within organisational cultures as well as fulfilling a practical function. A worker's uniform is an artefact that plays both a practical and a symbolic role, for example.

Authority Power which has been 'legitimised' or made acceptable to those subject to it.

Automation The application of machinery which is controlled and co-ordinated by computerised programmes to tasks previously done by direct human effort.

Bounded rationality See **Rationality, bounded.**

Bourgeoisie A Marxian category which includes all of those in a capitalist society whose ownership of capital enables them to subsist without selling their labour power (their capacity to work). The term is sometimes used in a more general way to refer to a 'middle class'.

Bullying at work Repeated actions towards people at work which have the effect of humiliating and mentally distressing them.

Bureaucracy The control and co-ordination of work tasks through a hierarchy of appropriately qualified office holders, whose authority derives from their expertise and who rationally devise a system of rules and procedures that are calculated to provide the most appropriate means of achieving specified ends.

Business process re-engineering (BPR) The restructuring of an organisation to focus on business processes rather than on business functions. Advanced management control information technologies are used together with team working and employee 'empowerment'.

Call centre work Work in which operators utilise computer terminals to process information relating to telephone calls which are made and/or received, these calls being mediated by various computer-based filtering, allocational and monitoring devices.

Capitalism See **Industrial capitalism.**

Capitalist labour process The design, control and monitoring of work tasks and activities by managers acting as agents of the capital owning class to extract surplus value from the labour activity of employees.

Career A sequence of social positions filled by a person throughout their life or through an aspect of their life such as their involvement in work.

Class An individual's class position is a matter of the part which they play (or the person upon whom they are dependent plays) within the division of labour of a society and the implications which this has for their access to those experiences, goods and services which are scarce and valued in that society.

Class consciousness A state of awareness of their common interests and situation by the members of an objectively existing social class.

Classical administrative principles Universally applicable rules of organisational design – structural and cultural – widely taught and applied, especially in the first half of the twentieth century.

Closed shop An arrangement whereby work in a particular setting is exclusively carried out by members of a specified trade union. Pre-entry closed shops required workers to be union members before they could be recruited whereas the new worker could join the union after entering the job in the case of the post-entry closed shop.

Closure, social The process whereby a group seeks to gain or defend its advantages over other groups by closing its ranks to those it defines as outsiders.

Collective bargaining A method of agreeing work conditions and rewards through a process of negotiation between employer representatives and the representatives of collectively organised employees.

Community Often used to mean more or less the same as 'society'. The word generally implies a smaller entity than does 'society', however. The essence of the idea of community is that people feel strongly aware of belonging to it and accept its traditions. It is small-scale and intimate and is characterised by face-to-face relationships.

Concepts Working definitions that are chosen or devised for use in scientific analysis. They are the way scientists define their terms for the purpose of a specific investigation. They therefore differ from dictionary definitions – these tending to have a much more general applicability.

Conflict A phenomenon that occurs at two levels. Conflict *at the level of interests* exists where there is a difference between different parties (employers and employees, say, or workers and customers) over desired outcomes; and conflict *at the level of behaviour* comes about when parties seeking different outcomes either directly clash over those differences and engage in open dispute or indirectly express their differences through such gestures as acting destructively or co-operating in a sullen or grudging manner.

Conjugal roles   The parts played in the household by husbands and wives.

Contingencies   In organisation theory: those circumstances which influence the ways in which organisations are structured. Examples are the size of the organisation, the nature of the technology used or the state of the organisation's environment.

Contradictions   Tendencies within a social or organisational structure for certain principles on which that structure is based to clash with each other in a way that undermines that structure.

Convergence thesis   Societies which industrialise become increasingly alike in their social, political and cultural characteristics as well as their work organisations.

Co-operatives, worker   Work enterprises jointly owned and controlled by those who work in them.

Corporatism   A political system in which major decisions, especially with regard to the economy, are made by the state in close association with employer, trade union and other pressure group organisations.

Cultural capital   The various linguistic and social competences derived from and certificated by the education system and manifested in a certain manner, ethos, know-how and set of aspirations.

Culture   The system of meanings which are shared by members of a society, organisation or other human grouping, and which define what is good and bad, right and wrong and what are the appropriate ways for members of that grouping to think and behave.

Deskilling   An approach to the redesign of jobs which involves a lowering of the skill levels required from those filling the job than had previously been the case.

Determinism   A way of thinking in which the causal factors behind whatever is being considered are seen to lie outside of human agency.

Deviance   The failure, deliberate or otherwise, of people to comply with the rules, standards or norms of any group, organisation or society in which they are involved.

Dialectic   The interplay between two potential opposites which leads to a third possibility. For example, the interplay between individual initiative and social constraint (which are often seen as opposing phenomena) can be seen as leading to a third phenomenon – 'society'.

Differentiation   The process in which a society or an organisation is divided into specialised parts which contribute to the functioning of the whole.

Direct and indirect management control attempts   Managers, in striving to achieve control over people's work efforts, may lean towards the adoption of either direct or indirect controls. *Direct controls* involve close supervision and monitoring of activities, tight rules, highly prescribed procedures, centralised structures, low commitment culture, low trust culture, adversarial culture and a tightly bureaucratic structure and culture. And *indirect controls* involve the 'empowering' or giving task discretion to workers, loose rules, flexible procedures, decentralised structures, high commitment culture, high trust culture, an emphasis on the mutuality of interests and a loosely bureaucratic structure and culture.

Dirty work An occupational activity which plays a necessary role in a society but which is regarded in some respects as morally doubtful.

Discourse A set of concepts, statements, terms and expressions which constitute a way of talking or writing about a particular aspect of life, thus framing the way people understand and act with respect to that area of existence.

Division of labour The allocation of work tasks to various groups or categories of individual. The **social division of labour** is the allocation of work tasks at the level of society, typically into trades and occupations; and the **technical division of labour** is task specialisation within an occupation or broad work task.

Domestic labour Household tasks such as cooking, cleaning, shopping and looking after dependent young, old or sick members of the household.

Dominant coalition The grouping of individuals within an organisation who effectively have greater influence over events than any other grouping.

Dualism The effective division of an economy into two major parts; typically a prosperous and stable 'core' sector of enterprises and jobs and a 'peripheral' sector which is relatively and systematically disadvantaged.

Effort bargain See **Implicit contract**.

Embourgeoisement The adoption by working-class people of the attitudes and lifestyle of middle-class groups.

Emotional labour An element of work activity in which the worker is required to display certain emotions in order to complete work tasks in the way required by an employer.

Emotions Feelings are sensations relating to a psychological state that are felt bodily and emotions are the way these sensations are culturally interpreted.

Empirical enquiry That part of social science activity which involves observation, experiment or other forms of data collection as opposed to the conceptual, theoretical and interpretative work.

Enacted environment Organisational environments exist for members of organisations by virtue of the interpretations they make of what is occurring 'outside' the organisation and the way their own actions influence or shape those occurrences.

Ethnography A style of social science research in which the subjects are directly observed in their normal setting and in their normal pattern of living, with a view to the researcher producing an account of the cultural lives of those research subjects.

Ethnomethodology The study of how ordinary members of society in their everyday lives make the world meaningful by achieving a sense of 'taken-for-grantedness'.

Flexibility for long-term adaptability The ability to make rapid and effective innovations through the use of job designs and employment policies that encourage people to use their discretion, innovate and work in new ways for the sake of the organisation – as circumstances require. This fits with *indirect control* managerial practices.

Flexibility for short-term predictability The ability to make rapid changes through the use of job designs and employment policies that allow staff to be easily recruited and trained or easily laid off – as circumstances require. This fits with *direct control* managerial practices.

Flexible firm A pattern of employment in which an organisation divides its workforce into *core* elements who are given security and high rewards in return for a willingness to adapt, innovate and take on new skills, and *peripheral* elements who are given more specific tasks and less commitment of continuing employment and skill enhancement.

Flexible specialisation An approach to employment and work organisation which offers customised products to diversified markets, building trusting and co-operative relationships both with employees, who use advanced technologies in a craft way, and other organisations within a business district and its associated community.

Fordism A pattern of industrial organisation and employment policy in which (a) mass production techniques and an associated deskilling of jobs is combined with (b) treatment of employees which recognises that workers are also consumers whose earning power and consumption attitudes – as well as their workplace efficiency – affect the success of the enterprise.

Function An action or an institution has a function within a social system if it contributes towards the maintenance or adaptation of that system. A 'dysfunction' exists when the effect is one 'harmful' to that system.

Functionalism An approach within sociology which explains aspects of societies or organisations in terms of the contribution they make to the functioning of that society or organisation as a whole.

Globalisation A trend in which the economic, political and cultural activities of people in different countries increasingly influence each other and become interdependent.

Harassment See **Sexual harassment**.

Human relations The term is used by sociologists almost exclusively to refer to a 'school' of industrial sociology and to managerial styles which follow its general recommendations. The school is that associated with the Hawthorne experiments carried out in the pre-war years in America. Its emphasis is on the ways in which the 'social needs' of workers are met or are not met in the work situation.

Human Resource Management (HRM) The HRM expression is sometimes used in a generic way to refer to all managerial activities that are concerned with employment (or 'personnel') aspects of work organisations. But it is also used to refer to one particular style of employment management, that involving a 'high commitment human resourcing strategy' (pp. 108–11). In such strategies, employers seek a close and psychologically involving relationship with workers; they build opportunities for personal development into people's careers; people's employment is expected to continue over a longer-term period, potentially covering a variety of different types of work, and workers are given discretion about how tasks are carried out. To complicate matters further, the HRM term is also used to refer to the study of employment management activities (giving us university departments, professors and journals of HRM).

Humour See **Workplace humour**.

Ideal type A model of a phenomenon or a situation which extracts its essential or 'pure' elements. It represents what the item or institution (capitalism, bureaucracy, instrumental work orientation, for example) would look like if it existed in a pure form.

Identity The conception which each individual develops, in relation to others, of who and what they are. A person's identity has two components: *self-identity* being an individual's own notion of self; and *social identity* being the notion others have of who and what that individual is.

Ideology/group ideology A set of ideas which are located within a particular social group and which fulfils functions for that group. It helps defend, justify and further the interests of the group with which it is associated.

Implicit contract The tacit agreement between an employed individual and an employing organisation about what the employee will 'put in' to their job and the rewards and benefits for which this will be exchanged.

Incorporation The process of directing the political and economic activities of groups who may threaten a social order or system so that they operate within that order instead of threatening it. This is often associated with the 'institutionalising' of conflict.

Indulgency pattern The ignoring of selected rule infringements by supervisors in return for those being supervised allowing supervisors to call for co-operation in matters which, strictly speaking, they could refuse.

Industrial capitalism A form of society in which large-scale or complex machinery and associated technique is widely applied to the pursuit of economic efficiency on a basis whereby the capacity for work of the members of some groups is sold to others who control and organise it in such a way that the latter groups maintain relative advantage with regard to those resources which are scarce and generally valued.

Industrial relations The activities and institutions associated with relationships between employers and groups of collectively organised employees.

Informal economy An area of economic exchange in which work, legal or illegal, is done for gain but is not officially 'declared' for such purposes as taxation.

Informating work ICTs can 'record' and hence can 'play back' or make visible the processes behind the operations that were once deep in the minds of the people doing that work.

Information and Communication Technologies (ICTs) The combination of micro-electronic and computing technologies with telecommunications to manipulate human information.

Institution, social A regularly occurring and therefore normal pattern of actions and relationships.

Instrumentalism An orientation to work which treats it as a means towards ends other than ones to do with work itself. It typically involves a primary concern with the money to be earned.

Interpretive conceptions of social science These see social science as requiring different procedures from physical sciences. The social world is regarded as a reality only accessible through the meanings developed by social actors. *Understandings* of social processes and the patterns within them are sought rather than *explanations* of social behaviour.

Jargon, work related Language use and terms that are peculiar to a specific organisational, occupational or technical context.

Job design The shaping of particular jobs, especially with regard to how narrow or broad the tasks associated with those jobs are and the extent to which jobholders exercise discretion in carrying out those tasks.

Job enrichment The expansion of the scope of jobs by such means as the re-integration of maintenance or inspection tasks; an extension of the work cycle; an increased degree of delegation of decision-making by job holders.

Just-in-time (JIT) production processes A way of organising production processes so that no buffer stocks are held in the factory, with materials and components only being delivered immediately before they are required.

Labour market, internal The creation by an employer of a stable and well-rewarded labour force through a policy of internal promotion and training.

Labour movement A coming together of such bodies as trade unions and associated political parties to represent the interests which employed people as a whole are believed to hold in common.

Labour process See **Capitalist labour process**.

Lean production A combining of teamworking with automated technologies. Workers are required both to initiate 'continual improvements' in quality and to ensure that every task is got 'right first time' and completed to a demanding 'just-in-time' schedule.

Legends, organisational Narratives about events that might or might not have happened in the organisation's past, which have a sense of wonder about them and which point to activities that the listener is encouraged to admire or deplore.

Leisure Those activities which people pursue for pleasure and which are not a necessary part of their business, employment or domestic management obligations.

Life-chances The ability to gain access to scarce and valued goods and services such as a home, food and education.

Logic of corporate management The logic of corporate management is one of shaping exchange relationships to satisfy the demands of the various constituencies, inside and outside the organisation, so that continued support in terms of resources such as labour, custom, investment, supplies and legal approval is obtained and the organisation enabled to survive into the long term.

Management The set of roles in an organisation and the activities associated with them which are primarily concerned with directing the organisation rather than with carrying out the tasks which make up the main work of the organisation.

Managerial manipulation of worker implicit contracts The attempts by managers to 'motivate' workers not by 'meeting needs' as in classic 'motivation theory' but by negotiating with and persuading workers that a particular bundle of rewards that is on offer is a fair and reasonable return for the bundle of 'efforts' that the management is asking them to put in.

Managerialism This term was once generally used to refer to the type of social system identified in the managerialist thesis. However, it is more often used nowadays to refer to approaches to public administration or government in which most problems are seen as soluble by managerial means – are seen, in effect, as administratively technical matters rather than as political, ideological or value matters.

Managerialist thesis The claim that the people who manage or 'direct' the corporations of modern societies have taken control away from those allegedly separate interests who own wealth.

Methodology A term often misused to refer to research techniques and which, more properly, refers to the philosophical issues raised by the attempt to investigate the world scientifically.

Micropolitics The political processes that occur within organisations as individuals, groups and organisational 'sub-units' compete for access to scarce and valued material and symbolic resources.

Mobility, social The movement of people between different positions in the pattern of inequality of any society. It may be intra-generational (the individual changes their position within their own life career) or inter-generational (where the individual moves into a position which differs from that of their parents). Movement may be upwards or downwards.

Models Analytical schemes which simplify reality by selecting certain phenomena and suggesting particular relationships between them.

Modernism An approach to dealing with the world based on the application of rational and scientific analysis to social, political, economic and industrial institutions in the belief that this can lead to greater human control over the world and thus bring about general progress in the condition of humankind.

Myths, organisational Narratives about events that are unlikely ever to have happened but which illustrate some important 'truth' about life in the organisation.

Narratives and stories Accounts of the world which follow a basic form of 'this, then that, then that' and which, when applied to human affairs, typically take on a more developed story-like form involving characters with interests, motives, emotions and moralities.

Negotiated order The pattern of activities which emerge over time as an outcome of the interplay of the various interests, understandings, reactions and initiatives of the individuals and groups involved in an organisation.

Non-standard employment Employment in which contracts between employers and employees are short-term and unstable with the worker taking part-time, temporary and, sometimes, multiple jobs – the work sometimes being at home rather than in an organisationally located workplace and there being little by way of employment benefits. See also **Standard employment**.

Norm, social Part of the underlying pattern of social life – the standards to which people are expected to conform or the rules of conduct whose infringement may result in sanctions intended to encourage conformity.

Occupation Membership of an occupation involves engagement on a regular basis in a part or the whole of a range of work tasks which are identified under a particular heading or title by both those carrying out these tasks and by a wider public.

Occupational career The sequence of positions through which the member of an occupation typically passes during the part of their life which they spend in that occupation.

Occupational community A form of local social organisation in which people's work and non-working lives are both closely identified with members of the occupation in which they work.

Occupational culture The set of ideas, values, attitudes, norms, procedures and artefacts characteristically associated with an occupation.

Occupational ideology A set of ideas developed by an occupational group, and especially by its leaders, to legitimate the pursuit of the group members' common occupationally related interests.

Occupational recruitment The typical processes and routes of entry followed by members of an occupation.

Occupational segregation A pattern of occupations in which some are predominantly male and others female. *Horizontal segregation* describes the tendency for male and female work to be separated into types of occupational activity, whilst *vertical segregation* sees gender differentiation in who takes the higher level and who takes the lower level jobs within an occupation.

Occupational socialisation The process whereby individuals learn about the norms, values, customs and beliefs associated with an occupation which they have joined so that they are able to act as a full member of that occupation.

Occupational structure The pattern in a society which is created by the distribution of the labour force across the range of existing types of work or occupation.

Official and unofficial aspects of organisations *Official* aspects of organisations are the rules, values and activities that are part of the formally managerial-sanctioned policies and procedures. *Unofficial* aspects are the rules, values and activities that people at all levels in the organisation develop but which do not have formal managerial sanction.

Official control apparatus of an organisation The set of roles, rules, structures, value statements, cultural symbols, rituals and procedures managerially designed to co-ordinate and control work activities.

Organisation man A male executive employee whose whole life is moulded by the corporation for whom he works.

Organisational culture The set of meanings and values shared by members of an organisation that defines the appropriate ways for people to think and behave with regard to the organisation.

Organisational mischief Activities occurring within the workplace that (a) according to the official structure, culture and rules of the organisation, 'should not happen' and (b) contain an element of challenge to the dominant modes of operating or to dominant interests in the organisation.

Organisational principle of work structuring Patterns of work activity which are the outcomes – intended and unintended – of institutional arrangements in which some people conceive of and design work and then recruit, pay, co-ordinate and control the efforts of other people to fulfil work tasks.

Organisational structure The regular or persisting patterns of action that give shape and a degree of predictability to an organisation.

Organisations See **Work organisations**.

Orientation to work The meaning attached by individuals to their work which predisposes them to think and act in particular ways with regard to that work.

Paradigm A 'model' in the very broadest sense in science which includes basic ideas about how investigation should proceed as well as what assumptions are to be made about the relationships between phenomena.

Paradox of consequences The tendency for the means chosen to achieve ends in social life to undermine or defeat those ends.

Paradox of organising The tendency for the means adopted by organisational managers to achieve particular goals to fail to achieve these goals since these 'means' involve human beings who have goals of their own which may not be congruent with those of the managers.

Patriarchy The system of interrelated social structures and cultural practices through which men exploit women.

Pluralism Social scientific perspectives which emphasise the multiplicity of interest groups within societies or organisations. It is often, unreasonably, used to refer to what is properly seen as just one type of pluralist perspective – that in which the various interest groupings in society are seen as being more or less equally powerful. See also **Radical pluralist frame of reference**.

Political economy Social scientific approaches which emphasise the power dimensions of social life and how these, together with the ways in which production is organised, influence whatever particular phenomena are being considered.

Population ecology A type of organisation theory which concentrates on how organisations adapt and evolve in order to survive within the general population of organisations of which they are a part.

Portfolio or **boundaryless careers** A pattern of working in which the individual does not enter an employment relationship with a single work organisation but is engaged by a variety of different organisations or clients, each for a segment of their working time.

Positivism The term is generally used to refer to a position which sees social science and the natural or physical sciences as equivalent and therefore as amenable to the same basic kind of investigative procedure. It sees the social world as an objective reality external to those who study it and seeks explanations in the form of general theories or *covering laws* which can be used to make predictions. For some, the essence of the positivism is the idea of social science as a means of predicting and therefore the controlling of social institutions and events.

Post-Fordism A pattern of industrial organisation and employment policy in which skilled and trusted labour is used continuously to develop and customise products for small markets.

Post-industrial society A type of economically advanced social order in which the centrally important resource is knowledge, service work has largely replaced manufacturing employment, and knowledge-based occupations play a privileged role.

Postmodernism An approach to the world which rejects attempts to build systematic explanations of history and human activity and which, instead, concentrates on the ways in which human beings go about 'inventing' their worlds, especially through language and cultural innovation.

Postmodernity An alleged state into which the world is moving which departs from the key organising principles of modernity.

Power The capacity of an individual or group to affect the outcome of any situation so that access is achieved to whatever resources are scarce and desired within a society or part of a society.

Problematic, A This is similar to a paradigm (above) but the term emphasises the role of certain problems or issues which give a focus to the process of selecting phenomena to concentrate on. A problematic is thus a set of linked concepts focusing on particular problems or issues.

Productive co-operation The achievement, in the light of the tendency of people involved in organisations to have their own projects, interests and priorities, of a degree of working together that ensures that tasks carried out in the organisation's name are fulfilled to sufficient a level to enable the organisation to continue in existence.

251

Professionalisation A process followed by certain occupations to increase its members' status, relative autonomy and rewards and influence through such activities as setting up a professional body to control entry and practice, establishing codes of conduct, making claims of altruism and a key role in serving the community.

Professions Occupations which have been relatively successful in gaining high status and autonomy in certain societies on the basis of a claimed specialist expertise over which they have gained a degree of monopoly control.

Proletarianisation A trend whereby members of a 'middle-class' occupational group move downwards in the class and status hierarchy, finding themselves located in a position more like that of working-class rather than middle-class people.

Proletariat This category, in the basic Marxian scheme, includes all of those who lack sufficient capital upon which they can subsist and who, therefore, are forced to 'sell their labour power' (capacity to work) on the market.

Psychologism A tendency to explain social behaviour solely in terms of the psychological characteristics of individuals.

Radical pluralist frame of reference This recognises the plurality of groups and interests in society (and welcomes social pluralism *in principle*) whilst observing the more basic patterns of power and inequality which tend to shape, as well as be shaped by it.

Rationalisation A trend in social change whereby traditional or magical criteria of action are replaced by technical, calculative or scientific criteria.

Rationality and change The criterion of rationality involves submitting decisions and actions to constant calculative scrutiny and produces a continuous drive towards change.

Rationality, bounded Human reasoning and decision-making is restricted in its scope by the fact that human beings have both perceptual and information-processing limits.

Rationality, instrumental The calculated choice of appropriate means to achieve specific ends.

Reification/personification An error in which an abstraction is treated as a 'thing' or a living person. The error is committed, for example, when one talks of 'society' or an 'organisation' *doing* something – or *making* people act in certain ways.

Responsible autonomy An approach to the design of work tasks which gives discretion to those doing the work on the understanding that they will choose to accept the managerial trust put in them and perform the tasks in accordance with managerial priorities. It can be contrasted with 'direct controls'. See **Direct and indirect management control attempts**.

Restructuring of work The changing patterns of work experience, organisational and occupational activity both resulting from and contributing to economic, political and cultural changes unfolding across the world.

Rites, organisational Rituals that are relatively formally (though not necessarily officially) organised and pre-planned.

Rituals, organisational Patterns of behaviour that regularly occur in particular circumstances or at particular times in an organisation.

Role, social People are said to be playing a role in social life whenever they act in a situation according to well-defined expectations.

Sabotage The deliberate disruption of work flows within an organisation or the undermining of the conditions whereby dominant management purposes are readily achieved.

Sagas, organisational Narratives with a series of events that are said to have unfolded over time and which constitute an important part of the organisation's history.

Science A formal, systematic and precise approach to building up a body of knowledge and theory which is rigorous in testing propositions against available evidence. Sociology is a science because it makes generalisations as systematically as possible in the light of available evidence.

Scientific management An approach to workplace organisation and job design associated with F.W. Taylor which is based on the principle of giving as much initiative about how tasks are done as possible to managerial experts who define precisely how each detailed aspect of every job is to be carried out.

Self-actualisation 'To become more and more what one is, to become everything that one is capable of becoming' (Maslow 1943).

Semi-autonomous work groups A work group or 'team' in which individual jobs are grouped to focus work activities on an overall 'whole task', with group members being fully trained and equipped so that they can be given discretion over how the task is completed.

Sexual harassment Unwanted and offensive expressions of sexual interest in a person or persons through words, gesture or touch.

Shop steward/union workplace representative A worker representative and 'lay' trade union official who represents to management the interests of fellow employees who elect them as their workplace spokesperson.

Social construction of reality The process in which people, through cultural interaction, give meaning to the world – a world that may well exist beyond language but which can only be known and communicated by people through language-based processes of cultural interpretation and sense-making.

Socialisation The process whereby individuals learn about the norms, values, customs and beliefs of a group, occupation, organisation or society.

Society The broad pattern of social, economic, cultural and political relationships within which people lead their lives, typically in the modern world as members of the same nation state.

Sociology The study of the relationships which develop between human beings as they organise themselves and are organised by others in societies and how these patterns influence and are influenced by the actions and interactions of people and how they make sense of their lives and identities.

Socio-technical systems An approach to work design in which the technical and the social/psychological aspects of the overall workplace are given equal weight and are designed at the same time to *take each other into account*.

Standard employment Employment in which the contract between the employer and employee is understood to be one in which the employee is likely to stay with the employer over the long term at a particular location, putting in a working day and week which is normal for that industry and receiving regular pay and the protection of pension and sick pay benefits. See also **Non-standard employment**.

State That set of institutions which, in a modern society, typically include government, parliament, civil service, educational and welfare apparatuses, the police, military and judiciary.

Status That aspect of social inequality whereby different positions are awarded different degrees of prestige or honour.

Stratification, social The patterns underlying the inequalities which exist between people in a society and form 'layers' on the basis of such factors as class or status.

Stress A sense of distress arising because of pressures experienced in certain social or economic circumstances that render the sufferer emotionally, and sometimes physically, incapable of continuing to behave in the ways expected of them in those circumstances.

Strike The collective withdrawal from work of a group of employees to exert pressure on the employer over any issue in which the two sides have a difference.

Structuration Ongoing processes in which individual initiatives are interwoven into the patterns of human interaction which sometimes constrain and sometimes enable those initiatives.

Subjective career The way an individual understands or makes sense of the way they have moved or are moving through various social positions or stages in the course of their life, or part of their life.

Subjectivity The notion that individuals are continually developing, in the light of the discourses surrounding them, of who they are and how they fit into the social world.

Symbol Any act, word, sound or object acts as a symbol when it stands for 'something else' that is not visible, audible or tangible.

Symbolic interactionism The study of social interaction which focuses on how people develop their concept of *self* through processes of communication in which symbols such as words, gestures and dress allow people to understand the expectations of others.

Systems thinking A way of viewing social entities such as societies or organisations as if they were self-regulating bodies exchanging energy and matter with their environment in order to survive.

Taylorism See **Scientific management**.

Teamworking A form of group-based work activity in which a degree of discretion is left to group members, acting in a co-operative manner, about how they perform the tasks allocated to them.

Technological implications A way of thinking about technology which sees it as determining, or at least closely constraining, the way in which tasks are organised with this, in turn, significantly influencing the attitudes and behaviour of workers.

Technology The tools, machines and control devices used to carry out tasks and the principles, techniques and reasoning which accompanies them.

Teleworking Work which is carried out away from the location of an employer or work contractor using electronic information and computing technology in either or both (a) carrying out the work tasks (b) communicating with the employing or contracting organisation with regard to those tasks.

Theories Systematic generalisations about the world resulting from the application of scientific procedures.

Total Quality Management (TQM) An approach to the production of goods and services in which employees at all levels focus on 'satisfying customers', use statistical and other techniques to monitor their work and seek continuous improvement in the processes used and the quality of what is produced.

Trade union An association of employees formed to improve their ability to negotiate working conditions and rewards with employers and, sometimes, to represent common interests within the political sphere beyond the workplace.

Trust relations *High trust* relations are said to exist in an organisation when employees and managers both feel able to take it for granted that broad mutual expectations established between them will be met and continue to be met, without the need closely to specify those expectations or to monitor their fulfilment. When this is lacking, *low trust* relations are said to prevail.

Uncertainty See also **Ambiguity**. A state in which the understanding of a future situation or event is unclear or confused and is therefore open to a variety of interpretations.

Values Notions of what is good and bad, right and wrong, within a society or a part of a society.

Virtual or networked organisations Sets of work arrangements in which those undertaking tasks carried under a corporate name largely relate to each other through electronic communications rather than through face-to-face interaction.

Work The carrying out of tasks which enable people to *make a living* within the social and economic context in which they are located.

Work design See also **Job design; Job enrichment**. General principles about how narrow or broad the tasks associated with jobs should be and the extent to which jobholders should use discretion in carrying out those tasks.

Work ethic A set of values which stresses the importance of work to the identity and sense of worth of the individual and which encourages an attitude of diligence, duty and a striving for success in the mind of the worker.

Work organisations Social and technical arrangements and understandings in which a number of people come together in a formalised and contractual relationship where the actions of some are directed by others towards the achievement of work tasks carried out in the organisation's name.

Work orientation See **Orientation to work**.

Workplace humour All forms of communication occurring in the work situation which create within people feelings of amusement and a predisposition to express that emotion through laughter.

Bibliography

Abell, P. and Reyniers, D. (2000) 'Review article: on the failure of social theory', *British Journal of Sociology*, 51: 739–50.

Abott, A. (1988) *The System of Professions: An Essay on the Division of Expert Labour*, Chicago: University of Chicago Press.

Ackers, P. (2002) 'Reframing employment relations: the case for neo-pluralism', *Industrial Relations Journal*, 33: 2–19.

Ackers, P. and Payne, J. (1998) 'British trade unions and social partnership: rhetoric, reality and strategy', *International Journal of Human Resource Management*, 9: 529–49.

Ackers, P., Smith, C. and Smith, P. (1996) *The New Workplace and Trade Unionism*, London: Routledge.

Ackroyd, S. and Fleetwood, S. (2000) *Realist Perspectives on Management and Organisations*, London: Routledge.

Ackroyd, S. and Procter, S. (1998) 'British manufacturing organisation and workplace industrial relations', *British Journal of Industrial Relations*, 36: 163–83.

Ackroyd, S. and Thompson, P. (1999) *Organisational Misbehaviour*, London: Sage.

Ackroyd, S., Burrell, G., Hughes, M. and Whitaker, A. (1988) 'The Japanisation of British industry?', *Industrial Relations Journal*, 19: 11–23.

Adkins, L. (1995) *Gendered Work*, Milton Keynes: Open University Press.

Aglietta, M. (1979) *A Theory of Capitalist Regulation: the U.S. Experience*, London: New Left Books.

Albrow, M. (1970) *Bureaucracy*, London: Macmillan.

Albrow, M. (1994) 'Accounting for organisational feeling', in L.J. Ray and M. Reed (eds) *Organizing Modernity: New Weberian Perspectives on Work*, London: Routledge.

Albrow, M. (1997) *Do Organisations Have Feelings?*, London: Routledge.

Aldrich, H.E. (1999) *Organizations Evolving*, London: Sage.

Allen, J. and du Gay, P. (1994) 'Industry and the rest: the economic identity of services', *Work, Economy and Society*, 8: 255–71.

Allen, S. and Wolkowitz, C. (1987) *Homeworking: Myths and Realities*, London: Macmillan.

Alvesson, M. and Deetz, S. (1996) 'Critical theory and postmodernist approaches to organizational studies', in S.R. Clegg, C. Hardy and W. Nord (eds) *Handbook of Organization Studies*, London: Sage, 191–217.

Alvesson, M. and Du Billing, Y. (1997) *Understanding Gender and Organizations*, London: Sage.

Alvesson, M. and Karreman, D. (2000) 'Varieties of discourse: on the study of organizations through discourse', *Human Relations*, 53: 1125–49.

Alvesson, M. and Willmott, H. (2002) 'Identity regulation as organizational control: producing the appropriate individual', *Journal of Management Studies*, 39: 619–44.

Anthony, P.D. (1977) *The Ideology of Work*, London: Tavistock.

Applebaum, H.A. (1981) *Royal Blue: The Culture of Construction Workers*, New York: Holt, Rinehart & Winston.

Arber, S. and Ginn, J. (1995) 'The mirage of gender equality: occupational success in the labour market and within marriage', *British Journal of Sociology*, 46: 21–44.

Arendt, H. (1959) *The Human Condition*, New York: Doubleday.

Armstrong, P. (1986) 'Management control strategies and interprofessional competition: the case of accountancy and personnel management', in D. Knights and H. Willmott (eds) *Managing the Labour Process*, Aldershot: Gower.

Armstrong, P. (1989) 'Management, labour process and agency', *Work, Employment and Society*, 3: 307–22.

Armstrong, P. (1993) 'Professional knowledge and social mobility: postwar changes in the knowledge-base of management accounting', *Work, Economy and Society*, 7: 1–21.

Arnold, J. (1997) *Managing Careers into the 21st Century*, London: Sage.

Arthur, M., Inkson, K. and Pringle, J. (1999) *The New Careers: Individual Action and Economic Change*, London: Sage.

Arthur, M.B. and Rousseau, D.M. (eds) (1996) *The Boundaryless Career: New Employment Principle for a New Organisational Era*, New York: Oxford University Press.

Arthur, M.B., Hall, D.T. and Lawrence, B.S. (1989) *Handbook of Career Theory*, Cambridge: Cambridge University Press.

Ashton, D.N. (1985) *Unemployment under Capitalism: The Sociology of British and American Labour*, Brighton: Wheatsheaf.

Atkinson, J. (1985) 'Flexibility: planning for an uncertain future', *Manpower Policy and Practice*, 1: 25–30.

Atkinson, J. (1987) 'Flexibility or fragmentation? The UK labour market in the eighties', *Labour and Society*, 12: 87–105.

Auster, C.J. (1996) *The Sociology of Work: Concepts and Cases*, Thousand Oaks, CA: Pine Forge Press.

Bacon, N. (1999) 'Union derecognition and the new human relations: a steel industry case study', *Work, Employment and Society*, 13: 1–17.

Bacon, N. (2001) 'Employee relations', in T. Redman and A. Wilkinson (eds) *Contemporary Human Resource Management*, Harlow: Prentice-Hall.

Badham, R. (1984) 'The sociology of industrial and post-industrial societies', *Current Sociology*, 32: 1–94.

Baechler, J. (1975) *The Origins of Capitalism*, Oxford: Blackwell.

Baechler, J., Hall, J.A. and Mann, M. (eds) (1988) *Europe and the Rise of Capitalism*, Oxford: Blackwell.

Bagguley, P. *et al.* (1990) *Restructuring: Place, Class and Gender*, London: Sage.

Bain, P. and Taylor, P. (2000) 'Entrapped by the "electronic panopticon"?: worker resistance in the call centre', *New Technology, Work and Employment*, 15: 2–18.

Baines, S. and Wheelock, J. (2000) 'Work and employment in small businesses: perpetuating and challenging gender traditions', *Gender, Work and Organization*, 5: 45–55.

Baldamus, W. (1961) *Efficiency and Effort*, London: Tavistock.

Banks, M., Bates, I., Breakwell, G., Bynner, J., Emler, N., Jamieson, L. and Roberts, K. (1992) *Careers and Identities*, Milton Keynes: Open University Press.

Banks, M.H. and Ullah, P. (1988) *Youth Unemployment in the 1980s: Its Psychological Effects*, London: Croom Helm.

Baritz, L. (1960) *The Servants of Power*, New York: Wiley.

Barker, J. (1993) 'Tightening the iron cage: concertive control in self-managing teams', *Administrative Science Quarterly*, 38: 408–37.

Barnard, C.I. (1938) *The Functions of the Executive*, Cambridge, MA: Harvard University Press.

Barnett, R. and Rivers, C. (1998) *She Works, He Works: How Two-Income Families Are Happy, Healthy and Thriving*, Cambridge, MA: Harvard University Press.

Barron, R.D. and Norris, G.M. (1976) 'Sexual divisions and the dual labour market', in D.L. Barker and S. Allen (eds) *Dependence and Exploitation in Work and Marriage*, London: Longman.

Barsoux, J-L. (1993) *Funny Business: Humour, Management and the Business Culture*, London: Cassell.

Batstone, E., Boraston, I. and Frenkel, S. (1977) *Shop Stewards in Action*, Oxford: Blackwell.

Baum, J.A.C. (1996) 'Organizational ecology', in S.R Clegg, C. Hardy and W. Nord (eds), *Handbook of Organization Studies*, London: Sage.

Baumann, Z. (1992) *Intimations of Postmodernity*, London: Routledge.

Baumann, Z. and May, T. (2001) *Thinking Sociologically*, Oxford: Blackwell.

Baxter, J. (2000) 'The joys and justice of housework', *Sociology*, 34: 609–31.

Bayliss, V. (1998) *Redefining Work*, London: Royal Society of Arts.

Bean, R. (1994) *Comparative Industrial Relations*, London: Routledge.

Bechhofer, F. (1973) 'The relation between technology and shopfloor behaviour', in D.O. Edge and J.N. Wolfe (eds) *Meaning and Control*, London: Tavistock.

Beck, U. (2000) *The Brave New World of Work*, Cambridge: Polity.

Beck, U., Giddens, A. and Lash, S. (1994) *Reflexive Modernization: Politics, Tradition and Aesthetics in the Modern Social Order*, Cambridge: Polity.

Becker, H.S. (1960) 'Notes on the concept of commitment', *American Journal of Sociology*, 66.

Becker, H.S. (1971) 'The nature of a profession', in *Sociological Work: Method and Substance*, London: Allen Lane.

Becker, H.S. and Geer, B. (1958) 'The fate of idealism in a medical school', *American Sociological Review*, 23.

Becker, H.S., Geer, B., Hughes, E.C. and Strauss, A.L. (1961) *Boys in White*, Chicago: University of Chicago Press.

Beer, M. and Spector, B. (1985) 'Corporatewide transformations in human resource management', in R.E. Walton and R.R. Lawrence (eds) *Human Resource Management: Trends and Challenges*, Boston: Harvard Business School Press.

Beetham, D. (1996) *Bureaucracy*, Milton Keynes: Open University Press.

Behrend, H. (1957) 'The effort bargain', *International Labor Relations Review*, 10.

Belanger, J., Berggrer, C., Björkman, T. and Köhler, C. (eds) (1999) *Being Local Worldwide: ABB and the Challenge of Global Management*, Ithaca and London: Cornell University Press.

Bell, D. (1974) *The Coming of Post-Industrial Society*, London: Heinemann.

Benders, J. and Van Hootegem, G. (1999) 'Teams and their context: moving the team discussion beyond existing dichotomies', *Journal of Management Studies*, 36: 609–28.

Bendix, R. (1963) *Work and Authority in Industry*, New York: Harper & Row.

Bendix, R. (1965) *Max Weber: A Sociological Portrait*, London: Methuen.

Bensman, J. and Lilienfeld, R. (1973) *Craft Consciousness*, New York: Wiley.

Berger, P.L. (1973) *The Social Reality of Religion*, London: Penguin.

Berger, P.L. and Luckmann, T. (1971) *The Social Construction of Reality*, Harmondsworth: Penguin.

Best, S. and Kellner, D. (1991) *Postmodern Theory: Critical Interrogations*, London: Macmillan.

Beynon, H. (1984) *Working for Ford* (2nd edn), Harmondsworth: Penguin.

Beynon, H. (1992) 'The end of the industrial worker?', in N. Abercrombie and A.Warde (eds) *Social Change in Contemporary Britain*, Cambridge: Polity.

Beynon, H. and Blackburn, R.M. (1972) *Perceptions of Work*, Cambridge: Cambridge University Press.

Beynon, H. *et al.* (2002) *Managing Employment Change: The New Realities of Work*, Oxford: Oxford University Press.

Beynon, H., Hudson, R. and Sadler, D. (1991) *A Tale of Two Industries: The Contraction of Coal and Steel in the North East of England*, Milton Keynes: Open University Press.

Beynon, J. and Dunkerley, D. (eds) (1999) *Globalisation: The Reader*, London: Athlone.

Bhaskar, R. (1986) *Scientific Realism and Human Emancipation*, London: Verso.

Bhaskar, R. (1989) *Reclaiming Reality*, London: Verso.

Bittner, E. (1965) 'The concept of organization', *Social Research*, 32: 239–55.

Bittner, E. (1973) 'The Police on Skid-row' in G. Salaman and K. Thompson (eds) *People and Organisations*, London: Longman.

Blackburn, P., Coombs, R. and Green, K. (1985) *Technology, Economic Growth and the Labour Process*, London: Macmillan.

Blackburn, R.M., Brooks, B. and Jarman, J. (2001) 'Occupational stratification: the vertical dimension of occupational segregation', *Work, Employment and Society*, 15: 511–38.

Blau, P.M. (1963) *The Dynamics of Bureaucracy*, Chicago: University of Chicago Press.

Blauner, R. (1960) 'Work satisfaction and industrial trends', in W. Galenson and S.H. Lipset (eds) *Labor and Trade Unions*, New York: Wiley.

Blauner, R. (1964) *Alienation and Freedom*, Chicago: University of Chicago Press.

Bobbit, P. (2002) *The Shield of Achilles: War, Law and Course of History*, London: Allen Lane.

Boddy, D. and Buchanan, D. (1986) *Managing New Technology*, Oxford: Blackwell.

Boddy, D. and Gunson, N. (1997) *Organizations in the Network Age*, London: Routledge.

Boje, D.M. and Winsor, R.D. (1993) 'The resurrection of Taylorism: total quality management's hidden agenda', *Journal of Organizational Change Management*, 6: 57–70.

Boje, D.M.G., Robert P. Jr and Thatchenkery, T.J. (eds) (1996) *Postmodern Management and Organization Theory*, London: Sage.

Boland, R.J. and Hoffman, R. (1983) 'Humor in a machine shop: an interpretation of symbolic action', in L.R. Pondy, P. Frost, G. Morgan and T. Dandridge (eds) (1983) *Organizational Symbolism*, Greenwich, CT: Jai Press.

Bolton, S.C. (2000) 'Emotion here, emotion there, emotional organisations everywhere', *Critical Perspectives on Accounting*, 11: 155–71.

Bond, S. and Sales, J. (2001) 'Household work in the UK: an analysis of the British Household Panel Survey 1994', *Work, Employment and Society*, 15: 233–50.

Bonney, N. and Reinach, E. (1993) 'Housework reconsidered: the Oakley thesis twenty years later', *Work, Employment and Society*, 7: 615–17.

Boris, E. and Prügl, E. (eds) (1996) *Homeworkers in Global Perspective: Invisible No More*, New York and London: Routledge.

Boxall, P. and Haynes, P. (1997) 'Strategy and trade union effectiveness in a neo-liberal environment', *British Journal of Industrial Relations*, 35: 567–92.

Boyer, R. (1988) *The Search for Labour Market Flexibility*, Oxford: Clarendon.

Bradley, H. (1989) *Men's Work, Women's Work*, Cambridge: Polity.

Bradley, H. (1996) *Fractured Identities: Changing Patterns of Inequality*, Cambridge: Polity.

Bradley, H. (1999) *Gender and Power in the Workplace: Analysing the Impact of Economic Change*, Basingstoke: Macmillan.

Bradley, H., Erickson, M., Stephenson, C. and Williams, S. (2000) *Myths at Work*, Cambridge: Polity.

Bradney, P. (1973) 'The joking relationship in industry', in D. Weir (ed.) *Men and Work in Modern Britain*, Glasgow: Fontana.

Braverman, H. (1974) *Labor and Monopoly Capital*, New York: Monthly Review Press.

Brewis, J. and Linstead, S. (2000a) '"The worst thing is the screwing": context and career in sex work', *Gender, Work and Organization*, 7: 168–80.

Brewis, J. and Linstead, S. (2000b) *Sex, Work and Sex Work: Eroticizing Organization?*, London: Routledge.

Bridges, W. (1995) *Jobshift: How to Prosper in a Workplace Without Jobs*, London: Brealey.

Brock, D., Powell, M. and Hinings, C.R. (eds) (1999) *Restructuring the Professional Organization – Accounting, Health Care and Law*, London: Routledge.

Brown, A.D. (1998) *Organisational Culture* (2nd edn), London: Pitman.

Brown, G. (1977) *Sabotage*, Nottingham: Spokesman Books.

Brown, R. (1997a) 'Introduction: work and employment in the 1990s', in R. Brown (ed.) *The Changing Shape of Work*, London: Macmillan.

Brown, R. (1997b) 'Flexibility and security: contradictions in the contemporary labour market', in R. Brown (ed.) *The Changing Shape of Work*, London: Macmillan.

Brown, R. (ed.) (1997c) *The Changing Shape of Work*, London: Macmillan.

Brown, R.K. (1983) 'From Donovan to where? Interpretations of industrial relations in Britain since 1968', in A. Stewart (ed.) *Contemporary Britain*, London: Routledge & Kegan Paul.

Brown, R.K. (1992) *Understanding Industrial Organisation*, London: Routledge.

Brown, W. (2000) 'Putting partnership into practice in Britain', *British Journal of Industrial Relations*, 38: 299–316.

Brown, W. *et al.* (2000) 'The employment contract: from collective procedures to individual rights', *British Journal of Industrial Relations*, 38: 611–29.

Bruegel, I. (2000) 'The full Monty? The feminisation of employment and the unemployment of men', in M. Noon and E. Ogbonna (eds) (2001) *Equality, Diversity and Disadvantage in Employment*, Basingstoke: Palgrave.

Bryan, J.H. (1965) 'Apprenticeships in prostitution', *Social Problems*, 12.

Buchanan, D. (1994) 'Cellular manufacture and the role of teams', in J. Storey (ed.) *New Wave Manufacturing Strategies: Organisational and Human Resource Management Dimensions*, London: Chapman.

Buchanan, D. and Badham, R. (1999) *Power, Politics, and Organizational Change: Winning the Turf Game*, London: Sage.

Buchanan, D.A. (1992) 'High performance: new boundaries of acceptability in worker control', in G. Salaman (ed.) *Human Resource Strategies*, London: Sage.

Buchanan, D.A. (2000) 'An eager and enduring embrace: the ongoing rediscovery of teamworking as a management idea', in S. Procter and F. Mueller (eds) *Teamworking*, Basingstoke: Macmillan.

Burawoy, M. (1979) *Manufacturing Consent*, Chicago: University of Chicago Press.

Burawoy, M. (1985) *The Politics of Production*, London: Verso.

Burchell, B. (1994) 'The effects of labour market position, job insecurity and unemployment on psychological health', in D. Gallie, C. Marsh and C. Vogler (eds) *Social Change and the Experience of Unemployment*, Oxford: Oxford University Press.

Burchell, B. *et al.* (1999) *Job Insecurity and Work Intensification: Flexibility and the Changing Boundaries of Work*, York: Joseph Rowntree Foundation.

Burchell, B. *et al.* (2001) *Job Insecurity and Work Intensification*, London: Routledge.

Burke, R.J. (2002) 'Organizational transitions', in C.L. Cooper and R.J. Burke (eds) *The New World of Work: Challenges and Opportunities*, Oxford: Blackwell.

Burnham, J. (1945) *The Managerial Revolution*, Harmondsworth: Penguin.

Burns, T. (1954) 'The directions of activity and communication in a departmental executive group', *Human Relations*, 7: 73–97.

Burns, T. (1955) 'The reference of conduct in small groups: cliques and cabals in occupational milieux', *Human Relations*, 8: 467–86.

Burns, T. (1957) 'Management in action', *Operational Research Quarterly*, 8: 45–60.

Burns, T. (1961) 'Micropolitics: mechanisms of institutional change', *Administrative Science Quarterly*, 6: 257–81.

Burns, T. (1962) 'The sociology of industry', in Welford *et al.* (eds) *Society: Problems and Methods of Study*, London: Routledge & Kegan Paul.

Burns, T. (1977) *The BBC: Public Institution and Private World*, London: Macmillan.

Burns, T. and Stalker, G. (1994) *The Management of Innovation* (2nd edn), Oxford: Oxford University Press.

Burrage, M. and Torstendahl, R. (eds) (1991) *The Formation of Professions*, London: Sage.

Burrell, G. (1984) 'Sex and organisational analysis', *Organisation Studies*, 5: 97–118.

Burrell, G. (1992) 'The organisation of pleasure', in M. Alvesson and H. Willmott (eds) *Critical Management Studies*, London: Sage.

Burrell, G. and Morgan, G. (1979) *Sociological Paradigms and Sociological Analysis*, London: Heinemann.

Butler, T. and Savage, M. (eds) (1996) *Social Change and the Middle Classes*, London: UCL.

Calas, M.B. and Smircich, L. (1996) 'From "the woman's" point of view: feminist approaches to organization studies', in S.R Clegg, C. Hardy and W. Nord (eds) *Handbook of Organization Studies*, London: Sage.

Campbell, C. (1987) *The Romantic Ethic and the Spirit of Modern Consumerism*, Oxford: Blackwell.

Carey, A. (1967) 'The Hawthorne Studies: a radical criticism', *American Sociological Review*, 32: 403–16.

Carlson, C. (1951) *Executive Behavior*, Stockholm: Strombergs.

Carroll, G.R. (ed.) (1988) *Ecological Models of Organisations*, Cambridge MA: Ballinger.

Carter, B. (2000) 'Adoption of the organising model in British trade unions: some evidence from MSF', *Work, Employment and Society*, 14: 117–36.

Carter, R. (1985) *Capitalism, Class Conflict and the New Middle Class*, London: Routledge & Kegan Paul.

Cascio, W.F. (2002) 'The virtual organization', in C.L. Cooper and R.J. Burke (eds) *The New World of Work: Challenges and Opportunities*, Oxford: Blackwell.

Casey, C. (1995) *Work, Self and Society: After Industrialism*, London: Routledge.

Castells, M. (1996) *The Information Age: Economy, Society and Culture, Vol. I: The Rise of the Network Society*, Oxford: Blackwell.

Castells, M. (1997) *The Information Age: Economy, Society and Culture, Vol. II: The Power of Identity*, Oxford: Blackwell.

Castells, M. (1998) *The Information Age: Economy, Society and Culture, Vol. III: End of Millennium*, Oxford: Blackwell.

Castells, M. (2000) 'Materials for an exploratory theory of the networked society', *British Journal of Sociology*, 51: 5–24.

Castillo, J.J. (1999a) 'Which way forward for the sociology of work?: an introduction', *Current Sociology*, 47: 1–4.

Castillo, J.J. (1999b) 'Sociology of work at the crossroad', *Current Sociology*, 47: 21–46.

Cavendish, R. (1982) *Women on the Line*, London: Routledge & Kegan Paul.

Chia, R.C.H. (1998) *Organized Worlds: Explorations in Technology and Organization with Robert Cooper*, London: Routledge.

Child, J. (1972) 'Organisational structure, environment and performance', *Sociology*, 6: 2–22.

Child, J. (1984a) *Organisation* (2nd edn), London: Harper & Row.

Child, J. (1984b) 'New technology and developments in management organisation', *Omega*, 12: 3.

Child, J. (1997) 'Strategic choice', in A. Sorge and M. Warner (eds) *The IEBM Handbook of Organizational Behaviour*, London: Thomson Learning.

Child, J. and Partridge, B. (1982) *Lost Managers*, Cambridge: Cambridge University Press.

Child, J. and Smith, C. (1987) 'The context and process of organisational transformation', *Journal of Management Studies*, 24: 565–93.

Child, J. *et al.* (1983) 'A price to pay? Professionalism and work organisation in Britain and West Germany', *Sociology*, 17: 63–78.

Child, J., Loveridge, R., Harvey, A. and Spencer, A. (1984) 'Microelectronics and the quality of employment in services', in P. Marstrand (ed.) *New Technology and the Future of Work Skills*, London: Pinter.

Chinoy, E. (1992) *Automobile Workers and the American Dream* (2nd edn), Urbana and Chicago: University of Illinois Press.

Chodorow, N. (1978) *The Reproduction of Mothering: Psychoanalysis and the Sociology of Gender*, Berkeley: University of California Press.

Clark, J. (1995) *Managing Innovation and Change: People, Technology and Strategy*, London: Sage.

Clark, P. (1999) *Organizations in Action: Competition across Contexts*, London: Routledge.

Clarke, J. and Newman, J. (1997) *The Managerial State*, London: Sage.

Claydon, T. (1989) 'Union derecognition in Britain in the 1980s', *British Journal of Industrial Relations*, 27: 214–23.

Clegg, S. (1990) *Modern Organisations: Organisation Studies in the Postmodern World*, London: Sage.

Clegg, S.R. and Hardy, C. (1996) 'Organizations, organization and organizing', in S.R. Clegg, C. Hardy and W. Nord (eds) *Handbook of Organization Studies*, London: Sage, 1–27.

Clegg, S.R., Hardy, C. and Nord, W. (eds) (1996) *Handbook of Organization Studies*, London: Sage.

Coates, R.V. and Pellegrin, R.J. (1962) 'Executives and supervisors', in B.H. Stoodley (ed.) *Society and Self*, New York: Free Press.

Cockburn, C. and Ormrod, S. (1993) *Gender and Technology in the Making*, London: Sage.

Coffey, A. and Atkinson, P. (eds) (1994) *Occupational Socialisation and Working Lives*, Aldershot: Ashgate.

Cohen, L. and Mallon, M.N. (1999) 'The transition from organisational employment to portfolio work: perceptions of "boundarylessness"', *Work, Employment and Society*, 13: 329–52.

Cohen, M.D., March, J.G. and Olsen, J.P. (1972) 'A garbage can model of organisational choice', *Administrative Science Quarterly*, 17: 1–25.

Colgan, F. and Ledwith, S. (2002) *Gender, Diversity and Trade Unions: International Perspectives*, London: Routledge.

Collin, A. (1986) 'Career development: the significance of subjective career', *Personnel Review*, 15: 22–8.

Collin, A. and Young, R.A. (eds) (2000) *The Future of Career*, Cambridge: Cambridge University Press.

Collins, J.C. and Porras, J.I. (1995) *Built to Last: Successful Habits of Visionary Companies*, New York: Random House.

Collinson, D.L. (1992) *Managing the Shopfloor*, Berlin: de Gruyter.

Collinson, D.L. (1994) 'Strategies of resistance', in J. Jermier, D. Knights and W.R. Nord (eds) *Resistance and Power in Organisations*, London: Routledge.

Collinson, D.L. (2000) 'Strategies of resistance: power, knowledge and subjectivity in the workplace', in K. Grint (ed.) *Work and Society: A Reader*, Cambridge: Polity Press: 163–98.

Collinson, D.L. (2002) 'Managing humour', *Journal of Management Studies*, 39: 269–88.

Collinson, D. and Hearn, J. (1996) *Men as Managers, Managers as Men*, London: Sage.

Collinson, D., Knights, D. and Collinson, M. (1990) *Managing to Discriminate*, London: Routledge.

Collinson, M. and Collinson, D.L. (1996) '"It's only dick": the sexual harassment of women managers in insurance sales', *Work, Employment and Society*, 10: 29–56.

Collinson, M., Edwards, M. and Rees, C. (1997) *Involving Employees in Total Quality Management*, London: DTI.

Cook, P. (1996) *The Industrial Craftsworker: Skill, Managerial Strategies and Workplace Relationships*, London: Mansell.

Cooper, C.L. and Burke, R.J. (eds) (2002) *The New World of Work: Challenges and Opportunities*, Oxford: Blackwell.

Cooper, C.L. and Rousseau, D.M. (1999) *The Virtual Organization, Trends in Organizational Behaviour*, Vol. 6, Chichester: Wiley.

Cotgrove, S., Dunham, J. and Vamplew, C. (1971) *The Nylon Spinners*, London: Allen & Unwin.

Creese, G. (1999) *Contracting Masculinity: Gender, Class, and Race in a White-Collar Union, 1944–1994*, Oxford: Oxford University Press.

Crompton, R. (1990) 'Professions in the current context', *Work, Employment and Society*, Additional Special Issue: 'The 1980's: a decade of change?'.

Crompton, R. (1997) *Women and Work in Modern Britain*, Oxford: Oxford University Press.

Crompton, R. (1998) *Class and Stratification. An Introduction to Current Debates* (2nd edn), Cambridge: Polity Press.

Crompton, R. (ed.) (1999) *Restructuring Gender Relations and Employment: The Decline of the Male Breadwinner*, Oxford: Oxford University Press.

Crompton, R. and Harris, F. (1998) 'Gender relations and employment: the impact of occupation', *Work, Employment and Society*, 12: 297–315.

Crompton, R. and Jones, G. (1984) *White-Collar Proletariat: Deskilling and Gender in Clerical Work*, London: Macmillan.

Crouch, C. (1982) *Trade Unions: The Logic of Collective Action*, Glasgow: Fontana.

Crouzet, F. (1985) *The First Industrialists: The Problem of Origins*, Cambridge: Cambridge University Press.

Crozier, M. (1964) *The Bureaucratic Phenomenon*, London: Tavistock.

Cullen, D. (1997) 'Maslow, monkeys and motivation theory', *Organization*, 4: 355–73.

Cully, M., Woodland, S., O'Reilly, A. and Dix, G. (1999) *Britain at Work*, London: Routledge.

Curtin, J. (1999) *Women and Trade Unions: A Comparative Perspective*, Aldershot: Ashgate.

Cyert, R.M. and March, J.G. (1963) *A Behavioural Theory of the Firm*, Englewood Cliffs, NJ: Prentice-Hall.

Czarniawska, B. (1998) *A Narrative Approach to Organization Studies*, London: Sage.

Dachler, H.P. and Hosking, D.-M. (1995) 'The primacy of relations in socially constructing organisational realities', in D.-M. Hosking, H.P. Dachler and K.J. Gergen (eds) *Management and Organisation: Relational Alternatives to Individualism*, Aldershot: Avebury.

Dahler-Larsen, P. (1994) 'Corporate culture and morality: Durkheim inspired reflections on the limits of corporate culture', *Journal of Management Studies*, 31: 1–18.

Dalton, M. (1951) 'Informal factors in career achievement', *American Journal of Sociology*, 56.

Dalton, M. (1959) *Men Who Manage*, New York: Wiley.

Danford, A. (1997) 'The "New Industrial Relations" and class struggle in the 1990s', *Capital and Class*, 61: 107–41.

Danford, A. (1998a) *Japanese Management Techniques and British Workers*, London: Mansell.

Danford, A. (1998b) 'Teamworking and labour regulation in the autocomponents industry', *Work, Employment and Society*, 12: 409–43.

Daniel, W.W. (1973) 'Understanding employee behaviour in its context', in J. Child (ed.) *Man and Organisation*, London: Allen & Unwin.

Darlington, R. (1994) *The Dynamics of Workplace Unionism: Shop Stewards' Organisation in Three Merseyside Plants*, London: Mansell.

Davidson, M.J. (1997) *The Black and Ethnic Minority Woman Manager: Cracking the Concrete Ceiling*, London: Paul Chapman.

Davidson, M.J. and Burke, R.J. (2000) *Women in Management: Current Research Issues Volume 11*, London: Sage.

Davis, F. (1959) 'The cabdriver and his fare', *American Journal of Sociology*, 65.

Davis, K. and Moore, W.E. (1945) 'Some principles of stratification', *American Sociological Review*, 10.

Davis, L.E. and Taylor, J. (1979) *The Design of Jobs* (2nd edn), Santa Monica, CA: Goodyear.

Dawes, L. (1993) *Long-term Unemployment and Labour Market Flexibility*, Leicester: University of Leicester Centre for Labour Market Studies.

Day, R.A. and Day, J.V. (1977) 'A review of the current state of negotiated order theory: an appreciation and a critique', *Sociological Quarterly*, 18: 126–42.

Deal, T.E. and Kennedy, A.A. (1982) *Corporate Cultures: The Rites and Rituals of Corporate Life*, Reading, MA: Addison-Wesley.

Deal, T. and Kennedy, A. (1999) *The New Corporate Cultures: Revitalizing the Workplace After Downsizing, Merger and Reengineering*, New York: Texere.

Delbridge, R. (1998) *Life on the Line in Contemporary Manufacturing: The Workplace Experience of Lean Production and the 'Japanese' Model*, Oxford: Oxford University Press.

Delbridge, R. and Lowe, J. (eds) (1998) *Manufacturing in Transition*, London: Routledge.

Delphy, C. and Leonard, D. (1992) *Family Exploitation: A New Analysis of Marriage in Contemporary Western Societies*, Cambridge: Polity.

Dent, M. and Whitehead, S. (eds) *Managing Professional Identities*, London: Routledge.

Desai, M. (2002) *Marx's Revenge*, London: Verso.

Deutsch, F. (1999) *Having It All: How Equally Shared Parenting Works*, Cambridge, MA: Harvard University Press.

Devine, F. (1992a) *Affluent Workers Revisited: Privatism and the Working Class*, Edinburgh: Edinburgh University Press.

Devine, F. (1992b) 'Gender segregation in the science and engineering professions: a case of continuity and change', *Work, Employment and Society* 6: 557–75.

Dex, S. (1988) *Women's Attitude Towards Work*, London: Macmillan.

Dex, S. and McCulloch, A. (1997) *Flexible Employment: The Future of Britain's Jobs*, Basingstoke: Macmillan.

DfEE (2000) *Work–Life Balance 2000*, London: Department for Education and Employment.

Ditton, J. (1974) 'The fiddling salesman', *New Society*, 28 November.

Ditton, J. (1977) *Part-time Crime*, London: Macmillan.

Doeringer, P.B. and Piore, M.J. (1971) *Internal Labor Markets and Manpower Analysis*, Lexington, MA: D.C. Heath.

Donaldson, L. (1996a) *For Positivist Organization Theory*, London: Sage.

Donaldson, L. (1996b) 'The normal science of structural contingency theory', in S.R Clegg, C. Hardy and W. Nord (eds) *Handbook of Organization Studies*, London: Sage.

Donaldson, L. (2001) *The Contingency Theory of Organizations*, London: Sage.

Donkin, R. (2001) *Blood, Sweat and Tears: The Evolution of Work*, London: Texere.

Doogan, K. (2001) 'Insecurity and long-term employment', *Work, Employment and Society*, 15: 419–41.

Dopson, S. and Stewart, R. (1990) 'What is happening to middle management?', *British Journal of Management*, 1: 3–16.

Draper, P. (1975), '!Kung women: contrasts in sexual egalitarianism in foraging and sedentary contexts', in R.R. Reiter (ed.) *Towards an Anthropology of Women*, New York: Monthly Review Press.

Drew, E., Emerek, R. and Mahon, E. (1998) *Women, Work and the Family in Europe*, London: Routledge.

Drucker, P. (1992) *Managing for the Future: The 1990s and Beyond*, Hemel Hempstead: Butterworth Heinemann.

Dubin, R. (1956) 'Industrial workers' worlds: a study of the central life interests of industrial workers', *Social Problems*, 3: 1312.

Dubin, R. *et al.* (1975) 'Central life interests and organisational commitment of blue-collar and clerical workers', *Administrative Science Quarterly*, 20: 411–21.

du Gay, P. (1995) *Consumption and Identity at Work*, London: Sage.

du Gay, P. (2000) *In Praise of Bureaucracy: Weber, Organization, Ethics*, London: Sage.

Dunlop, J.T. (1958) *Industrial Relations Systems*, New York: Holt.

Durkheim, E. (1984) *The Division of Labour in Society*, transl. W.D. Halls, London: Macmillan.

Edgell, S. (1980) *Middle Class Couples*, London: Allen & Unwin.

Edwards, P. (1986) *Conflict at Work*, Oxford: Blackwell.

Edwards, P. (2003a) 'The employment relationship and the field of industrial relations', in P. Edwards (ed.) *Industrial Relations: Theory and Practice* (2nd edn), Oxford: Blackwell.

Edwards, P. (ed.) (2003b) *Industrial Relations. Theory and Practice* (2nd edn), Oxford: Blackwell.

Edwards, P., Geary, J.H. and Sisson, K. (2001) 'Employee involvement in the workplace: transformative, exploitative or limited and controlled?', in J. Belanger *et al.* (eds), *Work and Employment Relations in the High Performance Workplace*, London: Cassell/ Mansell.

Edwards, P.K. (1990) 'Understanding conflict in the labour process: the logic and autonomy of struggle', in D. Knights and H. Willmott, *Labour Process Theory*, London: Macmillan.

Edwards, P.K. and Scullion, H. (1982) *The Social Organisation of Industrial Conflict*, Oxford: Blackwell.

Edwards, P.K. and Whitson, C. (1989) 'Industrial discipline, the control of attendance and the subordination of labour', *Work, Employment and Society*, 3: 1–28.

Edwards, R. (1979) *Contested Terrain*, London: Heinemann.

Ehrenreich, B. (2002) *Nickel and Dimed*, London: Granta Books.

Eisenstadt, S.N. (1973) *Tradition, Change and Modernity*, New York: Wiley.

Eldridge, J., Cressey, P. and MacInnes, J. (1991) *Industrial Sociology and Economic Crisis*, Hemel Hempstead: Harvester Wheatsheaf.

Eldridge, J.E.T. (1971a) *Sociology and Industrial Life*, London: Michael Joseph.

Eldridge, J.E.T. (1971b) 'Weber's approach to the study of industrial workers', in A. Sahay (ed.) *Max Weber and Modern Sociology*, London: Routledge & Kegan Paul.

Eldridge, J.E.T. (1975) 'Industrial relations and industrial capitalism', in G. Esland, G. Salaman and M. Speakman (eds) *People and Work*, Edinburgh: Holmes McDougall.

Elliot, P. (1972) *The Sociology of the Professions*, London: Macmillan.

Elliot, P. (1973) 'Professional ideology and social situation', *Sociological Review*, 21.

Enteman, W.F. (1993) *Managerialism: The Emergence of a New Ideology*, Madison, WI: University of Wisconsin Press.

Epstein, C.F. and Kalleberg, A.L. (2001) 'Time and the sociology of work', *Work and Occupations*, 28: 5–16.

Evans, P. and Bartolemé, F. (1980) *Must Success Cost So Much?* London: Grant McIntyre.

Eveline, J. (1999) 'Heavy, dirty and limp stories: male advantage at work', in M. Gatens and A. Mackinnon (eds) *Gender and Institutions: Welfare, Work and Citizenship*, Cambridge: Cambridge University Press.

Evetts, J. (1996) *Gender and Career in Science and Engineering*, London: Taylor & Francis.

Ezzy, D. (1997) 'Subjectivity and the labour process: conceptualising "good work"', *Sociology*, 31: 427–44.

Ezzy, D. (2001) 'A simulacrum of workplace community: individualism and engineered culture', *Sociology*, 35: 631–50.

Fairbrother, P. (2000) *Trade Unions at the Crossroads*, London: Mansell.

Fayol, H. (1949, orig. 1916) *General and Industrial Management* (transl. C. Stores), London: Pitman.

Felstead, A. and Jewson, N. (1999) *Global Trends in Flexible Labour*, Basingstoke: Macmillan.

Felstead, A. and Jewson, N. (2000) *In Work, At Home: Towards an Understanding of Homeworking*, London: Routledge.

Felstead, A., Jewson, N., Phizacklea, A. and Walters, S. (2001) 'Working at home: statistical evidence for seven key hypotheses', *Work, Employment and Society*, 15: 215–31.

Felstead, A., Jewson, A. with Goodwin, J. (1996) *Homeworkers in Britain*, London: HMSO.

Fernie, S. and Metcalf, D. (1998) (*Not*) *Hanging on the Telephone: Payment Systems in the New Sweatshops*, London: London School of Economics.

Filby, M.P (1987) 'The Newmarket racing lad: tradition and change in a marginal occupation', *Work, Employment and Society*, 1: 205–24.

Filby, M.P. (1992) '"The figures, the personality and the bums": service work and sexuality', *Work, Employment and Society*, 6: 23–42.

Finch, J. (1983) *Married to the Job: Wives' Incorporation into Men's Work*, London: Allen & Unwin.

Findlay, P. and Newton, T. (1998) 'Re-framing Foucault: the case of performance appraisal', in A. McKinlay and K. Starkey (eds) *Foucault, Management and Organization Theory: From Panopticon to Technologies of the Self*, London: Sage.

Fineman, S. (ed.) (1987) *Unemployment: Personal and Social Consequences*, London: Tavistock.

Fineman, S. (ed.) (1993) *Emotion in Organisations*, London: Sage.

Fineman, S. (1999) 'Emotion and organizing', in S.R. Clegg, C. Hardy and W. Nord (eds) *Handbook of Organization Studies*, London: Sage.

Fineman, S. (2003) *Understanding Emotion at Work*, London: Sage.

Fletcher, D. (2000) 'Family and enterprise', in S. Carter and D. Jones-Evans (eds) *Enterprise and Small Business: Principles, Practice and Policy*, Harlow: Prentice-Hall.

Fletcher, R. (1971) *The Making of Sociology, Vol. 1*, London: Joseph.

Foster, J. (1974) *Class Struggle and the Industrial Revolution*, London: Weidenfeld and Nicolson.

Foucault, M. (1980) *Power/Knowledge: Selected Interviews and Other Writings*, Brighton: Harvester.

Fournier, V. and Grey, C. (1999) 'Too much, too little, too often: A Critique of DuGay's Analysis of Enterprise', *Organization*, 6: 107–28.

Fox, A. (1966) *Industrial Sociology and Industrial Relations*, London: HMSO.

Fox, A. (1973) 'Industrial relations: a social critique of pluralist ideology', in J. Child (ed.) *Man and Organisation*, London: Allen & Unwin.

Fox, A. (1974) *Beyond Contract: Work, Power and Trust Relations*, London: Faber.

Fox, A. (1979) 'A note on industrial relations pluralism', *Sociology*, 13.

Fox, A. (1985) *History and Heritage: The Social Origins of the British Industrial Relations System*, London: Allen & Unwin.

Fraser, J. and Gold, M. (2001) 'Portfolio workers: autonomy and control amongst freelance translators', *Work, Employment and Society*, 15: 679–97

Freidson, E. (1994) *Professionalism Reborn: Theory, Prophecy and Policy*, Cambridge: Polity.

Freidson, E. (2001) *Professionalism: the Third Logic*, Cambridge: Polity.

Frenkel, S.J., Korczynski, M., Shire, K.A. and Tam, M. (1999) *On the Front Line: Organization of Work in the Information Economy*, Ithaca and London: Cornell University Press.

Friedman, A.L. (1977) *Industry and Labour*, London: Macmillan.

Friedmann, E.A. and Havighurst, R.J. (1954) *The Meaning of Work and Retirement*, Chicago: University of Chicago Press.

Frobe, F., Heinrichs, J. and Kreye, O. (1980) *The New International Division of Labour*, Cambridge: Cambridge University Press.

Fukuyama, F. (1992) *The End of History and The Last Man*, London: Hamilton.

Gabriel, Y. (1988) *Working Lives in Catering*, London: Routledge.

Gabriel, Y. (1993) 'Organizational nostalgia – reflections on "The Golden Age"', in S. Fineman (ed.) *Emotion in Organisations*, London: Sage.

Gabriel, Y. (ed.) (1999) *Organizations in Depth*, London: Sage.

Galbraith, J.K. (1972) *The New Industrial State*, Harmondsworth: Penguin.

Gall, G. (2003) *Union Organizing*, London: Routledge.

Gallagher, D.G. (2002) 'Contingent work contracts: practice and theory', in C.L. Cooper and R.J. Burke (eds) *The New World of Work: Challenges and Opportunities*, Oxford: Blackwell.

Gallie, D. (1985) 'Directions for the future', in B. Roberts, R. Finnegan and D. Gallie (eds) *New Approaches to Economic Life – Economic Restructuring: Unemployment and the Social Division of Labour*, Manchester: Manchester University Press.

Gallie, D. (1996) 'Changing patterns of skill and responsibility at work', in R. Crompton, D. Gallie and K. Purcell (eds) *Corporate Restructuring and Labour Markets*, London: Routledge.

Gallie, D. and Marsh, C. (1994) 'The experience of unemployment', in D. Gallie, C. Marsh and C. Vogler (eds) *Social Change and the Experience of Unemployment*, Oxford: Oxford University Press.

Gallie, D. and Paugam, S. (eds) (2000) *Welfare Regimes and the Experience of Unemployment in Europe*, Oxford: Oxford University Press.

Gallie, D. and Vogler, C. (1994) 'Unemployment and attitudes to work', in D. Gallie, C. Marsh and C. Vogler (eds) *Social Change and the Experience of Unemployment*, Oxford: Oxford University Press.

Gallie, D., Marsh, C. and Vogler, C. (eds) (1994) *Social Change and the Experience of Unemployment*, Oxford: Oxford University Press.

Gallie, D., White, M., Cheng, Y. and Tomlinson, M. (1998) *Restructuring the Employment Relationship*, Oxford: Oxford University Press.

Garrahan, P. and Stewart, P. (1992) *The Nissan Enigma*, London: Cassell.

Garsten, C. (1999) 'Betwixt and between: temporary employees as liminal subjects in flexible organizations', *Organization Studies*, 20: 610–17.

Geary, J.F. and Dobbins, A. (2001) 'Teamworking: a new dynamic in the pursuit of management control', *Human Resource Management Journal*, 11: 3–23.

Geer, B. *et al.* (1968) 'Learning the ropes', in J. Deutscher and J. Thompson (eds) *Among the People*, New York: Basic Books.

Gergen, K.J. (1992) 'Organisation theory in a postmodern era', in M. Reed and M. Hughes (eds) *Rethinking Organisation*, London: Sage.

Gergen, K.J. (1999) An *Invitation to Social Construction*, London: Sage.

Gershuny, J. (1978) *After Industrial Society*, London: Macmillan.

Gershuny, J. (1994) 'The psychological consequences of unemployment: an assessment of the Jahoda thesis', in D. Gallie, C. Marsh, and C. Vogler (eds) *Social Change and the Experience of Unemployment*, Oxford: Oxford University Press.

Gershuny, J. (2000) *Changing Times, Work and Leisure in Postindustrial Society*, Oxford: Oxford University Press.

Gerstl, J.E. and Hutton, S.P. (1966) *Engineers: The Anatomy of a Profession*, London: Tavistock.

Giddens, A. (1971) *Capitalism and Modern Social Theory*, Cambridge: Cambridge University Press.

Giddens, A. (1973) *The Class Structure of the Advanced Societies*, London: Hutchinson.

Giddens, A. (1982) *Sociology: A Brief but Critical Introduction*, London: Macmillan.

Giddens, A. (1984) *The Constitution of Society: Outline of the Theory of Structuration*, Cambridge: Polity.

Giddens, A. (1991) *Modernity and Self-Identity: Self and Society in the Modern Age*, Cambridge: Polity Press.

Gillespie, R. (1991) *Manufacturing Knowledge: A History of the Hawthorne Experiments*, Cambridge: Cambridge University Press.

Gini, A. (2000) *My Job, My Self*, London: Routledge.

Ginn, J., Arber, S., Brannen, J., Dale, A., Dex, S., Elias, P., Moss, C., Pahl, J., Roberts, C. and Rubery, J. (1996) 'Feminist fallacies: a reply to Hakim on women's employment', *British Journal of Sociology*, 47: 167–74.

Ginzberg, E.J., Sinzberg, S., Axelrad, S. and Herma, J.L. (1951) *Occupational Choice*, New York: Columbia University Press.

Glucksmann, M. (1995) 'Why "work"? Gender and the "total social organisation of labour"', *Gender, Work and Organisation*, 2: 63–75.

Glucksmann, M. (2000) *Cottons and Casuals: The Gendered Organisation of Labour in Time and Space*, Durham: Sociology Press.

Goffee, R. and Scase, R. (1985) *The Experience of Female Entrepreneurs*, London: Allen & Unwin.

Goffman, E. (1961) *Asylums*, Harmondsworth: Penguin.

Golden, L. and Figart, D.M. (eds) (2000) *Working Time: International Trends, Theory and Perspectives*, London: Routledge.

Golding, P. (2000) 'Forthcoming features: information and communications technologies and the sociology of the future', *Sociology*, 34: 165–84.

Goldner, F.H. (1970) 'The division of labor: process and power', in M. Zald (ed.) *Power in Organisations*, Vanderbilt: Vanderbilt University Press.

Goldthorpe, J. (1987) *Social Mobility and Class Structure in Modern Britain* (2nd edn), Oxford: Clarendon Press.

Goldthorpe, J.H. (1971) 'Theories of industrial society', *European Journal of Sociology*, 12.

Goldthorpe, J.H. (1974) 'Industrial relations in Great Britain: a critique of reformism', *Politics and Society*, 4: 419–52.

Goldthorpe, J.H. (1982) 'On the service class, its formation and future', in A. Giddens and G. Mackenzie (eds) *Social Class and the Division of Labour*, Cambridge: Cambridge University Press.

Goldthorpe, J.H. (1985) 'The end of convergence: corporatist and dualist tendencies in modern western societies', in B. Roberts, R. Finnegan and D. Gallie (eds) *New Approaches to Economic Life – Economic Restructuring: Unemployment and the Social Division of Labour*, Manchester: Manchester University Press.

Goldthorpe, J.H. (1995) 'The service class revisited', in T. Butler and M. Savage, *Social Change and the Middle Classes*, London: UCL Press.

Goldthorpe, J.H., Lockwood, D., Bechhofer, F. and Platt, J. (1968) *The Affluent Worker: Industrial Attitudes and Behaviour*, Cambridge: Cambridge University Press.

Goode, W.J. (1957) 'Community within a community: the professions', *American Sociological Review*, 22.

Gorz, A. (1999) *Reclaiming Work: Beyond the Wage-based Society*, Cambridge: Polity.

Gottlieb, B.H., Kelloway, E. and Barham, E. (1998) *Flexible Work Arrangements: Managing the Work-Family Boundary*, Chichester: Wiley.

Gouldner, A.W. (1957) 'Cosmopolitans and locals', *Administrative Science Quarterly*, 2.

Gouldner, A.W. (1964) *Patterns of Industrial Bureaucracy*, New York: Free Press.

Gouldner, A.W. (1971) *The Coming Crisis of Western Sociology*, London: Heinemann.

Graham, S. (1995) *On the Line at Subaru Isuzu: The Japanese Model and the American Worker*, Ithaca, NY: ILR Press.

Gray, J. (1998) *False Dawn: The Delusions of Global Capitalism*, London: Granta Books.

Greenfield, L. (2002) *The Spirit of Capitalism: Nationalism and Economic Growth*, Cambridge, MA: Harvard University Press.

Gregson, N. and Lowe, M. (1994a) *Servicing the Middle Clases: Waged Domestic Labour in Britain in the 1980s and 1990s*, London: Routledge.

Gregson, N. and Lowe, M. (1994b) 'Waged domestic labour and the renegotiation of the domestic division of labour within dual career households', *Sociology* 28: 55–78.

Grey, C. (1994) 'Career as a project of the self and labour process discipline', *Sociology*, 28: 479–97.

Grey, C. and Mitev, N. (1995) 'Reengineering organizations: a critical appraisal', *Personnel Review*, 24: 6–18.

Grieco, M. (1987) *Keeping it in the Family: Social Networks and Employment Chance*, London: Tavistock.

Grint, K. (1994) 'Reengineering history', *Organization*, 1: 179–202.

Grint, K. (1998) *The Sociology of Work* (2nd edn), Cambridge: Polity.

Grint, K. and Willcocks, L. (1995) 'Business process re-engineering in theory and practice: business: paradise regained?', *New Technology, Work and Employment*, 10: 99–108.

Grint, K. and Woolgar, S. (1997) *The Machine at Work: Technology, Work and Organisation*, Cambridge: Polity Press.

Grugulis, I. and Knights, D. (2001) 'Glossary', *International Studies of Management and Organization*, 30: 12–24.

Grugulis, I., Willmott, H. and Knights, D. (2001) *The Labor Process Debate – International Studies of Management and Organization*, 30.

Guerrier, Y. and Adib, A.S. '"No, we don't provide that service": the harassment of hotel employees by customers', *Work, Employment and Society*, 14: 689–705.

Guest, D. (1991) 'Personnel management: the end of an orthodoxy', *British Journal of Industrial Relations*, 29: 149–76.

Guest, D. (1995) 'Human resource management, trade unions and industrial relations', in J. Storey (ed.) *Human Resource Management: A Critical Text*, London: Routledge.

Guest, D. (1998) 'Is the psychological contract worth taking seriously?', *Journal of Organizational Behaviour*, 9: 649–64.

Guest, D. and Peccei, R. (2001) 'Partnership at work: mutuality and balance of advantage', *British Journal of Industrial Relations*, 39: 207–36.

Guiffre, P. and Williams, C. (1994) 'Boundary lines: labelling sexual harassment in restaurants', *Gender and Society*, 8: 374–401.

Gulick, L. and Urwick, L. (1937) *Papers on the Science of Administration*, New York: Columbia University Press.

Habermas, J. (1987) *Lectures on the Philosophical Discourse of Modernity*, Cambridge, MA: MIT Press.

Hakim, C. (1993) 'The myth of rising female employment', *Work, Employment and Society*, 7: 97–120.

Hakim, C. (1995) 'Five feminist myths about women's employment', *British Journal of Sociology*, 46: 429–55.

Hakim, C. (1996) *Issues in Women's Work*, London: Athlone Press.

Hakim, C. (1998) *Social Change and Innovation in the Labour Market*, Oxford: Oxford University Press.

Hakim, C. (2000) *Work-lifestyle Choices in the 21st Century: Preference Theory*, Oxford: Oxford University Press.

Halford, S. and Leonard, P. (2001) *Gender, Power and Organisations*, Basingstoke: Palgrave.

Halford, S., Savage, M. and Witz, A. (1995) *Gender, Careers and Organization*, London: Macmillan.

Hall, C. (1979) 'The early formation of Victorian domestic ideology', in S. Burman (ed.) *Fit Work for Women*, London: Croom Helm.

Hall, D.T. and associates (1996) *The Career is Dead: Long Live the Career: A Relational Approach to Careers*, San Francisco: Jossey-Bass.

Hall, D.T. and Moss, J.E. (1998) 'The new protean career contract: helping organisations and employees adapt', *Organizational Dynamics*, 26: 22–37.

Hall, E. (1993) 'Smiling, deferring and flirting: doing gender by giving "good service"', *Work and Occupations* 20: 452–71.

Halmos, P. (1970) *The Personal Service Society*, London: Constable.

Hamilton, R. (1978) *The Liberation of Women*, London: Allen & Unwin.

Hammer, M. and Champy, J. (1993) *Reengineering the Corporation*, London: Nicholas Bealey.

Hancock, P. and Tyler, M. (2001) *Work, Postmodernism and Organization: A Critical Introduction*, London: Sage.

Handy, C. (1994) *The Empty Raincoat: Making Sense of the Future*, London: Hutchinson.

Hanlon, G. (1998) 'Professionalism as enterprise: service class politics and the redefinition of professionalism', *Sociology*, 32: 43–63.

Hannan, M. and Freeman, J. (1989) *Organizational Ecology*, Cambridge, MA: Harvard University Press.

Harding, P. and Jenkins, R. (1989) *The Myth of the Hidden Economy: Towards a New Understanding of Informal Economic Activity*, Milton Keynes: Open University Press.

Hardy, C. (ed.) (1995) *Power and Politics in Organizations*, Aldershot: Dartmouth.

Harley, B. (2001) 'Team membership and the experience of work in Britain: an analysis of the WERS98 data', *Work, Employment and Society*, 15: 721–42.

Harris, M. (1998) 'Re-thinking the virtual organization', in P.J. Jackson and J.M. van der Wielen (eds) *Teleworking: International Perspectives*, London: Routledge.

Harris, R. (1987) *Power and Powerlessness in Industry*, London: Tavistock.

Haslam, C. *et al.* (1996) 'A fallen idol? Japanese management in the 1990s', in P. Stewart (ed.) *Beyond Japanese Management*, Trowbridge: Frank Cass.

Hassard, J. (1993) *Sociology and Organization Theory: Positivism, Paradigms and Postmodernity*, London: Sage.

Hassard, J. and Parker, M. (eds) (1993) *Postmodernism and Organisations*, London: Sage.

Hatch, M-J. (1997) *Organization Theory: Modern, Symbolic and Postmodern Perspectives*, Oxford: Oxford University Press.

Hatt, P.K. (1950) 'Occupations and social stratification', *American Journal of Sociology*, 55.

Hearn, J. and Parkin, W. (1987) *'Sex' at 'Work': The Power and Paradox of Organisation Sexuality*, Brighton: Wheatsheaf.

Heath, C., Knoblauch, H. and Luff, P. (2000) 'Technology and social interaction: the emergence of "workplace studies"', *British Journal of Sociology*, 51: 299–320.

Heery, E. and Kelly, J. (1994) 'Professional, participative and managerial unionism: an interpretation of change in trade unions', *Work, Employment and Society* 8: 1–22.

Heery, E. and Salmon, J. (2000) *The Insecure Workforce*, London: Routledge.

Held, D., McGrew, A., Goldblatt, D. and Perraton, J. (1999) *Global Transformations*, Cambridge: Polity.

Hendry, C. and Pettigrew, A. (1990) 'Human resource management: an agenda for the 1990s' *International Journal of Human Resource Management* 1(1).

Henry, S. (1978) *The Hidden Economy*, London: Robertson.

Herman, A. (2001) *The Scottish Enlightenment: The Scots' Invention of the Modern World*, London: Fourth Estate.

Herriot, P. and Pemberton, C. (1995) *New Deals: The Revolution in Managerial Careers*, Chichester: Wiley.

Herriot, P., Manning, W.E.G. and Kidd, J.M. (1997) 'The content of the psychological contract', *British Journal of Management*, 8: 151–62.

Herzberg, F. (1966) *Work and the Nature of Man*, Cleveland, OH: World Publishing Company.

Hickson, D.J., Hinings, C.R., Lee, C.A., Schneck, R.E. and Pennings, J.M. (1971) 'A strategic contingencies theory of intra-organisational power', *Administrative Science Quarterly*, 16: 216–29.

Hickson, D.J. (1999) 'Politics permeate', in R.H. Rosenfeld and D.C. Wilson, *Managing Organizations* (2nd edn), London: McGraw-Hill.

Hickson, D.J. and Pugh, D.S. (1995) *Management Worldwide: The Impact of Societal Culture on Organisations Around the Globe*, Harmondsworth: Penguin.

Hill, C. (1974) *Change and Continuity in Seventeenth Century England*, London: Weidenfeld & Nicolson.

Hill, L.A. (1992) *Becoming a Manager: Mastery of a New Identity*, Boston, MA: Harvard Business School.

Hill, S. (1988) *The Tragedy of Technology*, London: Pluto.

Hill, S. (1991) 'How do you manage a flexible firm? The total quality model', *Work, Employment and Society*, 5: 397–415.

Hinton, J. (1973) *The First Shop Stewards' Movement*, London: Allen & Unwin.

Hirschfeld, R.R. and Field, H.S. (2000) 'Work centrality and work alienation: distinct aspects of a general commitment to work', *Journal of Organizational Behaviour*, 21: 789–800.

Hirst, P. (1997) 'The global economy – myths and realities', *International Affairs*, 73: 409–25.

Hirst, P. and Thompson, G. (1996) *Globalization in Question*, Cambridge: Polity Press.

Hirst, P. and Zeitlin, J. (1991) 'Flexible specialisation versus Post-Fordism: theory, evidence and policy implications', *Economy and Society*, 20: 1–55.

Hobsbawm, E.J. (1969) *Industry and Empire*, Harmondsworth: Penguin.

Hochschild, A.R. (1985) *The Managed Heart: The Commercialisation of Human Feeling*, Berkeley: University of California Press.

Hochschild, A.R. (1989) *The Second Shift*, New York: Avon Books.

Hochschild, A.R. (2001) *The Time Bind: When Work Becomes Home and Home Becomes Work* (2nd edn), New York: Owl Books.

Hodson, R. (1996) 'Dignity in the workplace under participative management: alienation and freedom revisited', *American Sociological Review*, 61: 719–38.

Hodson, R. and Sullivan, T. (2001) *The Social Organization of Work* (3rd edn), London: Wadsworth.

Holliday, R. (1995) *Investigating Small Firms: Nice Work?*, London: Routledge.

Hollowell, P.G. (1968) *The Lorry Driver*, London: Routledge & Kegan Paul.

Holton, R.J. (1985) *The Transition from Feudalism to Capitalism*, London: Macmillan.

Hopper, E. and Pearce, A. (1973) 'Relative deprivation, occupational status and occupational "situs"', in M. Warner (ed.) *Sociology of the Workplace*, London: Allen & Unwin.

Hoskin, K. (1998) 'Examining accounts and accounting for management', in A. McKinlay and K. Starkey (eds) (1998) *Foucault, Management and Organization Theory: From Panopticon to Technologies of Self*, London: Sage.

Huczynski, A. and Buchanan, D. (2001) *Organisational Behaviour: An Introduction*, Harlow: Prentice-Hall.

Hughes, E.C. (1937) 'Institutional office and the person', *American Journal of Sociology*, 43: 404–13.

Hughes, E.C. (1958) *Men and their Work*, New York: Free Press.

Hughes, E.C. (1994) *On Work, Race, and the Sociological Imagination*, edited by Lewis A. Coser, Chicago: University of Chicago Press.

Hunter, L. and McInnes, J. (1992) 'Employers and labour flexibility: the evidence from case studies', *Employment Gazette*, June, 307–15.

Hutchinson, S., Purcell, J. and Kinnie, N. (2000) 'Evolving high commitment management and the experience of the RAC call centre', *Human Resource Management Journal*, 10: 63–78.

Hutton, W. (2002) *The World We're In*, London: Little, Brown.

Huws, U., Jagger, N. and O'Regan, S. (1999) *Teleworking and Globalisation*, Institute for Employment Studies Report 358.

Hyman, R. (1989) *The Political Economy of Industrial Relations*, London: Macmillan.

Hyman, R. (2003) 'The historical evolution of British industrial relations', in P. Edwards, (ed.) *Industrial Relations: Theory and Practice* (2nd edn), Oxford: Blackwell.

IES (2000) *Labour Force Survey*, Brighton: Institute for Employment Studies.

Israel, H. (1966) 'Some religious factors in the emergence of industrial society in England', *American Sociological Review*, 31.

Jackall, R. (1988) *Moral Mazes: The World of Corporate Managers*, New York: Oxford University Press.

Jackson, C. (ed.) (2001) *Men at Work: Labour, Masculinity, Development*, London: Frank Cass.

Jackson, N. and Carter, P. (2000) *Rethinking Organisational Behaviour*, Harlow: Prentice-Hall.

Jackson, P. (ed.) (1999) *Virtual Working: Social and Organisational Dynamics*, London: Routledge.

Jackson, P. and Suomi, R. (2001) *Business and Workplace Redesign*, London: Routledge.

Jackson, P.J. and Van der Wielen, J.M. (1998) *Teleworking: New International Perspectives from Telecommuting to the Virtual Organisation*, London: Routledge.

Jacobs, J.A. and Gerson, K. (2001) 'Overworked individuals or overworked families', *Work and Occupations*, 28: 40–63.

Jacques, R. (1996) *Manufacturing the Employee*, London: Sage.

Jahoda, M. (1982) *Employment and Unemployment: A Social Psychological Analysis*, Cambridge: Cambridge University Press.

James, L. (1973) 'On the game', *New Society*, 24 May.

Jaros, S.J. (2001) 'Labor process theory: a commentary on the debate', *International Studies of Management and Organization*, 30: 25–39.

Jenkins, R. (1986) *Racism and Recruitment: Managers, Organisations and Equality in the Labour Market*, Cambridge: Cambridge University Press.

Jenson, J., Hagen, E. and Reddy, C. (eds) (1988) *Feminization of the Labour Force*, Polity: Cambridge.

Jermier, J., Knights, D. and Nord, W.R. (eds) (1994) *Resistance and Power in Organisations*, London: Routledge.

Johnson, T.J. (1977) 'The professions in the class structure', in R. Scase (ed.) *Industrial Society*, London: Allen & Unwin.

Jones, B. (1982) 'Destruction or redistribution of engineering skills?', in S. Wood (ed.) *The Degradation of Work?*, London: Hutchinson.

Jones, B. (1997) *Forcing the Factory of the Future: Cybernation and Societal Institutions*, Cambridge: Cambridge University Press.

Jones, O. (1997) 'Changing the balance? Taylorism, TQM and the work organization', *New Technology, Work and Employment*, 12: 13–23.

Joyce, P. (1980) *Work, Society and Politics: The Culture of the Factory in Late Victorian England*, Brighton: Harvester Press.

Joyce, P. (ed.) (1987) *The Historical Meanings of Work*, Cambridge: Cambridge University Press.

Kalleberg, A.L. (2000) 'Nonstandard employment relations: part-time, temporary and contract work', *Annual Review of Sociology*, 26: 341–65.

Kanter, R.M. (1989) 'Work and family in the United States: a critical review and agenda for research and policy', *Family Business Review*, 2: 77–114.

Kelly, J. (1982) *Scientific Management, Job Redesign and Work Performance*, London: Academic Press.

Kelly, J. (1998) *Rethinking Industrial Relations: Mobilization, Collectivism and Long Waves*, London: Routledge.

Kelly, J. and Heery, E. (1994) *Working for the Union: British Trade Union Officers*, Cambridge: Cambridge University Press.

Kelly, J.N. and Gennard, J. (2001) *Power and Influence in the Boardroom: The Role of The Personnel/HR Director*, London: Routledge.

Kenney, M. and Florida, R. (1993) *Beyond Mass Production: The Japanese System and Its Transfer to the US*, New York: Oxford University Press.

Kerfoot, D. and Knights, D. (2000) *Management, Organization and Masculinity*, London: Sage.

Kerr, C. (1983) *The Future of Industrial Societies: Convergence or Continuing Diversity?*, Cambridge, MA: Harvard University Press.

Kerr, C. and Rostow, J.M. (eds) (1979) *Work in America: The Decade Ahead*, New York: Van Nostrand.

Kerr, C. and Siegal, A.J. (1954) 'The inter-industry propensity to strike', in Kornhauser *et al.* (eds) *Industrial Conflict*, New York: McGraw-Hill.

Kerr, C., Dunlop, J.T., Harbison, F. and Myers, C.A. (1973) *Industrialism and Industrial Man*, Harmondsworth: Penguin.

Klein, L. and Eason, K. (1991) *Putting Social Science to Work*, Cambridge: Cambridge University Press.

Knights, D. (2001) 'Hanging out the dirty washing: labor process theory and its dualistic legacy', *International Studies of Management and Organization*, 30: 68–84.

Knights, D. and McCabe, D. (1998) '"What *happens* when the phone goes wild?": staff stress and spaces for escape in a BPR telephone banking work regime', *Journal of Management Studies*, 35: 163–95.

Knights, D. and McCabe, D. (2000) '"Ain't Misbehavin"? Opportunities for resistance under new forms of "quality" management', *Sociology*, 34: 421–36.

Knights, D. and McCabe, D. (2001) '"A different world": shifting masculinities in the transition to call centres', *Organization*, 8: 619–45.

Knights, D. and Murray, F. (1994) *Managers Divided: Organizational Politics and Information Technology Management*, Chichester: Wiley.

Knights, D. and Willmott, H. (1985) 'Power and identity in theory and practice', *Sociological Review*, 33: 22–46.

Knights, D. and Willmott, H. (eds) (1986) *Managing the Labour Process*, Aldershot: Gower.

Knights, D. and Willmott, H. (eds) (1989a) *Labour Process Theory*, London: Macmillan.

Knights, D. and Willmott, H. (1989b) 'Power and subjectivity at work: from degradation to subjugation at work', *Sociology*, 23: 535–58.

Knights, D., Collinson, D. and Willmott, H. (eds) (1984) *Job Redesign: The Organisation and Control of Work*, Aldershot: Gower.

Kotter, J.P. (1982) *The General Managers*, New York: Free Press.

Kuhn, J.W. (1961) *Bargaining in Grievance Settlement*, Columbia University Press.

Kumar, K. (1978) *Prophecy and Progress*, Harmondsworth: Penguin.

Kumar, K. (1996) *From Post-industrial to Post-modern Society*, Oxford: Blackwell.

Kunda, G. (1992) *Engineering Culture: Control and Commitment in a High-tech Corporation*, Philadelphia: Temple University Press.

Land, H. (1981) *Parity Begins at Home*, London: EOC/SSRC.

Landsberger, H.A. (1958) *Hawthorne Revisited*, Ithaca, NY: Columbia University Press.

Landsberger, H.A. (1961) 'The horizontal dimension in bureaucracy', *Administrative Science Quarterly*, 6.

Lankshear, G., Cook, P., Mason, D., Coates, S. and Button, G. (2001) 'Call centre employees' responses to electronic monitoring: some research findings', *Work, Employment and Society*, 15: 595–605.

LaNuez, D. and Jermier, J. (1994) 'Sabotage by managers and technocrats', in J. Jermier, D. Knights and W.R. Nord (eds) *Resistance and Power in Organisations*, London: Routledge.

Larson, M.S. (1977) *The Rise of Professionalism: A Sociological Analysis*, Berkeley: University of California Press.

Larson, M.S. (1991) 'On the matter of experts and professionals, or how impossible it is to leave nothing unsaid', in M. Burrage and R. Torstendahl (eds) *The Formation of Professions*, London: Sage.

Lash, S. and Urry, J. (1987) *The End of Organised Capitalism*, Cambridge: Polity.

Latour, B. (1987) *Science in Action*, Milton Keynes: Open University Press.

Latour, B. (1993) *We Have Never Been Modern*, Brighton: Harvester Wheatsheaf.

Lawrence, P.R. and Lorsch, J.W. (1967) *Organisation and Environment*, Cambridge, MA: Harvard University Press.

Layder, D., Ashton, D. and Sung, J. (1991) 'The empirical correlates of action and structure: the transition from school to work', *Sociology*, 25: 447–64.

Layte, R. (1999) *Divided Time: Gender, Paid Employment and Domestic Labour*, Aldershot: Ashgate.

Ledwith, S. and Colgan, F. (1996) *Women in Organisations: Challenging Gender Politics*, Basingstoke: Macmillan.

Lee, D. (2000) 'Hegemonic masculinity and male feminisation: the sexual harassment of men at work', *Journal of Gender Studies*, 9: 141–55.

Legge, K. (1995) *Human Resource Management: Rhetorics and Realities*, Basingstoke: Macmillan.

Leidner, R. (1991) 'Serving hamburgers and selling insurance: gender, work and identity in interactive service jobs', *Gender and Society*, 5: 154–77.

Leidner, R. (1993) *Fast Food Fast Talk: Service Work and the Routinization of Everyday Life*, Berkeley: University of California Press.

Leisink, P. (ed.) (1999) *Globalisation and Labour Relations*, Cheltenham: Elgar.

Levinson, H., Price, C., Munder, K. and Solley, C. (1966) *Men, Management and Mental Health*, Cambridge, MA: Harvard University Press.

Likert, R. (1967) *The Human Organisation*, New York: McGraw-Hill.

Linstead, S. (1985) 'Jokers wild: the importance of humour in the maintenance of organisational culture', *Sociological Review*, 33: 741–67.

Lipietz, A. (1987) *Miracles and Mirages: The Crisis in Global Fordism*, London: Verso.

Lipset, S.M. (1976) 'Social structure and social change', in P.M. Blau (ed.) *Approaches to the Study of Social Structure*, London: Open Books.

Lipset, S.M., Trow, M. and Coleman, J. (1956) *Union Democracy*, Chicago: Free Press.

Littler, C. (1982) *The Development of the Labour Process in Capitalist Societies*, London: Heinemann.

Littler, C.R. and Salaman, G. (1982) 'Bravermania and beyond: recent theories of the labour process', *Sociology*, 16: 2.

Littler, C.R. and Salaman, G. (1984) *Class at Work: The Design, Allocation and Control of Jobs*, London: Batsford.

Littleton, S.M., Arthur, M.B. and Rousseau, D.M. (2000) 'The future of boundaryless careers', in A. Collin and R.A. Young (eds) *The Future of Career*, Cambridge: Cambridge University Press.

Lockwood, D. (1989, originally 1958) *The Blackcoated Worker: A Study in Class Consciousness* (2nd edn), Oxford: Oxford University Press.

Luff, P., Hindmarsh, L. and Heath, C. (eds) (2000) *Workplace Studies: Recovering Work Practice and Information System Design*, Cambridge: Cambridge University Press.

Lupton, T. (1963) *On the Shopfloor*, Oxford: Pergamon.

Lyotard, J.-F. (1984) *The Postmodern Condition*, Manchester: Manchester University Press.

Macdonald, C.L. and Sirianni, C. (eds) (1996) *Working in the Service Society*, Philadelphia: Temple University Press.

Madge, C. (1963) *The Origins of Scientific Sociology*, London: Tavistock.

Mair, A. (1994) *Honda's Local Global Corporation*, London: Macmillan.

Mangham, I.L. and Pye, A. (1991) *The Doing of Management*, Oxford: Blackwell.

Mann, M. (1973) *Workers on the Move*, Cambridge: Cambridge University Press.

Manning, P.K. (1977) *Police Work: The Social Organisation of Policing*, Cambridge, MA: MIT Press.

Marceau, J. (1989) *A Family Business? The Making of an International Business Elite*, Cambridge: Cambridge University Press.

March, J.G. and Olsen, J.P. (1976) *Ambiguity and Choice in Organisations*, Oslo: Universitetsforlagtt.

Marglin, S. (1980) 'The origins and function of hierarchy in capitalist production', in T. Nichols (ed.) *Capital and Labour*, Glasgow: Fontana.

Mars, G. (1974) 'Dock pilferage', in P. Rock and M. McIntosh (eds) *Deviance and Control*, London: Tavistock.

Mars, G. (1982) *Cheats at Work*, London: Allen & Unwin.

Mars, G. and Nicod, M. (1984) *The World of Waiters*, London: Allen & Unwin.

Marshall, G. (1997) *Repositioning Class: Social Inequality in Industrial Societies*, London: Sage.

Marshall, G., Newby, H., Rose, D. and Vogler, C. (1988) *Social Class in Modern Britain*, London: Hutchinson.

Marshall, J. (1995) *Women Managers Moving On*, London: Routledge.

Martin, J. and Roberts, C. (1984) *Women and Employment*, London: HMSO.

Martin, P.Y. (2001) '"Mobilising masculinities": women's experiences of men at work', *Organization*, 8: 587–618.

Maslow, A. (1943) 'A theory of human motivation', *Psychological Development*, 50: 370–96.

Maslow, A. (1954) *Motivation and Personality*, New York: Harper & Row.

Mason, G. (2000) 'Production supervisors in Britain, Germany and the United States: back from the dead again?', *Work, Employment and Society*, 14: 625–45.

Mayo, E. (1933) *The Human Problems of an Industrial Civilisation*, New York: Macmillan.

Mayo, E. (1949) *The Social Problems of an Industrial Civilisation*, London: Routledge & Kegan Paul.

McCabe, D. (1999) 'Total Quality Management: anti-union Trojan horse or management albatross?', *Work, Employment and Society*, 13: 665–91.

McCabe, D. (2000) 'Factory innovations and management machinations: the productive and repressive relations of power', *Journal of Management Studies*, 37: 931–53.

McGovern, P. (1998) *HRM, Technical Workers and the Multination Corporation*, London: Routledge.

McGovern, P., Hope-Hailey, V. and Stiles, P. (1998) 'The managerial career after down-sizing: case studies from the "leading edge"', *Work, Employment and Society*, 12: 457–77.

McGregor, D.C. (1960) *The Human Side of Enterprise*, New York: McGraw-Hill.

McKeganey, N. and Barnard, M. (1996) *Sex Work on the Streets: Prostitutes and their Clients*, Buckingham: Open University Press.

McKenzie, D. and Wajcman, J. (1985) *The Social Shaping of Technology*, Milton Keynes: Open University Press.

McKie, L., Bowlby, L. and Gregory, S. (eds) (1999) *Gender, Power and the Household*, Basingtoke: Macmillan.

McKinlay, A. and Starkey, K. (eds) (1998) *Foucault, Management and Organization Theory: From Panopticon to Technologies of Self*, London: Sage.

McKinlay, A. and Taylor, P. (2000) *Inside the Factory of the Future: Work, Power and Authority in Microelectronics*, London: Routledge.

McLoughlin, I. (1999) *Creative Technological Change: The Shaping of Technology and Organisations*, London: Routledge.

McLoughlin, I. and Harris, M. (eds) (1997) *Innovation, Organizational Change and Technology*, London: International Thomson.

Mead, G.H. (1962) *Mind, Self and Society*, Chicago: University of Chicago Press.

Mead, M. (1962) *Male and Female*, Harmondsworth: Penguin.

Meissner, M. (1971) 'The long arm of the job', *Industrial Relations*, 2.

Meissner, M. (1976) 'The language of work', in R. Dubin (ed.) *The Handbook of Work, Organisation and Society*, Chicago: Rand-McNally.

Merton, R.K. (1957) 'Bureaucratic structure and personality', in *Social Theory and Social Structure*, New York: Free Press.

Meyer, J. and Rowan, B. (1977) 'Institutionalised organisations: formal structure and myth and ceremony', *American Journal of Sociology*, 83: 340–63.

Miles, I. (1984) 'Work, well-being and unemployment', in P. Marstrand (ed.) *New Technology and the Future of Work Skills*, London: Pinter.

Miles, S. (2001) *Social Theory in the Real World*, London: Sage.

Milkman, R. (1991) *Japan's California Factories: Labor Relations and Economic Globalisation*, Los Angeles: Institute of Industrial Relations, University of California.

Milkman, R. (1997) *Farewell to the Factory: Auto Workers in the Late Twentieth Century*, Berkeley: University of California Press.

Miller, P. and O'Leary, T. (1987) 'Accounting and the deconstruction of the governable person', *Accounting, Organizations and Society*, 12: 235–65.

Miller, S.L., Hickson, D.J. and Wilson, D.C. (1996) 'Decision-making in organizations', in S.R. Clegg, C. Hardy and W. Nord (eds) *Handbook of Organization Studies*, London: Sage.

Millerson, G. (1964) *The Qualifying Associations*, London: Routledge & Kegan Paul.

Mills, C.W. (1953) *White Collar*, New York: Oxford University Press.

Mills, C.W. (1970a) 'The trade union leader: a collective portrait', in I.L. Horowitz (ed.) *Politics and People: The Collected Essays of C.W. Mills*, New York: Oxford University Press.

Mills, C.W. (1970b) *The Sociological Imagination*, Harmondsworth: Penguin.

Millward, N. *et al.* (1992) *Workplace Industrial Relations in Transition*, Aldershot: Dartmouth.

Millward, N., Bryson, A. and Forth, J. (2000) *All Change at Work? British Employment Relations 1980–1998, as Portrayed by the Workplace Industrial Relations Survey Series*, London: Routledge.

Mintzberg, H. (1973) *The Nature of Managerial Work*, New York: Harper & Row.

Moody, K. (1997) *Workers in a Lean World: Unions in the International Economy*, London: Verso.

Mooney, J.D. and Riley, A.C. (1931) *Onward Industry*, New York: Harper.

Moore, R. (1975) 'Religion as a source of variation in working class images of society', in M. Bulmer (ed.) *Working Class Images of Society*, London: Routledge & Kegan Paul.

Morgan, G. (1990) *Organisations in Society*, London: Macmillan.

Morris, L. (1988) 'Employment, the household and social networks', in D. Gallie (ed.) *Employment in Britain*, Oxford: Blackwell.

Morris, R.T. and Murphy, R.J. (1959) 'The situs dimension in occupational sociology', *American Sociological Review*, 24.

Morris, T. and Morris, P. (1973) 'The prison officer', in D. Weir (ed.) *Men and Work in Modern Britain*, Glasgow: Fontana.

Morse, N.C. and Weiss, R.S. (1955) 'The function and meaning of work and the job', *American Sociological Review*, 20.

Moses, J.A. (1990) *Trade Union Theory from Marx to Walesa*, New York: Berg.

Mott, J. (1973) 'Miners, weavers and pigeon racing', in M.A. Smith, S. Parker and C.S. Smith (eds) *Leisure and Society and Britain*, London: Allen Lane.

Moule, C. (1998) 'The regulation of work in small firms', *Work, Employment and Society*, 12: 635–54.

MOW International Research Team (1987) *The Meaning of Work*, London: Academic Press.

Mulkay, M. (1988) *On Humour: Style and Technique in Comic Discourse*, Cambridge: Polity.

Musgrave, P.W. (1967) 'Towards a sociological theory of occupational choice', *Sociological Review*, 15.

Neal, M. and Morgan, J. (2000) 'The professionalization of everyone? A comparative study of the development of the professions in the UK and Germany', *European Sociological Review*, 16: 9–26.

Newton, T. (1998) 'Theorizing subjectivity in organizations: the failure of Foucauldian studies', *Organization Studies*, 19: 415–47.

Newton, T. (1999) 'Power, subjectivity and British industrial and organizational sociology', *Sociology*, 33: 411–40.

Newton, T. with Handy, J. and Fineman, S. (1995) *'Managing' Stress: Emotion and Power at Work*, London: Sage.

Nichols, T. (1997) *The Sociology of Industrial Injury*, London: Mansell.

Nichols, T. and Beynon, H. (1977) *Living with Capitalism*, London: Routledge & Kegan Paul.

Nisbet, R. (1970) *The Sociological Tradition*, London: Heinemann.

Noble, D.F. (1984) *Forces of Production: A Social History of Industrial Automation*, New York: Alfred A. Knopf.

Noon, M. and Blyton, P. (2002) *The Realities of Work*, Basingstoke: Palgrave.

Noon, M. and Delbridge, R. (1993) 'News from behind my hand: gossip in organisations', *Organisation Studies*, 14: 23–36.

Nordenmark, M. and Strandh, M. (1999) 'Towards a sociological understanding of mental well-being among the unemployed: the role of economic and psychosocial factors', *Sociology*, 33: 577–97.

O'Connell Davidson, J. (1994) 'Resistance in a privatised utility', in Jermier, Knights and Nord (eds) *Resistance and Power in Organisations*, London: Routledge.

O'Connell Davidson, J. (1995) 'The anatomy of "free choice" prostitution', *Gender, Work and Organisation*, 2: 1–10.

O'Connell Davidson, J. (1998) *Prostitution, Power and Freedom*, Cambridge: Polity.

O'Connor, E. (1999) 'Minding the workers: the meaning of "human" and "human relations" in Elton Mayo', *Organization*, 6: 223–46.

O'Doherty, D. and Wilmott, H. (2001a) 'The question of subjectivity and the labor process', *International Studies of Management and Organization*, 30: 112–13.

O'Doherty, D. and Willmott, H. (2001b) 'Debating labour process theory: the issue of subjectivity and the relevance of poststructuralism', *Sociology*, 35: 457–76.

Oakley, A. (1974) *Housewife*, London: Allen Lane.

Offe, C. (1976) *Industry and Inequality*, London: Arnold.

Oliver, N. and Wilkinson, B. (1988) *The Japanisation of British Industry?* (2nd edn), Oxford: Blackwell.

Oppenheimer, M. (1973) 'The proletarianisation of the professional', *Sociological Review Monograph*, 20.

Orzack, L. (1959) 'Work as a central life interest of professionals', *Social Problems*, 6.

Pahl, J.M. and Pahl, R.E. (1972) *Managers and their Wives*, Harmondsworth: Penguin.

Pahl, R.E. (1984) *Divisions of Labour*, Oxford: Blackwell.

Pahl, R.E. (ed.) (1988) *On Work: Historical, Comparative and Theoretical Approaches*, Oxford: Blackwell.

Parker, B. (1996) 'Evolution and revolution: from international business to globalization', in S.R. Clegg, C. Hardy and W. Nord (eds) *Handbook of Organization Studies*, London: Sage.

Parker, M. (1993) 'Life after Jean-François', in J. Hassard and M. Parker (eds) *Postmodernism and Organizations*, London: Sage.

Parker, M. (1999) 'Capitalism, subjectivity, and ethics: debating labour process analysis', *Organization Studies*, 20: 25–45.

Parker, M. (2000) *Organizational Culture and Identity: Unity and Division at Work*, London: Sage.

Parker, S. (1982) *Work and Retirement*, London: Allen & Unwin.

Parker, S. (1983) *Leisure and Work*, London: Allen & Unwin.

Parkin, F. (ed.) (1974) *The Social Analysis of Class Structure*, London: Tavistock.

Peccei, R. and Rosenthal, P. (1997) 'The antecedents of employee commitment to customer service', *International Journal of Human Resource Management*, 8: 66–86.

Peiperl, M., Arthur, M., Goffee, R. and Morris, T. (eds) (2000) *Career Frontiers: New Conceptions of Working Lives*, Oxford: Oxford University Press.

Pendleton, A. (2000) *Employee Ownership, Participation and Governance*, London: Routledge.

Perrow, C. (1970a) 'Departmental power', in M. Zald (ed.) *Power in Organisations*, Vanderbilt: Vanderbilt University Press.

Perrow, C. (1970b) *Organisational Analysis*, London: Tavistock.

Perrow, C. (1977) 'Three types of effectiveness studies', in P.S. Goodman and J.M. Pennings (eds) *New Perspectives on Organizational Effectiveness*, San Francisco: Jossey-Bass.

Perrow, C. (1986) *Complex Organisations: A Critical Essay*, New York: Random House.

Peters, T.J. and Waterman, R.H. Jr (1982) *In Search of Excellence*, New York: Harper & Row.

Pettigrew, A. and Fenton, E. (eds) (2000) *The Innovating Organization: Process and Practice in New Forms of Organizing*, London: Sage.

Pettigrew, A.M. (1973) *The Politics of Organisational Decision Making*, London: Tavistock.

Pettigrew, A.M. and McNulty, T. (1995) 'Power and influence in and around the boardroom', *Human Relations*, 48: 845–73.

Pfeffer, J. (1993) 'Barriers to the advance of organizational science: paradigm development as a dependent variable', *Academy of Management Review*, 18: 599–620.

Pfeffer, J. and Salancik, G.R. (1978) *The External Control of Organisations: A Resource Dependence Approach*, New York: Harper & Row.

Phizacklea, A. (1990) *Unpacking the Fashion Industry: Gender, Racism and Class in Production*, London: Routledge.

Phizacklea, A. and Wolkowitz, C. (1995) *Homeworking Women*, London: Sage.

Phoenix, H. (1999) *Making Sense of Prostitution*, Basingstoke: Macmillan.

Pickford, L.J. (1985) 'The superstructure of myths supporting the subordination of women', in B.A. Stead (ed.) *Women in Management* (2nd edn), Englewood Cliffs, NJ: Prentice-Hall.

Pilcher, J. (2000) 'Domestic divisions of labour in the twentieth century: "change slow a coming"', *Work, Employment and Society*, 14: 771–80.

Piore, M.J. (1986) 'The decline of mass production and challenge to union survival', *Industrial Relations Journal*, 17: 207–13.

Piore, M. and Sabel, C.F. (1984) *The Second Industrial Divide: Possibilities of Prosperity*, New York: Basic Books.

Poggi, G. (1983) *Calvinism and the Capitalist Spirit*, London: Macmillan.

Pollert, A. (1981) *Girls, Wives, Factory Lives*, London: Macmillan.

Pollert, A. (ed.) (1991) *Farewell to Flexibility*, Oxford: Blackwell.

Powell, G.N. (1999) *Handbook of Gender and Work*, London: Sage.

Poynter, G. (2002) *Restructuring in the Service Industries: Management Reform and Workplace Reform and Workplace Relations in the UK Service Sector*, London: Mansell.

Preece, D., McLoughlin, I. and Dawson, P. (eds) (2000a) *Technology, Organizations and Innovation: Critical Perspectives on Business and Management, Vol. I, The Early Debates*, London: Routledge.

Preece, D., McLoughlin, I. and Dawson, P. (eds) (2000b) *Technology, Organizations and Innovation: Critical Perspectives on Business and Management, Vol. II, Theories, Concepts and Paradigms*, London: Routledge.

Preece, D., McLoughlin, I. and Dawson, P. (eds) (2000c) *Technology, Organizations and Innovation: Critical Perspectives on Business and Management, Vol. III, Critical Empirical Studies*, London: Routledge.

Preece, D., McLoughlin, I. and Dawson, P. (eds) (2000d) *Technology, Organizations and Innovation: Critical Perspectives on Business and Management, Vol. IV, Towards 'Real Virtuality'?*, London: Routledge.

Preece, D., Steven, G. and Steven, V. (1999) *Work, Change and Competition: Managing for Bass*, London: Routledge.

Pringle, R. (1989) *Secretaries Talk: Sexuality, Power and Work*, London: Verso.

Procter, S. and Ackroyd, S. (1998) 'Against Japanization: understanding the reorganisation of British manufacturing', *Employee Relations*, 20: 237–48.

Procter, S.J. and Mueller, F. (eds) (2000) *Teamworking*, Basingstoke: Macmillan.

Procter, S.J., Rowlinson, M., McArdle, L., Hassard, J. and Forrester, P. (1994), 'Flexibility, politics and strategy: in defence of the model of the flexible firm', *Work, Employment and Society*, 8: 221–42.

Pugh, D.S. (ed.) (1995) *History of Management Thought*, Aldershot: Dartmouth.

Pugh, D.S. and Hickson, D.J. (1976) *Organisational Structure in its Context: The Aston Programme I*, Farnborough: Saxon House.

Pugh, D.S. and Hinings, C.R. (eds) (1976) *Organisation Structure: Extensions and Replications, the Aston Programme II*, Farnborough: Gower.

Pugh, D.S. and Payne, R.L. (1977) *Organisational Behaviour in its Context: The Aston Programme III*, Farnborough: Saxon House.

Punch, M. (1996) *Dirty Business: Exploring Corporate Misconduct: Analysis and Cases*, London: Sage.

Purcell, J. and Ahlstrand, B. (1994) *Human Resource Management in the Multi-Divisional Company*, Oxford: Oxford University Press.

Purcell, K. (1982) 'Female manual workers: fatalism and the reinforcement of inequality', in D. Robbins (ed.) *Rethinking Inequality*, Aldershot: Gower.

Purcell, K. (ed.) (2000) *Changing Boundaries in Employment*, Bristol: Bristol Academic Press.

Purcell, K., Hogarth T. and Simm, C. (1999) *Whose Flexibility?: the Costs and Benefits of 'Non-Standard' Working Arrangements and Contractual Relations*, York: Joseph Rowntree Foundation.

Quinney, E.R. (1963) 'Occupational structure and criminal behaviour', *Social Problems*, 11.

Radcliffe-Brown, A.R. (1965) *Structure and Function in Primitive Society*, New York: Free Press.

Rainnie, A. (1989) *Industrial Relations in Small Firms*, London: Routledge.

Ram, M. (1994) *Managing to Survive: Working Lives in Small Firms*, Oxford: Blackwell.

Ram, M., Edwards, P., Gilman M. and Arrowsmith, J. (2001) 'The dynamics of informality: employment relations in small firms and the effects of regulatory change', *Work, Employment and Society*, 15: 845–61.

Ray, C.A. (1986) 'Corporate culture: the last frontier of control?', *Journal of Management Studies*, 23: 287–97.

Ray, L.J. and Reed, M. (eds) (1994) *Organizing Modernity: New Weberian Perspectives on Work*, London: Routledge.

Reed, M. (1992) *The Sociology of Organisations: Themes, Perspectives and Prospects*, Hemel Hempstead: Harvester Wheatsheaf.

Ribeiro, V.E. and Blakely, J.A. (1995) 'The proactive management of rumor and gossip', *Journal of Nursing Administration*, 25: 43–50.

Rice, A.K. (1958) *Productivity and Social Organisation*, London: Tavistock.

Richman, J. (1969) 'Busmen v. the public', *New Society*, 14 August.

Richman, J. (1983) *Traffic Wardens: An Ethnography of Street Administration*, Manchester: Manchester University Press.

Rifkin, J. (1996) *The End of Work*, New York: Tarcher/ Putnam Press.

Rinehart, J., Huxley, J. and Robertson, D. (1997) *Just Another Car Factory? Lean Production and its Discontents*, Ithaca, NY: Cornell University Press.

Ritzer, G. (1993) *The McDonaldization of Society*, Thousand Oaks, CA: Pine Forge.

Ritzer, G. (1998) *The McDonaldization Thesis*, London: Sage.

Ritzer, G. (1999) 'Assessing the resistance', in B. Smart (ed.) *Resisting McDonaldization*, London: Sage.

Ritzer, G. (2000) *Sociological Theory*, New York: McGraw-Hill.

Roberts, K. (1975) 'The developmental theory of occupational choice', in G. Esland, G. Salaman and M. Speakman (eds) *People and Work*, Edinburgh: Holmes McDougall.

Roberts, K. *et al.* (1977) *The Fragmentary Class Structure*, London: Heinemann.

Robertson, R. (1992) *Globalisation: Social Theory and Global Culture*, London: Sage.

Roethlisberger, F.J. (1945) 'The foreman: master and victim of double talk', *Harvard Business Review*, 23.

Roethlisberger, F.J. and Dickson, W.J. (1939) *Management and the Worker*, Cambridge, MA: Harvard University Press.

Rojek, C. (ed.) (1989) *Leisure for Leisure*, London: Macmillan.

Roper, M. (1994) *Masculinity and the British Organisation Man since 1945*, Oxford: Oxford University Press.

Rose, D. and O'Reilly, K. (eds) (1997) *Constructing Classes: Towards a New Social Classification for the UK*, Swindon: Economic and Social Research Council/ Office for National Statistics.

Rose, M. (1985) *Re-Working the Work Ethic*, London: Batsford.

Rose, M. (1988) *Industrial Behaviour*, London: Allen Lane.

Rose, M. and Jones, B. (1984) 'Managerial strategy and trade union response in plant level reorganisation of work', in D. Knights, D. Collinson and H. Willmott (eds) *Job Redesign: The Organisation and Control of Work*, Aldershot: Gower.

Rosenbrock, H. (1982) 'Technology and policy options', in N. Bjorn-Anderson, M. Earl, O. Holst and G. Mumford (eds) *Information Society for Richer or Poorer*, Amsterdam: North Holland Publishing Company.

Rosenthal, P., Hill, S. and Peccei, R. (1997) 'Checking out service: evaluating excellence, HRM and TQM in retailing', *Work, Employment and Society*, 11: 481–503.

Rothman, R. (1997) *Working: Sociological Perspectives*, London: Prentice-Hall.

Rousseau, D.M. (1995) *Psychological Contracts in Organisations: Understanding Written and Unwritten Agreements*, Thousand Oaks, CA: Sage.

Rowlinson, M. (1997) *Organisations and Institutions*, Basingstoke: Macmillan.

Roy, D. (1952) 'Quota restriction and goldbricking in a machine shop', *American Journal of Sociology*, 57: 427–42.

Roy, D. (1953) 'Work satisfaction and social reward in quota achievement: an analysis of piecework incentives', *American Sociological Review*, 18: 507–14.

Roy, D. (1954) 'Efficiency and "the Fix": informal inter-group relations in piecework machine shops', *American Journal of Sociology*, 60: 255–66.

Roy, D. (1958) 'Banana time: job satisfaction and informal interaction', *Human Organization* 18: 158–68.

Royle, T. (2000) *Working for McDonald's in Europe: The Unequal Struggle?*, London: Routledge.

Rubenstein, D. (1978), 'Love and work', *Sociological Review*, 26.

Rubery, J., Smith, M., Fagan, C. and Grimshaw, D. (1998) *Women and European Employment*, London: Routledge.

Sabel, C. and Zeitlin, J. (1997) *World of Possibilities: Flexibility and Mass Production in Western Industrialisation*, Cambridge: Cambridge University Press.

Salaman, G. (1974) *Community and Occupation*, Cambridge: Cambridge University Press.

Salaman, G. and Thompson, K. (1978) 'Class culture and the persistence of an elite', *Sociological Review*, 26.

Salutin, M. (1971) 'Stripper morality', *Transaction*, 8.

Sandberg, A. (ed.) (1995) *Enriching Production: Perspectives on Volvo's Uddevalla Plant as an Alternative to Lean Production*, Aldershot: Avebury.

Saussure, F. de (1974) *Course in General Linguistics*, London: Fontana.

Savage, M. (2000) *Class Analysis and Social Transformation*, Buckingham: Open University Press.

Savage, M., Barlow, J., Dickens, P. and Fielding, A. (1992) *Property, Bureaucracy and Culture: Middle Class Formation in Contemporary Britain*, London: Routledge.

Sayles, L.R. (1958) *The Behavior of Industrial Work Groups*, New York: Wiley.

Scarborough, H. (1996) (ed.) *The Management of Expertise*, Basingstoke: Macmillan.

Scarborough, H. and Corbett, J.M. (1992) *Technology and Organisation*, London: Routledge.

Scase, R. (2003) 'Employment relations in small firms', in P. Edwards (ed.) *Industrial Relations: Theory and Practice* (2nd edn), Oxford: Blackwell.

Scase, R. and Goffee, R. (1982) *The Entrepreneurial Middle-Class*, London: Croom Helm.

Scase, R. and Goffee, R. (1989) *Reluctant Managers: Their Work and Lifestyles*, London: Unwin Hyman.

Schacht, R. (1970) *Alienation*, London: Allen & Unwin.

Schein, E. (1978) *Career Dynamics: Matching Individual and Organizational Needs*, Reading, MA: Addison Wesley.

Schienstock, G. (1981) 'Towards a theory of industrial relations', *British Journal of Industrial Relations*, 19: 2.

Schmidt, G. (1976) 'Max Weber and modern industrial sociology', *Sociological Analysis and Theory*, 6.

Schor, J. (1991) *The Overworked American: The Unexpected Decline of Leisure*, New York: Basic Books.

Schwartzman, H.B. (1993) *Ethnography in Organisations*, Newbury Park, CA: Sage.

Scott, A. (1994) *Willing Slaves? British Workers Under Human Resource Management*, Cambridge: Cambridge University Press.

Scott, J. (1996) *Stratification and Power*, Cambridge: Polity Press.

Scott, J. (1997) *Corporate Business and Capitalist Classes*, Oxford: Oxford University Press.

Scott, W.R. (1995) *Institutions and Organizations*, London: Sage.

Scott, W.R. and Meyer, J.W. (1994) *Institutional Environments and Organisations*, Newbury Park, CA: Sage.

Selznick, P. (1949, 1966) *TVA and the Grassroots*, Berkeley: University of California Press.

Selznick, P. (1957) *Leadership in Administration: A Sociological Interpretation*, New York: Harper & Row.

Senker, P. (1994) 'Supervision in manufacturing organisations', *Journal of General Management*, 20: 44–61.

Sennett, R. (1998) *The Corrosion of Character: The Personal Consequences of Work in the New Capitalism*, New York: Norton.

Sennett, R. and Cobb, J. (1977) *The Hidden Injuries of Class*, Cambridge: Cambridge University Press.

Sewell, G. and Wilkinson, B. (1992) '"Someone to watch over me": surveillance, discipline and just-in-time labour process', *Sociology*, 26: 271–89.

Sharpe, S. (1984) *Double Identity: The Lives of Working Mothers*, Harmondsworth: Penguin.

Shenav, Y. (1999) *Manufacturing Rationality: The Engineering Foundations of Managerial Rationality*, Oxford: Oxford University Press.

Silverman, D. (1970) *The Theory of Organisations*, London: Heinemann.

Silverman, D. (1994) 'On throwing away ladders: rewriting the theory of organisations', in J. Hassard and M. Parker (eds) *Towards a New Theory of Organisations*, London: Routledge.

Silverman, D. and Jones, J. (1976) *Organisational Work*, London: Collier Macmillan.

Simon, H.A. (1957) *Models of Man*, New York: Wiley.

Simpson, R. (1998) 'Presenteeism, power and organisational change', *British Journal of Management*, 9, 37–50.

Sisson, K. (1993) 'In search of HRM', *British Journal of Industrial Relations*, 31: 201–9.

Skipper, J. and McCaghy, C. (1970) 'Stripteasers', *Social Problems*, 17.

Smart, B. (ed.) (1999) *Resisting McDonaldization*, London: Sage.

Smith, A. (1974, orig. 1776) *The Wealth of Nations*, Harmondsworth: Penguin.

Smith, C. and Thompson, P. (1998) 'Re-evaluating the labour process debate', *Economic and Industrial Democracy*, 19: 551–77.

Smith, C., Child, J. and Rowlinson, M. (1990) *Reshaping Work: The Cadbury Experience*, Cambridge: Cambridge University Press.

Smith, J.H. (1987) 'Elton Mayo and the hidden Hawthorne', *Work, Employment and Society*. 1: 107–20.

Smith, V. (1990) *Managing in the Corporate Interest: Control and Resistance in an American Bank*, Berkeley: University of California Press.

Snow, C.C., Lipnack, J. and Stamps, K. (1999) 'The virtual organization: promises and payoffs, large and small', in C.L. Cooper and D.M. Rousseau (eds) *The Virtual Organization, Trends in Organizational Behaviour*, Vol. 6, Chichester: Wiley.

Sorge, A. and Warner, M. (eds) (1997) *The Handbook of Organizational Behaviour*, London: International Thomson Business Press.

Sosteric, M. (1996) 'Subjectivity and the labour process: a case study in the restaurant industry', *Work, Employment and Society*, 10: 297–318.

Spencer, D.A. (2000) 'Braverman and the contribution of labour process analysis to the critique of capitalist production – twenty-five years on', *Work, Employment and Society*, 14: 223–43.

Spradley, J.P. and Mann, B.J. (1975) *The Cocktail Waitress*, New York: Wiley.

Stanworth, J. and Stanworth, C. (1992) *Telework: The Human Resource Implications*, London: IPM.

Starkey, K. (1998) 'Durkheim and the limits of corporate culture: whose culture? which Durkheim?', *Journal of Management Studies*, 35: 125–37.

Starkey, K. and McKinlay, A. (1989) 'Beyond Fordism: strategic choice and labour relations in Ford UK', *Industrial Relations Journal*, 20: 93 100.

Stoner, C.R., Hartman, R.I. and Arora, R. (1990) 'Work–home conflict in female owners of small businesses: an exploratory study', *Journal of Small Business Management*, 29: 30–8.

Storey, J. (1992) *Developments in the Management of Human Resources*, Oxford: Blackwell.

Storey, J. (ed.) (1994) *New Wave Manufacturing Strategies: Organisational and Human Resource Management Dimensions*, London: Chapman.

Storey, J. (ed.) (2001) *Human Resource Management: A Critical Text* (2nd edn), London: Thomson Learning.

Storey, J. and Harrison, A. (1999) 'Coping with world class manufacturing', *Work, Employment and Society*, 13: 643–64.

Storey, R. (1989) *New Perspectives on Human Resource Management*, London: Routledge.

Strangleman, T. (1999) 'The nostalgia of organisations and the organisation of nostalgia: past and present in the contemporary railway industry', *Sociology*, 33: 725–46.

Strangleman, T. and Roberts, I. (1999) 'Looking through the window of opportunity: the cultural cleansing of workplace identity', *Sociology*, 33: 47–67.

Strati, A. (2000) *Theory and Method in Organization Studies*, London: Sage.

Strauss, A. (1978) *Negotiations*, New York: Wiley.

Strauss, A., Schatzman, L., Erlich, D., Bucher, R. and Sabsin, M. (1963) 'The hospital and its negotiated order', in E. Friedson (ed.) *The Hospital in Modern Society*, New York: Macmillan.

Sturdy, A. (1992) 'Clerical consent: "shifting" work in the insurance office,' in A. Sturdy, D. Knights and H. Willmott (eds) *Skill and Consent: Contemporary Studies in the Labour Process*, London: Routledge.

Sullivan, O. and Gershuny, J. (2001) 'Cross-national changes in time-use: some sociological (hi)stories re-examined', *British Journal of Sociology*, 52: 331–47.

Super, D.E. (1957) *The Psychology of Careers*, New York: Harper & Row.

Swingewood, A. (2000) *A Short History of Sociological Thought*, Basingstoke: Macmillan.

Sykes, A.J.M. (1969) 'Navvies: their work attitudes', *Sociology*, 3.

Tailby, S. and Whitson, C. (1989) 'Industrial relations and restructuring', in S. Tailby and C. Whitson (eds) *Manufacturing Change: Industrial Relations and Restructuring*, Oxford: Blackwell.

Tailby, S. and Winchester, D. (2000) 'Management and trade unions: towards social partnership?', in S. Bach and K. Sisson (eds) *Personnel Management: A Comprehensive Guide to Theory and Practice*, Oxford: Blackwell.

Taksa, L. (1992) 'Scientific Management: technique or cultural ideology?', *Journal of Industrial Relations*, 34: 365–97.

Taylor, F.W. (1911a) *The Principles of Scientific Management*, New York: Harper.

Taylor, F.W. (1911b) *Shop Management*, New York: Harper.

Taylor, I. and Walton, P. (1971) 'Industrial sabotage: motives and meanings', in S. Cohen (ed.) *Images of Deviance*, Harmondsworth: Penguin.

Taylor, P. *et al.* (2002) 'Work organisation, control and the experience of work in call centres', *Work, Employment and Society*, 16: 133–50.

Taylor, R. (1982) *Workers and the New Depression*, London: Macmillan.

Taylor, R. (1998) 'Emotional labour and the new workplace', in P. Thompson and C. Warhurst (eds) *Workplaces of the Future*, Basingstoke: Macmillan.

Taylor, R. (2002) *Managing Workplace Change*, Swindon: Economic and Social Research Council.

Taylor, S. and Tylor, M. (2000) 'Emotional labour and sexual difference in the airline industry', *Work, Employment and Society*, 14: 77–95.

Tebbut, M. and Marchington, M. (1997) '"Look before you speak": gossip and the insecure workplace', *Work, Employment and Society*, 11: 713–35.

Terkel, S. (1977) *Working*, Harmondsworth: Penguin.

Terry, M. (2000) *Redefining Public Sector Unionism: Unison and the Future of Trade Unions*, London: Routledge.

Terry, M. (2003) 'Employee representation: shop stewards and the new legal framework', in P. Edwards (ed.) *Industrial Relations: Theory and Practice* (2nd edn), Oxford: Blackwell.

Thomas, A.M. and Kitzinger, C. (eds) (1997) *Sexual Harassment: Contemporary Feminist Perspectives*, Buckingham: Open University.

Thomas, R. and Linstead, A. (2002) 'Losing the plot? Middle managers and identity', *Organization*, 9: 71–93.

Thompson, E.P. (1967) 'Time, work discipline and industrial capitalism', *Past and Present*, 38.

Thompson, E.P. (1968) *The Making of the English Working Class*, Harmondsworth: Penguin.

Thompson, J.A. and Bunderson, J.S. (2001) 'Work-nonwork conflict and the phenomenology of time', *Work and Occupations*, 28: 17–39.

Thompson, J.D. (1967) *Organisations in Action*, New York: McGraw-Hill.

Thompson, P. (1983) *Living the Fishing*, London: Routledge & Kegan Paul.

Thompson, P. (1989) *The Nature of Work: An Introduction to Debates on the Labour Process* (2nd edn), London: Macmillan.

Thompson, P. (1993) 'Fatal distraction: postmodernism and organisational analysis', in J. Hassard and M. Parker (eds) *Postmodernism and Organizations*, London: Sage.

Thompson, P. and Ackroyd, S. (1995) 'All quiet on the workplace front: a critique of recent trends in British industrial sociology', *Sociology*, 29: 615–33.

Thompson, P. and Smith, C. (2001) 'Follow the redbrick road: reflections on pathways in and out of the labor process debate', *International Studies of Management and Organization*, 30: 40–67.

Thompson, P. and Warhurst, C. (eds) (1998) *Workplaces of the Future*, Basingstoke: Macmillan.

Tichy, N.M., Fombrun, C.J. and Devanna, M.A. (1982) 'Strategic human resource management', *Sloan Management Review*, 23.

Tilgher, A. (1930) *Work: What it has Meant to Men through the Ages*, New York: Harcourt Brace.

Tilly, C. and Tilly, C. (1998) *Work under Capitalism*, Oxford: Westview Press.

Tilly, L. and Scott, J. (1978) *Women, Work and Family*, New York: Holt, Rinehart & Winston.

Tolbert, P.S. and Zucker, L.G. (1996) 'The institutionalization of institutional theory', in S.R. Clegg, C. Hardy and W. Nord (eds) *Handbook of Organization Studies*, London: Sage.

Towers, B. (1997) *The Representation Gap: Change and Reform in the British and American Workplace*, Oxford: Oxford University Press.

Toynbee, P. (2002) *Hard Work*, London: Bloomsbury.

Trist, E.L., Higgin, G.W., Murray, H. and Pollock, A.B. (1963) *Organisational Choice*, London: Tavistock.

Tsoukas, H. (1992) 'Postmodernism, reflexive rationalism and organizational studies: a reply to Martin Parker', *Organization Studies*, 13: 643–9.

Tunstall, J. (1962) *The Fishermen*, London: MacGibbon & Kee.

Turnbull, P. and Sapsford, D. (1992) 'A sea of discontent: the tides of organised and "unorganised" conflict on the docks', *Sociology*, 26: 291–309.

Turner, B.S. (1996) *For Max Weber: Essays in the Sociology of Fate*, London: Sage.

Turner, J.H. (2001) 'The origins of positivism: the contributions of Auguste Comte and Herbert Spencer', in G. Ritzer and R. Smart, *Handbook of Social Theory*, London: Sage.

Undy, R., Fosh, P., Morris, H., Smith, P. and Martin, R. (1996) *Managing the Unions: The Impact of Legislation on Trade Unions' Behaviour*, Oxford: Clarendon Press.

Vail, J., Wheelock, J. and Hill, M. (eds) (1999) *Insecure Times: Living and Insecurity in Contemporary Society*, London: Routledge.

Van Maanen, J. (1991) 'The smile factory: work at Disneyland', in E.J. Frost, L.F. Moore, M.R. Louis, C.C. Lundberg and J. Martin (eds) *Reframing Organizational Culture*, Newbury Park, CA: Sage.

Van Maanen, J. (1995) 'Fear and loathing in organization studies', *Organization Science*, 6: 687–92.

Vokins, N. (1993) 'The Minerva matrix women entrepreneurs: their perceptions of their managerial style', in S. Allen and C. Truman (eds) *Women in Business: perspectives on Women Entrepreneurs*, London: Routledge.

Vosko, L.F. (2000) *Temporary Work: The Gendered Rise of a Precarious Employment Relationship*, Toronto: Toronto University Press.

Wacjman, J. and Martin, B. (2001) 'My company or my career: managerial achievement and loyalty', *British Journal of Sociology*, 52: 559–78.

Waddington, J. (2003) 'Trade union organization', in P. Edwards (ed.) *Industrial Relations: Theory and Practice* (2nd edn), Oxford: Blackwell.

Wainwright, D. and Calnan, M. (2002) *Work Stress: The Making of a Modern Epidemic*, Buckingham: Open University Press.

Wajcman, J. (1998) *Managing Like a Man: Women and Men in Corporate Management*, Cambridge: Polity Press.

Walby, S. (1986) *Patriarchy at Work: Patriarchal and Capitalist Relations in Employment*, Oxford: Polity.

Walby, S. (1997) *Gender Transformations*, London: Routledge.

Walker, C.R. and Guest, R.H. (1952) *The Man on the Assembly Line*, Cambridge, MA: Harvard University Press.

Walsh, J. (1999) 'Myths and counter-myths: an analysis of part-time female employees and their orientations to work and working hours', *Work, Employment and Society*, 13: 179–203.

Walton, R.E. (1985) 'From control to commitment in the workplace', *Harvard Business Review*, March-April: 76–84.

Ward, R. (1987) 'Resistance, accommodation and advantage: strategic development in ethnic business', in G. Lee and R. Loveridge (eds) *The Manufacture of Disadvantage*, Milton Keynes: Open University Press.

Warde, A. and Hetherington, K. (1993) 'A changing domestic division of labour? Issues of measurement and interpretation', *Work, Employment and Society*, 7: 23–45.

Warhurst, C. and Thompson, P. (1998) 'Hands, hearts and minds: changing work and workers at the end of the century', in P. Thompson and C. Warhurst (eds) *Workplaces of the Future*, Basingstoke: Macmillan.

Warr, P. (1983) 'Unemployment and mental health', *SSRC Newsletter*, 48.

Warwick, D. and Littlejohn, G. (1992) *Coal, Capital and Culture: A Sociological Analysis of Mining Communities in West Yorkshire*, London: Routledge.

Waters, M. (1995) *Globalization*, London: Routledge.

Watson, D.H. (1988) *Managers of Discontent: Trade Union Officers and Industrial Relations Managers*, London: Routledge.

Watson, D.H. (1992) 'Power, conflict and control at work', in J. Allen, P. Brayham and P. Lewis (eds) *Political and Economic Forms of Modernity*, Cambridge: Polity.

Watson, D.H. (1996) 'Individuals and institutions: the case of work and employment', in M. Wetherell (ed.) *Identities, Groups and Social Issues*, London: Sage.

Watson, T.J. (1977) *The Personnel Managers: A Study in the Sociology of Work and Employment*, London: Routledge.

Watson, T.J. (1982) 'Group ideologies and organisational change', *Journal of Management Studies*, 19: 259–75.

Watson, T.J. (1986) *Management, Organisation and Employment Strategy*, London: Routledge & Kegan Paul.

Watson, T.J. (1994) 'Management "flavours of the month": their role in managers' lives', *The International Journal of Human Resource Management*, 5: 889–905.

Watson, T.J. (1995a) 'In search of HRM: beyond the rhetoric and reality distinction or the dog that didn't bark', *Personnel Review*, 24: 6–16.

Watson, T.J. (1995b) 'Rhetoric, discourse and argument in organisational sense-making: a reflexive tale', *Organisation Studies*, 16: 805–21.

Watson, T.J. (1995c) 'Entrepreneurship and professional management: a fatal distinction', *International Small Business Journal*, 13: 33–45.

Watson, T.J. (1996) 'Motivation: that's Maslow, isn't it?', *Management Learning*, 27: 447–64.

Watson, T.J. (1997a) 'Theorising managerial work: a pragmatic pluralist approach to interdisciplinary research', *British Journal of Management*, 8: 3–8.

Watson, T.J. (1997b) 'Human resource management, industrial relations and theory – standing back and starting again', *The New Zealand Journal of Industrial Relations*, 22: 7–21.

Watson, T.J. (1998) 'The labour of division: the manager as "self" and "other"', in K. Hetherington and R. Munro (eds) *Ideas of Difference*, Oxford: Blackwell.

Watson, T.J. (2000) 'Discourse and organisation' (review article), *Human Relations*, 53: 559–97.

Watson, T.J. (2001a, originally 1994) *In Search of Management: Culture, Chaos and Control in Managerial Work* (2nd edn), Harlow: Prentice-Hall.

Watson, T.J. (2001b) 'Formal and informal organization', in N.J. Smelser and P.B. Baltes (eds) *International Encyclopedia of the Social and Behaviour Sciences*, Amsterdam: Elsevier.

Watson, T.J. (2001c) 'Negotiated orders, in organizations', in N.J. Smelser and P.B. Baltes (eds) *International Encyclopedia of the Social and Behaviour Sciences*, Amsterdam: Elsevier.

Watson, T.J. (2001d) 'The emergent manager and processes of management pre-learning', *Management Learning*, 32: 221–35.

Watson, T.J. (2002a) *Organising and Managing Work: Organisational, Managerial and Strategic Behaviour in Theory and Practice*, Harlow: Prentice-Hall.

Watson, T.J. (2002b) 'Speaking professionally – occupational anxiety and discursive ingenuity among human resourcing specialists', in S. Whitehead and M. Dent (eds) *Managing Professional Identities*, London: Routledge.

Watson, T.J. (2002c) 'Professions and professionalism: should we jump off the bandwagon better to study where it is going?', *International Studies of Management and Organization*, 32: 94–106.

Watson, T.J (2003a) 'Ethical choice in managerial work: the scope for managerial choices in an ethically irrational world', *Human Relations*, 56: 167–85.

Watson, T.J. (2003b) 'Strategists and strategy-making: strategic exchange and the shaping of individual lives and organisational futures', *Journal of Management Studies*, 40: 1305–23.

Watson, T.J. and Bargiela-Chiappini, F. (1998) 'Managerial sensemaking and occupational identities in Britain and Italy', *Journal of Management Studies*, 35: 285–301.

Watson, T.J. and Harris, P. (1999) *The Emergent Manager*, London: Sage.

Watson, T.J. and Rosborough, J. (1999) 'Teamworking and the management of flexibility: local and social-structural tensions in high performance work design initiatives', in S. Procter and F. Mueller, F. (eds), *Teamworking*, Basingstoke: Macmillan.

Watson, T.J. and Tansley, C. (2000) 'Strategic exchange in the development of human resource information systems', *New Technology, Work and Employment*, 15: 108–22.

Watson, T.J. and Watson, D.H. (1999) 'Human resourcing in practice: managing employment issues in the university', *Journal of Management Studies*, 36: 483–504.

Watson, W. (1964) 'Social mobility and social class in industrial communities', in M. Gluckman and E. Devon (eds) *Closed Systems and Open Minds*, Edinburgh: Oliver & Boyd.

Webb, J. (1996) 'Vocabularies of motive and the "new" management', *Work, Employment and Society*, 10: 251–71.

Weber, M. (1927) *General Economic History*, New York: Free Press.

Weber, M. (1965) *The Protestant Ethic and the Spirit of Capitalism*, London: Allen & Unwin.

Weber, M. (1978) *Economy and Society*, Berkeley: University of California Press.

Webster, F. (1995) *Theories of the Information Society*, London: Routledge.

Webster, F. and Robbins, K. (1993) '"I'll be watching you": comment on Sewell and Wilkinson', *Sociology*, 27: 243–52.

Wedderburn, D. and Crompton, R. (1972) *Workers' Attitudes and Technology*, Cambridge: Cambridge University Press.

Weick, K.E. (1979) *The Social Psychology of Organizing*, Reading, MA: Addison-Wesley.

Weick, K.E. (1995) *Sensemaking in Organisations*, Thousand Oaks, CA: Sage.

Westergaard, J., Noble, I. and Walker, A. (1989) *After Redundancy*, Oxford: Polity.

Wheelock, J. (1990) *Husbands at Home: The Domestic Economy in a Post Industrial Society*, London: Routledge.

Whipp, R. (1990) *Patterns of Labour: Work and Social Change in the Pottery Industry*, London: Routledge.

Whitehead, T.N. (1938) *The Industrial Worker*, New York: Oxford University Press.

Whitfield, K. and Strauss, G. (eds) (1998) *Researching the World of Work: Strategies and Methods in Studying Industrial Relations*, Ithaca, NY: Cornell University Press.

Whitley, R. (1994) 'The internationalisation of firms and markets: its significance and institutional structuring', *Organisation*, 1: 101–34.

Whitley, R. (2000) *Divergent Capitalisms: The Social Structuring and Change of Business Systems*, Oxford: Oxford University Press.

Whyte, W.H. (1961) *The Organisation Man*, Harmondsworth: Penguin.

Wicks, D. (2001) *Nurses and Doctors at Work Rethinking Professional Boundaries*, Buckingham: Open University Press.

Wild, R. and Birchall, D.W. (1975) 'Job structuring and work organisation', *Journal of Occupational Psychology*, 48: 169–77.

Wilkinson, A. and Willmott, H. (eds) (1994) *Making Quality Critical*, London: Routledge.

Wilkinson, A., Marchington, M., Goodman, J. and Ackers, P. (1992) 'Total Quality Management and employee involvement', *Human Resource Management Journal*, 2: 1–20.

Wilkinson. A., Redman, T., Snape, E. and Marchington, M. (1998) *Managing with Total Quality Management: Theory and Practice*, London: Macmillan.

Wilkinson, B. (1983) *The Shopfloor Politics of New Technology*, London: Heinemann.

Williams, C.C. (1988) *Examining the Nature of Domestic Labour*, Aldershot: Avebury.

Williams, C.L., Giuffre, P.A. and Dellinger, K. (1999) 'Sexuality in the workplace: organizational control, sexual harassment and the pursuit of pleasure', *Annual Review of Sociology*, 25: 73–93.

Williams, K., Cutler, T., Williams, J. and Haslam, C. (1987) 'The end of mass production', *Economy and Society*, 16: 405–39.

Willis, P.E. (1977) *Learning to Labour*, London: Saxon House.

Willman, P. (1980) 'Leadership and trade union principles: some problems of management sponsorship and independence', *Industrial Relations Journal*, 11.

Willmott, H. (1994) 'Business process re-engineering and human resource management', *Personnel Review*, 23: 34–46.

Willmott, H. (1995) 'Strength is ignorance; slavery is freedom: managing culture in modern organisations', *Journal of Management Studies*, 30: 511–12.

Willmott, H. (1998) 'Recognizing the other: reflections on a new sensibility in social and organization studies', in R. Chia (ed.) *In the Realm of Organization*, London: Routledge.

Wilson, F. (1999a) 'Genderquake? Did you feel the earth move?', *Organization*, 6: 529–41.

Wilson, F. (1999b) *Organizational Behaviour: A Critical Introduction*, Oxford: Oxford University Press.

Wise, S. and Stanley, L. (1987) *Gorgie Porgie: Sexual Harassment in Everyday Life*, London: Pandora.

Witz, A. (1992) *Professions and Patriarchy*, London: Routledge.

Womack, J. and Jones, D. (1996) *Lean Thinking*, New York: Simon & Schuster

Womack, J.P., Jones, D.J. and Roos, D. (1990) *The Machine that Changed the World*, New York: Rawson.

Woodfield, R. (2000) *Women, Work and Computing*, Cambridge: Cambridge University Press.

Woodward, J. (1965) *Industrial Organisation*, Oxford: Oxford University Press.

Woolgar, S. (1988) *Science: The Very Idea*, London: Ellis Horwood.

Worrall, L. and Cooper, C.L. (1999) *The Quality of Working Life: The 1999 Survey of Managers' Experiences*, Institute of Management Research Report, London: Institute of Management.

Worrall, L., Cooper C. and Campbell, F. (2000) 'The new reality for UK managers: perpetual change and employment instability', *Work, Employment and Society*, 14: 647–68.

Wray, D. (1949) 'Marginal men of industry: the foremen', *American Journal of Sociology*, 54.

Wray, D. (1996) 'Paternalism and its discontents', *Work, Employment and Society*, 10: 701–71.

Wray-Bliss, E. (2002) 'Abstract ethics, embodied ethics: the strange marriage of Foucault and positivism in labour process theory', *Organization*, 9: 5–39.

Zeitlin, M. (1989) *The Large Corporation and Contemporary Classes*, Oxford: Polity Press.

Zimmerman, D.H. (1973) 'The practicalities of rule use', in G. Salaman and K. Thompson (eds) *People and Organisations*, London: Longman.

Zuboff, S. (1988) *In the Age of the Smart Machine*, Oxford: Heinemann.

Zucker, L.G. (ed.) (1988) *Institutional Patterns and Organisations*, Cambridge, MA: Ballinger.

Zugbach, von R. (1995) *The Winning Manager: Coming out on Top in the Organization Game*, London: Souvenir Press.

Author index

Subject index